Twentieth-Century Germany

Politics, Culture and Society 1918–1990

EDITED BY

MARY FULBROOK

Professor of German History, University College London

A member of the Hodder Headline Group
LONDON
Co-published in the United States of America by
Oxford University Press Inc., New York

Learning Resources
Centre

121 6507 7

First published in Great Britain in 2001 by
Arnold, a member of the Hodder Headline Group
338 Euston Road, London NW1 3BH
Except for Ch. 6, originally published as part of
Mary Fulbrook, ed., *German History since 1800*

http://www.arnoldpublishers.com

Co-published in the United States of America by
Oxford University Press Inc.,
198 Madison Avenue, New York, NY 10016

British Library Cataloguing in Publication Data
A catalogue record for this book is available from the British Library

Library of Congress Cataloging-in-Publication Data
A catalog record for this book is available from the Library of Congress

ISBN 0 340 76330 2 (hb)
ISBN 0 340 76331 0 (pb)

1 2 3 4 5 6 7 8 9 10

Production Editor: Rada Radojicic
Production Controller: Martin Kerans
Cover Design: Terry Griffiths

Typeset in 10/13pt Plantin by Phoenix Photosetting, Lordswood, Chatham, Kent
Printed and bound in Great Britain by MPG Books, Bodmin, Cornwall

What do you think about this book? Or any other Arnold title?
Please send your comments to feedback.arnold@hodder.co.uk

Contents

Part I   1918–1945

Part II   Germany since 1945

List of maps

List of figures

List of tables

Introduction

Mary Fulbrook

The history of Germany in the twentieth century has been a history of dramatic contrasts, repeatedly reappearing in different guises: militarist imperialism and subjugation; strident nationalisms and critical cultures of shame; varieties of dictatorship and democracy; capitalism in crisis and capitalism triumphant; communist visions and communist perversions; reactionary and radical forms of culture. Twentieth-century Germany has profoundly affected not only European, but indeed world history: from its role in unleashing both the First and Second World Wars; provoking the USA out of isolationism and into a titanic battle with the Soviet Union over world power status; through to the quieter, more benign, but no less powerful role in the drive towards (initially western) European integration. The breaching of the Berlin Wall in the 'gentle revolution' of autumn 1989 came to function as a powerful image of the dramatic way in which the 'short' twentieth century came to a close.

It is almost easy to forget that the 14 troubled years of the Weimar Republic and the dozen years of Nazi dictatorship, or the 40 years of division and cold war, were not all that twentieth-century German history is about. Alongside the dramatic visible political upheavals and ruptures, the genocide of the Third Reich and the near-fratricide of the cold war, which have caught the public imagination and captured political debate, there have been longer, more subterranean processes of change. Some major and minor hiccups notwithstanding, and with striking regional contrasts, the face of Germany has been radically transformed over the twentieth century by processes of economic growth, industrialization, urbanization, commercialization and the communications revolution.

Participants may have been much less consciously aware of these underlying trends and currents, but they have been no less important, not least in the ways in which perceptions and attitudes have themselves been trans-formed. The affluent cosmopolitan German of 2000, equipped with mobile phone (or *Handy*, to use the extraordinarily anglophone German word for this instrument), hooked up to internet, e-mail and fax, capable of speed-ing down the autobahn or hopping on a cheap flight to destinations far and wide, bears little resemblance to, say, his or her grandparents bringing in the hay, milking the cows, or sweating in the factories – or standing in the soup queues of the unemployed – of the 1920s. Radical changes in the structure of family life, the roles of women, the status of organized religion and the churches, alongside the introduction and development of new mass media (radio, film, television, satellite and cable TV), have accompanied – in some cases despite, in some cases to a greater or lesser extent because of – political changes and associated social policies.

No single, simple 'grand narrative' can readily encompass these develop-ments. If one sought still to account for German history in terms of some out-dated notion of a 'national character', one would have to posit a Jekyll-and-Hyde character deeply driven by schizophrenic tendencies. Attempts to resurrect versions of the 'uniqueness of German culture' argument fail to account for radical ruptures with previous traditions after 1945. Notions of a German 'special path' to modernity, characterized by 'belated nation-hood', or alleged disjunctures between rapid economic modernization and outmoded social and political structures, have come under increasing fire for both substantive and theoretical reasons. Indeed, on the view of some historians influenced by postmodernism, it has been a century of such intrinsic chaos and 'rupture' (to deploy a favourite postmodernist term) that any attempt to impose retrospective order on historical accounts is to do an injustice to the complexities of reality.

This book does not draw this conclusion. As the chapters below demon-strate, historical analysis needs to be clearly focused, conscious of the truly significant wider questions, constantly on the active search for relevant empirical material, and concerned to situate – and challenge – received interpretations in the context of new findings and ongoing debates. Rejection of the imposition of any single 'grand narrative' does not entail rejection of any rational attempt to order, interpret, and explain. The chapters which follow not only present each author's own view of the topic under discussion, but also each seek to address the range of relevant contemporary debates.

Given the sheer immensity of the historic upheavals, and the ways these have profoundly affected the lives of millions of people both within the shifting boundaries of 'Germany', and across Europe and the world, attempts by historians at ordering and explanation become even more urgent. This is not least because of the acute politicization and contemporary sensitivity – still – of this most deeply problematic history. There is virtually no area of twentieth-century German history that has not, at one time or another, been the subject of fierce public debates as well as – and interacting with – scholarly discussions among members of the historical profession.

This is a past which, in the words of one (notoriously controversial) commentator 'refuses to become history'.[1] Clashes of interpretation in the public sphere have, in a myriad of ways, both informed as well as been informed by the research agendas and interpretive frameworks of historians. And the conclusions of the latter have, in different ways under different circumstances, often been of considerable public significance.

Views on the causes and character of Nazism played a role, alongside current political considerations, in the ways in which denazification and restructuring took place in the early post-war years, and in the war crimes trials of the 1950s and 1960s. Competing historical interpretations were key elements in the new official legitimations and constructions of national identity in East and West Germany, laying the foundations for a public culture of collective shame and penance in the West, of triumphant anti-fascism in the East. A variety of 'historical pictures' (*Geschichtsbilder*) lay behind differing historical representations. For example, the view of Nazism as carried by Hitler and his small gang of evil henchmen, adopted by West Germany's first Chancellor, Konrad Adenauer, conveniently exonerated the vast mass of the German people while castigating a small group of individual perpetrators who had been supposedly brought to justice in the various post-war trials. In very different substantive form, a similar function was fulfilled by the class theory of 'fascism' adopted in Ulbricht's GDR, which cast the German workers and peasants as victims rather than accomplices of Nazism, which was, on this view, carried by 'monopoly capitalists and imperialists' who continued to exercise power in the capitalist West.

Official and private perceptions of the recent past changed over time in both East and West. Historical consciousness was affected by a multiplicity of factors: not only the private tales told in families and among friendship circles, but also, increasingly, cultural representations of the past shaped patterns of collective memory. In the works not only of survivors, such as Primo Levi, but also in the prose and drama of writers such as Bertolt Brecht, Christa Wolf, Günther Grass, Peter Weiss, Rolf Hochhuth, Ingeborg Bachmann, Anne Duden, or the films of Rainer Werner Fassbinder, Hans Syberberg, Claud Lanzmann (*Shoah*), Roberto Benigni (*Life is Beautiful*), not to mention Stephen Spielberg (*Schindler's List*), reflections on and of the Nazi period have played a recurrent role in the creative literature, poetry, theatre and film of the latter half of the twentieth century. Often bitter controversies over the character of the Nazi dictatorship, the relations between the regime and the people, or the role of the Army in genocidal atrocities, increasingly dogged public debates in the West, often unleashed by particular incidents: the showing of a particular television show (most notably the American television series *Holocaust* in 1979) or exhibition (such as the *Wehrmacht* exhibition of the 1990s), or a sudden flurry of newspaper slanging matches among historians (as in the notorious *Historikerstreit* of 1986–7); or political incidents such as US President Ronald Reagan's would-be exonerative visit, alongside West German Chancellor Helmut Kohl, to the Bitburg military cemetery, with its graves of members of the former Waffen-SS, in 1985; or Philip Jenninger's ill-judged remarks to the Bundestag on the anniversary of *Kristallnacht* in 1988.[2]

Perhaps oddly, the Third Reich cast a new and longer shadow in the new circumstances of united Germany in the 1990s. The incorporation of the reconstituted east German Länder into an enlarged Federal Republic was accompanied by renewed and quite bitter controversies over how to 'overcome' what was dubbed the 'second German dictatorship', with new attributions of heroes and victims, new critiques of an *Unrechtsstaat*, new accusations of complicity and guilt. This was often accompanied by a (frequently unacknowledged) new national pride among West Germans, who felt that their constitution had proved itself in practice, and that they had learned how to overcome a dictatorial past, a lesson that would now have to be repeated by their eastern brethren. The concept of 'totalitarianism', which had for some time been out of favour for Third Reich history, experienced a renaissance with respect to the GDR; and the latter was perceived in some circles in far more black-and-white denunciatory tones than had generally been the case in the era of détente. But there were often bitter controversies over competing interpretations of this most recent German dictatorship – not least in respect of the widespread comparisons made between the communist and the Nazi dictatorships.

Given the acute and continuing public sensitivity of the recent past, political opinions and moral positions muddied virtually all attempts at professional historical interpretations of 'contemporary history' (*Zeitgeschichte*). Even debates over issues of method could not be abstracted from their political and moral implications. Attempts at comparative history were mired in widespread confusions between 'comparison' and 'comparable' (as encapsulated in the eventual dogma 'vergleichen heisst nicht gleichsetzten', to compare is not to equate), as evidenced in debates of the 1950s and 1960s over the comparability of Nazism and Stalinism under the rubric of totalitarianism, or, later, debates over the comparability of the GDR and the Third Reich, under the same rubric of totalitarianism. Controversies over questions such as the 'normalization' of Third Reich history, or approaches rooted in the history of everyday life, or structural analyses of socio-economic and political configurations versus narrative histories of high politics, were intimately connected to clashes between perceived political positions, as theoretical sides were taken with associated political colours very much in mind – radical, left-liberal, conservative, hostage to far-right, and so on. In more acute ways than in most countries, historical consciousness and historical research in Germany were – to put it at its most basic – intrinsically politically relevant.

In the light of all this, it seems all the more important that professional historians – for all the concerns about the historian's 'imposition of narrative' on the 'buzzing blooming confusion' of the past – do not take flight in postmodernist rejections of rationality and celebrations of chaos and rupture, but rather make strenuous and systematic efforts to seek out and engage with all available relevant evidence in pursuit of honest solutions to current historical controversies. This is, perhaps, casting the historian in the role of detective and barrister rather than myth-monger, purveyor of national or other collective identity, or writer of fiction.

If historical consciousness is intrinsically related to contemporary politics and cultural sensibilities, the publication of professional history is also subject to market forces. This volume is, in the main, a slightly revised version of what first appeared as Parts III and IV of *German History since 1800* (1997). The latter proved sufficiently popular for two reprints to be required within three years of initial publication; but the modularization of many history courses, combined with the production costs and hence price of a volume amounting to over 600 pages, suggested that a further reprint should be as two slimmer volumes, one for the 'long' nineteenth century and one for the 'short' twentieth century, losing, alas, the final thematic chapters of the original.[3] Hence the current version.

As in the earlier volume, the intention has been to provide coverage of key areas of debate on culture, politics, social history and economic development by scholars who are at the cutting edge of research in each field. In each case, authors have been given the opportunity to up-date their discussions and bibliographies. Richard Bessel and Niall Ferguson tackle, with different explanatory emphases, the immense political and economic legacies and challenges faced by Germany after the First World War, while Jill Stephenson traces the ways in which the NSDAP was able to exploit the weaknesses of the Weimar Republic, culminating in Hitler's appointment as chancellor. Weimar was, despite (or in part because of?) the economic and political turmoil also a time of extraordinary cultural creativity; Elizabeth Harvey examines some of the fascinating and complex ways in which modern culture was expressed and refracted in what was still a highly fragmented and diverse society. Ian Kershaw, whose brilliant two-volume biography of Hitler has appeared since the first publication of this collection, here provides a concentrated vignette of Hitler's role in the Nazi state, explicating his interpretation of Hitler's 'charismatic authority' which beautifully brings together a focus on Hitler's personality on the one hand, and the increasingly chaotic, overlapping structures of power in this 'polycratic' regime on the other.[4]

There then follow the two significant changes in this revised edition. We have included an essay by Omer Bartov filling a crucial gap on the Second World War. Bartov's work on German soldiers and the German Army has served in many ways to bring together two areas which have previously been treated quite separately, in the historiography: experiences at the front, and the experiences of Germans at home. In the essay reprinted here, Bartov brings together several further areas of debate, linking realities and images of war, particular types of warfare with the domestic economic and political situation, and war with modernity and genocide. The explosion of research on the Holocaust in the 1990s prompted Nick Stargardt into writing a wholly new version of his chapter on a topic which is perhaps the epitome of the ultimately inexplicable in history. Stargardt's thoughtful synthesis of recent research on the Holocaust, reformulating the terms in which debates have been carried out and showing how some interpretations approximate better to the available evidence than others, superbly illustrates the ways in which, despite the enormity and intrinsic unthinkability of the issues, it is not only possible, but essential, to continue the search for a comprehensive historical explanation of this most difficult part of a difficult past.

The two post-war states founded on this problematic legacy were very different from one another. Despite continuities of both structure and personnel in certain areas, particularly the economy, the Federal Republic of Germany represented a complete break with Germany's previous record of political instability and authoritarian rule. Many external commentators have perceived it as a model in terms of both its affluent social market economy and its (often self-doubting, if at times almost immobile) democracy. Mark Roseman's chapter addresses explanations for West German stabilization, and measures the extent of change in West German political culture over forty years. Despite the widespread label of 'Germany's second dictatorship', the break with the past was arguably even more dramatic in communist East Germany: the GDR was not only founded on a very different political ideology, and with a very different economic structure, from that of the Third Reich; it also (almost paradoxically) had a rather different, more streamlined political structure and quite different patterns of relations between party and state on the one hand, economy and society on the other. Any simplistic equation of the two German dictatorships under the common heading of totalitarianism misses the extent of their differences, as Mark Allinson's differentiated analysis of the GDR makes abundantly clear. Indeed, what is perhaps most striking about post-war German history is the sheer malleability of politics and society, undermining any attempts at defining notions of a persistent German identity across the centuries. Differing patterns of social change and constructions of collective identity in West and East Germany are treated in the chapters by Mary Fulbrook and Erica Carter respectively, revealing the extent of divergence on either side of the Wall. Finally, Jonathan Osmond examines the interplay of domestic and international factors in the collapse of the communist dictatorship and the course of German unification.

These chapters do not seek, cumulatively, to present a new, single narrative of this extraordinary history. Rather, they reflect the state of play on some of major issues. In some areas developments within the historical profession have been more far-reaching than others. Thus, for example, debates on the character of the Third Reich have moved forwards dramatically over the last two or three decades, through leaps both in conceptualization and in the unearthing of new evidence. And while unification in 1990 appears to have made little major difference to the general outlines of interpretations of West German history (though there are developments in detail), the controversial and arguably increasingly polarised historiography of the GDR is only beginning to acquire clear contours.[5] The chapters which follow reflect the diversity and liveliness of the field, and provide informed and informative points of entry to key issues and debates with which all students and scholars of the period must engage.

Notes:

1. Cf. the title of Ernst Nolte's essay, 'Die Vergangenheit, die nicht vergehen will', which played a role in unleashing the *Historikerstreit*: see the Piper collection, *Historikerstreit* (1987).
2. For further discussion of the topics briefly mentioned in the last few paragraphs, see Mary Fulbrook, *German National Identity after the Holocaust* (1999).

3. M. Fulbrook (ed. with J. Breuilly), *German History since 1800* (1997); Breuilly, *Nineteenth-Century Germany: Politics, Culture and Society 1780–1918* (2001).
4. See for the full exposition Ian Kershaw, *Hitler. Hubris* (1998) and *Hitler. Nemesis* (2000).
5. See further M. Fulbrook, *Interpretations of the Two Germanies 1945–1990* (2000).

Part I

1918–1945

1

Germany from war to dictatorship

Richard Bessel

> There are times in which conditions that were thought to be unshakeable
> and eternal all are called into question. The feeling spreads that the
> ground is being pulled out from under people's feet. Such a time
> descended upon Germany after 1918. Germany's great-power status was
> gone; the social strata which had identified themselves with it found that
> there was no longer any air for them to breathe. One lived from hand to
> mouth and saw oneself time and again on the edge of the abyss and
> catastrophe.[1]

'The population is beginning to go crazy.' ('*Die Einwohnerschaft fängt an,
verrückt zu werden.*') Thus the police director in Stuttgart began a directive
to the city's police in early August 1914, a few days after war had been
declared.[2] He was referring to the panic about suspected spies and alleged
acts of sabotage which had accompanied the excitement with which the
German public greeted the outbreak of war. The wild, unfounded rumours
circulating around the city, the Stuttgart Police Director wrote, gave one
the impression of being 'in a lunatic asylum', and he observed, more
prophetically than he possibly could have imagined: 'There is no telling
what will happen if times really become more difficult'.

As we know, times did become more difficult. August 1914 was a turning
point even more profound than could have been predicted at the time,
shattering the apparent certainties of the pre-1914 world and marking the
beginning of a period 'in which conditions that were thought to be
unshakeable and eternal all are called into question' and in which the
feeling spread 'that the ground is being pulled out from under people's
feet'. Few nation states have tumbled more precipitously into catastrophe
than did Germany between 1914 and 1933. A prosperous, apparently
stable and self-confident nation plunged into a world war and lost it,

experienced the collapse of monarchic and then of democratic government, saw its economy ravaged by the worst inflation and then the worst depression the world had ever seen, and succumbed to a vicious racist political movement which led the country down the path to dictatorship, world war and mass murder. The tragic history of Germany in the two decades which followed the outbreak of the First World War is a history of political, economic and social instability, and of a profoundly misplaced search for a return to stability and security.

For many years it has been a commonplace to describe the events of 1914 as an outpouring of popular enthusiasm for war, with cheering crowds confidently wishing the nation's young men a glorious and speedy march to Paris, as the declaration of war 'released a heady excitement that swept the whole country'.[3] As we have come to appreciate more recently, however, what occurred in the summer of 1914 was rather more complex and the emotions stirred up by the outbreak of war rather more ambivalent than often has been assumed. Alongside demonstrations of patriotic enthusiasm there were manifestations of anxiety and fear. In late July 1914 hundreds of thousands of Germans took part in peace demonstrations; while many Germans rushed to the colours once war was declared, many others desperately sought to have their sons exempted from military service; many rushed to remove their savings from banks and hoarded food; and many more found themselves thrown out of work as unemployment reached unprecedented levels with the economic dislocation which followed the military mobilization. Already at the outbreak of war tensions were present which would grow to tear German society and the German polity apart in the next few years. While the nervous hopes for a quick and glorious victory initially overwhelmed the less positive reactions to the outbreak of war, once the quick and glorious victory failed to materialize the public mood turned progressively darker. As Gerhard A. Ritter and Klaus Tenfelde have observed in their mammoth account of the condition of German workers in the Empire, 'seldom do social-historical caesura allow themselves to be fixed so clearly as for the year 1914'.[4] To which may be added (and perhaps even more importantly), psychological-historical caesura as well.

With the outbreak of world war, the pursuit of which required the mobilization of the whole of society, the mass of the German people no longer could be excluded from or marginalized in political life; the old order, in which government remained largely insulated from popular representation, was not going to emerge from the war intact. The problem of how to integrate the German people into German political life surfaced in wartime discussion about reforming the (Prussian three-class) franchise, the participation of the trade-union leadership in drafting and operating the Auxiliary Service Law of 1916, the Peace Resolution passed by a majority of the Reichstag in July 1917, the mobilization of popular annexationist opinion with the Vaterlandspartei in 1917, and the mounting social and industrial unrest of 1917 and 1918. The old order proved woefully inadequate to deal with the new challenge. The Kaiser was marginalized from government and military planning, and by late 1918 had become so loathed that abdication and flight formed his only remaining option; the civil administration had abdicated responsibility to the military, which with the declaration of war had taken over domestic administration in accordance with the Prussian Law of Siege of 4 June 1851 and which tried and failed to subordinate the German economy completely to military needs with the 'Hindenburg programme' of 1916. Failure to manage the wartime economy in a manner regarded as either efficient or fair, while millions of men were being slaughtered on the battlefield, brought the political system into disrepute. The basic political question put on the table by wartime mobilization and its failure was: what would take its place?

The course and conduct of Germany's First World War made it difficult, and finally impossible, to come up with an answer which might have preserved political stability and social cohesion. Germany's pursuit of war exacerbated existing social, economic and political divisions, and thus undermined chances for achieving political stability in the aftermath of the conflict. Obviously, losing the war did not help, but given the unrealistic expectations which had been aroused and the wartime sacrifices which had been demanded, it is difficult to imagine *any* post-war settlement which the German people generally would have regarded as satisfactory. (The case of Italy, which achieved first its 'mutilated victory' and then Fascism, certainly suggests that victory would not necessarily have led to stable democracy.) The *leitmotiv* of Germany's war was not political or spiritual unity in the sense of some 'spirit of 1914' or 'front community'; it was division. The conduct of the war exacerbated conflicts between government and people, between the civil authorities and the military, between front and home front, between rich and poor, between producers and consumers, between employers and employees, between town and country. Failure to achieve quick victory and mounting casualties and suffering made the issue of war aims all the more difficult and divisive, leading on the one hand to the formation and rapid expansion of the radically annexationist Vaterlandspartei and on the other to the split of the Social Democratic Party, and provoked mounting social and industrial unrest, a 'covert military strike' involving soldiers who shirked dangerous military service in their hundreds of thousands from the spring of 1918, and, finally, revolution.

Parliamentary government – the great goal of the revolutionaries of 1848 – was inaugurated in Germany on 28 October 1918, when the Reichstag passed a law stipulating that henceforth the Reich government was dependent upon the confidence of the parliament. By the time the Kaiser abdicated and fled to Holland, Germany already had had effective parliamentary government for over a month – in the form of the government of Prince Max von Baden, which rested on majority support in the Reichstag rather than the confidence of the Emperor. Yet the depth of the social and political divisions which had grown since 1914 was such that when Germany's military rulers Paul von Hindenburg and Erich Ludendorff – realizing that the war was lost and that Germany needed a parliamentary government in order to negotiate with the Allies – opened the door to a genuine parliamentary system, the change was almost superfluous. Indeed, on the same day that Germany finally formally achieved parliamentary government, 28 October 1918, the first naval mutiny began in Wilhelmshaven. Political reform very quickly gave way to political revolution.

The divisions exacerbated by the war not only undermined the imperial political system; they also constituted an extraordinarily difficult and damaging legacy for the democratic system put into place following defeat in 1918. Four aspects of the emergence of democracy from the 'German revolution' proved particularly important for its subsequent development and demise:

- The precipitate collapse of the old regime meant that political power essentially fell into the laps of the Majority Social Democrats around Friedrich Ebert, who were far from being enthusiastic revolutionaries and who found themselves having to take responsibility for the mess left behind by their predecessors. This, of course, was essentially what Ludendorff had had in mind when, on 29 September, he admitted the game was up, demanded that Germany seek an armistice on the basis of Wilson's 14 Points, and urged the formation of a government with majority support in the Reichstag. Instead of those who had led Germany into war and left her defeated and bankrupt being blamed for the unrest which followed the end of the war, it was the unwilling revolutionaries of November 1918 who became identified with the disorder which accompanied the birth of democracy.

- The collapse of the old regime in the autumn of 1918 and the revolution which gave birth to the Weimar Republic were in large measure a consequence of war weariness and military collapse. As the great mass of Germany's soldiers knew well, once it became clear that victory was not on the cards, the only way to get out alive was to jettison the Kaiser and capitulate to the Allies. And this is what they did: when the final military collapse came, the navy mutinied and the army disintegrated, and the one thing of which the old army remained capable in November and December 1918 was carrying out its own demobilization. This was the military reality behind the famous 'Ebert-Groener Pact' – initiated on 10 November 1918, when General Wilhelm Groener, who had been named Ludendorff's successor as Chief Quartermaster General on 29 October, telephoned the new Chancellor Friedrich Ebert and promised the army's support for the new government provided the new government oppose left-wing radicalism. Thus, at the moment of its birth, the new democratic political system did not have a reliable armed force at its disposal.

- The financial and economic problems left behind by the war were colossal, yet their dimensions were not fully appreciated by a war-weary, impoverished, fed-up population which looked to peace and to a new democratic government for rapid improvements. The German people did not understand that the task of Germany's post-war government, whatever its composition or constitution, would be less to distribute the material benefits of peace than to distribute poverty. In the event this was done by taking the oft-trodden economic path of least resistance chosen by weak governments: inflation. Whether or not the choice of such a path was avoidable (and Niall Ferguson, in the following chapter, asserts that it was), it was a response to an extraordinarily difficult political predicament. One of main burdens which the new democratic system faced was the accumulation of unrealistic popular expectations – hardly a sound basis for successful democratic government.

- From the outset the new governmental system lacked the support of a large proportion of the German population, many of whom had been shocked by defeat and revolution, still felt loyalty to the Kaiser, regretted the crumbling of the rigid social and political lines of authority embodied in the imperial system, and refused to accept the legitimacy of the new regime. Thus, from the moment of its birth, the first successful attempt to establish a governmental system in Germany on the basis of popular sovereignty was burdened by the fact that a large proportion of the German people did not recognize its legitimacy.

Against such an unpromising background, Germany's new political masters generally opted for continuity rather than change, and in the crucial months after the November Revolution (and before the Weimar constitution was drafted), key decisions were reached which shaped the Weimar Republic for the whole of its short life. The first was the decision in effect to maintain the existing state administrative structure. The assumption of power by the 'Council of People's Representatives' in November 1918 notwithstanding, and despite the radical changes instituted with regard to labour relations (including the abolition of the restrictive *Gesindeordnungen* governing agricultural workers), the predominant tendency in German government during 1918–19 was continuity. The November Revolution was a revolution in which senior civil servants continued to run their departments with the agreement of the provisional government and in which, although the police momentarily disappeared from view, local government officials remained at their posts (and, in the months which followed easily marginalized the 'council movement').

The second key decision was to postpone, which essentially meant to reject, a radical restructuring of the economy. After state controls had provoked such hostility during wartime, it was unlikely that extending state direction of the economy would win widespread support. Furthermore, the economic demobilization, combined with the frightening shortages of food and fuel and the continuing blockade pursued by the victorious Allies, undercut the case for structural change; the needs of the moment appeared too pressing to allow for experiments whose outcome was uncertain. On 15 November 1918, a few days after the Kaiser's abdication, a key decision was reached when leaders of industry and the socialist trade unions signed the Stinnes-Legien Agreement: the employers conceded trade-union recognition and the eight-hour day while the trade unions implicitly abandoned demands for wholesale nationalization and a socialist transformation of the economy. This presaged the main outlines of Weimar economic policy: preservation of the capitalist system, with grudging acceptance of the interests of labour when necessary. Agreement by employers and unions and the opting for pragmatic emergency measures rather than a fundamental restructuring effectively postponed any possible socialization until after the National Assembly elections of 19 January 1919. These elections resulted in a majority for democratic parliamentary government, not for socialism: the Majority Social Democrats received 37.9 per cent of the vote, and the Independent Social Democrats 7.6 per cent. Henceforth if Germany was going to be governed democratically, it was not going to be socialist.

The third area of decision concerned the constitutional framework. This too was largely fixed before the Weimar constitution was ratified, or even written. Just two days after the National Assembly convened in Weimar at the beginning of February – Berlin was considered too dangerous a venue following the Spartacist uprising in the capital during January – the Reich government submitted a bill 'Concerning the Provisional Exercise of Political Power'. Two days later, on 10 February 1919, the National

Assembly passed it, and thus confirmed the essential constitutional outlines of the Weimar Republic: the National Assembly was empowered to adopt both a new constitution and 'other urgent national laws' (i.e. it could act as a legislature); the individual states were represented in an upper house; and a Reich president, who was responsible for conducting government business, was to be elected by the National Assembly and in turn was to appoint a cabinet which needed to possess the confidence of the Assembly. As Eberhard Kolb has pointed out, 'while all these arrangements were designated "provisional", in practice the basic structure of the constitution – with the Reichstag, president and cabinet – was thus predetermined before formal discussion about the constitution had begun.'[5]

In parallel with the political arrangements which emerged in the months following the November Revolution, the Weimar constitution was far from being the constitution of a socialist republic. It was essentially a liberal document, written largely by Hugo Preuß, a leading left-liberal jurist whom Ebert named as state secretary in the Department of the Interior in November 1918 and who became Reich Minister of the Interior from January 1919. However, it did not reflect a single, consistent picture of how a society was or should be governed and structured. Rather, it was, at once, a stirring declaration of democratic principles and a contradictory collection of compromises which reflected the divisions which characterized German politics. The main areas of compromise were:

- Centralism/federalism. Originally the framers of the Weimar constitution had hoped to make a radical break with the Prussian-dominated federal structure of the Empire and to construct a more strongly centralized, unitary state. This would have meant the break-up of Prussia and the creation of a very different set of administrative subdivisions of the Reich. However, the various state governments were able to mobilize effectively against this change. Many of their old prerogatives indeed were abolished: Bavaria and Württemberg no longer could maintain their own postal and railway administrations and, most importantly, the military became a central government (as opposed to essentially Prussian) institution. (The Reichswehr thus became the first *German* – as opposed to Prussian or Bavarian – army in modern German history.) But the *Länder* retained considerable executive powers with regard to the courts, education and the police.
- Parliamentary/presidential government. The Weimar constitution essentially combined parliamentary and presidential democracy. On the one hand, the Reichstag was to be the central institution of government, the expression of the sovereign people's will and the organ responsible

for legislation. On the other hand, and partly to offset fears that a parliament with a socialist majority (which never materialized) might become dominant, the Reich president was given considerable powers: supreme command of the armed forces, the power to appoint and dismiss governments as well as to dissolve the Reichstag, and (in accordance with Article 48 of the constitution) the power to rule by decree, bypassing the Reichstag, in the event of a national emergency.

- Public/private ownership. The Weimar constitution effectively looked both ways on the question of property ownership. In the articles on basic rights (Articles 109–64) the constitution guaranteed the economic status quo and the right to private property. At the same time, however, it provided for the possibility of taking private concerns into public ownership.
- Church/state. Here too the Weimar constitution looked in two directions at once. On the one hand, it reflected long-standing liberal and social-democratic desires by stating that there was to be 'no state church'. On the other hand, however, the hopes of radical anti-clerics – such as the Independent Social Democrat Adolf Hoffmann, who as head of the Prussian Culture Ministry in late November 1918 banned religious education from schools and provoked vociferous protest – were rejected, and important points about church privileges and religious instruction in the schools were conceded.

The constitutional system put into place in 1918 and 1919 was thus a compromise, which reflected the social and ideological divisions of the country and which itself was compromised in the years which followed.[6] The same may be said for the first parliamentary government, which was formed after the National Assembly elections: a coalition of the Majority Social Democrats (with seven members in the new cabinet, including Chancellor Philipp Scheidemann and Reichswehr Minister Gustav Noske), the left liberals of the DDP (with three cabinet members, including Interior Minister Hugo Preuß) and the Catholic Centre (the Christian People's Party, with three cabinet members, including Matthias Erzberger, Minister without Portfolio, who was responsible for the Armistice negotiations). (The new Foreign Minister, Count Ulrich von Brockdorff-Rantzau, had no party affiliation.) The three parties which comprised the 'Weimar coalition' each entered government with different motives: the Social Democrats wanted to defend the gains, as they saw them, of the revolution, and to ensure a strong position for organized labour; the Liberals wanted to support parliamentary democracy and act as a brake on socialist initiatives; and the Centre was concerned to protect private property and to prevent nationalization, to protect the position of the Catholic Church, and to preserve the federal structure of the Reich. What united all three parties was concern to prevent further radicalization.

It may be easy, with the benefit of hindsight, to criticize the compromises which created the shaky foundations of the Weimar state. However, the challenges facing Germany's new rulers were considerable: the sudden, and largely unplanned demobilization of roughly six million soldiers who flooded into Germany between November 1918 and January 1919; the abrupt termination of wartime production; the huge overhang of war-related debt; catastrophic shortages of coal and food during a period of continued Allied naval blockade; precipitous declines in labour productivity; Polish insurrections which led to most of the provinces of Posen and West Prussia becoming part of the new Polish state; the loss of Alsace-Lorraine and concern that the Allies might dismember Germany; a serious refugee problem as Germans flooded into the Reich from territories lost to France and Poland; and, in early 1919, an upsurge of industrial unrest and radical protest which erupted in serious outbreaks of violence in Berlin, the Ruhr, Munich and a number of other places. Against such a background, it is hardly surprising that the 'Council of People's Representatives', which had assumed provisional responsibility for the Reich government in November 1918, was desperate to keep the wheels of state administration turning, marshal some armed force behind itself and to re-establish order – even if this meant keeping the bureaucracy inherited from the old regime at their desks, vastly overestimating the revolutionary threat and sending in right-wing *Freikorps* units against militant workers. When Gustav Noske took on the role of 'bloodhound' of the revolution and hired the *Freikorps* to suppress real and imagined revolutionary threats to the new government, it was an expression of a deep, at once both understandable and paranoid, concern to re-establish order at a time of extreme uncertainty.

Given the acute difficulties which Germany faced after the First World War, it is hardly surprising that the compromises which framed the establishment of the Weimar Republic soon began to unravel. The German people's search for security and stability was profoundly disappointed.

On the domestic political front, Germany experienced mounting instability. While the collapse of the old regime in November 1918 had been largely free of violence, the same could not be said of the events which followed. On 28 December the three USPD members of the six-man 'Council of People's Representatives' left the provisional government in protest at the suppression of unrest in Berlin by the military. (USPD members left the Prussian government on 3 January 1919.) This was followed by the 'January Uprising' of the revolutionary shop stewards and the newly formed Communist Party (Spartacus League) in Berlin, which was easily and brutally suppressed (and the two leaders of the Spartacists, Rosa Luxemburg and Karl Liebknecht, were murdered). A wave of unrest spread across the country during the first half of 1919, with strikes, open challenges to government authority and, in Bremen and Munich for example, short-lived attempts to set up radical 'council republics'. In March 1920, the military *putsch* engineered by Wolfgang Kapp, the former chairman of the Vaterlandspartei, and General Walther Freiherr von Lüttwitz was defeated by a general strike, but not before armed conflict had broken out in a number of cities and after which tens of thousands of militant workers in the Ruhr formed a ramshackle 'Red Army'. In March 1921 a communist uprising in the central German industrial region around Merseburg was suppressed by police acting effectively as a military force. Three armed uprisings of Polish insurgents, in 1919, 1920 and 1921, punctuated the history of post-war Upper Silesia. Political demonstrations frequently ended in violent confrontations. Crime reached epidemic proportions during the post-war and inflationary years. And political life in the early Weimar years was characterized by a large number of political murders: in addition to Luxemburg and Liebknecht in January 1919, among those who fell victim to political assassins was Hugo Haase, the Independent Social Democratic leader who joined Ebert in the 'Council of People's Representatives' in November 1918 and who was shot in front of the Reichstag on 8 October 1919 (and died of his wounds a month later); in August 1921 Matthias Erzberger, the Centre Party politician who had been the driving force behind the Peace Resolution of 1917, who had signed the Versailles Treaty on behalf of the German government in 1919, and who as Finance Minister (from June 1919 to March 1920) had initiated a fundamental reform of Germany's taxation system, was murdered by two members of the right-wing terrorist Organization Consul; and on 24 June 1922 Germany's Foreign Minister, Walther Rathenau, the Jewish industrialist who had organized Germany's war economy, was shot dead as he left his home in Grunewald for the Foreign Office. Altogether, German political life experienced a marked decline in peaceful civilized behaviour in the aftermath of war and revolution.

On the party political front, the apparently broad support for democratic politics indicated in the 1919 National Assembly elections soon faded. Already in the Reichstag elections of June 1920 there emerged a pattern which became a defining characteristic of Weimar politics: parties which accepted governmental responsibility, and thus responsibility for necessarily unpopular decisions, subsequently lost massively at the polls. The SPD lost nearly half its 11.5 million votes (37.9 per cent) in 1919,

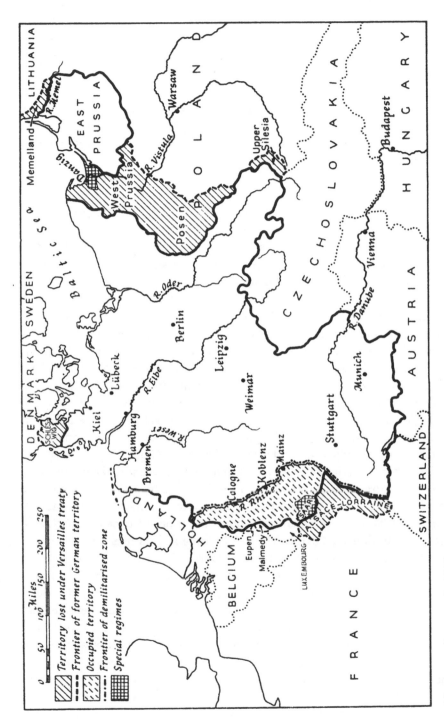

Map 1.1 Germany in 1919

falling to barely six million (21.7 per cent) in 1920 while the Independent Social Democrats (who had left government) saw their vote mushroom; the DDP lost more than half its 5.6 million votes (18.5 per cent), falling to just over 2.3 million (8.3 per cent); and the Centre Party captured 3.8 million (13.6 per cent), as opposed to the nearly six million (19.7 per cent) which the 'Christian People's Party' had attracted in 1919. With that, the 'Weimar Coalition', which had captured roughly three-quarters of the popular vote at the outset of the Weimar Republic, no longer commanded a majority in parliament. It was never to do so again.

On the economic front, the surprising success of the demobilization was undermined by inflation. In the short term, the post-war German economy appeared to perform rather well, with a rapid decline in unemployment (which virtually disappeared in 1921 and 1922) and a sharp recovery in economic activity. However, these apparent successes had their price. For one thing, sooner or later the government's massive deficit spending had to come to an end, and when it did so, and the inevitable bill had to be paid, the suffering created by a necessarily harsh currency stabilization was considerable. For another, the inflation provoked tension and conflict, not only in economic affairs but also political and social life. Rising prices were a constant source of friction, while price controls also often caused anger. The ramshackle continuation of wartime price controls for agricultural produce, for example, ensured the ongoing hostility of the farming community; rent controls ensured the continuation of a desperate housing shortage; and rapidly rising prices provided a constant stimulus to labour militancy and anger at the marketplace. Two particularly telling indications of the degree to which the inflation undermined Germany's political and social stability are the 'first (and last) major civil servant strike in Germany history' (Andreas Kunz), which occurred in February 1922 (and which the employees lost), and the upsurge in anti-Semitic attacks on businesses, which had its most ugly manifestation in the mob violence against Jewish shops in Breslau on 20 July 1923. The inflation damaged not only the German economy but also the civilized fabric of social and political life.

On the foreign political front, the unrealistic hopes which had accompanied the Armistice – that the Allies would deal generously with a democratic Germany which had jettisoned the Kaiser – were dashed when the draft of the Versailles Treaty was presented to the Germans on 7 May 1919. For once, Germany's political divisions were overcome: all parties were united in rejecting the treaty, and Chancellor Scheidemann dramatically declared that the treaty was unacceptable to the Reich government. However, German protests left the Allies unmoved, and on 16 June the final treaty terms were presented in the form of an ultimatum. The army leadership admitted its inability to prevent an Allied military advance, and, after Scheidemann's government resigned on 20 July rather than sign the treaty, a new SPD-led government (with Gustav Bauer as Chancellor but without DDP members) declared itself willing to accept the Versailles *Diktat*, as it became known in Germany. The treaty did not aim to create a Wilsonian 'peace without victors or vanquished' but rather to ensure that Germany no longer could be a military aggressor and that French security interests would be safeguarded. This meant imposing territorial losses (many of which had already occurred) – Alsace-Lorraine to France, Eupen-Malmedy to Belgium, much of Upper Silesia and most of Posen and West Prussia to Poland, and North Schleswig to Denmark; Germany lost her colonies; the size of the armed forces was limited to 100,000 men, and the manufacture or possession of offensive weapons was prohibited; the Allies occupied strategic bridgeheads across the Rhine, and the Rhineland was demilitarized; and Germany was saddled with (as yet unspecified) reparations. In order to provide a basis for these terms, Germany was compelled, with Article 231 (the notorious 'war-guilt clause'), to admit responsibility for launching the war. Among Germans there was near universal agreement that such treatment was unjust and intolerable – making the Versailles Treaty perhaps the only political issue around which there was widespread agreement in Weimar Germany.

Finally, on the military front, the Reichswehr came to occupy a peculiar position of domestic military dominance and foreign military impotence, which turned old conceptions of the role of the military upside down. Although the German military had disintegrated almost completely in 1918, it was reconstituted remarkably quickly thereafter, only to be sharply reduced in size by the terms of the Versailles Treaty. The reduction in the size of the army, and the concomitant growth of *Freikorps* units which were called upon to suppress domestic unrest and fight Polish insurrection in the eastern Prussian provinces, meant that, for a crucial period, the German army did not possess a monopoly of armed force in the country. The army response to this situation was ambivalent. This ambivalence was demonstrated painfully with the Kapp-Lüttwitz *putsch* in March 1920, when *Freikorps* commanders attempted to seize power in Berlin and Defence Minister Noske discovered that there were no army units at his disposal prepared to suppress the rebellion; the head of the *Truppenamt* (Troop Office – the disguised General Staff), General Hans von Seeckt, announced that it was impossible to commit troops to the government's defence; and army commanders throughout the country were prepared to support the right-wing insurgents. Despite its compromised behaviour in 1920, the Reichswehr was not subsequently harnessed to strict civilian control, however. Instead, power was consolidated in the hands of von Seeckt, who emerged during the crisis year of 1923 as the effective arbiter of German domestic politics.

In 1923 the compromises on which the republic initially had been based crumbled, and behind republican government loomed the spectre of military rule. It was the Reichswehr which was sent into Saxony and Thuringia in October and November 1923 to subdue their left-wing governments; and when Hitler staged his aborted coup attempt in Munich on 8/9 November, Ebert proclaimed a state of emergency and placed executive powers in the hands of von Seeckt, who quickly liquidated the Munich *putsch* and established central control over the maverick Bavarian Reichswehr. Yet paradoxically, the moment at which Germany came closest to military rule was also the moment when its military was at its weakest, for the impotence of the Reichswehr as a military force had been exposed with brutal clarity when, on 11 January 1923, French and Belgian troops marched unopposed into the Ruhr in order to secure overdue reparations. The response of the German government to the Ruhr occupation, passive resistance (subsidized by recourse to the printing press and accompanying the complete destruction of the German currency), was perhaps necessary given popular opinion, but it offered no way out of the political, economic, diplomatic and military cul-de-sac into which Germany had marched.

In the autumn of 1923, the Weimar Republic faced a crisis which called its survival into question and which, as Gerald Feldman has observed, 'threatened the very existence of civil society itself as well as the political order and the integrity of the German state'.[7] The currency had become completely worthless; the unwillingness of rebellious German farmers to sell their produce for paper marks threatened the urban population with starvation; employer–employee relations in industry had broken down; the French had occupied Germany's most important industrial area, and passive resistance to that occupation was bankrupting the country; economic activity was declining rapidly, and unemployment was rising; criminality was increasing; social and political unrest reached a post-war peak; the desperate need of the Reich government for armed force at its disposal brought Germany close to military dictatorship; and effective government had become possible only through repeated recourse to emergency legislation which effectively marginalized the Reichstag. Stresemann's Vice-Chancellor, the Socialist Robert Schmidt, was quite candid about this, when he admitted that a 'measure of dictatorship would have to be exercised by the government in order to gain control of the situation'.[8] By the autumn of 1923 there seemed very little of Weimar democracy left.

Yet the republic survived. Why? In part, one might explain the survival by the fact that there was little real alternative. With French troops in Essen, the idea of the Reichswehr openly assuming control of government was not really an option; nor was the installation of a revanchist right-wing regime openly committed to breaking the 'chains' of the Versailles *Diktat*. With the mark totally debauched and complete economic collapse staring Germany's rulers in the face, there was no real alternative but to take the hard decisions about government finance and seek an accommodation with the French which would allow the establishment of a stable currency. The depth of the crises of late 1923 made the politics of the 'republicans of reason' (*Vernunftrepublikaner*) the only viable option. This is not to deny that overcoming the 1923 crisis and the political and economic stabilization of 1923–4 formed a considerable achievement, however. And credit for this achievement is owed first and foremost to Gustav Stresemann, during whose 'hundred days' as Reich Chancellor, from 13 August to 23 November 1923, the difficult and indeed heroic task of stabilization was achieved in the face of unprecedented chaos and without Germany yet slipping into dictatorship.

Stresemann's service to the Weimar Republic during his lengthy tenure as Foreign Minister (beginning in August 1923, when he was also Chancellor, and lasting until his death on 3 October 1929) was no less important than his brief tenure in the Reich Chancellery. In both the short and the medium term, the emergence from crises of 1923 and the subsequent stabilization rested on a settlement of Germany's foreign political position no less than it did on a domestic–political settlement. (Post-war Germany's first great diplomatic coup, the Rapallo Treaty signed with Soviet Russia in April 1922, may have been successful in upsetting the western Allies and in providing a foundation for cooperation between the Reichswehr and the Red Army, but it was no substitute for re-integration with her neighbours to the west.) The two were closely interrelated. An end to the inflation and the restoration of Germany's financial position rested on settling the reparations issue, which in turn rested on coming to terms with the French – in effect recognizing French security interests and coming to terms with the fact that Germany had lost the war. By demonstrating the bankruptcy of a policy of intransigence and unwillingness to face the consequences of wartime defeat, the hyperinflation and the Ruhr occupation in effect paved the way for a provisional settlement of the reparations issue. The repayment plan drawn up by the commission under the chairmanship of the American banker Charles Dawes opened the door to massive foreign, largely American, investment which helped fuel Germany's economic upturn in the mid-1920s; to the Locarno Treaty of

1925, which provided a framework for the peaceful settlement of disputes between Germany and her western neighbours and ended Germany's foreign political isolation; to the Allied military evacuation of the Ruhr; and to Germany's entry into the League of Nations in September 1926 as a permanent council member.

Notwithstanding the advantages which reaching agreement with France brought to Germany, Stresemann attracted criticism from the right for in effect accepting the conditions of the hated Versailles Treaty. The fragility of the foreign political *rapprochement* achieved during the mid-1920s became apparent when, in 1929, the ratification of what was to be a permanent settlement to the reparations issue, prepared under the chairmanship of Owen D. Young (chairman of the board of the American General Electric Company), provoked a storm of protest in Germany and provided a focus around which the radical right could coalesce in a vicious plebiscite campaign against the 'enslavement of the German people' allegedly brought about by the Young plan. Although ratification of the Young plan made possible the final evacuation by the French military of the Rhineland on 30 June 1930, and even if, as Steven Schuker has claimed, once all payments and defaults on debts are tallied the Americans in effect paid 'reparations' to Germany, the benefits of the settlement were far from apparent to many Germans.

From 1924 until the end of the decade, the Weimar Republic enjoyed a measure of domestic social and political stability. These were the republic's 'golden years' of relative stabilization. The unrest and violence which had characterized public life in Germany between 1919 and 1923 ebbed. The political extremes of left and right were the big losers in the Reichstag elections of December 1924, while the parties which supported the republic – the SPD, DDP, DVP and the Centre – saw their representation in the Reichstag increase; the SPD-led Weimar coalition continued to offer Prussia, which comprised roughly two-thirds of the Reich, stable democratic government firmly committed to the republic; the conservative right, initially resolutely hostile to the republic, appeared to have become reconciled, as the conservative DNVP joined a Reich government coalition for the first time in January 1925 and began to play by the rules of the republican game; and Friedrich Ebert's successor as (and first popularly elected) Reich president, Field Marshal Paul von Hindenburg – while bringing a conservative, military-minded approach to the office of head of state – acted within the constitution and by his presence appeared to reconcile many conservative Germans to a republic which had been born in defeat and revolution. Thus supporters of Weimar democracy appeared to have had some good reasons to take heart when, in the Reichstag elections of May 1928, the Nazis were able to gather a mere 2.6 per cent of the popular vote and the SPD emerged as the party with by far the largest vote and was able, in June, to form a Reich government under the leadership of Hermann Müller. To some extent, the stability and security which had been blown apart after July 1914 appeared to have been reconstituted or replaced.

Nevertheless, all was not well even during the Weimar Republic's brief sunny spell. The German electorate had not entirely been converted to the republican cause. The extreme racialist right, although subdued after its support declined in the second Reichstag elections of 1924, had not gone away; the Communists continued to attract the support of millions of voters; the conservative DNVP, although participating in Reich government coalitions from the beginning of 1925, had not completely jettisoned its anti-republican disposition (which would re-surface with a vengeance after 1928); and the inflation and stabilization had left a residue of bitterness among hundreds of thousands of people who had lost out and blamed the Weimar 'system' for their plight. Once the clouds of economic crisis began again to gather over Weimar Germany, the cracks in the democratic polity would widen dangerously.

The economic and political stabilization realized in the mid-1920s gave scope for the development of what has become known as the Weimar 'welfare state'. The achievements of the Weimar Republic during the period of 'relative prosperity' (1924–28) were impressive, especially after the turbulence of the republic's early years. Living standards, which had plummeted during the final stages of the hyperinflation, rose considerably. Housing construction, which had virtually come to a halt during the war and had not fully recovered during the inflation (when rent controls acted as a great disincentive to building new dwellings), rose substantially (with considerable state financial involvement) (see Table 1.1). Municipal

Table 1.1 Housing construction in Germany, 1919–33 (showing net increase in dwellings)

1919	56,714	1924	106,502	1929	317,682
1920	103,092	1925	178,930	1930	310,971
1921	134,223	1926	205,793	1931	233,648
1922	146,615	1927	288,635	1932	141,265
1923	118,333	1928	309,762	1933	178,039

Source: Statistisches Jahrbuch für das Deutsche Reich 1924/25 (1925), pp. 101–2; *Statistisches Jahrbuch für das Deutsche Reich 1926* (1926), p. 89; *Statistisches Jahrbuch für das Deutsche Reich 1934* (1934), p. 155.

governments undertook impressive public works schemes, which gave their cities new airports, exhibition centres, housing estates and swimming pools. On 16 July 1927 the crowning achievement of the Weimar 'welfare state', the 'Act on Labour Exchanges and Unemployment Insurance' was enacted, to cover the major area left uncovered by Bismarck's social insurance programmes of the 1880s: by extending statutory unemployment insurance to roughly 17.25 million employees, this scheme embraced more people than did such insurance in any other country.

However, as Werner Abelshauser has pointed out, 'the Weimar Republic was an overstrained welfare state',[9] and the achievements of the years of 'relative stability' became damaging liabilities once the depression arrived. The 1927 unemployment insurance legislation had been enacted at a time when unemployment was quite low, and the envisaged level of employee and employer contributions allowed for the support of about 800,000 unemployed; a further 600,000 could have been supported from a need fund of the Reich Office for Unemployment Benefits and Unemployment Insurance. However, as we know, unemployment soon far surpassed these levels. Within a year the unemployment insurance scheme was up against its financial limits, and by 1930 the critical financial position of the Reich Unemployment Office meant that a rise in contributions was urgently required – the issue which precipitated the split between the SPD and DVP which destroyed the last truly parliamentary Weimar government.

The unhappy history of unemployment insurance points to a fundamental problem which plagued the Weimar Republic: the changed relationship of the German people to the German state which had emerged from the First World War. Popular expectations of what the state could and should provide for its citizens outstripped what the Weimar system was able to deliver. The resulting bitterness, and its political ramifications, may be illustrated well by the case of the war dependants. The war had left behind hundreds of thousands of widows, orphans and invalids, who looked to the state for support. Not only did this cast a shadow over the lives of many people; the resulting pensions burden also put enormous demands on government finances. In Germany, for example, Robert Whalen has claimed that 40 per cent of national (i.e. Reich) government expenditure went towards paying war-related pensions. Yet, despite all the money paid to war widows and invalids, almost everyone involved was left dissatisfied: on the one hand, war victims who felt that they were being inadequately compensated; on the other, officials who saw government expenditure spinning out of control. Not surprisingly, attempts to limit such expenditure provoked angry protest, particularly in the early 1930s when the economic crisis reduced government revenues and added to pressure to cut expenditure. Between 1928 and 1933 the budget for war victims' pensions was cut by one-third, leaving hundreds of thousands of people – who had been promised during the war that 'You can be sure of the thanks of the Fatherland' – deeply angry. Yet there was no democratic way to square the circle. Neither the funds nor the parliamentary majorities existed on which to base taxation and spending policies which might have satisfied war victims. Expectations of what the German state could and should provide had been raised to such an extent that they could not be met.

This suggests that even during the years of 'relative stabilization' all was not well with the Weimar Republic. The profound social, economic, political and psychological destabilization which had set in with the First World War had not really been overcome; underlying economic problems remained, and the relative political stability of Weimar's 'golden years' rested on shaky foundations. This was particularly apparent in the German countryside, where a combination of high farm indebtedness, low prices for agricultural produce and high taxes was driving farm producers into bankruptcy and political radicalism – a disturbing sign of which was the terror campaign of rural radicals in Schleswig-Holstein in 1928. No less damaging was the fact that participation in government did not cement German conservatism into republican politics. As the two liberal parties – the DDP and the DVP – had found in the early years of the republic, the conservative DNVP discovered that its reward for accepting the responsibilities of government was a sharp decline in popular support: compared with the result in December 1924, the DNVP lost nearly a third of its vote in May 1928. Consequently the party returned to radical opposition to the republic. Under the intransigent leadership of media magnate Alfred Hugenberg, who became chairman of the DNVP in October 1928, Germany's conservatives set out on a path which led to the formation of a common front with the Nazis in the campaign against the Young plan in 1929 and in the Harzburg Front in 1931, and to the formation of a coalition government with Adolf Hitler in 1933. And while the two liberal parties saw their popular support dwindle and the conservatives lost roughly a third of their supporters, many voters turned to special-interest parties – betraying a lack of faith in a democratic politics which focused on the common good.

These developments, and the rapid growth of the Nazi Party from 1929 onwards (discussed by Jill Stephenson in Chapter 4 below), reflected a decomposition of popular support for traditional elite politics. This was accompanied by a crisis of state and government of unparalleled proportions in the early 1930s. On 27 March 1930, with the collapse of the coalition government led by Hermann Müller, the Weimar parliamentary system effectively ceased to function. Its successor, put together on 30 March by the Centre Party politician Heinrich Brüning, rested not on a coalition in the Reichstag but instead depended ultimately on the confidence of the Reich president and his willingness to sign emergency legislation as sanctioned under Article 48 of the constitution. Following the elections of 14 September 1930, when the NSDAP captured over six million votes to become the second largest party in the Reichstag, forming any government based on a stable parliamentary coalition became almost impossible. Brüning faced a rapidly deteriorating economic situation and mounting political unrest; the Social Democrats found there was little they could do but to tolerate Brüning's attempts to deal with the mounting financial difficulties with deeper and deeper expenditure cuts, for fear of opening the door to a government even further to the right and in order to protect its own 'Weimar' coalition (with the Centre Party) in Prussia; and the conviction was growing that the mounting problems facing Germany could not be tackled within a strictly democratic framework.

There has been much debate about Brüning's intentions – whether he was in effect a 'heroic' figure desperately struggling against economic catastrophe and political radicalism, or whether he was concerned to use the crisis to reshape government in a more authoritarian direction and pursued policies which made a bad situation even worse. Much of this debate revolves around the economic policies of the Brüning government, which are discussed in the following chapter by Niall Ferguson. However, two points are worth stressing here.

First, whatever his motives and however limited his room for manoeuvre, Brüning's was an essentially authoritarian project. Effectively removing the Reichstag from the business of government and undercutting the autonomy of local government, which was overwhelmed by the effects of the economic slump, were not accidental or unfortunate side effects of an idealistic attempt to preserve Weimar democracy. After the collapse of the Müller government, it was fairly clear that there would be no going back to the political system created through the compromises of 1918–19 or the settlements of 1923–24.

Second, during his period as Chancellor, Brüning's focus remained very largely upon foreign policy, in particular the goal of freeing Germany from reparations. For Brüning, harsh emergency measures were not only a (perhaps unavoidable) means by which to cope with an economic and fiscal crisis of unprecedented proportions, nor were his policies only an attempt to instrumentalize the crisis in order to achieve constitutional reform of a more authoritarian mould. (In his memoirs, published in 1970, Brüning revealed that if he had had his way constitutional reform would have ended with a monarchist restoration).[10] They also were designed to demonstrate to the Allies that the reparations burden was intolerable, and thereby to get the burden of reparations lifted entirely – that is, to achieve a major foreign–policy success, to take a decisive step towards undoing the Versailles Treaty, to win a major economic victory, and thus to gain popularity at a single stroke.

That is not quite how things turned out. The reparations burden was indeed lifted: in July 1931, with the Hoover Moratorium, international debt payments were suspended for one year; and a year later, at the Lausanne Conference of June–July 1932, Germany's reparations were cancelled. However, Brüning – who had gambled his own and his country's future to achieve this victory – did not survive in office long enough to reap the benefits of this success. Instead, that fell to his successor, Franz von Papen. However, von Papen's right-wing 'cabinet of barons' faced problems of such magnitude – mass unemployment, a rising tide of political extremism and violence, and an almost complete breakdown of parliamentary business once the Nazi Party had emerged from the elections of July 1932 with 230 Reichstag deputies – that the victory in Lausanne was hardly sufficient to tip the scales. Von Papen, whose power rested solely on his ability to gain approval for emergency legislation from the aged Reich President and who suspended the SPD-led government of Prussia on 20 July, aimed for authoritarian government in the place of the discredited democratic system. However, his authoritarian project had negligible popular support, and his short, turbulent period in the Reich Chancellery demonstrated the impossibility of establishing stable government without support of – or against – the mass of the German people. Similar lessons could be drawn from the unhappy history of von Papen's successor, Reichswehr General Kurt von Schleicher, whose attempts to gather support across the political spectrum – from the NSDAP's organizational leader Gregor Strasser to the Christian and socialist trade unions – came to nothing and who lasted in office less than two months before making way for the coalition headed by Adolf Hitler.

The attempts during the early 1930s to use the crisis to replace Weimar democracy with a more authoritarian state structure misfired, for a number of reasons. First, they aroused little popular support, and, short of a staging a successful military coup, it was probably impossible to impose a system of rule against the wishes of virtually the entire population. Second, the Reichswehr was ultimately unwilling to intervene actively to impose authoritarian rule. That is to say, the army wanted to develop its armaments programmes and lay the ground for future expansion, not get involved in a domestic civil war. Third, the problems facing German governments in 1931 and 1932 probably were beyond the ability of *any* government to master. Not until the economic cycle had begun to turn (as we now know it did towards the end of 1932), Germans' expectations had been reduced, and foreign–political limitations to Germany's room for manoeuvre had been removed, could a government hope to put a new political settlement into place. Thus, the achievement of Brüning, von Papen and von Schleicher essentially was to remove important obstacles to the establishment of a Nazi dictatorship bent on repression at home and expansion abroad. By eliminating reparations from the foreign-policy agenda, they helped to remove an important constraint on the foreign policy of their successor; by demonstrating the bankruptcy of authoritarian elite politics without substantial popular support, they paved the way for an extraordinarily dangerous authoritarian populism; by failing to impose their own solutions they put themselves in a weak position to prevent Hitler from imposing his – with substantial popular support – in 1933.

It is a remarkable feature of the collapse of the Weimar Republic that the left played so marginal a role. As German democracy withered, neither the Social Democrats nor the Communists really offered a practicable alternative. For the Communists, who drew on the jobless and the inhabitants of urban slums for support and whose electoral support grew as the economic crisis deepened, apparent strength was in fact testimony to the political weakness of a German working class stricken by mass unemployment. The real function of the KPD consisted of (1) providing a spectre of unrest and red revolution which frightened respectable Germans, and (2) splitting the left. The division of the left did not so much serve to prevent successful resistance to German fascism; for such resistance to have overcome the combined forces of the Nazi Party and the German state even the combined SPD and KPD probably would have been too weak. Rather the division effectively prevented the SPD from making the overtures to a middle-class electorate which might have permitted its successful transformation into a 'people's party' (as finally occurred in the Federal Republic), for fear of losing working-class support to the Communists. For the Social Democrats, who drew support from among the 'respectable' working class, the economic crisis undercut what was left of their once powerful position in Weimar politics. As the main pillar of the original Weimar coalition, the dominant coalition partner in Prussia, and allied with Germany's largest trade-union movement, the SPD had been a serious contender for political power. But it was precisely this which made the established elites so determined to keep the Social Democrats out of government in the early 1930s. Clinging to their faith in legality as the republic disintegrated, watching their electoral support dwindle while mass unemployment cut the ground from under the trade unions, the SPD became a helpless onlooker as the crisis deepened.

With the party system in disarray, the economy spiralling downward, the left crippled, governments in Berlin lacking parliamentary or popular support, and the social and political culture corroded by a breakdown in civilized behaviour, the grave of the Weimar Republic had already been dug by the time Adolf Hitler was handed the keys to the Reich Chancellery on 30 January 1933. The Nazis did not so much destroy the Weimar Republic as take advantage of its prior decomposition. The failure to achieve a solid democratic stabilization during the 1920s had left an opening for a radical, anti-democratic political movement which could appeal across the class, confessional and regional divides which hitherto had characterized German politics. Once the depression struck with full force, the ground had been well prepared for the NSDAP to become the largest political party that Germany had ever seen.

What the Nazis promised was an end to the divisions which characterized German society and politics – a 'folk community' (*Volksgemeinschaft*) in the place of a divided class society, an end to paralysis of government and to disorder (which was provoked in no small measure by the Nazis themselves). That is to say, the Nazis appeared to offer an end to the 'times in which conditions that were thought to be unshakeable and eternal all are called into question', when 'the feeling spreads that the ground is being pulled out from under people's feet', when Germans saw themselves 'time and again on the edge of the abyss and catastrophe'. The tragedy, of course, is that in fact the Nazis offered no such thing. Instead they pulled the ground from under people's feet more effectively than any political movement has done before or since, and drove Germany – and eventually the entire European continent – headlong into catastrophe.

Notes:

1. Niekisch, Ernst, *Gewagtes Leben* (1958), pp. 173–4.
2. The directive was published subsequently in the Berlin press: *B.Z. am Mittag*, Nr. 186, 9 August 1914: 'Ein schwäbischer Dienstbefehl'. Reproduced in Bernd Ulrich and Benjamin Ziemann, eds., *Frontalltag im Ersten Weltkrieg. Wahn und Wirklichkeit* (1994), p. 29.
3. Thus Gordon A. Craig in his *Germany 1866–1945* (1978), p. 339.
4. Ritter, Gerhard A. and Tenfelde, Klaus, *Arbeiter im Deutschen Kaiserreich 1871 bis 1914* (1992), p. 3.
5. Kolb, Eberhard, *The Weimar Republic* (1988), p. 17.
6. This formulation, 'the compromised compromise', comes from Lutz Niethammer, *Bürgerliche Gesellschaft in Deutschland, Historische Einblicke, Fragen, Perspektiven* (1990).

7. Feldman, Gerald D., *The Great Disorder, Politics, Economics and Society in the German Inflation 1914–1924* (1933), p. 699.
8. Quoted in Feldman, *The Great Disorder*, p. 700.
9. Abelshauser, Werner, 'Die Weimarer Republik – Ein Wohlfahrtsstaat?', in Werner Abelshauser, ed., *Die Weimarer Republik als Wohlfahrtsstaat. Zum Verhältnis von Wirtschafts- und Sozialpolitik in der Industriegesellschaft* (1987), p. 31.
10. Brüning, Heinrich, *Memoiren 1918–1934* (1970), p. 194.

Select bibliography

Bessel, Richard, *Germany after the First World War* (1993).
Bessel, Richard, and Feuchtwanger, E. J., eds., *Social Change and Political Development in Weimar Germany* (1981).
Carsten, F. L., *The Reichswehr and Politics, 1918–1933* (1966).
Childers, Thomas, ed., *The Formation of the Nazi Constituency, 1918–1933* (1986).
Evans, Richard J., and Geary, Dick, eds., *The German Unemployed. Experiences and Consequences of Mass Unemployment from the Weimar Republic to the Third Reich* (1987).
Feldman, Gerald D., *Army, Industry, and Labor in Germany 1914–1918* (1966).
Feldman, Gerald D., *The Great Disorder. Politics, Economics and Society in the German Inflation 1914–1924* (1993).
Feuchtwanger, E. J., *From Weimar to Hitler: Germany, 1918–33* (1993).
Fowkes, Ben, *Communism in Germany under the Weimar Republic* (1984).
Fritzsche, Peter, *Rehearsals for Fascism. Populism and Political Mobilization in Weimar Germany* (1990).
Harsch, Donna, *German Social Democracy and the Rise of Nazism* (1993).
Heiber, Helmut, *The Weimar Republic* (1993).
Kolb, Eberhard, *The Weimar Republic* (1988).
Kershaw, Ian, ed., *Weimar: Why Did German Democracy Fail?* (1990).
Kocka, Jürgen, *Facing Total War: German Society 1914–1918* (1984).
Kunz, Andreas, *Civil Servants and the Politics of Inflation in Germany 1914–1924* (1986).
James, Harold, *The German Slump. Politics and Economics 1924–1936* (1986).
Jones, Larry Eugene, *German Liberalism and the Dissolution of the Weimar Party System 1918–1933* (1988).
Lee, Marshall, and Michalka, Wolfgang, *German Foreign Policy 1917–1933: Continuity or Break?* (1987).
Lee, W. R., and Rosenhaft, Eve, eds., *The State and Social Change in Germany, 1880–1980* (1990).
Moeller, Robert G., *German Peasants and Agrarian Politics, 1914–1924. The Rhineland and Westphalia* (1986).
Mommsen, Hans, *The Rise and Fall of Weimar Democracy* (1996).
Mommsen, Hans, *From Weimar to Auschwitz: Essays in German History* (1991).
Mommsen, W. J., ed., *The Emergence of the Welfare State in Britain and Germany* (1981).
Nicholls, A. J., *Weimar and the Rise of Hitler* (3rd edn, 1991).
Peukert, Detlev J. K., *The Weimar Republic. The Crisis of Classical Modernity* (1991).

Schuker, Stephen A., *American 'Reparations' to Germany 1919–33: Implications for the Third-World Debt Crisis* (1988).

Stachura, Peter D., ed., *Unemployment and the Great Depression in Weimar Germany* (1986).

Stargardt, Nicholas, *The German Idea of Militarism. Radical and Socialist Critics 1866–1914* (1994).

Whalen, Robert Weldon, *Bitter Wounds. German Victims of the Great War, 1914–1939* (1984).

2

The German inter-war economy: political choice versus economic determinism

Niall Ferguson

Berthold Brecht and Kurt Weill's musical *The Rise and Fall of the City of Mahagonny* received its premier in Leipzig on 9 March 1930. Unemployment in Germany at that date, according to the contemporary figures based on trade union members, stood at 20 per cent. The annual inflation rate was negative: the cost of living had fallen by around 4 per cent in the previous 12 months. Output in most sectors of the economy had been falling for around a year and a half. The German economy was in the grip of a deep recession, with no sign of recovery in view. Yet only seven months before, the German government had been obliged to accept the recommendation of the Young committee that it should continue to pay annual reparations to the victors of the First World War until 1988. The sum transferred as reparations in 1930 alone was equivalent to around 2.4 per cent of national income, rather more than the entire German trade surplus for the year. It is in this context of deepening economic gloom that Mahagonny's nihilistic 'Alabama Song' is perhaps best seen:

> Oh, show us the way to the next little dollar,
> Oh, don't ask why, oh, don't ask why,
> For if we do not find the next little dollar,
> I tell you we must die, I tell you we must die.

With its jarring rhythms and discordant melody, the 'Alabama Song' is, of course, one of the 'classic' products of Weimar culture, and deserves its place in cultural histories of inter-war Germany. But the song is of interest to economic historians too, for there is an influential line of argument which maintains that the rise and fall not only of the city of Mahagonny, but also of the Weimar Republic itself, was a function of an increasingly desperate hunt for 'the next little dollar' to service the country's external debts.

Even if they do not accept this particular diagnosis, most historians would at least accept that economic factors were at the root of the violent political fluctuations which characterized German history in the period between 1918 and 1933. Indeed, many writers have drawn a direct causal link from Weimar's dismal economic performance to the failure of parliamentary democracy. According to this view, the twin crises of inflation and depression – separated by a few, less-than-golden years of 'relative stagnation' – alienated so many voters from the parliamentary system that its collapse was inevitable.

At first sight, such hypotheses have much to recommend them. After all, it was in the same month that 'Mahagonny' received its premiere that the last properly parliamentary government of the inter-war period – that of Hermann Müller – resigned because of unbridgeable differences between the coalition partners on the subject of unemployment insurance. However, the direction of causation often assumed – from the economic to the political – is open to question. It can just as persuasively be argued that the direction was, in fact, the other way around, with political factors causing the violent economic fluctuations of the period. Indeed, historians of the period can roughly be divided into two groups: those who maintain that politicians and other decision-makers had 'room for manoeuvre' – that politics, in short, was paramount – and those for whom essentially uncontrollable economic or 'structural' factors were decisive. To a large degree, the historiography of the inter-war German economy has been dominated by this basic dichotomy between belief in political 'free will' and economic determinism. Was the hyperinflation of 1923 inevitable, or was it the result of errors of fiscal and monetary policy? Was the deflationary crisis of 1930–2 inevitable, or was it deliberately exacerbated by Müller's successor as Chancellor, Heinrich Brüning, for political reasons?

Another (closely linked) division of historiographical opinion is between those who see Germany's position as externally determined – by the Versailles Peace Treaty of 1919 and other foreign impositions – and those who see internal factors as being of greater importance. For most Germans during the 1920s, it was an article of faith that Germany's problems were primarily a function of the 'shameful peace'. Above all, the reparations demanded by the victorious Allies were seen as a crushing burden on the economy.

There are some historians who still take the view that reparations – that search for 'the next little dollar' – doomed the republic. However, there has been a growing tendency since the war to question this view, and to seek the causes of Weimar's failure within Germany itself. Within the literature which concentrates on internal politics, the clearest sub-division of opinion is between those historians who see the excessive power of labour as a source of economic and political weakness, and those who see the excessive power of big business as the real problem. Although other social divisions have been studied by historians (for example, religious, gender and generational divisions), class conflicts, or at least the distributional conflicts between interest groups, remain of primary concern to historians of the interwar economy.

I   The problem: twin crises

That inter-war Germany suffered severe economic instability can be easily illustrated. Between 1890 and 1914, the German Reich had experienced a period of relatively good economic performance. The economy as a whole had grown at an average annual rate of around 2.8 per cent. Inflation had been negligibly low – a little more than 1 per cent per annum – and there had been relatively little unemployment. To be sure, the fruits of this economic expansion had been distributed quite unequally by modern standards. There had also been considerable cyclical fluctuation. But wages had certainly kept pace with inflation and in some sectors actually grew faster. Moreover – a point often overlooked – the period saw a significant shift towards more progressive taxation at the state and local levels.

These 'golden years' ended abruptly with the First World War, and Germany did not experience anything comparable until after the Second. It is important to emphasize this, if only to point out that economic crisis preceded the creation of the Weimar Republic by nearly five years. For the period 1914–18, the best available index suggests that, in real terms (i.e., allowing for inflation) net national product fell at an average annual rate of around 4 per cent during the war, with both agricultural and industrial production declining steeply. At the same time, a serious inflationary problem developed: the official cost-of-living index rose at annual rates of 32 per cent during the war, twice the comparable figure for Britain. Prices on the large black market rose even more rapidly. The crisis period of 1918–19 saw a still worse deterioration.

There were, it is true, some positive developments after 1919. The economy grew rapidly between 1920 and 1922. Moreover, unemployment was relatively low in Germany in the immediate post-war years, especially compared with Britain and the United States. However, these years also

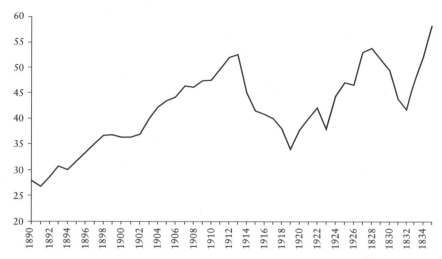

Figure 2.1 German net national product at market prices, adjusted for inflation and territorial changes, 1890–1935 (billion marks)

saw accelerating inflation, the annual rate exceeding 100 per cent for most of 1920 (though it did drop sharply in the first half of 1921). Thereafter, prices rose rapidly again and in July 1922 the monthly rate of inflation for the first time passed 50 per cent – the technical threshhold of hyper-inflation. For nearly two years thereafter, there was economic chaos. Output once again fell and unemployment soared to more than 25 per cent (with more than 45 per cent of trade union members on short-time).

The years between 1924 and 1928 were once thought of as Weimar's 'golden years'; but on closer inspection the most that can be said is that things were not quite as bad as they were in the periods immediately before and after. The economy grew rapidly in 1924, 1925 and 1927, but there was virtually no growth in 1926 and 1928. Unemployment in 1926 reached a peak of more than 20 per cent. It was only a meagre consolation that inflation was low – indeed, had fallen below zero in 1926.

From March 1929 onwards, however, this downward trend became unstoppable as the economy plunged into a severe deflationary crisis. At its lowest point in June 1932, the annual rate of deflation reached minus 12 per cent. This was just one symptom of a second great economic collapse. Overall in the period of the slump, prices fell by more than one-fifth and output by about the same amount. At its worst in the summer of 1932, more than 45 per cent of trade union members were recorded as being out of work. No other major economy suffered such a severe downturn. Unemployment rates were calculated in different ways from country to

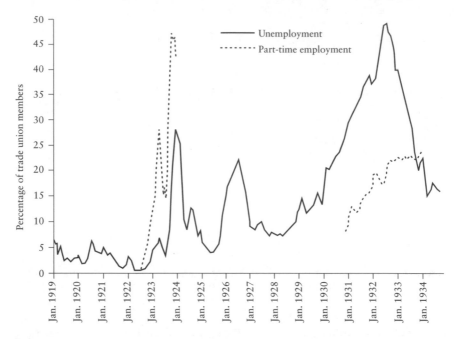

Figure 2.2   Unemployment among trade union members, 1919–1934

country, but appropriately adjusted figures suggest that the German
unemployment rate was two-thirds higher than the British in 1932.

   In short, compared not only with its past and later performance but also
with the contemporary performance of other economies, the German
economy was extremely unstable in this period. In this light, it is not
surprising that so many historians have seen the political collapse of
Weimar as essentially economically determined. The only real debate
about the consequences of economic instability concerns the relative
importance of inflation and unemployment. It is a popular misconception
that because high unemployment coincided with rising Nazi support, the
unemployed must have voted for Hitler. Although some did, unemployed
workers were more likely to turn to Communism than to Nazism, whereas
middle-class voters were relatively more important to National Socialist
electoral success; and in their case, the memory of inflation was at least as
traumatic as the immediate experience of the slump. The social burdens of
the slump were, after all, to a significant degree concentrated on those –
predominantly workers – who lost their jobs. The effects of the inflation, by
contrast, had been universally felt, but with a disproportionate impact on
people living on savings or higher salaries. Certainly, middle-class observers
often seem to have been more shocked by the earlier crisis – even those

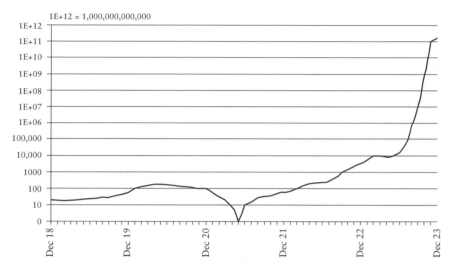

Figure 2.3   Annual inflation rate (cost of living index, log. scale), 1919–1923

businessmen who managed to avoid the worst effects of inflation were appalled by the wiping out of savings, the sudden levelling of income and wealth distribution, the increased criminality. The Hamburg banker Max Warburg described Germany in 1922 as 'a society divided into three classes of society: one that suffers and goes under in decency; another that profiteers cynically and spends recklessly; and another that writhes in desperation, and wishes to destroy in blind fury whatever is left of a government and society that permits such conditions'. At around the same time – as if to illustrate his point – a still obscure South German demagogue named Adolf Hitler was blaming 'the distress of the small rentier, pensioner and war cripple' squarely on 'this weak republic [which] throws its pieces of worthless paper about wildly in order to enable its party functionaries and like-minded good-for-nothings to feed at the trough'. Simply because it took until 1930 for the losers of the inflation to be effectively mobilized by the Nazis does not mean that the economist Lionel Robbins was wrong when he called Hitler 'the foster-child of the inflation'.

II   External pressures: can't pay versus won't pay

How are we to account for Weimar's twin economic crises? For most Germans, ranging right across the political spectrum, it was an article of faith that Weimar's principal economic problem was the Treaty of Versailles, and the reparations imposed on Germany by the victorious powers in 1919. Some historians continue to share that view, which found its most influential expression in the English economist John Maynard Keynes's book, *The Economic Consequences of the Peace*.

There is much to be said for the 'can't pay' thesis. From 1914 onwards, there were severe external pressures on the German economy and these did not cease until 1932. Even before the armistice had been signed, the Reich debt had risen to 150 billion marks – 85 billions in 'gold marks' (or 1913 marks, adjusting for wartime depreciation), compared with less than 5 billion before the war. In addition, state and local debts amounted to around 22 billion gold marks. Moreover, the state was already committed to paying pensions to more than 800,000 war wounded, 530,000 war widows and 1.2 million war orphans, as well as compensation to the owners of certain kinds of property lost during the war.

The peace simply added to these existing burdens; but it added much more than most Germans had anticipated. This was because most Germans did not fully grasp that the war had been lost, whereas from the moment Ludendorff demanded his 'immediate armistice to avoid a catastrophe' – arguably 'the stab in the front' which caused the hitherto relatively firm home front to collapse – the western powers acted as if Germany had surrendered unconditionally. For nearly a month, the American President Woodrow Wilson chose to ignore the parliamentary legitimacy of the new government of Max von Baden, as good as demanding a political revolution against the monarchy as a precondition of peace. And even after such a revolution broke out in early November, the British navy continued its blockade of German ports, ensuring that conditions in German cities worsened rather than improved during the first half of 1919. The Versailles peace – itself a muddled compromise between the victors – was thus imposed on a thoroughly destabilized country.

In economic terms, the peace was not all bad: the loss of Germany's colonies and most of her army and navy implied a considerable financial saving as well as strategic setback. But in other respects the burdens were heavy indeed. The loss of around 11 peripheral chunks of territory, the equivalent of 13 per cent of the Reich's area, mattered economically because that territory included important industrial regions. Germany also lost virtually all that remained of its merchant marine and a substantial number (5,000) of locomotives. These losses in themselves appalled the German delegation, but there was worse to follow. On the legalistic rather than historical premise that Germany had started the war, the treaty required indemnification not only for damage to occupied territory, but also (at the insistence of the Australian government) for the costs of Allied war pensions. So astronomical was the total implied – a figure of 480 billion gold marks was mentioned, which would have made the Reich's total liabilities equivalent to over 1,700 per cent of national income – that it was decided to leave the bill blank pending further discussion. Until then, the Germans were supposed to pay the costs of any occupying forces and 20 billion gold marks by way of a down payment. Keynes – echoing the German delegates at Versailles – denounced all of this, arguing on the basis of detailed calculations about the German balance of payments that the most Germany could pay was some 41 billion gold marks spread over 30 years. If more was asked, he warned:

> vengeance . . . will not limp. Nothing can then delay . . . that final civil war between the forces of Reaction and the despairing convulsions of Revolution . . . which will destroy . . . civilisation and progress.

When a total of 132 billion marks was finally agreed in 1921 he naturally dismissed it – as did most Germans – as far too high.

Keynes's dire prophecy after Versailles was extremely influential at the time in Britain; and subsequent events appeared, at least superficially, to vindicate him. Yet there was always a good deal of suspicion (especially in France) that German protestations of insolvency were fraudulent, or at least exaggerated. In recent years, this charge has been reiterated by a number of writers, including Sally Marks and Stephen Schuker. The 'can't pay? won't pay!' school makes two telling points. Firstly, the 1921 total was in fact closer than Keynes admitted to the sum he had considered realistic two years before. According to Marks, 82 of the 132 billions were purely 'notional', in that so-called 'C bonds' to that value would only be issued at some unspecified future date when German economic recovery was sufficiently advanced. Thus Germany's immediate obligations in 1921 were less than 50 billion marks – as little, in fact, as 41 billion (taking account of what had been paid after 1919). That had been Keynes's idea of a viable total in *The Economic Consequences*. Moreover, inflation had substantially reduced the real value of Germany's internal debt by mid-1921 to around 24 billion gold marks. So as a percentage of national income, total public sector liabilities including reparations were around 160 per cent.

The second point (made by Schuker) is that the Germans received at least as much in the form of loans from abroad which were never repaid as they themselves paid in reparations. Altogether, between 1919 and 1932, Germany paid around 19.1 billion gold marks in reparations (the Germans insisted it was much more, but tended to overvalue assets they handed over). But in the same period, net capital inflows to Germany totalled around 27 billion gold marks. Of this money, much was never repaid, because it took the form of investments denominated in paper marks which were reduced to worthlessness by hyperinflation in 1923; or deposits in German banks which were effectively frozen after the 1931 banking crisis.

There is no question that reparations need to be put in perspective. Germany was not alone in emerging from the war weighed down with debts and shorn of valuable assets and territories. Indeed, Germany was in some respects better off than its former allies, the Ottoman and Habsburg Empires, and better off than the Russian Empire too. Indeed, even France and Britain had total debt burdens – including substantial sums owed to a foreign power – of a similar order to that of Germany. As a proportion of national income, the British national debt in 1921 was in fact almost exactly the same as total German liabilities as calculated above. On the other hand, the German balance of payments was much weaker than the British because of the loss of overseas investments and the merchant marine, all of which had been important sources of foreign currency before the war. Although foreign lending allowed the Germans to run trade deficits and pay reparations for much longer than he had expected, Keynes was right that at some point the system was bound to break down. Even in the absence of the depression, there would have been a German debt crisis eventually. For even if German exports had picked up sufficiently to exceed imports for a sustained period – unlikely in the absence of global free trade – the 'C bonds' would then have ceased to be notional. In the sense that foreign investors could not ignore this *potential* 82 billion gold marks of debt when assessing Germany's future creditworthiness, the C bonds were always a more onerous burden than Marks claims.

At the same time, the fact that France and Britain were also heavily burdened with debts meant that, from the outset, there were limits to what they could afford to do to impose their peace terms on Germany. Full-scale occupation of Germany was never seriously contemplated: the most the French were able to do was to occupy the Rhine ports and later the Ruhr area when the Germans defaulted on reparation payments, and these sanctions in no way facilitated the collection of the indemnity; quite the reverse. Thus the Allies expected the Germans to execute the punitive terms of the treaty on their behalf – a novelty, since the reparations imposed on France in 1815 and 1870–1 had been combined with military occupation. Reparations after 1919 were treated as part of the Reich budget, and, not surprisingly, democratically elected politicians were extremely reluctant to approve taxes for this purpose. The fact that the sums actually transferred in the 1920s were less as a proportion of national income than (for example) the sums transferred by France to Germany between 1940 and 1944 or the sums transferred from East Germany to the Soviet Union after 1945 is thus beside the point; in both these cases the collecting power was far more coercive. The short answer to the 'can't pay? won't pay!' argument is 'won't pay? can't collect!'

This brings us back to the question of determinism versus free will. Historians like Marks and Schuker are quite right that the Germans sought to avoid paying reparations. Between 1919 and 1923, there seems little doubt that at least some politicians saw currency depreciation as a way of undermining the Versailles system, believing that a weak mark would boost German exports so much that the western powers would be forced to revise the treaty, if only to defend their own economies from German 'dumping'. In the mid-1920s, the liberal Foreign Minister Gustav Stresemann saw the conclusion of trade treaties in a not dissimilar light, aiming to 'conduct foreign policy by economic means, as this is the only respect in which we are still a great power'. And, after 1930, Brüning sought (as he later put it) 'to make use of the world crisis to put pressure on all the other powers', in the belief that deflation would, once again, boost German exports and thereby force revision. In short, no Weimar government seriously wanted to 'fulfil' the terms of the London Ultimatum, the Dawes plan or the Young plan. But two points must be made. First, all these efforts to get rid of reparations had only very limited success. Only after inflation, stagnation, deflation and complete economic collapse were reparations finally suspended in 1932. If nothing else, this suggests that avoiding payment was less easy than historians have sometimes made it sound: a case of 'won't pay? can't not pay!', perhaps. Second, to argue that the Germans could have paid even more than they did begs the question: what constitutes a tolerable level of unrequited transfer? For a democratic state, the majority of whose population refused to recognize that Germany had lost the war, much less surrendered unconditionally, it might be said that *any* reparations were intolerable. The so-called 'Chancellor of fulfilment' Joseph Wirth expressly ruled out a new tax on property because it would 'declare the [London] Ultimatum [of 1921] to be 80 per cent possible'. Such views, more than anything else, determined the maximum sum which German governments were able to transfer as reparations. It is to the domestic politics of Weimar that we must therefore turn – and to the other, less well-known reparations which the Germans wished to pay to themselves.

III   Internal factors: politics versus economics

If external factors are ultimately inseparable from internal factors, then much the same can be said about the dichotomy between economics and politics within Germany itself. The reality of the inter-war period was that the two became entangled as never before. In many ways, this politicization

of economic life – and economization of political life – was a legacy of the
First World War. It was the war which caused the role of government to
expand, so that the state not only became the economy's biggest customer
for labour, goods and services, but also vastly extended its powers of legal
regulation to cover trade, capital exports, the internal distribution of raw
materials, prices, rents and, to some extent, wages. In 1914, public
spending had accounted for 18 per cent of net national product. In 1917, it
reached a peak of 76 per cent. The tide of state economic power receded
substantially after the collapse of Germany's military position, but it never
returned to its pre-war level. Between 1919 and 1932, total public spending
was equivalent to, on average, 34 per cent of NNP, nearly twice its pre-war
level. Nor did the state wholly relinquish its new powers of regulation.

At the same time, increasing power was wielded after 1914 by organized
economic interest groups. The strength of cartells and associations was a
distinctive feature of German industry even before the war, when they had
mainly been concerned with (relatively modest) price-fixing and (relatively
unsuccessful) resistance to the demands of organized labour. When the war
came, however, it seemed sensible to delegate considerable amounts of
regulatory power to them, rather than create entirely new state organs.
Some economic associations thus acquired a public, statutory character –
allocating raw materials in a particular sector, for example, or controlling
prices and exports. As Gerald Feldman has shown, such tendencies were
especially pronounced in the iron and steel sector. This system of 'self-
regulation' was partly but not entirely wound up after the war and there
remained a number of areas in which private and public sector responsibilities continued to overlap – notably in the process of wage negotiation.
The assumption remained pervasive that business interests should be given
special consideration in all matters relating to the economy. The very fact
that the words *die Wirtschaft* signified both 'big business' and 'the economy'
in Weimar politics was indicative of this.

However, it was not only heavy industry which was able to influence the
making of economic policy. The traditional influence of Prussian
landowners did not end with the revolution. Indeed, the acute plight of the
agricultural sector – constantly sinking into debt as commodity prices
plummeted – in some ways served to increase agrarian influence in politics.
At the same time, the various social groups which Germans lump together
as the *Mittelstand* – small businessmen, white-collar employees and so on –
were also able to exert at least as much political pressure as they had been
able to do in the Wihelmine period – though the fissiparous tendency which
characterized all middle-class politics in the 1920s was especially evident
here. Finally, there is no question that the organizations of manual labour,

whose influence had been much circumscribed before 1914, came to exercise an influence over policy-making every bit as important as that played by big business.

This was a consequence of the war and the revolution of November 1918. Although the likelihood of a Bolshevik-style revolution in Germany now tends to be played down by historians, fear of such a descent into civil war was strong enough to persuade German business leaders (as well as some senior military officers and civil servants) of the expediency of a post-war understanding with the socialist trade unions, whose leaders generally shared their aversion to the radical left. The agreement of 15 November 1918 between the industrial magnate Hugo Stinnes and the trade union leader Carl Legien was one of four vital compromises which the majority Social Democrat leaders made in the first days after the proclamation of the republic. (The others were with the army, the federal states and the constitutional liberals.) Formally, it meant the concession to workers of the eight-hour day and large nominal wage increases; in practice it meant that business and the new government would do everything possible to avoid high post-war unemployment and serious falls in working-class living standards, which it was widely feared would lead to a second revolution. As far as men like Legien were concerned, ambitious plans for 'socialization' (meaning everything from nationalization to the institutionalization of workers' power within works' councils) were of less importance than these basic commitments to reduce working hours, maintain full employment and raise wages. These, in conjunction with redistributive taxation and increased public spending on housing, health and education, were the reforms they had always hoped to achieve in Germany without the upheaval of revolution. For their part, Stinnes and other businessmen certainly did not relish concessions on such issues, but saw them as preferable to the sort of wholesale expropriation taking place in Russia. In the short run, they also opened up the possibility of continuing state subsidies, loans at low real interest rates, liberalized exports and tax breaks – so long as these could be justified as being necessary to maintain employment.

The institutional arrangements which developed out of this hastily concluded compact between big business and organized labour were exceedingly complex. National organs like the Central Community of Labour and the Reich Economic Council jostled for influence over economic policy with new Reich ministries for Labour, the Economy and Reconstruction, traditional organs of economic management like the Reichsbank, wartime relics like the price control boards and new bureaucratic excrescences like the foreign trade control bureaux. At the local level, firms had to deal with a multiplicity of institutions and, especially in the early 1920s, a torrent of regulations. Often, decision-making was simply stalemated by the application of the principle of 'parity', whereby employers' and employees' interests had to be equally represented wherever economic matters were being debated. In short, Weimar's political economy was a tangle to which no simple label – 'corporatism', 'organized capitalism' 'welfare state' – can do justice. Even to sub-divide industry into rival light and heavy industrial blocs, following David Abraham, is to do a violence to the convoluted and fragmented reality.

Perhaps the most obvious focus for distributional conflicts was the Reich budget, for it was the budget which determined tax rates and social security contributions, pensions and benefits, subsidies to industry and certain kinds of social expenditure. As we have seen, reparations accounted for a significant proportion of total Reich spending each year between 1920 and 1932, and they actually exceeded the deficits for the period 1924–31. But they do not explain the full extent of government deficits in the inflation period: if one simply deducts reparations from total expenditures (adjusting domestic spending for inflation), large deficits remain for the years 1919, 1920 and 1923.

True, as Eichengreen and Webb have pointed out, inflation would have been lower in the absence of reparations and thus revenue would have been higher in real terms (the reverse of the 'Tanzi effect' whereby higher inflation reduces the real value of tax receipts). The temptation is strong to conclude, as they do, that reparations were therefore the key to Weimar's financial problem. Yet the implication that without reparations there would have been no deficits is open to question. For Weimar's political economy was as much riven by internal as by external distributional conflicts. Even if there had been no reparations, it is easy to imagine the various competing interest groups simply bidding up total expenditure to take up the slack.

The trouble was that German politics in the 1920s was not just a zero-sum game; in fiscal terms, it was a negative-sum game. As the debates on Matthias Erzberger's tax reforms of 1919–20 showed, there was no real willingness to balance the budget, even before the publication of the London Ultimatum and even at a time when inflation was levelling off. Radical – perhaps too radical – increases in direct taxation were accompanied or followed by even larger increases in expenditure on the railways or on the reconstruction of the merchant marine, the main objective of which was to create jobs. In short, the republic existed to pay not only reparations to the victorious Allies but also reparations to the Germans themselves. Had the former been reduced, it is probable that the latter would simply have been increased.

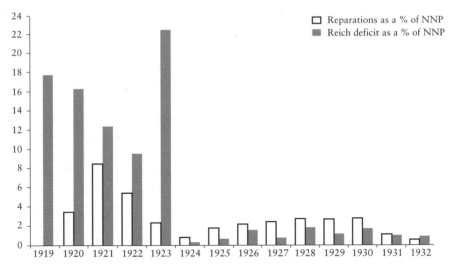

Figure 2.4   Reparations and Reich deficits as a percentage of NNP, 1919–1932

Between 1919 and 1923, reparations to the working classes not only meant that post-war unemployment was postponed. Because it led to inflation, it also meant that the distribution of income and wealth in Germany was considerably equalized, even allowing for the fact that an elite of enterpreneurs protected their wealth from erosion by investing in 'real values' and foreign currency. For, if foreign lenders ended up paying for foreign reparations, it was domestic lenders who ended up paying for much of the cost of domestic reparations. By the end of 1923, people who had invested in pre-war bonds and shares or war loans – any financial asset, in fact, which was denominated in paper marks – found the value of their investments reduced to virtually nothing. The revaluation legislation which was subsequently enacted did something to make good these losses; but ultimately it could not possibly alter the fact that a massive transfer – in the form of an inflationary tax on savings – had been effected.

After 1924, 'domestic reparations' continued to be paid, though in a less spectacular fashion. The reforms to the tax system introduced by Luther in 1924 made the overall impact of the Reich budget slightly less progressive than it would have been had Erzberger's reforms worked. But they had not: in the later inflation years, tax deducted at source from employees' wages had been about the only direct tax efficiently collected. If anything, then, the end of inflation probably reduced the share of the tax burden which fell on workers. Inasmuch as 'social expenditures' by the Reich, states and local government tended to rise during the mid-1920s, there was a further redistributive effect.

However, transfers to workers were not only effected through taxation and expenditure, but also through wages which, if unions and employers could not agree, were often imposed by the Labour Ministry's system of binding arbitration. One of the most important debates in modern economic history was precipitated by the publication in 1979 of an article by Knut Borchardt, which argued that this system made the economy inherently 'sick' in the mid-1920s because arbitration led to excessive real wages, which squeezed company profits and thus reduced investment. In saying this, Borchardt appeared to endorse the contemporary argument advanced by the Reich Association of German Industry that nothing short of a dismantling of the post-revolutionary arrangements governing industrial relations could have restored the economy to health.

The evidence that labour costs were excessive in the 1920s seems, at first sight, quite convincing. For example, the share of wages as a proportion of national income (as compared with income from capital) rose sharply between 1914 and 1932. However, it is one thing to say that Weimar Germany was a more equal society than Wilhelmine Germany and another to say that this was why investment tailed off in the 1920s (especially as the share of wages in national income was not so very different in the years of the 'economic miracle' after 1947). Recent research on this point by Theo Balderston has arrived at rather different conclusions.

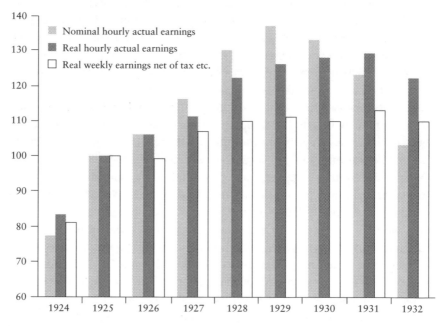

Figure 2.5   Collectively contracted earnings, 1924–1932 (1925=100)

Balderston acknowledges that real wages were rising relative to productivity and export prices, though the rise was less than spectacular when shorter hours, tax and insurance deductions are taken into account. But he denies that this was what caused profits to stagnate and investment to fall. He maintains that rising real wages were needed to increase the 'participation ratio' – i.e., to attract additional men and women into the workforce – at a time when world demand for German exports was rising.

So if the 'real wage position' was not the problem, how are we to explain the undoubted decline in investment and the relatively greater severity of the slump in Germany? Balderston finds the most plausible culprit not in the labour market but in the capital market. Of course, for some historians of the left – such as Dick Geary – there has always been a strong preference for any explanation for the slump which blames capital rather than labour for it. He and others have attached considerable significance to decisions taken in 1928 by industrial employers to adopt a tougher line with labour which culminated in the Ruhr lock-out of that year, arguing that this marked the breakdown of that corporatist partnership between capital and labour on which Weimar rested. This may be true in a political sense, but it is not a satisfactory economic explanation of the fall in investment and general business pessimism of which the Ruhr lock-out was a consequence, rather than a cause. Balderston's argument is more sophisticated. He stresses the damage done to the German capital market by the inflation. Savers and investors who lost out in the crisis of 1923–4 were wary of making the same mistake twice – especially those who had bought public sector bonds, which had been exceptionally bad investments. When the Reich, states or local authorities wished to borrow money after 1924, they thus found the market for new bonds extremely weak even when high yields were offered. This (combined with the low liquidity of the banking sector) obliged governments at all levels to reduce their deficits and attempt to balance their budgets. And the first items of expenditure to be reduced were local authorities' budgets for housing and other infrastructure investment – precisely the sector which fuelled British recovery in the 1930s.

IV   Real and imaginary alternatives

Whether the labour market or the capital market was to blame for reducing investment will doubtless continue to be debated. There still remains, however, the further question of whether governments could possibly have done anything to stop the downward economic spiral which ensued. And here we return once again to the debate between economic determinism and political room for manoeuvre.

There is little doubt that fiscal and monetary policy made the slump worse between 1930 and 1932. Attempts to balance the budget and to preserve the convertibility of the Reichsmark clearly had the effect of exacerbating deflation. According to critics of the Chancellor at the time, Brüning, there was no economic need for this; his motives were primarily political (to get rid of reparations and alter the constitution). Economic historians such as Holtfrerich claim that the government could instead have increased borrowing, rather than trying to balance the budget, giving a proto-Keynesian stimulus to demand through public works schemes; or it could have devalued the Reichsmark, allowing a reduction in interest rates and boosting exports. It is certainly pleasant, if tantalizing, to imagine such Keynesian policies being adopted five years before the publication of Keynes's *General Theory*. But to these suggestions Borchardt and James have given three answers. First, contemporary alternative policies came too late in the day and did not envisage a big enough counter-cyclical boost; even if they had been tried, therefore, they would not have had much success. Second, they could not have been tried: the government was not free to act as it wished, because of restrictions on the Reichsbank's reserve law imposed by the Allies after the inflation. And third, the memory of the inflation meant that there would have been public panic at the news of increased Reich deficits, leading, self-defeatingly, to cash withdrawals from banks and further deflation. These arguments are largely endorsed by Balderston.

The determinist view thus seems to have prevailed, at least for Weimar's last years. However, simply because there was no *effective* alternative to a policy of deflation, does not mean that Weimar's economic collapse was inevitable from the outset. For, as both Balderston and Borchardt show, what really constrained both investors and politicians in the slump was the fear of a second great inflation. A question which needs urgently to be addressed is therefore whether there were alternatives to the inflation. As with all counterfactual hypotheses, the suggestion that there might have been can only be tentative. Nevertheless, it seems a more plausible scenario than the alternatives to deflation discussed above.

As we have seen, the key to the inflation was monetary expansion caused principally by uncontrolled short-term government borrowing. Was this avoidable? Conceivably. In early 1920, prices stopped rising and actually began to fall, mainly as a result of speculative capital in-flows, but also because price increases had largely absorbed the wartime monetary over-hang. This presented a real opportunity to stabilize the currency – not, as happened in Britain, to deflate to the pre-war exchange rate, but merely to stabilize at the existing rate, which was around 10 per cent of the pre-war rate. (This was roughly what happened in France.) Such a formal devaluation, in conjunction with cuts in spending and increases in indirect taxes, could have effectively avoided the descent into hyperinflation, particularly if combined with the deregulation of trade and the labour market. Although such a policy would have meant a cut in living standards and an increase in unemployment, it would have been a significantly 'softer landing' than actually happened in 1923. Although it would have disappointed foreign investors, the experience of 1924 – when they returned to the German market despite far greater losses – suggests that the disappointment would soon have been forgotten.

It is not difficult to see why this was not done. Economically, it might have been possible, even preferable. Politically, it was impossible. First, the fear of unemployment was too great. Second, the belief that financial stabilization would make the collection of reparations easier was too widespread. This might seem to consign any counterfactual hypothesis to the realm of idle speculation. Yet with hindsight, there are good reasons for questioning the rationality of such contemporary assumptions. It seems unlikely that a rise in unemployment in 1920 would have led to anything as serious as the disorder and violence unleashed in 1923. Moreover, the evidence suggests that the strategy of trying to get rid of reparations by means of inflation was misconceived. Allowing the mark to depreciate may have boosted German exports, but it boosted Allied exports to Germany even more (hence the huge trade deficit of 1922). This was hardly an inducement to treat Germany more generously. Thus we are bound to conclude that hyperinflation happened not just because it was the line of least political resistance, but also because its benefits were exaggerated and its costs understated. Tragically, its legacy seems to have compelled Brüning to take the line of greatest economic resistance.

There is of course an easier way of answering the question: was there an alternative to the extremes of inflation and deflation which characterized the Weimar period? The answer is that there was, and it was called National Socialism. The nature of the economic recovery which took place in Germany after 1933 illustrates not so much what ought to have been done by a democratic regime, but why a democratic regime could not have done it. Although there is some evidence of an increase in industrial output in the second half of 1932, there is little reason to believe that Germany would have recovered any more successfully than France without the massive programme of state investment undertaken by Hitler. Between 1933 and 1938, the public sector accounted for between 44 and 49 per cent of gross investment. The lion's share of this had a military purpose, as the increase of military spending from just 1.5 per cent of gross national product in 1933 to 20 per cent in 1938 suggests – though even this under-states the importance of rearmament, since many apparently non-military investments in transport and infrastructure (most famously, the *Autobahnen*) had strategic objectives.

The results were, at least by comparison with what had gone before, impressive. Between 1928 and 1932, gross national product had fallen by about a fifth in real terms. Between 1932 and 1938 it rose by three-quarters. Industrial output in the same periods had fallen by 42 per cent, then rose by 110 per cent. Unemployment fell from its appalling peak in 1932 to a negligible level in 1938: just 400,000. Yet there was only the most moderate inflation, in itself not unwelcome after the deflation of the slump. How was this possible? Public spending rose by more than 120 per cent. Although taxes and social insurance were increased, total public debt went up from 14 billion Reichsmarks to 42 billion Reichsmarks, and 60 per cent of new debt was short-term. The money supply expanded by more than 70 per cent. Yet wholesale prices rose by no more than 16 per cent between 1933 and 1937; and although the trade deficit widened, the consequences were in fact far less dire than pessimists like the Reichsbank President Hjalmar Schacht feared. Moreover, actual weekly wages rose by around 18 per cent. Although that figure reflects longer working hours rather than higher real hourly rates, it demonstrates the limits of Schacht's warning that 'the standard of living and the extent of armament production are in inverse ratio'. If aggregate output increased enough, both could go up without drastically compromising the rearmament programme.

The explanation for the relative success of Nazi economic policy lies in the fact that private consumption was restrained in a way which had been more or less impossible under Weimar. The bulk of industrial output was accounted for by producer goods, not consumer goods. As investment rose, so private consumption as a percentage of national income fell from 83 per cent to 59 per cent. To give a striking example: in 1937, beer consumption per capita was 60 per cent lower than it had been ten years before. The Germans were never so sober as they were under Hitler. In other words, the Nazi recovery was not 'Keynesian': the state was not engaged in 'kick-starting' a stalled market economy by boosting demand. On the contrary, private consumption was actually reined in to allow rearmament to proceed with minimal inflationary consequences. (The restoration of price controls and the extension of exchange controls served the same purpose.) In addition, considerable ingenuity was expended on disguising the extent of the fiscal stimulus: government borrowing was concealed behind the bogus

Metallurgical Research Office, which effectively took over from the Reichsbank the discounting of treasury bills.

Although many of the economic controls used by the Nazis had in fact been developed in the Weimar period, none of this would have been possible without a radical transformation of the German political system, to eradicate that institutional pluralism which had ultimately been responsible for the extreme 'go-stop' swings of Weimar economic policy. Hitler's earliest political statements show that he understood the need for political centralization. As early as 1920, he and his associates in the German Workers' Party had called for 'the creation of a strong central power for the Reich; the unconditional authority of the political central parliament over the entire Reich and its organizations; and the formation of corporations based on estate and occupation for the purpose of carrying out the general legislation passed by the Reich in the various ... states'. Of course, by 1933 he had replaced any notion of parliamentary centralization with the 'leader principle'; and in practice, as is well known, political centralization in the Third Reich was always to some extent compromised by the uneasy dualism of party and state and the 'polycratic' tendencies which Hitler's style of leadership encouraged. The deficiencies of Nazi organization were laid bare by war. Nevertheless, there is an important sense in which the Nazi state was less polycratic than its predecessor. The destruction of the trade unions and the creation in their stead of the Labour Front and the subordination of the employers' associations to the Reich Estate of German Industry marked the end of 'corporatism' as it had evolved in the 1920s. It is important to emphasize that these changes marked the end of autonomy for both organized labour and business, though the freedom of the latter was more gradually eroded. In particular, restrictions on private sector access to the capital market and on the distribution of profits meant that even before the promulgation of the Four Year Plan, most firms' economic freedom of action was severely limited. Hitler's famous declaration in the Four Year Plan memorandum – 'the job of the Reich Economics Ministry is simply to set out the national economic tasks; private industry has to fulfil them' – perfectly encapsulated the subordination of economics to politics which had been achieved.

Between 1918 and 1939, the German economy was capable of one of three things: it could pay reparations to the victors; it could pay 'reparations' to its own working class; or it could rearm for 'a war of revenge'. It could not do all three; nor could it do just two of these. Weimar failed because it attempted to do the second while pretending to do the first (as well as secretly beginning the third). This confusion was less the product of conscious political decision-making than the spontaneous outcome of an overcomplex political process in which economic interests were given too much weight. By contrast, Hitler saw what Weimar politicians had failed to see: that economics should come second to politics. True, he had one obvious advantage: the changed international situation after 1932 meant that he did not need to pay reparations or even conceal rearmament. But he still needed to make a choice between rearmament and working-class living standards. It can be argued that he sought to avoid such a choice – that was certainly the view of Tim Mason. But the evidence for a successful restriction of living standards to allow a non-inflationary programme of rearmament – and rearmament sufficient to bring Germany a decisive victory in Europe – is overwhelming. German workers in the 1930s were no longer being paid domestic reparations, as they had been in the 1920s; they were getting a slowly diminishing share of a quite rapidly growing cake. And although Hitler's Third Reich ultimately lasted even less time than Weimar's 'city of Mahagonny', it was not its internal economic weakness which determined that – reassuring though the notion of Nazi self-destruction might be. In the final analysis, it was the superior organizational efficiency of its enemies which was decisive.

Select bibliography

Abraham, David, *The Collapse of the Weimar Republic. Political Economy and Crisis* (1981).

Balderston, Theo, 'War Finance and Inflation in Britain and Germany', *Economic History Review*, 42 (1989).

Balderston, Theo, *The German Economic Crisis, 1923–1932* (1993).

Borchardt, Knut, 'Constraints and Room for Manoeuvre in the Great Depression of the Early Thirties: Towards a Revision of the Received Historical Picture', in Balderston, Theo, *Perspectives on Modern German Economic History and Policy* (1991).

Eichengreen, Barry, *Golden Fetters. The Gold Standard and the Great Depression, 1919–1939* (1992).

Feldman, Gerald D., *Iron and Steel in the German Inflation, 1916–1923* (1977).

Feldman, Gerald D., *The Great Disorder. Politics, Economics and Society in the German Inflation* (1993).

Ferguson, Niall, *Paper and Iron. Hamburg Business and German Politics in the Era of Inflation, 1897–1927* (1995).

Geary, Dick, 'Employers, Workers and the Collapse of the Weimar Republic', in Ian Kershaw, ed., *Weimar: Why did German Democracy Fail?* (1990).

Holtfrerich, Carl-Ludwig, *The German Inflation, 1914–1923* (1986).

James, Harold, *The German Slump. Politics and Economics 1924–1936* (1986).

Kaiser, David E., Tim W. Mason and Richard J. Overy, 'Debate: Germany, "Domestic Crisis" and War in 1939', *Past and Present* 12 (1989).

Kershaw, Ian, ed., *Weimar: Why did German Democracy Fail?* (1990).

Keynes, John Maynard, *The Economic Consequences of the Peace* (1919).

Kruedener, J. Baron von, ed., *Economic Crisis and Political Collapse. The Weimar Republic, 1924–1933* (1990).

Maier, Charles S., *Recasting Bourgeois Europe. Stabilisation in France, Germany and Italy in the Decade after World War I* (1975).

Marks, Sally, 'The Myths of Reparations', *Central European History* 11 (1978).

Mason, Tim W., 'The Primacy of Politics: Politics and Economics in National Socialist Germany', in S. Woolf, ed., *The Nature of Fascism* (1968).

Noakes, Jeremy and Geoffrey Pridham, eds., *Nazism, 1919–1945*, vol. II: *State, Economy and Society, 1933–1939* (1984).

Overy, Richard J., *The Nazi Economic Recovery, 1932–1938* (2nd edition, 1996).

Overy, Richard J., 'Germany, Domestic Crisis and War in 1939', *Past and Present* 116 (1987).

Schuker, Steven, 'American Reparations to Germany, 1919–1933', in Gerald D. Feldman and Elisabeth Müller-Luckner, eds., *Die Nachwirkungen der Inflation auf die deutsche Geschichte, 1924–1933* (1985).

Webb, Stephen B., *Hyperinflation and Stabilisation in Weimar Germany* (1989).

Witt, Peter-Christian, 'Tax Policies, Tax Assessment and Inflation: Towards a Sociology of Public Finances in the German Inflation, 1914 to 1923', in Witt, ed., *Wealth and Taxation in Central Europe. The History and Sociology of Public Finance* (1987).

3

Culture and society in Weimar Germany: the impact of modernism and mass culture

Elizabeth Harvey

The history of cultural life in Weimar Germany is usually, and rightly, associated with upheaval and transformation. Accounts of Weimar culture have emphasized the way in which forces for change – the upsurge in the aftermath of the First World War of the reformist and revolutionary left, the establishment of democracy, and longer-term economic and technological modernization – interacted with each other to foster modernism in the arts and to promote the development of a new 'mass culture'. The new mass culture, for contemporaries a crucial sign of the arrival of 'modernity', transformed the context of artistic production and consumption, shaking the dominance of the educated bourgeoisie as arbiters and consumers of culture. Germany in the 1920s, torn by political and economic crises but outstanding for its pluralist and cosmopolitan cultural climate and its cultural innovation, became the object of fascination for foreign observers and visitors.

It also became the object of intense self-analysis by its own critics and cultural commentators. Contemporaries were highly sensitive to the cultural changes they were witnessing. An outpouring of comment and criticism greeted the various manifestations of cultural modernity and documented the fascination, ambivalence and often fierce hostility aroused by phenomena as diverse as jazz, twelve-tone music, plays about abortion, anti-war paintings, film palaces and pulp fiction. In the eyes of their enemies, these types of cultural output, which were in different ways products of economic and social modernization, became the scapegoat for those changes: cultural conservatives accused them of contributing to a comprehensive national crisis, and of undermining social stability, moral values and cultural standards. At the same time, right-wing attacks on modernism in the arts and mass culture became attacks on the republic itself, which because it provided a framework for cultural innovation became identified with it. Through such attacks, cultural debates in Weimar Germany became polarized to an extreme and politically destabilizing degree.

In recent years much effort has gone into refining our understanding of the cultural transformations of the Weimar period and of the positions adopted by the participants in contemporary debates on cultural issues. There is, however, a risk of allowing the polarized contemporary debate to distort our perceptions of German cultural life in the Weimar years. It is possible to focus exclusively on discourses about modern art, the new media and mass entertainments without examining assumptions about their social impact and their distribution beyond the big cities, in particular beyond Berlin. This essay therefore places particular emphasis on the issue of cultural transmission and reception. It focuses for the most part on the arts and entertainments which were publicly shown or performed, though it also considers the new medium of radio; for reasons of space, it leaves aside the novels and poetry of the period. It emphasizes the significance of innovations in cultural life, and of Berlin as a focus of cultural experiment, but it also considers how far developments in artistic modernism shaped cultural life in the provinces, and considers how social class and regional differences affected the reception of the new media and mass entertainments. When looking at cultural conservatism, it draws attention not only to the ideas of individual conservative theorists and the arguments of conservative parties or organizations at national level, but also to the practice of cultural conservatism at the grass-roots, particularly in provincial Germany. Looking at the social history of Weimar culture from these angles may, it is hoped, enhance our understanding of it as a history of uneven development.

I Cultural innovation and experiment

To draw attention to the limits and unevenness of the breakthrough of 'cultural modernity' is not to deny the momentum of innovation which so impressed or alarmed contemporary observers. Artistic conventions and established assumptions about the function of art had already been widely challenged in Wilhelmine Germany. However, the republic provided a context in which aesthetic experiment and committed left-wing art flourished as never before. The revolutionary upheavals of 1918–19 and the advent of democracy inspired artists and politicians to draw up programmes of cultural revolution and cultural reform. Expressionist poets, painters and architects greeted the revolution with enthusiasm, believing a new age had dawned. When a certain disillusion with its consequences set in, artists sympathetic to the left, together with journalists and critics, continued to provoke the bourgeoisie and the new republican establishment with work which was frequently satirical and deliberately shocking or shrill. Some looked to the newly founded KPD as the source of a class-conscious proletarian counter-culture and to the Soviet Union as an alternative model of modernity to western capitalism. Meanwhile, the republican state itself fostered a degree of political and artistic pluralism. The Weimar constitution declared, albeit with some qualifications, that censorship 'does not take place' and proclaimed the freedom of the arts and scholarship. Censorship did in fact continue, but the boundaries of what was tolerable to the state authorities were extended. The newly democra-tized municipal and regional governments became a source of patronage, in a number of cases favouring the performance or display of avant-garde works as a badge of their progressiveness. Despite the strain on public finances in the early years of the Weimar Republic, reaching a crisis at the height of the inflation, politicians at local and *Land* level continued to channel substantial public funding into the arts. As Gerald Feldman has commented, it was remarkable that an impoverished Germany in the wake of the First World War continued to maintain so many theatres and more than 30 opera houses.

The impact of the avant-garde was felt most in the world of 'high' culture, which remained a sphere dominated by an educated bourgeois public. Changes in the cultural sphere which had a greater impact on the mass of the population were those taking place in the entertainments industry through technological advances and new investment. Home entertainment began from 1923–4 onwards to include radio. Cheap entertainment outside the home could be found at variety theatres, at the new sports stadia, in bars and dance halls, and above all at the cinema, the commercial mass entertainment *par excellence*. By the end of the 1920s there were more than 5,000 cinemas in Germany; in 1928, the peak year for cinema-going, around 353 million cinema tickets were sold. By comparison, attendance figures for the performances staged by municipal theatres in 87 towns and cities in 1926–7 were just under 12 million.[1]

The new cinemas and sports stadia were part of the changing urban landscapes of the 1920s. Local government efforts to improve the urban environment focused on the construction of new public parks, libraries, transport and housing schemes. Such reforms, often advocated and implemented by Social Democrats in cooperation with bourgeois politicians, were fuelled by an optimistic vision of the hygienic management of cities and their populations. But at the same time department stores and advertising hoardings were shaping cities in a different way as sites of consumerism, stimulating aspirations – even though the dream of American-style mass consumption was still far from being realized in Weimar Germany – towards a fast-moving urban consumer lifestyle. In this process, women – as wage-earners and as housewives, as salesgirls and shoppers – played key roles.

The salesgirl and the woman shopper represented facets of the potent composite myth of the Weimar 'new woman'. The myth was widely propagated in the media: illustrated magazines revelled in images of cigarette-smoking, motorbike-riding, silk-stockinged or tennis-skirted young women out on the streets, in bars or on the sports field. To an extent there was a social reality underlying the image: women had gained formally equal rights under the Weimar constitution, a growing number of middle-class as well as working-class women in the 1920s were working outside the home in jobs in the professions and in the service sector; a growing number of (particularly young and single) women spent their leisure at sports clubs and cinemas. Women thus constituted a more visible presence in the public sphere and in the economy than they had done before 1914 or 1918. But the myth as concocted by and debated in the media overlaid this reality with a mixture of fantasies and fears about women's increasing sexual independence (or voraciousness) and sexual knowledge, and about their presence on the street or in the cinema, dance-hall or lecture room. In the end, any and every facet of 'modern womanhood' became incorporated into the 'new woman': 'she' was both a devouring *femme fatale* and a cross-dressing lesbian, a sportswoman and an efficient housewife, a movie-going typist and a bluestocking student. But incoherent as it was, the 'new woman' myth expressed perceptions of cultural change and represented to Germans of both sexes many of the intoxicating and threatening dimensions of modernity.

If the 'new woman' was one powerful symbol of cultural change, Berlin came to embody it in terms of a geographical location. The capital of the republic became the site on which competing and conflicting visions of its modernity were – at least partially – realized. One strand of this perceived modernity was the cultivation of iconoclasm and experiment in the arts. Much of the artistic avant-garde gravitated to Berlin, and as the new 'insiders' of Weimar culture (to borrow Peter Gay's image) they found institutional footholds and receptive audiences there. Thus Schoenberg began teaching master classes in composition at the Prussian Academy of Arts in 1925, while Hindemith taught composition at the Staatliche Musikhochschule from 1927 onwards. Meanwhile at the Staatsoper major milestones of the new music were premiered, for instance Berg's *Wozzeck* in 1925. The Nationalgalerie promoted the work of contemporary German painters, while powerful private gallery directors vied with each other to sell 'difficult' contemporary art to public galleries and private collectors and to market their 'star' artists. Beyond the world of the arts establishment, fringe art forms flourished in clubs, bars and cabarets. Such venues provided outlets for lesser-known and experimental performers and pieces, and a place where a sub-culture such as that of Berlin's homosexual community could thrive.

At the same time, Berlin was developing as a centre of mass cultural production – in journalism, film and fashion – and as a showcase for the latest cultural imports from abroad. Of the big publishing houses, Ullstein stood out: it produced from its new printing house in Tempelhof newspapers and periodicals which ranged from the quality *Vossische Zeitung* to the popular *BZ am Mittag*, and included the most successful Ullstein publication of all, the *Berliner Illustrirte Zeitung*, whose circulation peaked at over 1.8 million in July 1929. As a city of cinema, Berlin had the giant studio complex of UFA at Neubabelsberg as the major German centre of film production; and a plethora of cinemas, ranging from the pseudo-rococo palaces of the Kurfürstendamm seating a thousand or more apiece to the smaller cinemas in working-class neighbourhoods. Fashion design and production was concentrated around the Hausvogteiplatz, where small firms – many of them Jewish – competed fiercely with each other to turn the latest Paris lines into wearable women's fashions – 'Berliner Chic' – for the elite and for the mass market. The different branches of cultural production in Berlin fed off each other: stars of stage and cinema had their images reproduced and amplified by the illustrated press, women could study the designs of Berlin fashion houses as worn by an actress in a Pabst film, by a revue singer or a model in the *Berliner Illustrirte* – even if their budget only ran to buying cheaper imitations in the nearest department store.

American cultural influence on Germany in the Weimar period was by no means restricted to Berlin. However, cultural imports from the USA found particularly enthusiastic audiences in the capital. The Tiller Girls and Josephine Baker drew Berlin audiences and evoked images of America and Americans as capable of technical brilliance as well as energy, expressiveness and daring. Jazz was one of the most popular, but also one of the most controversial, cultural imports from the United

States: jazz-playing dance bands could be found all over Berlin in hotels, cafés and bars. And American films seemed to go down better in Berlin than in Germany as a whole. Remarking on the disappointing box-office figures in Germany for the films made by Ernst Lubitsch in America after 1923, one contemporary observer remarked in 1926 that 'The Kurfürstendamm and Germany are two very different things'.[2] In its embracing of American culture, Berlin seemed to some observers more American than America.

In contrast both to the image of Berlin as centre of revolutionary art and bohemian lifestyles, and the view of the city as the capital of commercialized mass entertainment, the public authorities promoted a different vision of the city as a progressive polity providing an efficient urban infrastructure, combating social evils through appropriate welfare intervention and encouraging a democratic culture based on a rational lifestyle balancing work, domesticity and healthy leisure pursuits. Modern architects associated with the Bauhaus believed such a culture would be fostered by functionally designed mass housing projects, and they began from the mid-1920s onwards to gain major contracts in Berlin: building societies and the electrical engineering company Siemens commissioned housing projects, and under Martin Wagner as director of the municipal central building administration from 1927 onwards police stations and public swimming baths came to be designed in the new style as well. Even if these projects comprised only a fraction of new building in the city, they were striking symbols of the 'New Berlin'.

To contemporaries, developments in Berlin clearly embodied important shifts in culture and society which were affecting Germany generally. Accepted norms governing the form, content and exclusivity of 'high culture' were being challenged by the avant-garde. 'Mass culture' was becoming more pervasive, and its spread was seen as contributing to social homogenization: the rise of entertainments such as the cinema and the radio appeared to be loosening people's ties to traditional cultural milieux. In hindsight, however, these processes appear less straightforward. Recent studies which have focused on cultural life in the provinces, and on questions of class and cultural consumption, have been helpful in adding to and modifying the picture of cultural change.

II Keeping pace with the capital? The avant-garde in provincial Germany

It is generally agreed that the various competing styles and versions of modernism, though flourishing spectacularly in the Weimar years, never actually dominated German cultural output in quantitative terms or in terms of public performances, exhibitions or bestseller lists. As far as the production and reception of modernist work in different parts of Germany are concerned, local and regional studies have contributed to a history of Weimar modernism which takes into account the different cultural conditions in different parts of Germany, while avoiding an oversimplified view of the provinces as constantly lagging behind the pace-setter, Berlin. At the same time, they acknowledge the extent to which some provincial contexts really did prove less receptive than the capital to aspects of avant-garde artistic production.

There were in the Weimar period, as had been the case in Wilhelmine Germany, important centres of avant-garde creativity outside Berlin. The Bauhaus, for instance, was set up in Weimar and moved to Dessau in 1925, only leaving Dessau after a Nazi motion passed by the city authorities in August 1932 forced the school to relocate to Berlin. The emergence in the mid-1920s of the 'New Objectivity' movement (*Neue Sachlichkeit*) in the visual arts – which can be seen in part as a reaction against the intensity, rage and emotionalism of Expressionism – was by no means centred on Berlin, though important *Neue Sachlichkeit* painters such as Georg Grosz, Rudolf Schlichter and Christian Schad were based there. It flourished rather in a number of provincial centres, notably Karlsruhe, Dresden, Munich, Hanover, Cologne and Düsseldorf, as Sergiusz Michalski emphasizes in his recent study.

Artistic modernism was promoted by some (though certainly not all) provincial city politicians who sought to overcome the stigma of provincialism and wanted to 'catch up with the metropolis' not only in the quality of their town's cultural facilities but in the content of its publicly subsidized arts programme. Thus, for instance, the Wiesbaden city authorities appointed the progressive theatre directors Carl Hagemann and subsequently Paul Bekker, the latter overseeing productions of Křenek's jazz-inspired opera *Jonny spielt auf* and the German premiere of Schoenberg's *Erwartung*. In the Ruhr, as Matthias Uecker has shown, the city councils of Bochum and Essen backed the conductor Rudolf Schulz-Dornburg in his campaign to convert local audiences and music critics to the work of Schoenberg, Webern, Honegger, Stravinsky and Bartok. However, few involved in the arts world of the Ruhrgebiet shared Schulz-Dornburg's commitment to the vision of a gigantic Ruhr metropolis which would dwarf London and New York in size and be united by the 'new art': as an out-and-out advocate of modernism, the conductor remained an exception in the generally more conservative cultural climate of the region.

On the whole, theatre directors and conductors in provincial towns and cities tempered their enthusiasm for new work with consideration for the preferences of subscription-buying audiences. Despite the growth of the Social Democratic *Freie Volksbühne*, which supplied cut-price theatre tickets to its largely working-class membership, concert and theatre audiences were still predominantly middle-class and tended to be middle of the road in taste. The institutions of provincial cultural life remained – despite the buffeting taken by the middle classes during the inflation – what they had been in the *Kaiserreich*, a focus of middle-class sociability, bound by middle-class conventions. (Whether audiences which were more socially mixed would have been more adventurous in their tastes is another question.) Theatre schedules and concert programmes including more advanced contemporary works tended to be cushioned, just as they are today, by more familiar and reassuring items to keep audiences happy. Thus it was reported that in Wiesbaden in 1927 the subscription audience reacted to Darius Milhaud's experimental three-part miniature opera (*opéra minute*) with bewilderment, but was 'compensated and cheered' by the next item on the programme, a 'very graceful' performance of a piece by Pergolesi.[3] Studies of the theatre schedules in Heidelberg and Bochum show a predominance of light contemporary comedies and farces, operettas (increasing as a proportion of productions during the depression as public subsidies were cut and the pressure grew to maximize ticket sales), and classic plays and operas from the eighteenth and nineteenth centuries: serious contemporary drama comprised a minority of productions. At the Heidelberg city theatre, only one work by Brecht was performed during the whole of the Weimar era.

The need for caution in programme planning was underlined by cases where the scheduling of consciously progressive and avant-garde work provoked outright hostility. One such case was the world premiere of Bartok's 'musical pantomime' *The Miraculous Mandarin* at the Cologne Opera House in November 1926. Bartok had wanted the work premièred in Germany as he had expected its reception there to be particularly favourable; however, he had hoped for a première in Berlin or Munich, and took up the offer from Cologne only with some trepidation as, according to one biographer, Bartok 'did not trust the Cologne audience'.[4] The première ended in uproar, with the audience yelling and booing in the auditorium. Konrad Adenauer, the then mayor of Cologne (and later first Chancellor of the Federal Republic of Germany), then intervened personally to ban further performances. The work was never performed in Germany again during the composer's lifetime.

Sometimes rejection of new work was coupled with a quite explicit hostility to Berlin and a sense of provincial self-assertion against the decadence of the centre. In 1929, for example, the Heidelberg city theatre organized a one-off performance of the new play by Peter Martin Lampel, *Revolte im Erziehungshaus*, a work inspired by scandals concerning the maltreatment of inmates in reformatories. Reaction in the Catholic local daily *Pfälzer Bote* was withering: 'And if one result of this performance in the "provinces" is clear, then it is that it arouses horror at the moral nihilism of a certain Berlin.'[5]

Generally, therefore, the influence of artistic modernism extended well beyond the avant-garde mecca of Berlin, making its mark on publicly subsidized and publicly consumed art in smaller provincial towns as well as in larger cities. This process was aided by consciously progressive municipal and *Land* authorities, public and private galleries and art societies, and by theatre and orchestra directors committed to promoting the work of the avant-garde alongside the traditional repertoire. Public reaction to the works of the modernists was predictably diverse, ranging from enthusiasm (*Jonny spielt auf*, for instance, was an enormous popular hit), through respectful curiosity to suspicion, bewilderment or straight-forward hostility.

III   Mass culture: a force for social and regional homogenization?

The extent to which the emergence of a mass culture in Weimar Germany lessened social and regional differences in cultural consumption, taste and expectations is a question that has aroused debate. Assessing the notion that new forms of entertainment acted as a force for regional and social homogenization involves looking both at the pattern of take-up and availability of these entertainments, and at the question of how far the shared experience of the same entertainment might have had a socially 'unifying' effect.

One strand of the discussion of the social impact of mass culture revolves around the extent to which it eroded class differences. 'High' culture, as already mentioned, continued to be a predominantly middle-class pursuit. But contemporaries were also struck by the revolutionary sight of cinema audiences where the wives of bank managers sat alongside sales assistants, or of the crowd at the Berlin six-day cycle races where high society and low life alike watched, cheered and got drunk. However, historians have argued that even within the working class, social differences continued to deter-mine patterns of cultural choice: unskilled workers, for instance, were more likely than skilled workers to be attracted by the new commercial entertainments, while skilled workers were more inclined to devote leisure time to activities offered by the flourishing labour movement organizations.

Nor is the notion of a specifically female type of 'classless' consumer without its problems. Weimar's 'new woman' was constructed in such a way as to embody, among other things, the 'classless' consumer of fashion and of modern entertainments, particularly cinema; conversely, recent research (for instance by Patrice Petro) has emphasized the way in which the cinema in Weimar Germany targeted female audiences. But the powerful images dating from the period of women as consumers of modern entertainments should not obscure the financial and time constraints on working-class women's leisure. Admittedly, girls and young single women from the working class, even when they lived with their parents and were expected to do housework, had opportunities for cultural consumption in terms of time, if not in terms of spending power. However, contemporary surveys indicated that for working-class mothers real leisure time, as opposed to the time spent outside the place of paid employment, was minimal.

The extent to which audiences for the new entertainments spanned social classes and the degree to which working-class women had access to them have therefore to be assessed carefully. Even the experience of seeing the same film could be class-specific: workers might see it poorly projected in the local fleapit while the middle classes would be more likely to see it in a film palace, perhaps accompanied by a full orchestra. Moreover, if working-class and middle-class cinema-goers were mingling in the same cinema or sports stadium the classes were still likely to have been segregated on the basis of ticket prices.

Some scepticism may also be appropriate with regard to any subjective sense of cross-class unity which might have been gained from a common experience of the same entertainment – say the latest Charlie Chaplin film or a sporting event. It is plausible that any feeling of community transcending class in the auditorium or on the stands was likely to be fleeting in the face of the acute social and political divisions in Weimar society. A popular Berlin journalist reported, for example, that when at the six-day cycle races the band played *Deutschland, Deutschland über alles*, the public in the best seats applauded and the crowd on the stands whistled and booed.[6]

Looking at cultural life in smaller provincial towns and cities provides another useful perspective on the availability, take-up and social impact of mass culture. Modern forms of entertainment were certainly extending the range of leisure activities available to small-town populations. However, access to the new entertainments varied greatly depending on the region and the size of the locality. Rural Pomerania, to take an extreme example, was hardly touched by modern leisure customs or facilities. Dime novels, village taverns and sports competitions – as 'modern' as leisure pursuits got in Pomerania – were in evidence to the extent that the Pomeranian clergy felt called upon to complain about them, but church holidays, in particular the harvest festival, were the prime source of popular entertainment. Radio, that supposed force for cultural homogenization across classes and regions, was scarcely known.

Radio is a particularly striking case in which assumptions about the impact of new mass media across different classes and across the country as a whole become qualified when the evidence is looked at closely. Superficially, the story of the rise of radio in the Weimar Republic is one of the triumphs of the new medium. The first public radio programme began broadcasting in October 1923 from Berlin; other regional stations also started up in 1923–4, while the nationwide Deutsche Welle was established in 1926. The number of registered radio listeners increased steadily and by 1932 there were 4.2 million registered radio sets. However, as Karl Christian Führer has demonstrated, these figures showing an impressive overall growth in radio use concealed both high drop-out rates during the 1920s by (presumably disappointed) listeners abandoning their radio licences, and significant disparities across the Reich in the distribution of listeners. For most of the 1920s, the regional transmitters emitted such weak signals that to pick them up outside a certain radius (in 1926 around 50–70 kilometres) would-be listeners needed an elaborate and expensive radio set: the cost of such a set would in the late 1920s have swallowed half of the average monthly income for the average working-class urban household. In 1927 only 31 per cent of the German population lived in areas within which the cheaper 'detector' sets could be used.

The difficulties with reception and the resulting costs of buying adequate radio sets, together with the often stodgy and highbrow programmes offered, made radio a medium which was used disproportionately by the middle classes: only about a quarter of the radio audience by the end of the Weimar Republic was working-class. Radio can therefore hardly be seen as a major force bridging the class divide. In regional terms, the difficulties with reception made radio a medium of urban-dwellers. Of the Berliner Funkstunde's registered listeners, 83 per cent lived in Berlin and Stettin, the cities where the company's two transmitters were located. In April 1932, radio ownership in big cities of more than half a million inhabitants had reached 46 per cent of households; in villages of fewer than 2,500 inhabitants, only 10 per cent of households had a radio. The sluggish take-up of radio in rural areas was in spite of the efforts of 'radio vans' (*Werbewagen*) equipped with demonstration sets which travelled round rural areas trying to drum up interest in the medium. It confounded the hopes of radio companies and politicians that radio above all was the medium with the potential to bring the wider world to rural Germany and perhaps even counteract the flight from the land by making rural life less monotonous.

When considering the impact of new media and entertainments on German cultural life it is also important to stress the local context in which they were consumed. A case study by Konrad Dussel and Matthias Frese of leisure in the town of Weinheim in Baden (population *c*. 16,000) shows for the Weimar years the impressive variety of leisure activities and facilities available to such a small town. These included cinema, though only from 1925: in that year Weinheim's first cinema was opened by a café owner who built an extension onto his café, and by early 1930 three cinemas were in operation. Their typical offerings at this time included detective films and, with sound film a relative novelty, operetta films such as *Der Zarewitsch*, shown in Weinheim in March 1930 with a musical prelude on gramophone record. 'Educational' films, dealing discreetly but suggestively with themes of 'forbidden love' and venereal disease, featured at late showings on Saturday nights. The jazz craze, too, hit Weinheim in the 1920s: revellers going out on Whit Monday 1926 could find a 'Jazzband Concert' either at the tavern 'Zum Goldenen Bock' or at the Café Vogel.

However, even with the novelty of films at the local 'Alhambra' and jazz in the local tavern, leisure in Weinheim in the 1920s and early 1930s continued, as was the case before the war, to revolve around pubs and clubs, with men constituting the majority of regular pub-goers and club members. Once women got married, it seems, they stayed at home while their husbands went out in the evenings. With 'bourgeois' and 'proletarian', Catholic and Protestant clubs, Weinheim's associational life reflected the political, social and confessional divisions of the town. Commercial entertainments, even if consumed by a socially heterogeneous audience, did not substantially erode these divisions. This could be seen as confirmation of the continuing strength in the small-town context of cultural milieux based on class and political allegiance.

While the role of Weinheim's clubs and associations in structuring its members' leisure time and providing public entertainments did decline in the 1930s, this appears to have been due not so much to the rise of 'mass entertainments' as the destructive impact of Nazi rule on associational life after 1933. The effects of the regime having wiped out much of Weinheim's locally organized cultural life, the organization *Kraft durch Freude* ('Strength through Joy') could come in and fill the vacuum.

IV   The reaction against modernism and mass culture

Partial though it was, the impact of artistic modernism and mass culture in the Weimar period was sufficient to provoke a powerful backlash, especially among a section of the middle classes: only a section, it must be emphasized, since after all the enthusiastic audiences for avant-garde art and the new music, such as they were, were drawn largely from the educated bourgeoisie. Nevertheless, it has been remarked that while in other countries similar changes were occurring in cultural life, in Weimar Germany a particularly sharp middle-class reaction against them could be observed. This, Detlev Peukert has suggested, could have been because the idea of the nation being degraded by foreigners took root so strongly in post-First World War Germany; because domestic developments in the republic threatened the security of the middle classes politically and economically as well as culturally; and because middle-class Germans were accustomed to an idea of Germany as an outstanding 'cultural nation' (*Kulturnation*) with a heritage particularly meriting protection.

Admittedly, a sense of alienation from and alarm about the new cultural forces was not restricted socially to the middle classes nor politically to the parties of the right. There were also mixed reactions on the left to the works of the avant-garde. Although left-wing intellectuals such as those associated with the periodical *Weltbühne* – many of them, as their enemies noted, Jewish – were committed advocates of artistic modernism, Social Democratic cultural experts were more inclined to promote to workers the tried and tested products of the bourgeois cultural canon rather than the works of the avant-garde, while Communist cultural organizations pursued their own goals of creating a proletarian counter-culture. The left was also dubious about aspects of commercial mass culture. Social Democrats were as concerned as bourgeois organizations about the impact of pulp fiction on youthful minds, even if they did end up in 1926 opposing the law restricting the sale of pulp fiction. Both Social Democratic and Communist organizations regarded the rise of the cinema with concern, fearing that the labour movement would never be able to offer a socialist alternative to match the sophisticated products of the international film industry. Nor was anti-urbanism, though particularly associated with *völkisch* blood and soil myths and the idea of youth taking to the land as the route to national rebirth, a monopoly of the right. While municipal SPD politicians praised the social achievements of modern, progressively run cities, on the radical fringes of the left there were anarchists and socialists who denounced modern cities as irredeemably steeped in the evils of capitalism and who saw rural communes as the road to a classless and peaceful society: a number of such communes were founded as a consequence in the immediate post-war years and again in the depression. Left-wing responses to the cultural innovations of the Weimar years were thus complex and ambivalent. Nevertheless, there was on the whole more openness and curiosity on the political left than on the right regarding both avant-garde art and the new forms of mass communication: this can be seen for instance, in the efforts of the SPD and KPD to distribute films they regarded as progressive, and to use films as promotional material for members.

The harshest attacks on modernism and the greatest anxieties about the impact of modernization on cultural life emanated from bourgeois organizations and from the right. Much of the research on the cultural conservatism of the right has focused on its intellectual history, and in particular on that strand of cultural conservatism which labelled itself 'young conservatism', 'neo-conservatism' or 'conservative revolution'. Neo-conservatism was far from homogeneous, and was certainly not even wholeheartedly 'anti-modern'. Some theorists did indeed preach ruralism and racial mysticism, but others, as Jeffrey Herf in particular has shown, emphasized the need to harness technological progress to an authoritarian political framework. However, neo-conservative thinking had a number of common themes: that the stale and stiflingly bourgeois culture of Imperial Germany was better dead; that the republic had crushed and wasted the positive national energies unleashed by the war; that Weimar's cultural life was irredeemably debased by foreign and Jewish influence and 'shallow materialism'; and that a new order was needed, a 'Third Reich' in which elite rule would bring about class harmony, a restoration of gender differences, a synthesis of the 'best elements' in nationalism and socialism, and the victory of German *Kultur* over 'civilization'.

Politically, the neo-conservatives were a failure. Their interventions in Weimar politics were a shambles, and the futility of their attempts to influence Nazi policies after 1933 was brutally demonstrated when one of their main spokesmen, Edgar J. Jung, was shot dead as part of the regime's score-settling at the time of the Röhm purge in June 1934. However, as networkers and self-publicists they were highly effective. One particularly fertile 'ideas factory' of neo-conservatism was Motzstraße 22 in Berlin (just down the street from the bars and revue theatres of the Nollendorfplatz), where a number of right-wing clubs, circles and periodicals had their headquarters. Thanks to publishing houses such as Eugen Diederichs and J. F. Lehmanns, as Gary Stark has shown, neo-conservative ideology gained a clearer profile and reached an extensive readership, particularly among the ranks of the bourgeois youth movement (*bündische Jugend*).

Neo-conservatism was just one particularly vociferous strand of conservative cultural critique in the Weimar period. There were other interest groups and lobbies who took a gloomy view of contemporary cultural life. One group with an obvious axe to grind were those who continued to write tonal music, paint figuratively and design buildings in a more traditional style (trademark: the pitched roof): feeling sidelined and resentful of the avant-garde, conservative composers, artists and architects talked of 'fads', decried the quality of modernist work, and predicted that their time would come again.

Another grouping in the broad camp of cultural conservatism consisted of the churches and organizations such as the 'Working Party for the Restoration of the Health of the Nation' (*Arbeitsgemeinschaft für Volksgesundung*). These organizations campaigned against 'immorality' in modern life, whether this took the form of atheism, blasphemy, nudism, pornography, prostitution, homosexuality, birth control, abortion or companionate marriage. Cultural experts from the Zentrum and the DNVP railed against the 'tides of filth' engulfing Germany and Berlin in particular, and called for tougher censorship as a matter of cultural hygiene. One step in this direction was the passing by the Reichstag of a bill to 'protect youth from pulp fiction and pornography', the *Gesetz zur Bewahrung der Jugend vor Schund- und Schmutzschriften* of 18 December 1926. On the basis of this law, an index was set up of publications which were not to be sold to young people under 18: 'true crime' publications, erotic magazines and sex education books were among the 103 publications on the index by 1930.

As well as examining conservative theories and arguments, however, an analysis of the politics of cultural defence in the Weimar Republic also needs to take into account how conservative cultural attitudes at local level were reinforced by and articulated through associational life and local politics. Such a perspective can also raise the question of how the organized middle classes in Weimar Germany reacted to and sought to contain the process of cultural change, and how successfully they were able to do so.

Heimatvereine and the *Verein für das Deutschtum im Ausland* are two examples of middle-class 'cultural defence' organizations. Provincial *Heimatvereine*, as studies by Celia Applegate and Karl Ditt have shown, were typically run by schoolteachers and local history enthusiasts and often supported by local and regional governments. They offered the public-spirited middle classes a forum where they combined sociability with the 'idealistic' task of discovering and preserving (and, if necessary, inventing) local identities and traditions. Such associations put on folk evenings with dialect plays and folk dancing, set up *Heimat* museums featuring obscure 'bygones', agitated for nature conservation, and ran campaigns against the proliferation of advertising hoardings.

The idea of defending culture, though here culture was defined more in national than local terms, was also central to the work of the *Verein für das Deutschtum im Ausland* or VDA (Society for the Protection of Germandom Abroad) which set out to protect German culture against erosion by foreign influences, particularly in Germany's borderlands and beyond its borders: its 1,500 local groups, including local women's sections and youth groups run by schools, were, like the *Heimatvereine*, a presence in middle-class associational life dating back to the *Kaiserreich*. VDA events spanned the divide between the tradition of German classicism and contemporary German nationalism: lectures on 'Goethe in Bohemia' were juxtaposed with musical entertainment by the local Stahlhelm band.

All these activities can be seen as attempts to shore up middle-class cultural hegemony as well as the notion that authentic German culture was best preserved in locations remote from the big cities and above all Berlin. The VDA praised German communities abroad who seemed to be preserving cultural traditions (folk-dancing, church-going, family prayers) which were being increasingly challenged at home; *Heimatvereine* celebrated regional folk traditions as a bulwark against the homogenizing and centralizing influences of modern urban culture. The dilemma for these organizations, however, was how to reconcile a firm stance against the evils of modern culture without lapsing into nostalgia and escapism.

From 1929–30 onwards, the depression and the shift to the right in Weimar politics assisted the cause of cultural conservatism in a number of ways. With the country gripped by full-blown economic and political crisis, the vague but apocalyptic calls by the neo-conservatives for a 'new Reich' or a 'Third Reich' became more insistent. Such positions as had been won by the avant-garde were meanwhile being undermined both financially and politically. Although surprisingly few theatres and concert halls closed down altogether, cuts in local government spending forced theatres and orchestras to modify their programmes so as to ensure greater commercial viability, much as they had also done during the period of hyperinflation. Theatres increasingly substituted operettas for opera, concert organizers became more reluctant to programme contemporary works. Politically, the tide was running strongly against committed left-wing cultural efforts and against the avant-garde. In 1932 restrictions on the Communist press proliferated, and Communist freethinkers' organizations were banned by emergency decree. Even before the appointment of Hitler as Chancellor, a purge of those identified with the cultural avant-garde was beginning: thus, for instance, after the Reich government's coup against the *Land* government in Prussia in July 1932, two prominent advocates of the new music, Leo Kestenberg and Franz Schreker, were dismissed from their posts as music adviser in the Prussian Ministry of Education and director of the Staatliche Musikhochschule respectively.

The National Socialists, who emerged onto the battleground of cultural politics from around 1929 onwards, joined the bandwagon of cultural conservatism while giving it additional momentum. Laying claim to the leadership of the movement against mass culture, modernism, Americanism, Bolshevism, and female emancipation, the Nazis used their cultural activism – focused on the *Kampfbund für deutsche Kultur* – to try to enhance their standing among the propertied and educated middle classes. The self-styled Nazi cultural expert Alfred Rosenberg launched violent and scurrilous attacks, such as those in his 1930 polemic *Der Sumpf: Querschnitte durch das 'Geistes'-leben der November-Demokratie* ('The morass: a cross-section of "intellectual" life in the November-democracy') on all that was 'Jewish', 'nigger', 'Bolshevik', and 'perverse' in German cultural life. A foretaste of what would be in store if the National Socialists were to gain power in the Reich was provided in Thuringia in 1930–1. As Minister of the Interior and Education in the Thuringia *Land* government from January 1930 until April 1931, the National Socialist Wilhelm Frick presided over a campaign to remove modern art from museums and public buildings and impose restrictions on the performance of jazz music.

Thus before 1933 the contours of the National Socialists' cultural policy were visible, even if much of the detail emerged fully only after their takeover of government in the Reich. It was becoming evident that the footholds gained by the avant-garde in Weimar's cultural life would be destroyed, that the cultural organizations of the left would be smashed, and that both 'high culture' and mass entertainment would be made to serve Nazi purposes. But cultural conservatism would have to be brought under control and oriented towards Nazi ends as well. The 'struggle for German culture' had to be forward-looking, blending the traditional and the modern, and be based not merely on the celebration of folk culture and the diversity of *Heimat* traditions, but on the application of 'scientific' racism and the incorporation of all classes and all parts of Germany into a close-knit national whole. Where mass culture under the conditions of Weimar democracy might have partially eroded but certainly not eliminated class divisions and regional diversity in German cultural life, National Socialism set out to impose cultural homogeneity through coercion.

Notes:

1. *Statistisches Jahrbuch deutscher Städte* vol. 24 (= Neue Folge vol. 3) (1929), pp. 329–30.
2. 'Debatten über den deutschen Film', *Film-Kurier* 9 (1927), no. 76 (unpaginated). I am indebted to Karl Christian Führer for this reference.
3. Haddenhorst, Gerda, 'Das Wiesbadener Theater in der Zeit der Weimarer Republik', *Nassauische Annalen*, 100 (1989), pp. 243–64, here p. 246.
4. Zielinski, Tadeusz, *Bartok* (1973), p. 259.
5. Dussel, Konrad, 'Von Bert Brecht zu Hanns Johst? Deutsches Provinztheater 1918–1944 im Spiegel seiner Spielpläne', *Universitas* 9 (1988), pp. 976–89, here p. 985.
6. 'Sechstagerennen', in *Sling: Die Nase der Sphinx oder Wie wir Berliner so sind* (1987), p. 172.

Select bibliography

Abrams, Lynn, 'From Control to Commercialization: The Triumph of Mass Entertainment in Germany, 1900–25?', *German History* 8 (1990), pp. 278–93.

Alter, Peter, ed., *Im Banne der Metropolen: Berlin und London in den zwanziger Jahren* (1993).

Applegate, Celia, *A Nation of Provincials: The German Idea of Heimat* (1990).

Ditt, Karl, *Raum und Volkstum: Die Kulturpolitik des Provinzialverbandes Westfalen 1923–1945* (1988).

Dussel, Konrad, 'Von Bert Brecht zu Hanns Johst? Deutsches Provinztheater 1918–1944 im Spiegel seiner Spielpläne', *Universitas* 9 (1988), pp. 976–89.

Dussel, Konrad, and Frese, Matthias, *Freizeit in Weinheim. Studien zur Geschichte der Freizeit 1919–1939* (1989).

Feldman, Gerald D., *The Great Disorder: Politics, Economics and Society in the German Inflation, 1914–1924* (1993).

Führer, Karl Christian, 'Auf dem Weg zur "Massenkultur"? Kino und Rundfunk in der Weimarer Republik', *Historische Zeitschrift* 262 (1996), pp. 739–81.

Führer, Karl Christian, *Wirtschaftsgeschichte der deutschen Rundfunkgesellschaften 1923 bis 1932* (1996).

Gay, Peter, *Weimar Culture: The Outsider as Insider* (1974).

Gee, Malcolm., Kirk, Tim, and Steward, Jill, eds., *The City in Central Europe: Culture and Society from 1800 to the Present* (1999).

Haxthausen, Charles W., and Suhr, Heidrun, eds., *Berlin: Culture and Metropolis* (1990).

Herf, Jeffrey, *Reactionary Modernism: Technology, Culture and Politics in Weimar and the Third Reich* (1984).

Hermand, Jost, and Trommler, Frank, *Die Kultur der Weimarer Republik* (1988).

Jones, Larry Eugene, 'Culture and Politics in the Weimar Republic', in Gordon Martel, ed., *Modern Germany Reconsidered 1870–1945* (1992).

Kaes, Anton, Jay, Martin, and Dimendberg, Edward, eds., *The Weimar Republic Sourcebook* (1994).

Kater, Michael, 'The Revenge of the Fathers: the Demise of Modern Music at the End of the Weimer Republic', *German Studies Review* 15 (1992), pp. 295–315.

Kniesche, Thomas W., and Brockmann, Stephen, eds., *Dancing on the Volcano: Essays on the Culture of the Weimar Republic* (1994).

Lane, Barbara Miller, *Architecture and Politics in Germany 1918–1945*, 2nd edition (1985).

Laqueur, Walter, *Weimar: A Cultural History 1918–1933* (1974).

Meskimmon, Marsha, and West, Shearer, eds., *Visions of the Neue Frau. Women and the Visual Arts in Weimar Germany* (1995).

Michalski, Sergiusz, *New Objectivity: Painting, Graphic Art and Photography in Weimar Germany 1919–1933* (1994).

Nolan, Mary, *Visions of Modernity: American Business and the Modernization of Germany* (1994).

Petersen, Klaus, *Zensur in der Weimarer Republik* (1995).

Petro, Patrice, *Joyless Streets. Women and Melodramatic Representation in Weimar Germany* (1989).

Peukert, Detlev J. K., *The Weimar Republic: The Crisis of Classical Modernity* (1991).

Plummer, Thomas G., *et al.*, eds., *Film and Politics in the Weimar Republic* (1982).

Rosenhaft, Eve, 'Brecht's Germany, 1898–1933', in Peter Thomson and Glendyr Sacks, eds., *The Cambridge Companion to Brecht* (1994).

von Ankum, Katharine, ed., *Women in the Metropolis: Gender and Modernity in Weimar Culture* (1997).

von Saldern, Adelheid, 'Der Wochenend-Mensch: Zur Geschichte der Freizeit in den Zwanziger Jahren', *Mitteilungen aus der kulturwissenschaftlichen Forschung* 15, Heft 30, March 1992.

Stark, Gary, *Entrepreneurs of Ideology: Neoconservative Publishers in Weimar Germany* (1981).

Steinweis, Alan E., 'Weimar Culture and the Rise of National Socialism. The Kampfbund für deutsche Kultur', *Central European History* 24 (1991), no. 4, pp. 402–23.

Uecker, Matthias, *Zwischen Industrieprovinz und Großstadthoffnung. Kulturpolitik im Ruhrgebiet der zwanziger Jahre* (1994).

Wernecke, Klaus, 'Kinobesuch als Freizeitvergnügen. Der Spielfilm als klassenübergreifendes Medium in der Weimarer Republik', *Mitteilungen aus der kulturwissenschaftlichen Forschung* 15, Heft 30, March 1992.

Westphal, Uwe, *Berliner Konfektion und Mode 1836–1939. Die Zerstörung einer Tradition*, 2nd edition (1992).

4

The rise of the Nazis: *Sonderweg* or spanner in the works?

Jill Stephenson

I Contours of the debate

> It is a party without history which suddenly emerges in German political life,
> just as an island suddenly emerges in the middle of the sea owing to volcanic
> forces.[1]

Thus the Comintern agent Karl Radek characterized the effect on the
German political scene of the electoral success enjoyed by the National
Socialist German Workers' Party (NSDAP) in September 1930, when,
from a tiny political base, it achieved 6.4 million votes (18.3 per cent of the
total) and 107 seats in the Reichstag, as the second strongest party after
the Social Democrats (SPD). For Radek, normally an acute observer of
the German scene, the NSDAP suddenly came from nowhere. By contrast,
for some commentators in the 1950s and 1960s, most notoriously the
American William Shirer, it was all too clear where National Socialism had
come from: German history from Martin Luther to Frederick the Great and
the Kaiser – via Fichte, Hegel and Nietzsche, among others – formed a
logical continuum of subservience to authority, rampant nationalism and
inherent anti-Semitism. A more recent variant of this old-fashioned view,
focusing on the allegedly 'eliminationist mind-set that characterized
virtually all who spoke out on the "Jewish Problem" [in Germany] from the
end of the eighteenth century onward', has been expressed by Daniel J.
Goldhagen in his controversial book, *Hitler's Willing Executioners*.[2]

Between these two simplistic extremes, it is possible to tease out both

continuities from previous German history and a peculiar combination of
early twentieth-century circumstances which, together, created the
conditions in which National Socialism could take root and thrive. Both the
continuities and the peculiarities have their counterparts in the history of
other countries. In particular, anti-Semitism had deep roots in many
European societies. Further, the dislocation effected by industrialization,
and, more immediately around 1930, the catastrophic effects of the great
depression, produced extreme political responses across the continent. In
addition, the survival of Bolshevism in Russia was seen by many Europeans
as a threat, contributing to a conservative reaction and the emergence of
fascist movements on the political fringe in most countries in the inter-war
years.

But the German reaction to the problems of the early twentieth century
was so much more virulent than that anywhere else that there has, ever
since, been a quest to discover why Germany was different, or even
'peculiar'. Some have read the history of Germany in the entire modern
period as a prelude to the Third Reich, with the French historian, Edmond
Vermeil, giving an extreme example of this view:

> If, in addition to the influence of territorial Lutheranism, we take into
> account the influences of Counter-Reformation Catholicism and Romantic
> idealism, from which the twentieth-century national ideology stems, we can
> understand the German social *mystique*. To Germans this meant the organic
> State, the new Reich conceived as a planned community . . . . Here was the
> *Volkstum*, the popular totality of Germany.[3]

Others made intellectually disreputable assertions about the flawed nature
of the German 'national character', with A. J. P. Taylor claiming that, even
if its methods were widely disliked, the Third Reich 'was also a system
which represented the deepest wishes of the German people. . . . It was a
tyranny imposed upon the German people by themselves',[4] because only
thus could they achieve the domination of their neighbours which they
desired.

So, did modern Germany follow a 'special path' (*Sonderweg*) of
development which led logically to dictatorship, war and genocide? This
determinist and pessimistic view was challenged by historians like Gerhard
Ritter who argued, by contrast, that:

> It is a very great mistake to believe that the modern function of leader of the
> people is in any way the heritage and continuation of the old, monarchic
> power of the princes. Neither Frederick the Great, Bismarck, nor Wilhelm II
> were the historical precursors of Adolf Hitler. His precursors were the dema-
> gogues and Caesars of modern history, from Danton to Lenin and
> Mussolini.[5]

It followed that the National Socialists were able to come to power because of a strange coincidence of crises amounting almost to an 'industrial accident' – like dropping a spanner in the works. Yet to the new generation, writing in the 1960s and 1970s in the wake of the Fischer controversy about the First World War's origins, there seemed to be too much of a coincidence about Germany's central role in precipitating two major wars in 25 years. While rejecting crude prejudices about a German 'national character', some argued that Germany had taken a 'wrong' turning in the later eighteenth century. According to Wolfgang Mommsen, after 1945 'the Germans gradually rejoined the common stream of Western political culture from which they had gradually dissociated themselves since the Enlightenment'.[6] Karl Dietrich Bracher identified 'the deep schism between German and Western political thought, and the emergence of a special German sense of destiny with anti-Western overtones'.[7] Earlier, Werner Conze had argued that 'in the nineteenth century, elements were already recognizable in the early national movement which later emerged, grossly distorted, within National Socialism'.[8] Others found their explanation in what Volker Berghahn has described as 'the structural peculiarities'[9] of German society in the later nineteenth and earlier twentieth centuries. Germany's road to modernity combined the mutually contradictory forces of rapid, thoroughgoing industrialization with a political and social system inherited from *ancien régime* Prussia. According to Hans-Ulrich Wehler, the traditional elites devised cunning strategies for containing the new social forces, which merely delayed a critical domestic confrontation until after 1918.

Whatever its precise origins, this *Sonderweg* allegedly diverted Germans from 'normal' western development, which is characterized as progress towards a democratic, parliamentary and humanitarian polity and society, embodying values and standards deriving from the Enlightenment. Whether there was a common western model is doubtful, given the marked differences in development of France, Britain and the USA, for example. But here the question is: was there something peculiar about Germany's development as a modern society which predisposed its citizens to embrace National Socialism and its inhuman values? Or, conversely, was the fledgling democratic republic deprived of the chance to make a healthy start because of a combination of crises, from attempted revolution in 1918–19, through the Versailles Treaty and the great inflation of 1923, to the economic depression at the end of the 1920s?

The problems to which the singularity of the German experience have been attributed are, broadly, modernization, militarism and immaturity. While these features can be identified in other countries, it was their extreme form and their idiosyncratic interrelationships in Germany which seemed to create the preconditions for cataclysm. Certainly, modernization in the German Empire of 1871–1918 meant rapid, intensive and highly successful economic, industrial, technological and scientific development, which created new, assertive (urban) social classes and put some of the traditional (often rural) sections of society on the defensive. At the same time, political life was dominated by the pre-industrial elites, with an authoritarian monarchy reinforced by a powerful army and an influential landowning social class. This system allegedly deprived genuine democrats of political experience which, after 1918, was evident in their political 'immaturity' once a democratic system was established. The wider background for this development was the 'immaturity' of the German nation state, whose 'late development' in a *Mittellage* – in a central, encircled position in Europe – pushed the country's leadership into a defensive mentality which was manifested in an increasingly offensive foreign policy, with the accent on military superiority and preparation for war.

More recently, however, it has been argued – particularly by Anglophone historians of Imperial Germany – that a Prusso-centred approach does not reflect the diversity of experience throughout the Empire, that the picture of a co-opted industrial and professional middle class underestimates their self-confidence and autonomy, and that the variety of political and associational activities at local level gave many Germans experience of public life before the advent of parliamentary democracy at national level. The imperial government and its allies had to accommodate the aspirations of the new social forces in both the middle and the urban working classes, even if ultimate authority continued to rest with the Kaiser and his circle. It can further be argued that Germany was not a 'western' country but a central European country, sharing some characteristics with its western neighbours and also some with those in neighbouring areas of *eastern* Europe. While the 'modern' aspects of German development mirror those of some western countries, the continuing power and status of a traditional landed elite and the authoritarian system itself are recognizable as part of the eastern European pattern. The search for overseas colonies and the creation of an ocean-going navy show Germany in 'western' mode, while the desire for a contiguous land empire, as famously manifested in the 'September Programme' of Chancellor Bethmann Hollweg in 1914, matches the pattern of expansion of countries like Russia and Austria-Hungary. With its 'western' landholding small farmers and 'eastern' latifundia with tenant farmers or wage labourers, Germany straddled Europe as a hybrid nation. On the whole, these contrasting elements coexisted in uneasy tandem, but where their paths intersected there might be confrontation, or even collision, between urban Germany's industrial economy and society – the most modern in Europe – and the traditional 'backward' sections of society which felt increasingly threatened by new classes, institutions and practices.

II   Changes in the party-political landscape

Under the Empire, these differing regional and social patterns were represented in sociocultural structures which broadly reflected political allegiances. In the 1960s, Rainer Lepsius adopted the term 'milieu'[10] to describe these structures which, he argued, promoted remarkable party-political stability, from 1871 to 1928. For example, urban factory workers might belong to the Social Democratic milieu. Beyond merely voting for or even joining the SPD, this implied an entire lifestyle, with these workers and their families using local Social Democratic leisure and welfare facilities, reading the party's press and generally insulating themselves from the institutions and values of the Imperial German establishment. German Catholics comprised another major milieu, with their own sub-culture parallel to that of the Socialists. Liberals and Conservatives formed, for Lepsius, the two other major milieux, and while there were 'dissidents' who belonged instead to peasants' associations or regional parties, they were relatively small in number. But this did not indicate political coherence across the country: for example, 'conservatism' meant very different things to landowners in East Prussia, industrialists in the Ruhr and peasants in southern and western Germany. Thus party loyalty was often mediated through the milieu; that is, the milieu was the immediate focus of loyalty, with the political party a more distant construct.

While the First World War and its aftermath, including economic and social crises, disoriented many Germans in the 1920s, the political geography of the later Weimar Republic provided a hospitable environment for the growth of National Socialism. After 1918, the fault-lines in the existing milieux became ever more apparent, with substantial numbers deserting them for what Rudy Koshar has called 'apolitical'[11] social or single-issue associations which were not attached to a particular party but were, nevertheless, in many cases, highly political. The chief contribution of these special interest groups was to undermine the existing parties. With the fall of the monarchy, traditional Protestant conservatives, now assembled in the DNVP (German National People's Party), had lost the initiative, and their electoral fortunes in the 1920s (see Table 4.1) revealed that they had been reduced to a disaffected rump, leaving those who regarded themselves as Germany's rightful leaders without a secure

Table 4.1   Reichstag election results, 1928–33 (votes in millions with rounded percentages)

	1928	1930	1932 (July)	1932 (Nov.)	1933
SPD	9.15 (29.8%)	8.58 (24.5%)	7.96 (21.6%)	7.25 (20.4%)	7.18 (18.3%)
KPD	3.26 (10.6%)	4.59 (13.1%)	5.28 (14.3%)	5.98 (16.9%)	4.85 (12.3%)
DDP*	1.51 (4.9%)	1.32 (3.8%)	0.37 (1.0%)	0.34 (1.0%)	0.33 (0.8%)
DVP	2.68 (8.7%)	1.58 (4.5%)	0.44 (1.2%)	0.66 (1.9%)	0.43 (1.1%)
Centre/BVP	4.66 (15.2%)	5.19 (14.8%)	5.78 (15.7%)	5.32 (15.0%)	5.50 (14.0%)
DNVP	4.38 (14.2%)	2.46 (7.0%)	2.18 (5.9%)	2.96 (8.4%)	3.14 (8.0%)
NSDAP	0.81 (2.6%)	6.41 (18.3%)	13.75 (37.3%)	11.74 (33.1%)	17.28 (43.9%)
Others	2.30 (7.5%)	4.84 (13.8%)	1.20 (3.3%)	1.22 (3.4%)	0.63 (1.6%)
Total**	**30.75**	**34.97**	**36.88**	**35.47**	**39.34**
Percentage poll***	75.60%	82.00%	84.02%	80.57%	88.73%

Notes:
* In 1930, the DDP changed its name to 'Deutsche Staatspartei'.
** This is the total of *valid* votes cast, excluding spoilt papers.
*** This is the turnout – the percentage of those entitled to vote who did vote, including those who spoilt their ballot papers.
Source: Statistisches Jahrbuch für das Deutsche Reich (1933), p. 539.

powerbase. The DNVP's core of support in the East Elbian landowning class was both consistent in its opposition to the democratic republic and unable to comprehend the concept of a 'loyal opposition'. This was not critical while the DNVP languished on the margins of Weimar politics, but when it began to ally tactically with the growing battalions of the NSDAP, from 1929, it would prove fateful. Further, while young conservative intellectuals rejected the DNVP's old-fashioned nationalism, they aimed for a 'conservative revolution' and were susceptible to the appeal of what Kurt Sontheimer characterized as 'anti-democratic thought',[12] which bred attitudes which fatally undermined Weimar democracy. These young conservatives lacked the political organization to campaign effectively, and, again, some gravitated towards the NSDAP.

At the same time, as myriad tiny, single-issue splinter parties fragmented an already fissiparous landscape, support for the parties of the political centre haemorrhaged. Shifting coalitions of several parties became customary by the later 1920s, with the virtual eclipse of the republic's two liberal parties, the Democrats (DDP) and the People's Party (DVP). Admittedly, two of the three partners in the original 'Weimar coalition' of 1919, the SPD and the Roman Catholic Centre Party, remained substantial forces, with the Centre (in Bavaria, the BVP – Bavarian People's Party), especially, the establishment party in strongly Catholic areas, where it could sometimes command between a third and half of the

Table 4.2   The Centre Party in the Reichstag elections of July 1932 and March 1933 (electoral districts providing the strongest support for the Centre Party/BVP, in percentages of the total number of votes cast)

	July 1932	March 1933
Düsseldorf East	20.6	19.6
Württemberg	21.8	17.7
Westphalia South	23.6	22.5
Palatinate	23.8	22.7
Franconia	24.7	22.4
Baden	29.1	25.4
Westphalia North	32.9	28.7
Düsseldorf West	34.0	30.4
Oppeln	34.6	32.3
Upper Bavaria/Swabia	36.6	29.0
Cologne/Aachen	40.5	35.9
Koblenz/Trier	46.2	40.9
Lower Bavaria	48.0	37.6
National average	15.7	14.0

Source: *Statistisches Jahrbuch für das Deutsche Reich:* (1932), p. 542; (1933), pp. 540–1.

vote (see Table 4.2). But coalitions between the Centre and the SPD were always a marriage of convenience, and the depression's stresses rendered irretrievable the breakdown which had become increasingly likely by the later 1920s. Further, the rightward shift in the Centre's national leadership in the later 1920s repelled some supporters, including industrial workers in the central/southern Black Forest region in southwest Germany. At the same time, claims Oded Heilbronner, 'Catholic social life steadily disintegrated throughout the Weimar period'.[13] The result was that, in the 1920s, the Centre Party could attract barely half of the Catholic vote.

The Socialist milieu alone had traditionally enjoyed class homogeneity, but by the 1920s the SPD was not the only party claiming to represent proletarians. Although it had seemed the strongest party in the early Weimar years, the SPD was out of government during the years of relative stability in the mid to later 1920s, returning in 1928 to face the economic crisis (see Chapter 1, above). Its weakness lay partly in the increasing reluctance of other major parties to work with it, because it was associated with the 'social state', especially with the social welfare reforms which were resented by employers and many in the middle classes. By the later 1920s, the SPD could not attract even half of the working-class vote. According to Tim

Mason, the SPD and the Communist Party (KPD) together – not that they ever actually worked together – could attract only about one half of the total working-class vote. Nevertheless, some middle-class Germans were alarmed that several million of their compatriots voted either for the Communists or for the other party with a Marxist programme, the SPD. There was widespread dismay at the success of the revolutionary left in Russia in 1917, and at the establishment in Germany of a party, the KPD, whose first loyalty was to international revolution.

It is clear that during the 1920s many non-proletarian Germans became less rather than more confident in the new democratic political system which gave the mass of the people a voice, through elections to responsible authorities at local, *Land* (state) and Reich (national) levels. Their insecurity was enhanced by the massive economic and financial crises which struck twice in a decade and disposed many to seek stability in 'strong government'. While runaway inflation in the early 1920s had ruined some middle-class Germans and terrified many others, the great depression around 1930 was a crisis of modern economies which damaged Germany – the leading European industrial economy – particularly severely, creating acute hardship among industrial workers especially. At the same time, agricultural recession had bred poverty and insecurity, particularly in Germany's many small rural communities. Many blamed the republican system itself for their problems, and became susceptible to the siren call of the new radical right. As William Sheridan Allen has said 'they had no effective organization to express their often inchoate and even contradictory antipathies. More precisely, they had too many organizations – none of them effective – as radical Rightist grouplets sprang up all over the country'.[14]

Starting as just one of these 'grouplets', the NSDAP developed a formidable organizational structure which enabled it, in only a few years, to absorb other fringe political groupings as well as some of the 'apolitical' organizations – including peasants' leagues – which were the beneficiaries of both the breaking down of traditional milieux and discontent with the status quo. A party which could exploit popular fears, prejudices and aspirations, which could utilize modern technology to impart its message, and which campaigned with the zeal of a religious movement, could make a powerful impact in times that were, certainly in the view of contemporaries, abnormal. These tactics of harnessing modern methods to exploit often atavistic grievances proved successful in winning widespread electoral support for the NSDAP in the years 1930–2.

The question must be posed: why was it the Nazis who prevailed? Why, for example, did the KPD not reap the major political benefits of the 'crisis of capitalism' around 1930 in a country with a large and sophisticated urban working class? In a sense it did, with its vote increasing noticeably from the later 1920s through 1932 (see Table 4.1). But the KPD's modest success was overshadowed by the explosion of the Nazi vote, whose size was undoubtedly enhanced by those who were alarmed by the very fact of the Communists' gains. For the most part, the KPD could appeal to only a limited section of German society: proletarians who were disaffected with the SPD. It enjoyed success in the depression as the party of the unemployed, but its anti-capitalist rhetoric terrified almost anyone with a vested interest in the capitalist system – businessmen, shopkeepers, peasants and pensioners, among others. Its role in the attempted revolutions of 1918–19 was vividly remembered a decade or so later. Much is made of the enmity between the SPD and the KPD, with long memories of conflict between revolutionaries and 'revisionists' within the pre-1914 SPD, even before the wartime split and post-war recriminations. Certainly, *after* January 1933 some activists in the two socialist camps made common cause against Nazism even before the Comintern adopted 'Popular Front' policy in 1935. But before 1933 Communists and Social Democrats were sufficiently mutually hostile to rule out cooperation between them before the Nazi government's savage attacks on both. The mirage of two socialist parties, together commanding between 35 per cent and 40 per cent of the national vote, combining to thwart Hitler, remained just that. The most significant effect of this consistently strong show of support for the parties of the left was the fear it generated, in the minds of the God-fearing, property-owning, law-abiding classes, of a proletarian revolt of the kind that had (apparently) occurred in Russia.

III   The rise of the Nazis

Fear of the left was manipulated most successfully by the NSDAP, with its paramilitary wing, the SA (storm troopers), ostentatiously in the front line combating 'the reds' in the streets of Germany's towns in the early 1930s. The violence perpetrated by the SA alarmed some, but many others were relieved that someone was taking action against 'Bolshevism'; as Richard Bessel has said, the SA's very presence on the streets was propaganda for the Nazi cause. Nazi propaganda was a powerful weapon, particularly when it was deployed utterly unscrupulously, with mutually irreconcilable promises made to different social or regional groups at the same time but in different locations. But what enabled the NSDAP to disseminate its propaganda was the growing strength of its organization. The NSDAP was founded, as the German Workers' Party, in 1919. Even after changing its name in 1920 and Hitler's assumption of the leadership in 1921, it remained just another radical *völkisch* (ethnic nationalist) fringe party among many in the early 1920s. The notoriety gained following its attempted seizure of power in Munich in November 1923 and Hitler's subsequent trial and imprisonment was short-lived, but, with the refounding of the party in February 1925 and Hitler's assertion of supremacy as Führer (leader), the NSDAP embarked on a period of increasingly energetic recruitment, organization and electoral canvassing. Elections became vitally important to the party's strategy in this period because Hitler had decided, while in Landsberg prison in 1924, that: 'we shall have to hold our noses and enter the Reichstag against the Catholic and marxist deputies. If outvoting them takes longer than outshooting them, at least the results will be guaranteed by their own Constitution!'[15] That is, after the failure to seize power unconstitutionally, the NSDAP would work within the parliamentary system to try to achieve enough electoral support to enable it to claim power as its democratic right.

Particularly after the appointment in 1928 of Gregor Strasser as head of the party's organization office in the Brown House in Munich, a developing network of regional and local party organizations flourished across the country. But the NSDAP did not merely organize vertically, from the centre down through *Gaue* (regions), districts and local branches; it also created horizontal organizations to try to cater for the interests of virtually every social and occupational group. In the later 1920s, Nazi organizations for doctors, lawyers, teachers, students, war veterans, motor car drivers . . . and many more were created. There were Nazi organizations for both women and young people, and a Nazi Factory Cell organization aimed to bring industrial workers into the party. Strasser's aim was to create within the party a microcosm of society which would expand as more recruits joined, and which would eventually assume the organization of German society as a whole, once political power had been won. And these organizations did expand, particularly during the depression, as committed local activists spread the word that Adolf Hitler could and would bring a solution to Germany's problems. In the vertical organizations, although party discipline was strictly enforced, the *Gauleiter* (regional leader) had considerable scope for initiative, tailoring his activities and propaganda to local conditions. Thus the NSDAP could compete effectively with the SPD and KPD for working-class support in some industrial areas of the Ruhr and in Saxony, for example, even if there remained parts of Germany, like some Rhineland villages, where lack of support made it impossible to create more than a rudimentary network.

The party's work at local level was carried out by a skeleton staff of full-time officials reinforced by an army of volunteers of both genders who were unpaid enthusiasts. They canvassed and proselytized for the Nazi cause, making collections of money and goods to sustain party activities, including the provision of welfare assistance to needy fellow citizens who were casualties of the depression. But only speakers accredited by the leadership in Munich were permitted to make speeches publicizing the party's policies. The NSDAP excelled at other forms of propaganda, like posters, leaflets, parades, rallies. Its central office exploited modern technology, making slides and films which could be hired by local branches for use in recruiting drives. New local branches were established by activists from neighbouring localities, and leading Nazis toured the country to draw audiences to meetings in villages as well as cities. None was more indefatigable in this than Hitler himself, whose public appearances were carefully stage-managed to achieve the greatest effect. Over the years, Hitler developed a highly effective style of both public oratory and individual charm which won him a vast personal following. His stature within the party was elevated by the adoption of the *Führerprinzip* (leadership principle) which ensured that authority was imposed from the top, with obedience unconditionally required and indiscipline a cardinal sin.

In the country at large, his image was enhanced by the opportunistic relationship which he entered with the DNVP, initially in 1929 when they both campaigned against the new reparations settlement in the Young plan. Sharing a platform with the DNVP's leader, Alfred Hugenberg, at the meeting held at Bad Harzburg in October 1931 to attack the Weimar democratic system, and addressing industrialists at their club in Düsseldorf in January 1932, helped to raise Hitler's, and therefore the NSDAP's, acceptable public profile. Nevertheless, the DNVP and the NSDAP were often rivals for the same constituency, and, while united in their opposition to Hindenburg in the Presidential election of 1932, they failed to agree on a common alternative candidate. As the main, albeit unsuccessful, challenger to Hindenburg, Hitler enjoyed an enhanced public profile. And with the Nazis' electoral support mushrooming, especially in 1932, it was clear that rural conservative disillusionment with the DNVP was over-whelmingly to the NSDAP's benefit. Driving home its advantage, the NSDAP's propaganda portrayed '[t]he seamless web of Marxism, liberalism, international capitalism, and the Jew [which] allowed the party to transcend the contradictions in the social bases it strove to win over by presenting a unified, conveniently identified source of woe ... the Jew'.[16]

Looking back at the 1920s and 1930s through the filter of the Second World War and the Holocaust, it is perhaps hard to comprehend how a party with such repellent attitudes came to win massive electoral support.

But in its election campaigns the NSDAP was not offering the German people war and genocide. Anti-Semitism and xenophobia were certainly explicit in much of its propaganda, but, in addition, the party projected a variety of views with simple and attractive slogans and some messages that were, often deliberately, confusing. The pledge that Hitler would provide every German woman with a husband, for example, was manifestly specious in a population with some two million more women than men, but it sounded a note of optimism for some. Promising to overturn the Versailles Treaty of 1919 appealed to a much wider range of opinion than merely that of unreconstructed nationalists. Promising to reassert Christian moral standards, and to eradicate the decadence and immorality which, many believed, characterized Weimar (urban) society and culture appealed to many in both rural areas and the urban middle classes. Promising to combat the 'threat' of Bolshevism appealed to much the same constituency. Above all, promising to create jobs, with priority in employment for fathers of families, suggested the possibility of escape from the worst effects of the depression. Particularly once the electoral breakthrough had been achieved in September 1930, the Nazi leadership abandoned its early anti-capitalist and anti-Christian radicalism and constructed a new image for the party as the protector of all that was German, decent and stable, explicitly contrasting itself with both the internationalism and the alleged licentiousness of radicals and socialists on cultural and moral issues. The party whose ideology Hugh Trevor-Roper dismissed as 'this vast system of bestial Nordic nonsense'[17] courted the Christian churches and their congregations, with conspicuous success among Protestants, especially.

The archetypal Nazi voter has been described as a young middle-class male Protestant from a small town in northern or eastern Germany. Certainly, it has long been customary to blame the middle classes, in particular the *petite bourgeoisie*, for the rise to power of the National Socialists. Small shopkeepers, white-collar workers, peasant farmers and rootless ex-servicemen were deemed particularly susceptible to the Nazi message and some in these categories were among the party's earliest supporters, before the depression destabilized political life and made the NSDAP an attractive option for other groups. In addition, it has been argued, particularly by Richard F. Hamilton, that many in the upper bourgeoisie – substantial business, managerial and professional people – turned to Nazism from 1930, even if it is now doubted, following the massive findings of Henry A. Turner, that 'big business' made significant corporate donations to the NSDAP, in spite of Nazi attempts to solicit them. The mainstream Marxist view of Hitler as the lackey of big capital perhaps found support from one major businessman, Thyssen, who entitled his memoirs *I Paid Hitler*, but it is not a view that has recently been seriously entertained by more than the occasional scholar outside the former Soviet bloc.

By contrast, the work of a distinguished British Marxist historian, Tim Mason, showed in the 1970s that a significant number of 'proletarians' – perhaps 3.5 million, in July 1932 – actually voted for the NSDAP, constituting perhaps about 25 per cent of their support. Building on this, from about 1980 it has been increasingly argued that, in terms of both its membership and its electoral support, the NSDAP was a genuine *Volkspartei* (people's party), attracting both members and voters in significant proportions from all sections of society, including the manual working classes. While most historians now accept that some blue-collar workers voted Nazi, they tend to argue that these were non-unionized workers in smaller concerns, and that the KPD enjoyed better success in attracting unemployed former factory workers, while the SPD retained a strong base of support among the manual working class. Others, however, notably Jürgen Falter, have claimed, on the basis of sophisticated statistical studies, that the NSDAP received virtually *proportionate* support from manual workers – that workers, as about 45 per cent of the German population, by the early 1930s constituted between 40 per cent and 45 per cent of the Nazi electorate. If many historians remain sceptical about this, there is nevertheless now broad agreement that the traditional lower middle-class interpretation was too narrow. People from all social classes voted for the NSDAP, but it seems likely that proletarians were somewhat under-represented and non-proletarians rather overrepresented.

This distribution affects the extent to which Nazism was a 'small town' phenomenon because most proletarians lived in or around large towns and cities, and formed a significant proportion of their populations. Yet there were strong Nazi organizations in large cities like Berlin and Hamburg, as well as in the 'cradle' of the movement, Munich. In the depths of the depression the NSDAP could attract desperate voters in industrial centres like Chemnitz (Saxony) and the Ruhr towns. In these places, however, the parties of the left remained strong and dominant, whereas in small towns with a rural hinterland and widespread hostility to the left the Nazis could prosper. In rural villages the position was more complex. In some, the influence of the Catholic Church remained strong, and with it came adherence to the Centre Party, or, in Bavaria, the BVP. In others, like Heilbronner's Black Forest region, previous support for a peasant league transferred to the NSDAP as a national party which might have a better chance of representing their distress than a narrow local group. This was a pattern discernible in both north and south Germany, in both Protestant and Catholic villages.

As for the other 'archetypal' characteristics, there is little dispute that Protestants were more attracted to National Socialism than Catholics, at least until 1932–3. Hostility to the NSDAP on the part of the influential Catholic hierarchy, into the spring of 1933 at least, contributed to this, keeping rural Catholics relatively loyal to the Centre/BVP while urban Catholics proved particularly susceptible to National Socialism. Again, while contemporaries accused women of bringing Hitler to power, it became customary from the 1970s to deny that women had voted as strongly as men for the NSDAP. More recently, however, Helen Boak has shown that 'because of the preponderance of women in the electorate, the NSDAP received more votes from women than from men in some areas before 1932 and throughout the Reich in 1932'[18] (see Table 4.3). Further, while the NSDAP was explicitly an activist party of the young, some of its staunchest supporters were to be found in the oldest age-groups, among pensioners, or those living on rents or savings, who were over 65, although the next most loyal group was the under-25s, those who had grown up in the Weimar years. The young unemployed were more likely to vote for the KPD than for the NSDAP. Finally, in terms of region, the most enthusiastic support for the NSDAP was mainly to be found in

Table 4.3   The shares of the total vote (in %) cast by men (m) and women (w) for the NSDAP in selected areas in Reichstag elections, 1928, 1930, July 1932([1]), November 1932([2]) and 1933

	1930		1932[1]		1932[2]		1933	
	m	w	m	w	m	w	m	w
Bremen	12.9	11.1	29.9	30.9	20.8	20.9	30.8	34.4
Magdeburg	19.8	18.7	36.3	38.9	31.1	34.0	38.1	43.3
Leipzig	14.6	13.1					34.1	38.8
Wiesbaden	29.1	26.0	43.0	43.7	36.1	36.8	44.9	47.3
Bavaria	18.9	14.2	29.2	25.6	27.4	24.7	36.2	34.4
Augsburg	14.9	10.4	25.2	21.1	24.5	21.6	33.4	31.4
Regensburg	19.7	13.1	23.3	17.3	20.0	14.9	33.1	28.9
Ansbach	34.6	33.3			47.6	50.0	51.2	55.6
Dinkelsbühl	33.2	31.9			54.4	56.1	58.6	61.5
Ludwigshafen	17.4	14.0			28.6	27.7	34.5	34.9
Cologne	19.8	15.5	26.4	22.8	21.8	19.2	33.9	32.9
Konstanz			32.0	26.0	26.1	21.8	35.9	32.8

Source: Helen L. Boak, '"Our Last Hope": Women's Votes for Hitler – A Reappraisal', German Studies Review, XII, 2 (May 1989), Table III, p. 297. Figures are missing for some areas in individual elections.

northern areas like Schleswig-Holstein and in eastern areas, like Pomerania, which had a border with Poland, the region where the territorial effects of the Versailles Treaty were particularly keenly felt. Some parts of both southern and western Germany lagged behind, but even in Württemberg, hardly a stronghold of Nazism, electoral support trebled between 1930 and July 1932 (see Table 4.4).

Table 4.4   Percentage of votes cast in favour of the NSDAP (Reichstag elections of 1928, 1930, July([1]) and November ([2]) 1932 and 1933)

	1928	1930	1932[1]	1932[2]	1933
1 East Prussia	0.8	22.5	47.1	39.7	56.5
2 Berlin	1.4	12.8	24.6	22.5	31.3
3 Potsdam II	1.8	16.7	33.0	29.1	38.2
4 Potsdam I	1.6	18.8	38.2	34.1	44.4
5 Frankfurt a.d. Oder	1.0	22.7	48.1	42.6	55.2
6 Pomerania	1.5	24.3	48.0	43.1	56.3
7 Breslau	1.0	24.2	43.5	40.4	50.2
8 Liegnitz	1.2	20.9	48.0	42.1	54.0
9 Oppeln	1.0	9.5	29.2	26.8	43.2
10 Magdeburg	1.7	19.5	43.8	39.0	47.3
11 Merseburg	2.7	20.5	42.6	34.5	46.4
12 Thuringia	3.7	19.3	43.4	37.1	47.2
13 Schleswig-Holstein	4.0	27.0	51.0	45.7	53.2
14 Weser-Ems	5.2	20.5	38.4	31.9	41.4
15 East Hanover	2.6	20.6	49.5	42.9	54.3
16 South Hanover-Brunswick	4.4	24.3	46.1	40.6	48.7
17 Westphalia North	1.0	12.2	25.7	22.3	34.9
18 Westphalia South	1.6	13.9	27.2	24.8	33.8
19 Hesse-Nassau	3.6	20.8	43.6	41.2	49.4
20 Cologne-Aachen	1.1	14.5	20.2	17.4	30.1
21 Koblenz-Trier	2.1	14.9	28.8	26.1	38.4
22 Düsseldorf East	1.8	17.0	31.6	27.0	37.4
23 Düsseldorf West	1.2	16.8	27.0	24.2	35.2
24 Upper Bavaria-Swabia	6.2	16.3	27.1	24.6	40.9
25 Lower Bavaria	3.5	12.0	20.4	18.5	39.2
26 Franconia	8.1	20.5	39.9	36.4	45.7
27 Palatinate	5.6	22.8	43.7	42.6	46.5
28 Dresden-Bautzen	1.8	16.1	39.3	34.0	43.6
29 Leipzig	1.9	14.0	36.1	31.0	40.0
30 Chemnitz-Zwickau	4.3	23.8	47.0	43.4	50.0
31 Württemberg	1.9	9.4	30.3	26.2	42.0
32 Baden	2.9	19.2	36.9	34.1	45.4
33 Hesse-Darmstadt	1.9	18.5	43.1	40.2	47.4
34 Hamburg	2.6	19.2	33.7	27.2	38.9
35 Mecklenburg	2.0	20.1	44.8	37.0	48.0

Source: J. Noakes and G. Pridham, eds, *Nazism 1919–1945* (Exeter: Exeter University Press, 1983), vol. 1, p. 83.

IV The destruction of democracy

The National Socialists were able to triumph partly because of their opportunism and their industry, and partly because of the failings of others: for one thing, no other party, including the Communist Party, campaigned as effectively. On 30 January 1933, Adolf Hitler, the leader of the largest parliamentary party, was appointed Chancellor in the proper constitutional manner by President Hindenburg, although he had on 13 August 1932 declined to offer Hitler this post on the grounds that 'he could not justify . . . the transfer of the whole authority of government . . . to a party that was biased against people who had different views from their own'.[19] That understated refusal was made after the Nazis' spectacular performance in the July 1932 national elections, when they attracted 13.75 million votes, their highest total in a genuinely free election, making them by far the largest parliamentary party. In another Reichstag election in November

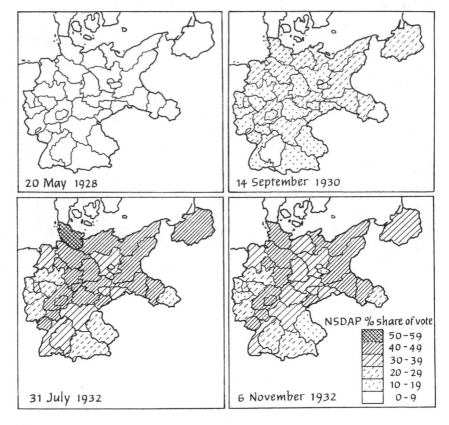

Map 4.1   The electoral fortunes of the Nazi Party, 1928–32

Table 4.5   Local elections in Saxony and Thuringia, November/December 1932 – the number of votes cast for the NSDAP

	Nov. 6	Nov. 14	Dec. 3
Urban areas			
Dresden	134,330	104,107	
Leipzig	128,558	101,690	
Plauen	33,720	26,840	
Chemnitz	79,766	69,538	
Weimar	11,003		7,122
Gera	16,577		13,809
Jena	8,420		6,459
Gotha	10,046		7,565
Eisenach	8,002		5,980
Apolda	6,389		4,430
Rural districts			
Weimar	20,570		15,778
Meiningen	22,180		16,193
Hildburghausen	16,616		12,839
Schleiz	22,835		8,941
Greiz	14,322		10,997
Gera	17,735		12,769
Saalfeldt	14,739		10,645
Rudolfstadt	11,381		8,102
Armstadt	18,821		15,693
Sondershausen	16,313		11,352

Source: Dietrich Orlow, *The History of the Nazi Party, 1919–1933* (Newton Abbott: David and Charles, 1971), pp. 288–9.

1932, their vote fell by two million, on a lower turnout (see Tables 4.1 and 4.4). While the NSDAP remained the largest parliamentary party, there were further signs, in local elections in November and December 1932, that their vote had peaked in July 1932 and was on a downward slide (see Table 4.5). Perceiving this, Gregor Strasser urged Hitler to accept the proffered vice-chancellorship before the party's position was further eroded. Hitler's insistence on holding out for the chancellorship and nothing less contributed to Strasser's resignation on 8 December 1932. Given the party's declining fortunes, Strasser should have been proved right: the time *should* have passed when it seemed necessary to offer Hitler the chancellorship. Yet seven weeks after Strasser's resignation, Hitler got what he wanted.

There was nothing 'inevitable' about Hitler's appointment as Chancellor, even if, as leader of the largest single party in the German parliament, it was perhaps his democratic right. Rather, the essential preconditions of Hitler's success were widespread disillusionment with the parliamentary system and the machinations of the clique of right-wing politicians and advisers around the aged President. It is now clear that the democratic parliamentary system established in 1919 was destroyed before Hitler came to power. Larry Jones believes that it never recovered from the economic and social crises of the immediate post-war years, while Detlev Peukert holds that, after the fall of the last SPD chancellor in March 1930, 'the real question . . . was no longer whether the republican constitutional system could be saved or restored: it was what would come in its stead'.[20] Genuine parliamentary government came to an end in March 1930, when Brüning accepted the chancellorship without a parliamentary majority. Thereafter, presidential power was used to justify and enforce the decisions of a minority government – including, under von Papen, the utterly illegal dismissal of the SPD-led caretaker government of Prussia on 20 July 1932. Some remnants of the Weimar system lingered on beyond January 1933: a parliamentary election was held, but in an atmosphere of intimidation, on 5 March 1933; the constitutionally necessary two-thirds Reichstag majority for the 'Enabling Law' on 23 March 1933 was engineered; and, finally, the President remained in office. Hindenburg's death, and the merging of the offices of chancellor and president in the person of the 'Führer', Hitler, on 2 August 1934, removed the last vestige of the democratic system of the Weimar Republic.

By 1931–2, then, Weimar democracy had been effectively destroyed, although the outward forms remained until Hitler liquidated them in the first half of 1933. It was already clear by then that an authoritarian government, without genuine parliamentary control, would be established – and indeed, was in the process of being established. But the old right, with more or less grudging acquiescence from the liberal parties and the Centre, faced a major problem, especially in the highly politicized atmosphere of the depression, with a high turnout (consistently over 80 per cent) at national elections. Could it, in a new authoritarian regime, force its will on the country, especially on a country where lawlessness was commonplace, with street battles being fought daily in Germany's towns and cities by rival paramilitary gangs? Certainly, the old right could, and did, destroy the Weimar Republic. But because of its own low level of popular support, evidenced in the poor showing of the DNVP, it could not construct a plausible and stable authoritarian system, although possibly Brüning and certainly von Papen used general elections to try to win support that would enable them to do so. That is why the conservatives turned to the NSDAP, with its still massive electoral support, in December 1932/January 1933. And that is why parliamentary democracy was replaced, not by a traditional right-wing authoritarian dictatorship (as happened in most of central and eastern Europe, and in the Iberian Peninsula), nor by Communism, as in the USSR, but by Nazism.

V   Conclusion

Where does all this leave the argument between *Sonderweg* and 'spanner in the works'? The NSDAP did not suddenly emerge from nowhere. There were countless small, radical right, fringe groups in existence during the 1920s, many of which came into the Nazis' orbit, often delivered by a leader – like Julius Streicher in Nuremberg – who was attracted by the idea of belonging to a larger and potentially more effective grouping, under dynamic leadership. It was the Nazis' singlemindedness and their skill that welded countless protest groups into a disciplined yet messianic political party. But they did not create the sense of grievance that motivated people to join these groups in the first place, and to desert traditional allegiances deriving from a particular milieu but only tenuously related to a genuine political party. Many Germans nursed a sense of both personal and national grievance long before the depression of the early 1930s, deriving from the lost war and the penalties that that loss incurred in terms of national humiliation and personal impoverishment, particularly through a worthless currency.

But, in the end, the idea of a 'special path' is also flawed because it implies that this was the path which Germany naturally followed because of its recent history and development. It suggests that the Weimar Republic could not have proved workable under any conditions because of ideas formulated in the early nineteenth century, or because of structures maintained, against the odds, under the Empire. Counterfactual propositions are rarely satisfactory, but had Germany been pursued to unmistakable defeat in 1918–19, as the American military leadership wished, then there might have been no room for the 'stab-in-the-back' myth which obsessed Hitler and served for many others as an excuse. Had early Weimar governments shown more responsibility, by not resigning in protest at the peace treaty or the reparations settlement, or by introducing deflationary policies before the currency lost its value altogether, then politics might have seemed more stable and a whole swathe of middle-class voters might not have been traumatized, making them highly susceptible to the Nazi appeal.

Yet there was a weakness in the German system, deriving from its hybrid nature as it straddled central Europe. The most advanced industrial economy coexisted with backward agriculture, both in the large East Elbian estates and in the small peasant farms of the west and south. There was not a single agrarian interest but rather both a politically reactionary landlord class and a potentially radical small peasant class. There were well-organized skilled workers, whose institutions offered little to unorganized workers in small concerns. There was a burgeoning professional class with too many well-educated recruits – including women and Jews – swelling the ranks of medicine, teaching and law. There were Protestants and Catholics, with memories of the *Kulturkampf* in the 1870s, and, in some cases, even longer memories of the Reformation and the Thirty Years War. Liberals were a dwindling group, yet still insisted on being divided into two political parties. Bavarians and Prussians had hardly a good word for each other. This, then, was Germany's special problem: that there were too many particularisms and too few grounds for consensus. Thus it was possible in Germany for a wrecking element to succeed: the democratic system of Weimar was sabotaged by those who had never believed in it and who were supported by a greater number who became disillusioned with it as democratic institutions like parliaments and trades unions failed to provide solutions to immediate economic, social and political problems. As Peukert has said, the democratic system was damaged before the depression struck. But it was the depression which gave the NSDAP its chance, with what Tom Childers has called its 'volatile constituency' attracted by its 'catch-all strategy' as a protest movement.[21] To that extent, perhaps the judgement of Karl Radek, quoted at the start of this essay, was sound enough after all.

Notes:

1. Quoted in Schulz, G., *Faschismus. National-Sozialismus. Versionen und theoretische Kontroversen* 1922–1972 (1974), p. 61.
2. Goldhagen, Daniel J. *Hitler's Willing Executioners. Ordinary Germans and the Holocaust* (1996), p. 69.
3. Vermeil, E., *The German Scene* (1956), p. 15.
4. Taylor, A. J. P., *The Course of German History* (1961), p. 248.
5. Ritter, G. (1955), quoted in J. C. G. Röhl, *From Bismarck to Hitler. The Problem of Continuity in German History* (1970), p. 9.
6. Mommsen, W. J., 'The Return to the Western Tradition: German Historiography since 1945', in Hartmut Lehmann, ed., *Occasional Paper No. 4* (1991), p. 7.
7. Bracher, K. D., *The German Dictatorship* (1971), p. 38.
8. Conze, W., *The Shaping of the German Nation* (1979), pp. 98–9.
9. Berghahn, V. R., *Modern Germany. Society, Economy and Politics in the Twentieth Century* (1982), p. viii.
10. Lepsius, M. R., 'Parteiensystem und Sozialstruktur. Zum Problem der Demokratisierung der deutschen Gesellschaft' (1966), republished in M. R. Lepsius, *Demokratie in Deutschland* (1993), pp. 32–50.

11. Koshar, Rudy, *Social Life, Local Politics, and Nazism. Marburg, 1880–1935* (1986), pp. 85–90, 126–66, 179–208.
12. Sontheimer, K., *Antidemokratisches Denken in der Weimarer Republik* (1962).
13. Heilbronner, Oded, 'Catholic Plight in a Rural Area of Germany and the Rise of the Nazi Party', *Social History*, 20, 2 (May 1995), p. 233.
14. Allen, W. S., *The Nazi Seizure of Power. The Experience of a Single German Town 1922–1945* (1st ed, 1965; here, 1989), p. 25.
15. Noakes, J., and Pridham, G., eds., *Nazism 1919–1945*, vol. 1 (1983), p. 37.
16. Baranowski, Shelley, *The Sanctity of Rural Life. Nobility, Protestantism, and Nazism in Weimar Prussia* (1995), p. 166.
17. Trevor-Roper, Hugh, *The Last Days of Hitler* (revised edn, 1962), p. 55.
18. Boak, Helen L., '"Our Last Hope"; Women's Votes for Hitler – A Reappraisal', *German Studies Review*, XII, 2 (May 1989), p. 303.
19. Noakes and Pridham, *Nazism*, vol. 1, p. 104.
20. Peukert, Detlev J. K., *The Weimar Republic. The Crisis of Classical Modernity* (1991), p. 249.
21. Childers, Thomas, 'The Limits of National Socialist Mobilisation: the Elections of 6 November 1932 and the Fragmentation of the Nazi Constituency', in Thomas Childers, ed., *The Formation of the Nazi Constituency* (1986), pp. 238, 240, 242, 244, 252, 254.

Select bibliography

In addition to the books cited in the notes:
Broszat, Martin, *Hitler and the Collapse of Weimar Germany* (1987).
Childers, Thomas, *The Nazi Voter* (1983).
Corni, Gustavo, and Gies, Horst, *Brot–Butter–Kanonen. Die Ernahrungswirtschaft in Deutschland unter der Diktatur Hitlers* (1997).
Eschenburg, Theodor, *et al.*, *The Road to Dictatorship. Germany 1918–1933* (1970).
Falter, Jürgen W., *Hitlers Wähler* (1991).
Farquharson, J. E., *The Plough and the Swastika. The NSDAP and Agriculture in Germany, 1928–1945* (1976).
Fischer, Conan, *The Rise of the Nazis* (1995).
Fischer, C. J. (ed.), *The Rise of National Socialism and the Working Classes in Weimar Germany* (1997).
Freeman, Michael, *Atlas of Nazi Germany* (1987).
Fritzsche, Peter, *Rehearsals for Fascism. Populism and Political Mobilization in Weimar Germany* (1990).
Grill, Johnpeter Horst, *The Nazi Movement in Baden 1920–1945* (1983).
Hamilton, Richard F., *Who Voted for Hitler?* (1982).
Harsch, Donna, *German Social Democracy and the Rise of Nazism* (1993).
Heberle, Rudolf, *From Democracy to Nazism* (1945).
Heilbronner, Oded, *Catholicism, Political Culture, and the Countryside. A Social History of the Nazi Party in South Germany* (1999).
Kater, Michael H., *The Nazi Party. A Social Profile of Members and Leaders, 1919–1945* (1983).
Kershaw, Ian, *Hitler, 1889–1936: Hubris* (1998).
Kolb, Eberhard, *The Weimar Republic*, trans. P.S. Falla (1988).

Koshar, Rudy, 'Cult of Associations? The Lower Middle Classes in Weimar Germany', in Rudy Koshar (ed.), *Splintered Classes. Politics and the Lower Middle Classes in Inter-war Europe* (1990).

Maier, Charles S., *The Unmasterable Past. History, Holocaust, and German National Identity* (1988).

Manstein, Peter, *Die Mitglieder und Wähler der NSDAP 1919–1933* (1989).

Mason, Tim, *Social Policy in the Third Reich. The Working Class and the 'National Community'* (1993), chs 1 and 2.

Mommsen, Hans, *The Rise and Fall of Weimar Democracy* (1996).

Mühlberger, Detlef, *Hitler's Followers* (1991).

Nicholls, A. J., *Weimar and the Rise of Hitler*, 3rd edn (1991).

Nicholls, Anthony and Matthias, Erich, eds., *German Democracy and the Triumph of Hitler* (1971).

Noakes, Jeremy, *The Nazi Party in Lower Saxony, 1921–1933* (1971).

Orlow, Dietrich, *The History of the Nazi Party, 1919–1933* (1971).

Patch, William L., Jr., *Heinrich Brüning and the Dissolution of the Weimar Republic* (1998).

Pridham, Geoffrey, *Hitler's Rise to Power. The Nazi Movement in Bavaria 1923–1933* (1973).

Schnabel, Thomas, ed., *Die Machtergreifung in Südwestdeutschland. Das Ende der Weimarer Republik in Baden und Württemberg 1928–1933* (1982).

Stachura, P. D., *Gregor Strasser and the Rise of Nazism* (1983).

Stachura, Peter D., ed., *The Nazi Machtergreifung* (1983).

Claus-Christian W. Szejnmann, *Nazism in Central Germany. The Brownshirts in 'Red' Saxony* (1999).

Turner, Henry Ashby, *Big Business and the Rise of Hitler* (1985).

5
Hitler and the Nazi dictatorship

Ian Kershaw

Despite libraries of books on the Third Reich, the questions posed by the rapid descent, within a few years, of a modern, civilized, economically advanced country into barbarism, war and systematic genocide still demand answers, and will continue to do so.

As research on the mechanisms of Nazi rule intensified during the 1960s and 1970s, and was followed by far-reaching analysis of the behaviour and attitudes of different social groups in the Third Reich, attempts were made to look afresh at the collapse of civilization in Germany. The focus shifted from a heavy concentration on the personality, ideology and actions of Hitler himself – which had sometimes been used to shore up exculpatory or apologetic interpretations of a nation driven to war and catastrophe by 'the will of an individual, of a madman'[1] – to analysis of the functioning of the 'system' of Nazi rule as a whole. Arising from this shift, a concept which has gained increasing recognition as a fruitful way of looking at the development of the Third Reich is that of 'cumulative radicalization', initially devised by Hans Mommsen.[2] It is suggestive of how forces unleashed by the National Socialist takeover of power and the often competing interests and policies of different powerful groups within the regime created a spiral of increasingly radical measures – a dynamic of racist persecution and expansionism culminating in war, genocide and unprecedented destruction. It implies, in addition, the unstoppable process of a regime careering more and more out of control, resorting to ever wilder urges to destroy and plunder, dependent increasingly on raw force as coherent structures of government and administration disintegrated and boats were recklessly burnt in an all-out genocidal war. Since that process ruled out any possibility of a compromise peace, 'cumulative radicalization' meant ultimately, therefore, self-destruction, as well as destruction on a monumental scale.

If the term offers a useful descriptive piece of shorthand for the process leading to the climacteric 'running amok' (as Mommsen calls it) of the Nazi regime,[3] it remains less than self-evident just why, exactly, the highly developed and sophisticated German state should have 'imploded' and capitulated to the irrational drive of 'cumulative radicalization'. Such a tendency does not appear to have been a feature of fascist (or quasi-fascist) states in general. Neither Mussolini's Italy nor Franco's Spain could be said to have offered similar cases of 'cumulative radicalization'. In a differently structured state, but one frequently compared with the National Socialist regime, that of the Soviet Union, there was certainly a dramatic escalation of terror and repression under Stalin. But that escalation ceased with the dictator's death. It was 'despotic radicalization' related to Stalin's form of dictatorship, rather than 'cumulative radicalization' inherent in the system itself.

The process of 'cumulative radicalization' appears, then, to be peculiar to the Third Reich. How should it be explained? A full answer would have to incorporate at least some of the following: expectations lodged in the vision of national renewal represented by Hitler; the drive of the Nazi movement's followers to implement the diffuse Party Programme; the pressure emanating from the security police to find new ideologically determined victims; the readiness of non-Nazi national-conservative elite groups to participate in the undermining of legality through the growing cancer of the police state, and to find wide areas of affinity with the regime's unfolding racial and expansionist goals; the willingness of much of society to collaborate in discrimination against minorities; the successful propagation among, especially, the younger generation of racist, militarist and extreme chauvinist ideas, all founded in beliefs in cultural superiority; and the self-reinforcing barbarism of the war itself and of complicity in genocidal actions.

Beyond these elements of an answer, it would also be important to consider the impact on government of the highly personalized, 'charismatic' rule of Hitler. Not least, it would also be vital to take account of the personal ideological 'vision' and the actions of Hitler himself. Historiographically, historians who have concentrated on the personal role of Hitler have seldom deployed the concept of 'cumulative radicalization'. Those 'structuralist' (or 'functionalist') historians, on the other hand, who have found the concept useful, have tended, on the whole, to downplay Hitler's personal role and to look instead to the functioning (or dysfunctioning) of the 'system' as a whole. Hans Mommsen, for instance, explicitly excludes Hitler as a causative force of 'cumulative radicalization' with the comment that 'it is a serious mistake to concentrate study of the Nazi tyranny on an analysis of the role which Hitler occupied in it'.[4] It would indeed be hard to argue convincingly that the will, whims, dictates or personality disorder of Hitler were all that mattered in pushing on the 'cumulative radicalization'. But to ignore or underrate the personal contribution of Hitler would surely be equally mistaken. Hitler needs to be fully incorporated in, rather than omitted from, an analysis of 'cumulative radicalization'.

A premiss of what follows is that 'cumulative radicalization' indeed provides a fruitful concept in analysis of the Third Reich. A further starting point is that the Nazi regime was a peculiar type of modern state, and that this peculiarity is closely and specifically related to the impact of Hitler's personal exercise of power upon existing channels of authority. This can be conceptualized – using Max Weber's terminology – as the superimposition of 'charismatic' upon 'bureaucratic' (or 'legal-rational') authority. ('Charismatic authority' is used here as a technical term, implying a sense of 'mission' associated by the 'following' with the perceived extraordinary qualities of the leader, and a highly personalized form of rule which, because of its dependence upon avoidance of failure or 'routinization', remains acutely unstable.) A further premiss, then, is that Hitler's power was real and immense, that he was neither a 'weak dictator' – a misleading implication[5] – nor a sort of front-man for other forces. The exercise of that level of power and autonomy – extraordinary even among modern dictatorships – had, so my argument runs, a direct and crucial bearing on the process of 'cumulative radicalization'. But – a final premiss – it is taken for granted that Hitler's power was not static, but expanded in consequence of the weakness, miscalculation, tolerance and collaboration of others, both inside and outside Germany.

It is important, therefore, to ask how Hitler came to be in a position to take or shape momentous decisions. This question has to be answered by looking to forces outside Hitler himself, since it is certainly true that dictators, including Hitler, 'are as dependent on the political circumstances which bring them to power as they in turn influence these'.[6] Hitler's role, in other words, has to be seen not simply in personal terms, but also as itself a 'structure' – and the most vital one – in the system of rule subject to the process of 'cumulative radicalization'.

Without the comprehensiveness of the crisis of the Weimar state, the speed and radicality of the collapse of civilization after 1933 would have been unthinkable. From the outset, the Weimar Republic had faced serious problems of legitimacy, both among wide sections of the population and within the very power elites on whom the state was dependent. Under the impact of the crippling depression beginning in late 1929, economic, social and governmental crises blended into an acute and unsustainable multidimensional legitimacy crisis of the state system itself. An authoritarian solution became increasingly inevitable. But the traditional national-conservative power elites were too weak to provide it.

An attack on civil liberties also became more and more likely, whatever the eventual outcome of the crisis. Liberal principles were under strong attack long before Hitler's takeover. One sign was growing paranoia about law and order at a time when, in fact, despite a sharp rise in political violence, actual criminality was far lower than it had been in the early 1920s. Another indicator was the growing pressure in the medical profession, strongly influenced by ideas of eugenics and 'racial hygiene', for legislation for the voluntary sterilization of those suffering from hereditary illnesses. A third example of the changing climate was the increasingly shrill clamour against 'double earners', aiming to hound women out of jobs if their husbands were also employed.

As each profession and social group increasingly felt itself disadvantaged and alienated by Weimar's failure, the attractiveness of a radical new start spread. Again, the links with an assault on human rights, including menacing signs of widening hostility towards Jews, were evident. Owners of shops and small businesses, threatened by consumer cooperatives and big department stores, found it easy to swallow the Nazi line of blaming Jewish ownership of such stores for their troubles. In the countryside, too, economic misery in the impoverished farming community readily translated itself into anger directed at 'inner enemies' and scapegoats – for the most part seen as Marxists and Jews. Many young Germans were swept into the path of the Nazis not only through misplaced idealism, but also because of poor job prospects. Once subjected to the prevailing ethos in the Hitler Youth or the SA (*Sturmabteilung* or stormtroopers), they could soon find themselves marching through the streets attacking the 'Reds' or singing 'When Jewish blood spurts from the knife'. Students, their career expectations often vanishing before their eyes, were frequently among the most radicalized of the younger generation. Many of those who came to run the Reich Security Head Office during the war, and were most closely implicated in genocidal policies and action, had imbibed *völkisch* ideals in universities during the early years of the Weimar Republic. In the early 1930s, during the depression, the progress made by the Nazis in universities was alarming. A climate hostile to Jews, Marxists, and 'the un-German spirit' in intellectual life increasingly took hold among students, and also among many of their professors who had seen their own careers blighted. Overlaying the interests of different social groups, the polarization of left and right in Weimar's 14-year 'latent civil war',[7] the explosion of political violence in the early 1930s, and the whipped-up anti-Marxist hysteria of a right now in the ascendancy, pointed in the direction of a potential blood-bath if the Nazis were to win power.

The expectations, in other words, of differing sections of society in a national rebirth were massively heightened by Weimar's terminal, comprehensive crisis. And frequently built into such expectations was an assault on liberal values and human rights. The radicalization that burst through after 1933 was, therefore, waiting to happen if a government could be found which was prepared to sanction it and release the pent-up forces.

Such a government, it was increasingly felt outside the ranks of Social Democrats and Communists, had to be a strong, authoritarian force on the right, capable of crushing Germany's internal 'enemies', establishing national unity, and restoring law and order. The more the pluralistic party system of Weimar was seen to have failed, the greater the feeling became that the party system should be done away with altogether and replaced by leadership that put the nation above party interest. The prospect of a restoration of the monarchy which, at least nominally, had represented the whole nation was not universally welcomed. But the two Reich Presidents during the Weimar Republic – the Social Democrat Friedrich Ebert and the monarchist war hero Paul von Hindenburg – had both been, in different ways, divisive figures. A new form of national leader capable of embodying the disparate social and political expectations and transcending – at first, it was widely recognized, by force against internal 'enemies' – the divisions, would, given some initial success, have a good chance of building an impressive platform of popular acclaim. That would be even more forthcoming following any success in overcoming the almost universally detested terms of the Versailles Treaty. Since revisionist hopes (of different kinds) were entertained in almost all sections of German society, success in the arena of foreign policy was guaranteed to win not only massive popular acclaim, but also the fervent backing of the national-conservative power elites – not least, in the army leadership. And during the terminal crisis of Weimar, the ending of reparations had opened up the possibility of rebuilding and modernizing the army and the return – at least gradually – to a more assertive foreign policy. This was all the more possible and likely in the event of a strong German nationalist government, given the self-evident fragility of the post-war settlement. In this, too, the Weimar crisis offered the preconditions for the subsequent rapid radicalization under Hitler.

During the terminal crisis of Weimar, of course, Hitler had increasingly appeared to many to offer the greatest hopes of national redemption. By 1932, over 13 million Germans – well over a third of the electorate, a substantial achievement in the Weimar electoral system – wanted a Hitler government. The radical demands for change – including a ruthless showdown with the Marxists and harsh discrimination against Jews – which formed central elements of the Nazi platform, were thereby assured of extensive, though far from universal, support. An army of activists in the huge National Socialist Movement – party membership numbered 850,000 by January 1933; the SA had by then around 425,000 members – ensured that there would never be any shortage of fanatics pressing for the implementation in government policy of the amalgam of phobias and prejudice that served as the Party Programme.

As a movement drawn from the most disparate social groups, with a catch-all appeal and utopian goals of national unity and resurgence, belief in a supreme leader who embodied the 'idea' and 'mission' of National Socialism was vital. Hitler himself, experiencing the fragmentation of the *völkisch* movement during his imprisonment in 1924, had recognized the need for the NSDAP, when it was refounded in 1925, to be built on principles of absolute obedience to the leader. Despite a constant tendency to factionalism and a number of internal crises, the growing prospect of attaining power had kept the movement intact in the following years. After the most serious of such crises, that surrounding the resignation from his party offices of Gregor Strasser in December 1932, Hitler had deliberately dismantled the organizational framework of the party that Strasser had created and once more put the emphasis solely on propaganda objectives focused, beyond the immediate task of getting to power, on vague and visionary goals of national resurgence. The party therefore entered the Third Reich not with a rationally devised organizational structure set to penetrate and take over the state, but purely as a vehicle for Hitler's 'charismatic leadership', incorporating diffuse and often contradictory social expectations of its vast following and demanding outlets for these in actionism directed at target groups for retaliation and discrimination.

Meanwhile, the deliberately and purposefully manufactured Führer cult had been embraced in differing degrees by over a third of the population. Many more, still hesitant at this stage, would be won after 1933 as Hitler's image was converted by saturation propaganda from that of party leader to 'great' national leader. And, at the centre of indescribable adulation and sycophancy, his already outsized ego swelling as success followed success – all attributed by propaganda to his own 'achievements' – not the least of the believers in the cult constructed around him was Hitler himself.

. . .

It is hard to exaggerate the significance of the Führer cult for the working of the regime. The traditional power elites had entered into their 'entente' with Hitler in January 1933 because he alone controlled the masses on the nationalist right. They had thought they could pen him in. But in reality, his position had been strong from the beginning. Though the conservatives outnumbered the Nazis in the coalition cabinet, Hitler, as Reich Chancellor, Goering, in charge of the Prussian police, and to a lesser extent Frick, as Reich Minister of the Interior, held the key positions. The anti-Communist hysteria – as prevalent among conservatives as among Nazis – played into Hitler's hands following the Reichstag fire in late February 1933, when draconian emergency decrees were promulgated, effectively abolishing civil liberties and setting aside the Weimar constitution. The takeover of power from below in the provinces after the election on 5 March, and, later that month, the passing of the Enabling Act, which empowered the cabinet to introduce legislation and removed thereby the dependence upon the Reichstag and the Reich President's willingness to grant emergency decrees, further bolstered Hitler's position from the outset. Already, the efflorescence of the Führer cult was remarkable. The naming of innumerable town squares and main streets after 'the people's Chancellor' was only one outward sign that no conventional change of government had taken place. The vicious onslaught on the left, bringing the internment of tens of thousands in prisons and makeshift new 'concentration camps' (the first set up at Dachau, outside Munich in March 1933), destroyed within weeks the seemingly powerful Socialist and Communist parties. Within six months of Hitler's appointment as Chancellor, the remaining parties had been suppressed or had dissolved themselves, leaving a one-party state. At the same time, institutions, organizations, clubs and associations throughout the country had been going through a process – for the most part voluntary rather than forced – of *Gleichschaltung* (or nazification). By the summer, Hitler's position *vis-à-vis* his conservative partners had already been strengthened inordinately.

Following his initial foreign policy coup – the withdrawal of Germany from the League of Nations in October 1933 – Hitler was for the first time to play the card of plebiscitary acclamation – seeking acclaim by plebiscite for an action already completed and known to be massively popular. Further plebiscites following the death of Reich President Hindenburg in 1934, the remilitarization of the Rhineland in 1936, and the Anschluß of Austria in 1938 brought, whatever the absurdity of the actual results, further demonstration inside and outside Germany of Hitler's unassailable popularity. This plebiscitary acclamation, which he could call upon almost at will, was a crucial basis of Hitler's power – demoralizing opposition, underlining his strength to the conservative elites, and showing the outside world that he had the overwhelming majority of the people behind him. It provided Hitler with a platform that enabled him to gain increasing autonomy from the traditional elites. Within a remarkably short time, their hopes of containing him and using him as a vehicle for the restoration of their own power had been shown to be vain ones.

Still, as long as Reich President Hindenburg, the hero of the First World War, lived, Hitler's power was relatively constrained. Hindenburg represented an alternative source of loyalty; the army owed its allegiance to the Reich President as head of state and supreme commander; and Hitler's position as head of government was dependent on the President's prerogative. The massacre of the SA leadership, an increasingly disruptive element threatening the consolidation of Nazi rule, at the end of June 1934 – carried out with the backing of the army – and the rapid assumption of the powers of head of state by Hitler at Hindenburg's death on 2 August amounted to a second 'seizure of power'. The position of Führer was now institutionalized, as Hitler's new title of 'Führer and Reich Chancellor' indicated. (The title became simply 'Führer' in 1939.) The army and civil servants swore an oath of loyalty not to an abstract constitution, but to Hitler personally. The Führer state was fully established.

Hitler's power now knew no formal bounds. Prominent constitutional theorists did their best to give legal meaning to his personalized authority. According to one of the foremost experts on constitutional law, Ernst Rudolf Huber, 'the power of the Führer' was 'comprehensive and total, . . . free and independent, exclusive and unlimited'.[8] Hans Frank, the leading Nazi lawyer, claimed that the Führer's will, resting on 'outstanding achievements', had replaced impersonal and abstract precepts as the basis of law.[9]

Forms and structures of collective cabinet government could scarcely remain intact in the face of such claims. Meetings of the cabinet became more and more infrequent following Hindenburg's death. That of 5 February 1938 turned out to be the last during the entire Third Reich. Government increasingly fragmented into separate offices of state, with no central coordination of policy, and with Hans-Heinrich Lammers, head of the Reich Chancellery, serving as the sole link between Hitler and individual government ministers. Legislation followed a laborious and inefficient process of circulation of written drafts to ministers until there was general agreement. Access to Hitler, apart from favoured ministers such as Goebbels, was often difficult, and made even more so because of the dictator's frequent absences from Berlin and his highly unbureaucratic and idiosyncratic style of working.

Usually, Hitler would get up late in the morning, read the press cuttings prepared for him, have a lengthy lunch (normally attended by regulars like Goebbels and Goering, other favoured party big-wigs, adjutants and other members of his immediate entourage, and some invited guests), see diplomats or other important visitors during the afternoon, spend the evening in a less formal meal, followed by a film, and then launch forth into a monologue until the small hours to those stifling their yawns and able to hold out. He seldom read documents and memoranda prepared by the state bureaucracy or submitted by ministers. These were usually summarized verbally by Lammers in his periodic audiences. Some ministers – Agriculture Minister Walther Darré is an example – were effectively barred from seeing Hitler for years. Nor did Hitler send out a regular stream of written missives and directives. 'He took the view that many things sorted themselves out on their own if one did not interfere', remarked one of his former adjutants after the war.[10] He dictated his own speeches, and signed formal laws, but apart from that wrote remarkably little. A less bureaucratic style of leadership from the head of a modern industrialized country would be hard to imagine. Orders were for the most part verbal, and transmitted – in so far as they concerned government ministers – through Lammers. The scope for misunderstanding and confusion was extensive. Significant policy decisions needed Hitler's approval. But for prestige reasons the Führer could not be dragged into factional in-fighting. The image of infallibility had to be preserved. Alongside his personal temperament, disdain for bureaucracy, and social Darwinist instinct of siding with the stronger in a conflict, this enhanced his detachment from the daily business of government. For the practice of government and administration this meant frequent delay, postponement or sometimes abandonment of proposed legislation which had been the subject of lengthy preparation.

Relations between the apparatus of state government – central, provincial and local – and the party at the differing levels were left unclarified and undefined. This provided a recipe for unending conflict. Headed by the weak and ineffectual Rudolf Hess, the Party's Political Organization interfered – with varying degrees of success – in policy formation in many areas. It was incapable of providing a coherent influence on rational policy choices. But in certain key areas central to the 'idea' of National Socialism, especially race policy and the persecution of the churches, the party subjected the state bureaucracy to relentless pressure through agitation aimed at putting the 'vision' of the Führer into practice. The concessions made by the government ministries to give legislative voice to such pressures, only to be followed by further agitation demanding new legislation, ensured the continued upward ratcheting of radicalization.

This process was further advanced by entrusting vital areas of policy, directly associated with the ideological goals of the regime, to special organizations outside the normal state administration, and directly subordinate to Hitler. The Office of the Four-Year Plan, for example, established in 1936, was meant to be a small and unbureaucratic unit to overcome the impasse in the economy which had built up. Goering's empire-building ensured that it developed into a huge, sprawling organization functioning alongside (and in practice dominating) the state Economics Ministry. The creation, also in 1936, of a centralized German police, headed by the fanatical and ambitious Heinrich Himmler and his right-hand man, the ruthless, ice-cold Reinhard Heydrich, and merged with the Nazi movement's most committed ideological elite, the SS, also spawned an enormous power-bloc – the most dynamic and ideologically driven sector of the regime.

The SS police empire stood outside the control of any government ministry. It was dependent solely upon Hitler, and justified itself as an executive agency of the 'will of the Führer'. This enabled it to develop its own agenda, legitimated by recourse to the Führer's 'mission', and to expand its target groups largely as it wished, thereby justifying the demand for still further expansion of its own activities and personnel. Hence, following Hitler's attacks on the homosexual activities of Röhm and other SA leaders in 1934 – actually a device to cover up the power-political reasons behind the liquidation of the SA leadership – the police could expand their persecution of homosexuals. In the wake of the 'church struggle', surveillance was extended even to minute Christian sects which were enthusiastic in their support of the regime. And in the crucial sphere of anti-Jewish policy, Eichmann was able to make his career, starting in an insigificant position (but in a vital policy area) in the SD's (*Sicherheitsdienst* or Security Service) Jewish Department, and ending as the manager of the 'final solution'.

The pressure from the police (in which, in a significant move in 1936, the criminal police had been blended in with the security police) to widen the net of surveillance and repression, and extend the target groups, was central to the process of 'cumulative radicalization', and took place with little or no direction from Hitler. The plans – already in 1937 when the number of internees had declined to its lowest point since 1933 and the reason for their existence was starting to become questionable – to expand the concentration camps provide a pointer to ways in which the self-feeding radicalization within the police organization operated. The expansion into Austria and Czechoslovakia in 1938–9 then brought new groups of victims and enlarged activities for the police. War and conquest from 1939 onwards gave the SS-police apparatus under Himmler and Heydrich unimaginable opportunities for unfolding the wildest, most megalomaniac schemes, resting on a continent-wide network of repression and terror.

The structures – perhaps 'structurelessness' would be a better description – of the Third Reich already briefly outlined provided the framework within which the 'idea' of National Socialism, located in the person of the Führer, became gradually translated from utopian 'vision' into realizable policy objectives. Territorial expansion and 'removal of the Jews', both central features of Hitler's ideology, had by 1938–9 come into the foreground as feasible policy options. In the following years they would escalate into genocidal war.

Anti-Jewish policy provides a telling illustration of the way 'cumulative radicalization' operated. There was no central coordination before 1939. But the aim of 'getting rid of the Jews', precisely because of its lack of precise definition, infused every aspect of the activity of the regime. The potential existed, therefore, for the unfolding of ever new discriminatory initiatives from the most diverse directions aimed broadly at the exclusion of Jews from German society and their forced emigration abroad. Hence, boycotts, legislation, 'aryanization' of the economy, physical violence, police measures, and party agitation guaranteed an escalation of the persecution of the Jews. Hitler needed to do little other than indicate his approval (or lack of disapproval) for such actions to gather momentum.

He was involved in 1935, for example, in the promulgation of the notorious Nuremberg Laws only following a summer of violence and agitation stirred up by party organizations. When, chiefly for economic reasons, the party's actions were seen to have become counter-productive, and he was under pressure on the one hand to introduce radical measures against the Jews and on the other to quell the disturbances which had punctuated the spring and summer, Hitler decided at the last minute to introduce legislation during the Nuremberg party rally. Some radicals wanted more draconian measures. But the legislation calmed down the agitation for the time being, while opening up countless further avenues for discrimination and persecution. It had, in other words, an immediate practical function in defusing dysfunctional activism while serving nevertheless as a step on the ladder of 'cumulative radicalisation' in the 'Jewish question'.

The subsequent wave of agitation unleashed from below in 1938, and accompanying the foreign-policy tension in the summer of that year, then had its own culmination in the nationwide pogrom of 9–10 November 1938, instigated by Goebbels but explicitly approved in its most radical form by Hitler. The consequence was not only draconian legislation excluding Jews from the economy, but also the placing of anti-Jewish policy henceforth under the control of the SS.

In foreign policy, Hitler played a much more direct and overt role. But here, too, the process of 'cumulative radicalization' cannot solely be attributed to his intentions and actions. The 'coups' that he pulled off between 1933 and 1936 were wholly in accord with the interests of the traditional power elites. Certainly, Hitler determined the timing and maximized the propaganda effect. But the withdrawal from the League of Nations, the reintroduction of

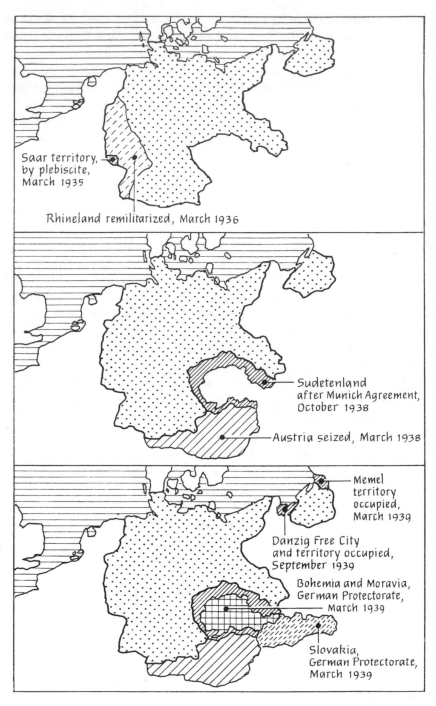

Map 5.1 Pre-war expansion

military service and expansion of the army, the bilateral naval treaty with Britain, and the remilitarization of the Rhineland were scarcely moves 'against the grain'. In the most spectacular demonstration of the weakness of the western powers – the remilitarization of the Rhineland – the army leaders certainly evoked Hitler's contempt through their anxiety over the possibility of French and British intervention. But they had nothing but approval for the aim of the Hitler's action. And the danger was in reality minimal – at any rate far lower than Hitler later claimed in order to play up the boldness of his move. As late as November 1937, when Hitler alarmed his top military leaders with his indications of early expansion into Austria and Czechoslovakia, there was no disagreement about the need to attain German hegemony in central Europe. The worry was solely about the risk of war with the great powers. Pressure, mainly on economic grounds, for the subsumption of Austria within the German orbit had up to then largely come from Goering, rather than Hitler. No section of the German elite differed with Hitler on the need to incorporate Austria in one form or another within the Reich. The Anschluß, when Schuschnigg forced matters to a head by his attempt to stage a plebiscite on Austrian autonomy, was as good as universally welcomed.

The Czechoslovakia crisis of summer 1938 was another matter. But by then Hitler's power had been substantially strengthened in relation to the army by the Blomberg–Fritsch affair, followed by his major triumph in Austria. As regards the prospect of military action against the Czechs, Ribbentrop, the new Foreign Minister, was outrightly hawkish. Himmler and Goebbels also backed Hitler's aggressive course. But otherwise, the worries about an unnecessary risk of war against the western powers prevailed. During the summer, General Beck, the chief of staff of the army, voiced his opposition in increasingly forthright memoranda, even advocating facing Hitler with a 'general strike' in the most literal sense – the collective refusal of the generals to obey an order to invade Czechoslovakia. But Beck was not supported by the commander-in-chief of the army, the weak and servile von Brauchitsch. In truth, the army leadership was divided. It had also been weakened by the Blomberg–Fritsch crisis at the beginning of the year. The resolution of this crisis – in which the War Minister Blomberg had been ousted because of his marriage to a woman with a shady past, and commander-in-chief of the army, Fritsch, had been forced out through trumped up charges (subsequently proved to have been based on mistaken identity) of homosexual practice – had effectively transformed the Wehrmacht leadership, the only powerful force left in the state capable of challenging Hitler, into no more than a functional elite, an executive agency of the Führer. When Beck resigned, no one followed him.

However, his replacement, Halder, found himself, together with the head of the Abwehr, Admiral Canaris, at the centre of the nascent conspiracy to have Hitler deposed in the event of an attack on Czechoslovakia that autumn. Whether the conspiracy would have come to anything is an open question. But it indicated the beginnings of a break with Hitler of a number of individuals who served, or had served, the regime in responsible positions in the Wehrmacht, the Foreign Ministry and elsewhere. In the event, of course, the appeasement policy of the western powers, desperate to avoid war, and the intervention by Mussolini (prompted by Goering – as anxious as any to rule out the prospect of war with Britain) forced Hitler to be content for the time being with a negotiated settlement to give him the Sudetenland rather than the war he wanted with the Czechs to gain the whole of Czechoslovakia at one fell swoop. But the West had shown it was unwilling to fight. Hitler had been correct in what he had claimed through-out the summer. Those who had opposed his line were, as a result of the readiness of the western powers to buy Hitler off, seriously weakened. The following summer, during the crisis over Poland, there was no opposition from the generals. Among ordinary people, too, who had been panic-stricken at the thought of war in summer 1938, the mood was far calmer. The Führer had pulled it off on every occasion before. He would do so again. The western powers had given in over the Sudetenland. They were hardly likely to go to war over Danzig. Hitler had, so he said, seen the western leaders at Munich, and they were no more than 'little worms'.[11] When asked by Goering on the eve of the war why it was necessary to gamble everything, Hitler replied: 'Goering, all my life I have gone for broke.'[12]

The war was, indeed, a gigantic gamble. But from Hitler's point of view, the risk had to be taken. Any delay – a characteristic argument – would merely strengthen the enemy. Time, he asserted, was not on Germany's side. The 'cumulative radicalization' of foreign policy over the previous years, and especially the triumphs of 1938, had gravely weakened those forces, above all in the Wehrmacht, which had pushed so strongly for expansion only to find themselves in the end inextricably bound up with a high-risk policy they had been instrumental in creating.

. . .

During the war, the 'structurelessness' of the regime – reflecting the impact of Hitler's 'charismatic authority' on the governmental system – became hugely magnified. Central government splintered. Lammers was less able to play a coordinating role as his own access to Hitler (now constantly shielded by Bormann) declined. Party interference in government under

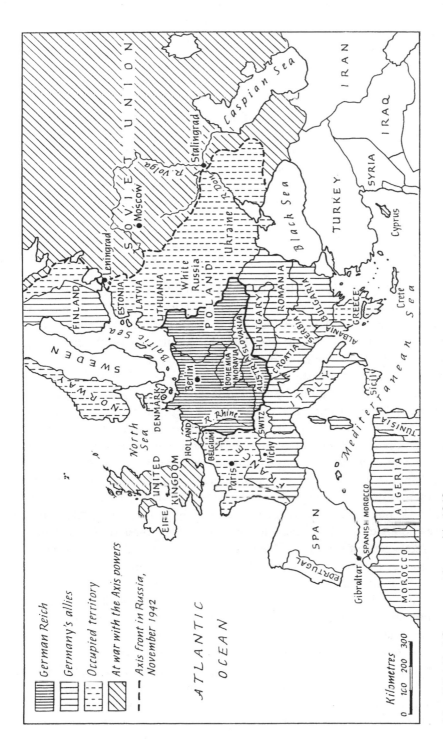

Map 5.2 Nazi Germany at its zenith 1942

Bormann as head of the re-named Party Chancellery from 1941 onwards, following Hess's flight to Scotland, intensified. Hitler himself became an increasingly remote figure, spending most of his time in his field head-quarters in East Prussia, physically detached from the centre of civil government in Berlin. The greatest chances of influencing him fell, apart from the ubiquitous Bormann, to those few who could always rely upon gaining access, such as Goebbels, Goering, Himmler, Ley and Speer. Not surprisingly, therefore, Hitler's interventions in policy-making, though frequent, were usually sporadic and arbitrary, based on one-sided and piecemeal information. Under the strains of total war from the end of 1942 onwards, the regime ran increasingly out of control. Hitler often seemed detached and out of touch, unable to or uninterested in resolving the overwhelming problems that were building up. It was little wonder that by early 1943 even Goebbels could hint not just at a 'leadership', but at a 'leader crisis'.[13]

During the first years of the war it had been different. The victories over Poland, then, especially, over France drove Hitler's power, standing and popularity to its zenith in the summer of 1940. But the triumphs (and the brutality that followed them) concealed for the time being the fragility of Germany's hold over much of Europe. The reality, acknowledged by Hitler and the German leadership, was that Britain was still undefeated; that intervention at some point by the USA with all its might and resources could not be ruled out; that the USSR – desperately preparing for the invasion it expected around 1942 – was bound to Germany only by the cynical opportunist pact of August 1939; and that the Reich's economic base, unless there were further expansion, was precarious indeed.

Without waiting for victory over Britain, Hitler had already, following the conquest of France, given orders to begin preparations for an attack on the Soviet Union – the ideological arch-enemy. In spring 1941, these preparations took concrete shape. This would be a different war to that in the west, a 'war of annihilation', as Hitler told his generals.[14] The army was complicitous in the orders for the shooting of Soviet commissars, who were not to be treated as comrades but were to be liquidated on capture. The army, brutalized by its experiences of the ruthless inhumanity in occupied Poland, its ranks infected by propaganda about the 'Jewish-Bolshevik world enemy', was also ready to collaborate in the operations of the SD's 'task forces' (*Einsatzgruppen*) to wipe out political enemies and Jews behind the front lines. With the orders to the *Einsatzgruppen*, given in the weeks before the invasion of the USSR, the 'quantum jump' into genocide was taken.[15] Once this jump had been made, the killing could only escalate.

'Operation Barbarossa' – the invasion of the Soviet Union – was meant to be over long before the end of the year. Despite the extraordinary advances initially made after it was launched on 22 June 1941, this was already looking unlikely before the German troops found themselves bogged down in the ice and the mud, condemned to exposure in a Russian winter without adequate clothing or provisions. With the entry of the USA into the war in December 1941, and the certainty of the conflict dragging on into the indefinite future with the balance of resources tipped heavily against Germany, Hitler's gamble was already effectively lost, even if the Wehrmacht continued to fight tooth and nail over every yard of ground and total defeat was still over three years away.

The 'cumulative radicalization' of anti-Jewish policy had meanwhile escalated into all-out systematic genocide. The power-crazed plans of the police and SS under Heydrich and Himmler for the mass removal of Jews in Poland to make way for the resettlement of ethnic Germans from the Baltic and other parts of eastern Europe had proved unrealizable. Ghettos – some, like Lodz and Warsaw, huge in size – had been hastily set up, initially meant as temporary measures, prior to further deportation eastwards to a huge Jewish reservation. The continuation of the war vitiated such schemes (which would doubtless in practice have resulted in a form of genocide, though not necessarily the form which actually emerged). Already in mid-1941 there were suggestions that the Jews in the ghettos should be liquidated rather than fed during the coming winter. By that time, the *Einsatzgruppen* were shooting thousands of Jews in the USSR. And pressure was building up meanwhile from police and party leaders within Germany to have Jews from the Reich deported eastwards – to ghettos already bursting at the seams. By autumn 1941, mass extermination was emerging as the solution, and killing by poison gas offered potential 'efficiency' in the plan to annihilate all the Jews in Nazi-occupied Europe. The first of the extermination camps in the General-Government was commissioned in September, at Belzec. Its personnel were drawn from those who had acquired expertise in killing by poison gas during the so-called 'euthanasia action' within Germany – the liquidation of around 100,000 mentally ill and incurably sick patients of asylums – which had been 'officially' ended (after doctors had nominated even more victims than the Nazis had imagined there to be) in August 1941. By December 1941, the first killing installations were in operation at Chelmno in the Warthegau, a part of western Poland annexed to the Reich. The following month, the orchestration of the 'final solution' was worked out at the Wannsee Conference. By spring 1942, the mass killing of Poland's big Jewish population in the extermination camps of what came to be called *'Aktion Reinhardt'* – Belzec, Sobibor, and Treblinka – was underway. By then, too, the enormous extermination camp at Auschwitz-Birkenau, with its huge capacity for production-line murder, was also in operation.

It is not credible to imagine that the 'final solution' as it emerged in the latter half of 1941 and the early months of 1942 – the attempt to exterminate the entire Jewish population of Europe – was implemented without the approval, let alone without the knowledge, of Hitler. The barbarous guidelines for the occupation of Poland, then for the invasion of the USSR, had been laid down by Hitler. Pressed for affirmation of his written authorization, in autumn 1939 he had explicitly, on his own headed notepaper, empowered his doctor, Karl Brandt, and the Philipp Bouhler head of the Chancellery of the Führer of the NSDAP, Viktor Brack, to carry out the killing of the mentally sick. Goebbels referred to Hitler in early 1942, as the death camps moved into full operation, as 'the undismayed champion of a radical solution' to the so-called 'Jewish question'.[16] Probably not least because of the difficulties which had arisen from the killing of the mentally sick and incurable, Hitler would have shied away from a written authorization in the case of the extermination of the Jews. But his verbal approval for initiatives in all probability emanating from Heydrich's office in the Reich Security Headquarters would have been necessary.

As military defeats mounted during the second half of the war, and as the bombs rained down ever more heavily on German cities, the popularity of the now distant figure of the Führer, who, without triumphs to announce, no longer wanted to face his once adoring public, went into steep decline. The 'successes' which had been essential to sustaining 'charismatic leadership' were by now a distant memory, the Führer cult a residual and ritualized propaganda product largely devoid of the spontaneous effusions of support which had been so vividly present during the early years of the regime.

Even so, strong reserves of popular support for Hitler remained. More important still: since all the power groups in the now crumbling regime had earlier committed themselves to Hitler, had become implicated in the criminal actions of the regime, and had burnt their boats with the Führer, they now felt no option other than to stick with him. This included most of the generals in the Wehrmacht – the one body capable of deposing Hitler. The minority of courageous officers, and of civilians from different backgrounds and positions, who at great peril joined the conspiracy to assassinate Hitler, did so in the recognition that they had to act without the backing of most of their colleagues, and without popular support. The chance of ending the regime from within collapsed with the failure of the attempted coup of 20 July 1944. In the gathering chaos as the war drew towards its finale, the complete fragmentation of authority below Hitler ruled out any alternative to following the dictator to the bitter end. Only in the last days were other leading Nazis prepared to challenge Hitler's authority. But even in these last days, in the unreal world of the bunker, generals awaited Hitler's orders to pass on to no longer existent army divisions.

. . .

A key to explaining the process of 'cumulative radicalization' in the Third Reich, I have suggested, can be found in the workings of the type of 'charismatic authority' embodied in Hitler's dictatorship. As Führer, Hitler was the linchpin of the entire 'system' – which, in reality, was fragmenting ever more under the impact of his leadership. He was the only link with its various, usually competing, parts. But, outside the realm of foreign and military policy, his direct intervention was seldom needed in order to drive forward the escalating radicalization of the regime. All that was required was for him to set the tone, give the green light, provide the broad guidelines for action, and sanction initiatives of others.

Such initiatives usually fell within the process which one leading Nazi described as 'working towards the Führer'.[17] This meant anticipating what Hitler wanted, second-guessing his intentions, doing everything possible to push forward his loosely defined long-term goals, not waiting for instructions before using one's own initiative. Hitler's presumed aims and intentions served, therefore, to activate the activists and to legitimate their actions. At the grass-roots of the party, this could mean, for example, agitation to hound out Jews from the economy and turn them into social pariahs. In the state bureaucracy, it justified ever more radical attempts to turn vicious but open-ended ideological imperatives into specific and concrete discriminatory legislation. Not least, in the ever-expanding SS and police organization, the tasks associated with the Führer's 'mission' offered endless scope for the unfolding of new, inhumane 'projects' (and accompanying power, status and enrichment), especially in the conquered eastern territories.

Among ordinary citizens, far removed from the centres of power, 'working towards the Führer' also had its meaning – if a more metaphorical one. Ideological motives were not necessarily dominant, or even present, when neighbours or workmates were denounced to the Gestapo. But the screw of repression was none the less tightened by countless such acts. Doctors looking for more 'modern' ways of creating a 'healthier' society could take a lead in pressing for measures on sterilization and recommend their patients for the 'euthanasia' programme. Or businessmen, anxious to rid themselves of competition, could use anti-Jewish legislation to close down a rival concern. These few examples illustrate how 'working towards the Führer' – unforced collaboration, using the broad ideological aims embodied in Hitler as a legitimation – could contribute to driving on an unstoppable radicalization which saw the gradual conversion of an ideological 'mission' into concrete policy objectives.

The 'idea' personified in the quasi-deified figure of the Führer held together the antagonistic forces within the Nazi movement itself. It also incorporated the distinct but related aims of the national-conservative elites in the economy, state administration, and – not least – army. The lack of definition of the 'idea' was itself an advantage. Building a united, racially homogeneous 'national community', restoring national strength and pride, establishing a 'Greater Germany', bringing ethnic Germans 'home into the Reich': all these aims corresponded with the hopes of millions. War to attain 'living space' (*Lebensraum*) and racial extermination were by no means seen by the mass of Hitler admirers during the rise to power or at the height of his triumphs in the 1930s as implicit in them. But the boundaries were fluid. The 'idea', represented by Hitler, provided a plebiscitary base and underlying consensus for the regime, whose aggressive dynamic was increasingly spiralling out of control.

The 'charismatic' nature of Hitler's position as Führer – a quasi-messianic personalized form of rule that arose from the desire for national rebirth and unity in a country traumatized by national humiliation and paralysed by political collapse – could of its essence not settle into 'normality' or routine, or sag into mere conservative authoritarianism. Visionary goals of national redemption through European domination and racial purification were at the heart of the regime. These meant constant dynamism and self-perpetuating, intensifying radicalism. The longer the regime lasted, the more megalomaniac were its aims, the more boundless its destructiveness. Its gamble for world supremacy meant war against an alliance of extremely powerful allies. It was a gamble against the odds, in which the regime risked its own destruction and that of Germany itself. This was Nazism's essential irrationality. Hitler's 'charismatic' leadership implied, therefore, not just an unprecedented capacity for destruction, but also an inbuilt tendency towards self-destruction. In this sense, the suicide of the German dictator on 30 April 1945 was not merely a welcome, but also a logical, end to the Third Reich.

Notes:

1. Ritter, Gerhard, *Das deutsche Problem. Grundfragen deutschen Staatslebens gestern und heute* (1962) (extended edition of *Europa und die deutsche Frage*, 1948), p. 198.

2. Mommsen, Hans, 'Der Nationalsozialismus. Kumulative Radikalisierung und Selbstzerstörung des Regimes', in *Meyers Enzyklopädisches Lexikon*, vol. 16 (1976), pp. 785–90. And see now Hans Mommsen, 'Cumulative Radicalization and Progressive Self-Destruction as Structural Determinants of the Nazi Dictatorship', in Ian Kershaw and Moshe Lewin eds., *Stalinism and Nazism. Dictatorships in Comparison* (1997).

3. Mommsen, Hans, 'Hitlers Stellung im nationalsozialistischen Herrschaftssystem', in Gerhard Hirschfeld and Lothar Kettenacker, eds., *Der 'Führerstaat': Mythos und Realität* (1981), p. 70.

4. Mommsen, 'Hitlers Stellung', p.70; translated, Hans Mommsen, *From Weimar to Auschwitz* (1991), p. 187.

5. I explore the limitations of this concept at length in *The Nazi Dictatorship*, 3rd edn. (1993), ch. 4.

6. Mommsen, Hans, 'Hitlers Stellung', p. 70; *From Weimar to Auschwitz*, p. 187.

7. Bessel, Richard, *Germany after the First World War* (1993), p. 262.

8. Huber, Ernst Rudolf, *Verfassungsrecht des Großdeutschen Reiches* (1939), p. 230; translated in Jeremy Noakes and Geoffrey Pridham eds., *Nazism 1919–1945: A Documentary Reader*, 3 vols. (1983, 1985, 1988) (= N&P), vol. 2, p. 199.

9. Frank, Hans, *Im Angesicht des Galgens* (1953), pp. 466–7; trans. N&P, vol. 2, p. 200.

10. Wiedemann, Fritz, *Der Mann, der Feldherr werden wollte* (1964), p. 69; trans. N&P, vol. 2, p. 208.

11. International Military Tribunal, *Trial of the Major War Criminals*, 42 vols. (1949), vol. 26, p. 343; trans. N&P, vol. 3, p. 742.

12. Hill, Leonidas E., ed., *Die Weizsäcker-Papiere 1933–1950* (1974), p. 162.

13. Speer, Albert, *Erinnerungen* (1969), p. 271.

14. Halder, Franz, *Kriegstagebuch*, 3 vols. (1962–4), vol. 2, pp. 336–7.

15. The phrase is that of Christopher Browning, *The Final Solution and the German Foreign Office* (1978), p. 8.

16. Lochner, Louis, ed., *The Goebbels Diaries* (1948), p. 103; Elke Fröhlich, ed., *Die Tagebücher von Joseph Goebbels*, Part II: *Diktate 1941–1945*, vol. 3, p. 561.

17. Speech by Werner Willikens, State Secretary in the Ministry of Food, 21 Feb. 1934, Niedersächsisches Staatsarchiv, Oldenburg, Best. 131, Nr. 303, Fol. 131v; trans. N&P, vol. 2, p. 207.

Select bibliography

Aly, Götz, *'Final Solution'. Nazi Population Policy and the Murder of the European Jews* (1999).

Balfour, Michael, *Withstanding Hitler* (1988).

Bartov, Omer, *Hitler's Army: Soldiers, Nazis, and War in the Third Reich* (1991).

Bessel, Richard, ed., *Life in the Third Reich* (1987).

Bracher, Karl Dietrich, *The German Dictatorship* (1971).

Broszat, Martin, *Hitler's State* (1981).

Browning, Christopher, *Fateful Months* (1985).

Browning, Christopher, *The Path to Genocide* (1992).

Buchheim, Hans, *et al.*, *Anatomy of the SS State* (1968).

Bull, Hedley, ed., *The Challenge of the Third Reich* (1986).

Bullock, Alan, *Hitler. A Study in Tyranny* (1952).
Bullock, Alan, *Hitler and Stalin. Parallel Lives* (1991).
Burleigh, Michael, and Wippermann, Wolfgang, *The Racial State* (1991).
Burrin, Philippe, *Hitler and the Jews. The Genesis of the Holocaust* (1994).
Caplan, Jane, *Government without Administration* (1988).
Carr, William, *Hitler: A Study in Personality and Politics* (1972).
Dülffer, Jost, *Nazi Germany. Faith and Annihilation* (1996).
Fest, Joachim C., *The Face of the Third Reich* (1972).
Fest, Joachim C., *Hitler* (1974).
Fleming, Gerald, *Hitler and the Final Solution* (1986).
Frei, Norbert, *National Socialist Rule in Germany* (1993).
Geary, Dick, *Hitler and Nazism* (1993).
Gellately, Robert, *The Gestapo and German Society* (1990).
Graml, Hermann, *Antisemitism in the Third Reich* (1992).
Hildebrand, Klaus, *The Third Reich* (1984).
Hiden, John, and Farquharson, John, *Explaining Hitler's Germany*, 2nd edn. (1989).
Hirschfeld, Gerhard, ed., *The Policies of Genocide* (1986).
Hoffmann, Peter, *The German Resistance to Hitler* (1988).
Jäckel, Eberhard, *Hitler in History* (1984).
Jäckel, Eberhard, *Hitler's World View* (1981).
Kater, Michael, *The Nazi Party* (1983).
Kershaw, Ian, *Popular Opinion and Political Dissent in the Third Reich* (1983).
Kershaw, Ian, *The Hitler Myth* (1987).
Kershaw, Ian, *Hitler. A Profile in Power* (1991).
Kershaw, Ian, *The Nazi Dictatorship*, 3rd edn. (1993).
Kirk, Tim, ed., *Nazi Germany* (1995).
Large, David Clay, ed., *Contending with Hitler* (1991).
Mason, Tim, *Social Policy in the Third Reich* (1993).
Mommsen, Hans, *From Weimar to Auschwitz* (1991).
Müller, Klaus-Jürgen, *Army, Politics, and Society in Germany, 1933–1945* (1987).
Noakes, Jeremy, ed., *Government, Party, and People in Nazi Germany* (1980).
Noakes, Jeremy, and Pridham, Geoffrey, eds., *Nazism. A Documentary Study*, 4 vols. (1983–98).
Overy, Richard, *War and Economy in the Third Reich* (1994).
Overy, Richard, *Why the Allies Won* (1995).
Peterson, Edward, *The Limits of Hitler's Power* (1969).
Peukert, Detlev, *Inside Nazi Germany* (1987).
Stachura, Peter, ed., *The Shaping of the Nazi State* (1975).
Stephenson, Jill, *Women in Nazi Society* (1975).
Stephenson, Jill, *The Nazi Organisation of Women* (1981).
Stoakes, Geoffrey, *Hitler and the Quest for World Dominion* (1987).
Weinberg, Gerhard, *The Foreign Policy of Hitler's Germany*, 2 vols. (1970, 1980).
Welch, David, ed., *Nazi Propaganda* (1983).
Welch, David, *The Third Reich. Politics and Propaganda* (1993).

6

From *Blitzkrieg* to total war*

Omer Bartov

The German *Wehrmacht* conducted two distinct, though not unrelated and at times overlapping types of warfare between 1939 and 1945. One was based on massive, concentrated, and well-coordinated attacks along narrow fronts, leading to encirclements of large enemy forces and aimed at achieving a rapid military and political disintegration of the opponent by undermining both his logistical apparatus and psychological determination at a minimum cost to the attacking force. The other constituted a stubborn and costly defence, along huge, static, or gradually retreating fronts, normally launching only local attacks and counter-attacks with relatively limited elements of the armed forces, and relying increasingly on fortifications and doggedness rather than on speed and daring. The first type, which came to be known as *Blitzkrieg*, or lightning war, since it assumed a brief, though intense military confrontation, called for the preparation of limited stocks of armaments (without any major, long-term changes in the economy) needed for the implementation of such shock tactics, namely tanks, armoured personnel carriers, motorized artillery and anti-aircraft guns, as well as fighter planes and tactical support light and medium bombers. The second type, generally called total war, and closely related to the experience of 1914–18 (whose repetition so many European countries, and especially Germany, had hoped to avoid), necessitated a much more profound restructuring of the economy and the industrial organization of the nation, as well a greater participation of, and a heavier burden on, the population, so as to be able to produce the endless quantities of *matériel*, to use most efficiently the existing material resources, and to mobilize the

* This chapter was originally published as 'From Blitzkrieg to Total War: Controversial Links Between Image and Reality' in Kershaw and Lewin, eds., *Stalinism and Nazism: Dictatorships in Comparison* (CUP, 1997).

largest possible numbers of men and women, in order to satisfy the voracious appetite of total industrial warfare.[1]

As long as Germany pursued political and military goals that could be achieved by resorting to a series of brief, albeit highly brutal, *Blitzkrieg* campaigns, it remained victorious. Once it moved beyond these relatively limited goals (by continuing the war with Britain and attacking the Soviet Union), Germany found itself increasingly embroiled in a total world war, which it had no hope of winning because of the much greater industrial and manpower capacities of its opponents. Hence we can say that the transition from *Blitzkrieg* to total war spelt the end of German military and political hegemony in Europe, even though at the time there were those in Germany (including such rational technocrats as Albert Speer) who argued that only a truly total mobilization of the nation would save it from defeat.[2] There is, however, controversy over the *nature*, *degree* and *implications* of German military preparation. Whereas one school claims that the Nazi regime launched a *Blitzkrieg* campaign due to the domestic economic, social and political cul-de-sac into which it had manoeuvred itself, the opposing thesis holds that the regime was motivated by foreign political and expansionist ambitions, showed no signs of anxiety over any alleged domestic crisis, did not seem unduly worried about its popularity, and was all along preparing for a total war rather than a *Blitzkrieg*, a war it finally launched not because it felt constrained to do so but because it seized what seemed to be the best opportunity.[3]

Debates over the nature and meaning of *Blitzkrieg*, not only as a military tactic, but also a type of war favoured by certain kinds of regimes and hence a strategic concept to be understood only as a combination of political, economic, and military factors, have to a large extent been moulded by the images it has produced ever since its inception. Images, in the case of *Blitzkrieg*, have been especially important, since the very success of this type of war has depended to a large extent on the image it projected, just as much as on its reality. Indeed, it would be more accurate to say that the image of *Blitzkrieg* was *part* of its reality, though precisely for that reason it is, nevertheless, important to distinguish between the more quantifiable facts of specific *Blitzkrieg* campaigns and their perception by contemporaries and later generations.[4] Such an analysis may tell us more about the relationship between the material aspects of war, on the one hand, and the power of myth and psychological suggestion, on the other.

In this chapter I will discuss several aspects of this issue. First, I will point out some of the implications of the disparities between the facts of *Blitzkrieg* as it was conducted by the *Wehrmacht* in the initial phases of the Second World War, and the impression it made not only on those subjected to its violence but also on its practitioners. Second, I will present some of the main controversies over the nature and meaning of *Blitzkrieg* and note their wider implications for the historiography of the Third Reich. Finally, I will briefly examine the images of *Blitzkrieg* both during the war and following the collapse of the Nazi regime, and remark on some of the more problematic and disturbing manifestations of the representation of the German war machine.

I Realities and impressions

The concept of *Blitzkrieg* was developed as an attempt to avoid the recurrence of a static, costly, and, especially for Germany, unwinnable war such as the Western Front of 1914–18. In order to prevent a similar stalemate along well-defended lines of trenches and fortifications, new types of weaponry and tactics were needed. Such ideas were already emerging during the latter part of the Great War, and during the inter-war period they were widely discussed and in some cases put into practice. All European nations were intrigued by the new technologies developed during the period and the manner in which they could be put to military use. But their conclusions as to organizing their armed forces and rethinking their strategic and tactical concepts differed greatly. While there is no doubt that the major European powers, namely the Soviet Union, Germany, France and Britain, recognized the importance of using modern tanks and aircraft in any future war, for a variety of reasons, which had to do both with their different experience during the war and with the domestic and foreign conditions in each country, it was only the newly established *Wehrmacht* which ultimately practised the new form of *Blitzkrieg* warfare in the initial phases of the Second World War.[5]

From the very beginning, it was clear to all those involved in conceptualizing and planning *Blitzkrieg* that this type of warfare depended to a large extent on the impression it made on the opponent, since it was aimed just as much at demoralizing the enemy troops as at destroying them. And, while the enemy was to be given the *coup de grâce* after being debilitated by a combination of deep thrusts into the rear, thereby severing the contact between the enemy's combat elements and logistics, as well as by bombing of control centres and civilian targets, one's own troops were expected to be greatly energized by the constant, if ultimately exhausting, momentum of the fighting. Hence *Blitzkrieg* was intended to create the impression of an invincible army both among its enemies and among its own soldiers.[6]

In this the Germans were highly, perhaps even dangerously successful. While the campaign in the West culminated in one of the greatest and cheapest victories in modern warfare, it created a new and vastly more confident perception of the German capacities for war among those *Wehrmacht* generals who had previously been somewhat reluctant to accept the risks of *Blitzkrieg*. The result was that the Western campaign was not analysed clearly enough, and those aspects of the fighting that might have turned a great German victory into a disastrous defeat were neglected or ignored. Nor did the failure of the Battle of Britain deter German military leaders from planning an even vaster and much riskier campaign in the Soviet Union, where precisely those elements which had formed the potential Achilles' heel of the German army's Western campaign were greatly accentuated. To make matters worse, the industrial output of military wares remained far below the rate needed by such an unprecedented operation, so that in terms of the ratio between space and material, the German Eastern Army was actually weaker than its Western counterpart of the previous year.[7]

The irony of this turn of events is obvious. While the Germans drew the correct military conclusions from the First World War, and prepared themselves better than anyone else for the fighting in the first part of the Second World War, it was their victories during those early campaigns that blinded them to the limitations of their own strategy. Hence their final and greatest *Blitzkrieg* ended in catastrophe, and had to be followed by a reversion to total war strategies highly reminiscent of 1914–18, with the unavoidable conclusion of a complete and total German defeat. The impression created by the swift victories and tremendous energies unleashed by *Blitzkrieg* therefore debilitated not only the enemy, but also the minds of those who had launched it. From being a means to preventing total war it came to be seen as a magic formula for German victory, and found its own nemesis in bringing about precisely what it had been intended to thwart. The concentration of forces at a given point, which formed the essence of *Blitzkrieg*, appeared to both sides as reflecting total strength, rather than relative power limited to a specific time and space.[8]

The fact that Germany chose *Blitzkrieg* in the first place was, of course, related to its severe industrial and manpower constraints, which were not fully appreciated abroad and forgotten in the flush of early victory by the Germans themselves. We will have occasion to discuss the debates on this issue in the next section, but for now let us examine the relative strengths of the armies and armaments industries of the major powers involved in the Second World War.

It is now generally accepted that contrary to the image disseminated (for different reasons) both by the Germans and their foes at the time, and indeed popularly accepted for a long time after the end of the war, the

Wehrmacht's armoured forces during its most successful *Blitzkrieg* operation were in fact numerically, and in some respects also qualitatively, inferior to those of its opponents. Germany attacked in the West with some 2,500 tanks, while the combined forces of the Allies had about 3,400 machines. Moreover, only 700 German tanks had the speed, armour, and calibre of guns to be effective against the heavier types of enemy machines. However, whereas most French tanks were subjugated to the infantry and the few existing tank formations were lacking both training and support, the Germans concentrated their tanks in large and well-integrated Panzer divisions. These divisions were then organized in powerful Panzer groups which could be used to punch through the enemy's front and thrust deep into the enemy's rear, dislocating and isolating the enemy forces from their logistical support. Hence it was thanks to a combination of innovative (but not entirely unknown) organizational and tactical concepts that the *Wehrmacht* overwhelmed its enemy. Nevertheless, the impression created was of overall numerical preponderance and technological superiority.[9]

This impression was enhanced by the much more highly developed air doctrine of the *Luftwaffe*, which in this case also enjoyed a numerical and technological advantage, as well as being able to deploy types of aircraft best suited for its strategy (but not for later phases of the war such as the Battle of Britain and the strategic bombing of Germany). Facing the *Luftwaffe*'s 4,000 operational airplanes were about 3,000 Allied machines, including those aircraft stationed in Britain. And, compared to the *Luftwaffe*'s crucially important 1,500 bombers, the Allies had only 700 mostly obsolete machines. Nevertheless, in this case too it was largely the use made of air power which decided the issue, rather than its numbers and quality. The fact that by the end of the campaign the French air force had more aircraft on the ground than it had had at the beginning of the fighting, testifies to the timidity and incompetence with which existing airplanes were employed at a time when their proper use could have made a crucial difference. The *Luftwaffe*, on the other hand, used its aircraft as 'flying artillery', and due to good planning, training and cooperation with the ground units, achieved its goal of unhinging the enemy forces' front, disorienting their command, sowing chaos in their logistical system, and demoralizing both the front and the rear, thus greatly contributing to their rapid military and political collapse. The much-hailed Maginot Line, where a high proportion of the numerically superior Allied artillery was to be found, played no role in the fighting, apart from tying down large numbers of inactive French troops.[10]

In spite of the initial impression created by the swiftness and decisiveness of the German victory, it would be a mistake to view it as inevitable. First, we should note that only some 7 per cent of the German force was truly modernized (10 Panzer out of a total of 141 mostly infantry divisions). Second, and as a consequence of the previous observation, the kind of breakthrough demanded by *Blitzkrieg* tactics necessitated the concentration of almost all tank formations along a very narrow front, and the exploitation of the initial penetration further called for a growing gap between the armoured thrust and its infantry and logistical support. Hence, while the Germans did manage to drive a wedge into the Allied Force, the Allies were in a position to do the same to the Germans by driving a wedge between the nine Panzer divisions rushing to the Channel and the mass of the German army trudging far behind. To a large extent, then, the success of the German *Blitzkrieg* in the West depended both on its novelty and on the incompetence of the other side's command. Had the Allies understood the essence of *Blitzkrieg* tactics (an example of which had been already given to them in Poland), had they organized their existing manpower and *matériel* appropriately, and, had they shown a slightly greater degree of cooperation and tactical skill, the *Wehrmacht* would have had a much harder time confronting their forces.[11]

Because the Germans were taken in by their representation of their own successes in the West as inevitable, and due to their prejudices about the nature of both the Russians in general and the Bolsheviks in particular, they had little doubt that a *Blitzkrieg* against the Soviet Union would lead to an even greater victory than the campaign just won in the West. This hope proved to be an illusion. Indeed, within a few weeks of fighting it became clear that the *Wehrmacht* could not conduct a war on the mammoth scale demanded by the Soviet Union by using the same tactics and equipment of the Western campaign. Here, both the ratio between manpower and machines on the one hand, and space on the other, as well as between the German and Soviet armed forces, was much less favourable than in the West. The tremendous victories achieved nevertheless by the *Wehrmacht* in the initial phases of 'Barbarossa' were thus not only a tribute to the tactical ability of the German officers and the fighting skills of their soldiers, but could also be attributed to the incompetence of the Soviet commanders and the lack of training (but not of determination) among their troops. It should be noted that while the *Wehrmacht* attacked Russia with 3,600 tanks (of which only 450 could confront modern Soviet armour), the Red Army in the West had 15,000 tanks (of which close to 2000 were excellent modern machines). The *Luftwaffe* deployed only 2,500 aircraft in the East, significantly fewer than during the Western campaign, while the Red Army deployed 9,000 admittedly mostly inferior aircraft. It is interesting to point out that in fact the Red Army had a better ratio between men and machines than the *Wehrmacht*, that is, it was more modern, since it had only 2.9 million soldiers along the Western front of the Soviet Union as opposed to the 3.6 million attacking German (and allied) troops.[12]

The attempt to repeat its *Blitzkrieg* tactics over a vastly larger space than in the West compelled the *Wehrmacht* to split its relatively limited forces into even smaller groupings, and to allot its modern elements to each of these separate bodies with the result of further weakening its punch. Worse still, in the central sector of the front, the huge tracts of land to be covered meant that the *Wehrmacht*'s armour had to be split once again in order to encircle the large Soviet forces in Belorussia. Meanwhile, as the Germans drove ever deeper into Russia, the front tended to extend, so that by late autumn 1941 it had doubled in length, from 800 to 1,500 miles, while supply lines stretched 1,000 miles to the rear. Insufficient motorization of the *Wehrmacht*'s logistical apparatus, the primitive road infrastructure of the Soviet Union, and the different gauge used by the Russian railroad, all made for growing chaos and eventually totally paralysed the German *Blitzkrieg*. The fact that about half of the German divisions deployed in Soviet Russia relied solely on horse-drawn wagons for their provisions meant that even when supplies arrived at the railheads, it was difficult to bring them to the front. Considering these factors, as well as the shortage of spare parts for the modern elements of the army, and the lack of replacement horses for the more backward formations, one can only wonder how the *Blitzkrieg* got as far as it did.[13]

After the failure of *Blitzkrieg*, production, industrial capacity, material and manpower resources, organization and technical skill all became more important than tactics, training, and courage. Of course, *Blitzkrieg* itself depended on technology, indeed, it made a fetish of modern fighting machines. But now technological innovation had to be paralleled by quantities produced, while the initial psychological impact of mass (but spatially and temporally limited) use of modern weaponry lost much of its force. In this area Germany had no chance of competing successfully with its enemies. One interesting consequence of this change was a transformation of the image of the war, to be discussed in the last section of this chapter. But this change took time, and although in retrospect one could find its origins in the pre-war period, it became increasingly obvious only during the latter part of the war.

The growing gap between Germany and the Allies can be gauged from some revealing figures. Between 1940 and 1941 Germany's tank production rose from more than 2,000 to well over 5,000. Consequently the *Wehrmacht* doubled the number of its armoured divisions, but reduced the number of tanks per division by a third. Nevertheless, this expansion of the armoured forces was insufficient in view both of the growing amounts of *matériel* on the Soviet side, and the immense losses of equipment suffered by the Germans. It is indicative, for instance, that while in 1940 less than 400 modern tanks were built in the Soviet Union, in the first half of 1941 alone their number rose to 1,500. Even more impressively, in the second half of that year, and in spite of the loss of Russia's primary industrial regions, almost 5,000 advanced models were turned out.[14] At this point Germany was apparently still not committed to fighting a total war, since between 1940 and 1941 its expenditure on war production hardly rose (although this may be partly explained by its previously high investment in armaments). During the same period the expenditure on armaments in Great Britain, the Soviet Union, and the United States put together almost doubled; even more significantly, this total was already three times larger than that of the Reich, although the United States was certainly not close to the peak of its war effort.[15]

In the wake of the terrible fighting of winter 1941–42, Germany greatly expanded its armaments production, and over the next few years also made significant improvements in the technology of its weapons. But by this point the nature of the fighting had already changed irreversibly. While in the West it had been possible (though not without risks) to maintain military effectiveness with a few well-equipped divisions followed by the great bulk of infantry formations, in the East, because of the vast spaces that had to be occupied, the infantry proved unable to keep up with the armour over such long distances. This meant that the armour had either to wait for the infantry, or to operate independently from its support (and logistical apparatus). Both options meant the end of *Blitzkrieg*, since the first dictated loss of momentum, and the second weakened the power of the punch by dispersing the forces and exposing them to the constant threat of encirclement and annihilation. *Blitzkrieg* operations could have been resumed only if the *Wehrmacht* had been motorized on a scale which was far beyond the capacities of the Reich. Hence, as a more or less stable front emerged in the East, it became clear that it had to be held by the *Wehrmacht*'s ill-equipped infantry formations, joined now by a growing number of armoured divisions which had lost most of their tanks over the winter and could no longer be replenished. Some elite army and *Waffen*-SS units were, of course, constantly supplied with modern fighting machines, but attempts to bring about fundamental changes in the overall situation repeatedly failed. Thus, while the summer offensive of 1942 already limited itself to the southern sector of the Eastern Front (where it met with disastrous defeat), the summer offensive of 1943 (the last time the Eastern Army took the initiative) was limited only to the area of Kursk and was stopped within a few days without any hope of success. Similarly, the winter offensive of 1944 in the West relied chiefly on surprise and cloud cover, and once more had to be given up shortly after it was launched. Consequently, during most of the years of fighting on the Eastern Front (where the bulk of the German army was engaged), conditions became increasingly similar to those on the Western Front of the First World War. However, while the *Wehrmacht* had to contend with a growing demodernization of its front-line forces, the Red Army was rapidly modernized as it prepared for its own *Blitzkrieg* to the West.[16]

A few figures will suffice to demonstrate that in spite of Germany's tremendous efforts to increase armaments production, it had little chance of catching up with its foes. If by 1944 the Third Reich had raised the annual production of tanks to 27,000, already in 1943 the Soviet Union had reached an annual production rate of 30,000 tanks, while the British produced 36,000 tanks in 1942–43, and the total American tank production by the end of the war reached 90,000. Similarly, while Germany produced 40,000 aircraft in 1944, the Soviet Union was already producing aircraft at an annual rate of 30,000 in last years of the war, and the United States put out a total of 100,000 fighters and 90,000 bombers, many of which were strategic four-engined aircraft of a type Germany was unable to produce. Add to this the four million vehicles of all kinds put out by the American motor industry, and we can see that Germany stood little chance of winning the war once it had been transformed into a total world confrontation.[17]

II   Controversies and historiography

Two main controversies have developed around the concept of *Blitzkrieg*, its causes, consequences and implications. One has to do with the relationship between domestic pressures and foreign policy, especially the decision to go to war.[18] The second concerns the relationship between war and the implementation of criminal policies by the Nazi regime, especially the decision on the 'final solution'.[19] Both controversies are of crucial importance, not merely for our understanding of the wider implications of *Blitzkrieg* but, more importantly, for the analysis of the nature of the Third Reich, and, even more generally, the relationship between modern war and the state.

For the first two decades following the end of the Second World War it was generally believed that *Blitzkrieg* had been simply utilized as the most fitting strategy for the Third Reich to accomplish its policy of military expansion. There was no appreciation of the fact that this might have been a way to resolve or prevent domestic tensions, or to wage war without further exacerbating popular discontent. Because Germany had reaped such amazing successes in its first military campaigns in Poland, Scandinavia, the West, south-east Europe, and the initial phases of 'Barbarossa', it was deemed natural that it had prepared a military machine most suitable for such battles, and that it was only because of unforeseen natural and political factors, as well as blunders by the political leadership of the Reich, that this series of triumphs finally turned into defeat. In the mid-1960s, however, this convention was challenged by a number of historians who claimed, on the basis of either new evidence, or new interpretations of old evidence, that in fact both the timing of the German decision to go to war, and the nature of the war conducted by the *Wehrmacht*, were anything but a matter of choice. Rather, they argued, the Nazi leadership was compelled to follow this course by a combination of economic constraints, popular pressures and political anxieties, along with the better-known aspirations of conquest and expansion. Surveys of the condition of the German economy during the initial phases of the war seem to have indicated that the Reich had not at all been as totally mobilized as had been assumed up to then. While it did build up an impressive military machine, and produced modern armaments for a portion of the armed forces, Germany failed to create the economic basis necessary to sustain a long-term military commitment, but rather used only certain sectors of industry, and even those could be shifted to peacetime production relatively rapidly. The question thus arose, what were the reasons for this obvious lack of preparation in a country apparently set upon waging a large-scale war, indeed, a war which it had itself initiated? Further examination of economic conditions in Germany on the eve of the war appeared to show that a major transformation had taken place from a state of widespread unemployment in the early 1930s to severe shortages of labour and resources by 1938. It was also noted that the Nazi leadership, and Hitler in particular, were profoundly anxious about the possibility of popular anger and unrest in case the regime attempted to make the same demands on the population associated with the First World War, namely both blood sacrifices and domestic economic hardship and privation. The German public, not unlike the population of France and England, was anything but enthusiastic about the prospect of another war, knowing full well the horrific toll it would take on each and every member of the nation (even if some suffered more than others).[20]

Combining all these findings, a new interpretation of the relationship between domestic and foreign policy in Nazi Germany was proposed.[21] According to this thesis, by 1938 Hitler realized that he was faced with the choice of either slowing down the rapid rearmament of Germany, for which he had neither sufficient manpower nor resources, or unleashing a war which would bring in more (slave) labour and (requisitioned) resources from newly conquered territories. The first option entailed giving up, or at least greatly postponing, his plans for expanding Germany's territories, an idea with which he was obsessed and therefore could in no way agree to give up, quite apart from the political repercussions such a decision might have had on his own stature and the Nazi regime in general.[22] The second option, however, meant that Germany would have to go to war before it had completed its rearmament programme and hence at a point in which it was still unready for a full-scale, potentially two-front confrontation.[23] Moreover, while discontent, especially among the working class, was already troubling the Nazi regime, it was feared that total war would greatly increase such manifestations of opposition, to the point of threatening the stability of the regime.[24] The choice was therefore made, not untypically for Hitler, to unleash a limited, but ferocious war, against selected targets and along specific fronts, while doing all that was possible to keep other nations out of the conflict until it was too late to intervene. This was to be carried out at a minimum cost to the population, without mobilizing the whole industrial infrastructure of Germany for war, but rather by producing, in certain sectors of industry, only those types of military hardware deemed necessary for the campaign. Hence, the idea was to fight a victorious war without paying the price Europeans had come to expect since 1914–18.[25]

This plan worked until the collapse of the German invasion of Russia in winter 1941–42. At that point it became clear that if Germany wished to stay in the war, it had to strive in all earnestness for a total mobilization of its resources. Paradoxically, just as Hitler's natural inclination to avoid such measures, motivated by his fear of unpopularity, was overcome, and total war was both declared and eventually also practised, the fate of Germany was sealed.[26] This was not, however, due to unrest among the German population, as Hitler had feared, nor to any attempted 'stab in the back' but rather to the fact that the Reich could only hope to win in a series of *Blitzkriege*, a type of warfare which, ironically, had initially been chosen for reasons of domestic constraints, not strategic calculation. Not uncharacteristically for the murderous absurdity that increasingly dominated the Reich, it was now such cool, rational technocrats as Albert Speer who insisted on making ever greater efforts for total mobilization of the nation's resources, and thereby simply prolonged the war and the suffering and destruction it entailed without being able to prevent Germany's ultimate defeat, an outcome already anticipated by far less brilliant minds no later than winter 1941/42.[27]

This complex analysis of the wider implications and underlying motives of *Blitzkrieg* has been accepted by a large number of scholars, and has served as an important interpretative tool in explaining both the domestic and foreign/military policy of the Reich. Only in recent years have the data on which it was established come under increasing scrutiny and criticism. The argument has been made that there was no such widespread opposition to the regime among the working classes as had been previously assumed, that the labour and resources shortage was not as severe as it had been depicted, and that Germany had actually done its very best, under the circumstances, to mobilize as totally as it could. Hence *Blitzkrieg* was not practised *instead* of total war, but was rather a new manner of deploying and employing forces without giving up the notion of total mobilization. In other words, *Blitzkrieg* was merely a tactical innovation, not a new strategy. The timing of the war, it has been said, had to do much more with the opportunities Hitler felt he had been presented with, than with the alleged domestic crisis, which in fact never existed, or at least was not perceived as such by the Nazi leadership.[28]

The criticism of the 'domestic crisis' thesis is of some importance not only because it questions several of the basic contentions about the nature of *Blitzkrieg*, but also since it constitutes part of a larger trend in recent scholarship on the Third Reich. The previous Marxist-oriented interpretation of *Blitzkrieg* had rejected the Nazi notion of *Volksgemeinschaft* as a mere propagandistic myth, and strove to document the workers' adherence to their interests and consequent opposition to the regime. While this view of society under the Nazi regime appears now to have resulted, at least in part, more from wishful thinking than from a balanced analysis, recent interpretations have similarly questioned the *Volksgemeinschaft* as a social reality, preferring for their part to concentrate more on passive resistance to the regime by widespread (often middle-class) sectors of society, or on non-conformist fringe groups made up mainly of youths of both middle- and working-class origins.[29] From another perspective of inquiry, the insistence on the primacy of domestic factors, typical of Marxist interpretations, was also shown to be at least not as foolproof as it had seemed in the past.[30] Finally, *Blitzkrieg* has always remained for many political and military historians, soldiers and intelligent laymen a military tactic rather than the outcome of complex forces and pressures and the expression of a totalitarian regime in crisis.[31] To be sure, this criticism, persuasive as it is in many ways, has not been able to demolish altogether the previous interpretation, and has left untouched many of the more intricate and subtle connections drawn between war, society, totalitarian regimes and economic preconditions. What is most important in this critique for our own argument, however, is that it blurs the distinction between *Blitzkrieg* and total war, and presents the former only as a version or elaboration of the latter, without denying that it was a crucial aspect of the Nazi state.

In the meantime, the importance of the ties between war and domestic policy has been highlighted from a different, even more disturbing, but nevertheless related perspective. In the course of debating the origins of the so-called 'final solution of the Jewish question,' it was suggested by some scholars that the decision to initiate mass murder had been taken only after the invasion of the Soviet Union. Consequently it was argued that the realization of genocide might well be related to the progress of the Russian campaign. The various versions of this interpretation belonged, generally speaking, to what has been called the 'functionalist,' or 'structuralist' school, a term coined, interestingly enough, by the same scholar who had insisted on the relationship between the decision to go to war and domestic policy.[32] Conversely, the so called 'intentionalist' school viewed operation 'Barbarossa' at best as the occasion, but certainly not the cause of or impetus for, the plan of genocide. Rather, the 'intentionalists' argued that the plan had been conceived years earlier, perhaps even long before Hitler came to power.[33]

The 'functionalists', however, precisely because they rejected such teleological interpretations, needed to find the point at which a decision *was* reached by the top echelons of the regime. Alternatively, since the more extreme representatives of this school maintained that genocide was first begun as a series of local initiatives from the middle ranks in the field and only then adopted and expanded as a general policy by the regime, it became necessary to provide the chronological and geographical context within which this process took place (the assumption being that there had in fact never been a specific decision on the 'final solution').[34] Since there was no doubt that the killing of Jews by mass shootings began only following the invasion of Russia, and since the construction of death camps began only in the fall of 1941, with the first installations being put into operation in winter 1941–42 and spring 1942, it seemed likely that there was some connection between the military operations and the 'final solution'.[35] But while it is clear that the occupation of a huge territory, and the vicious nature of the fighting in the East, provided the context in which genocide could be carried out, partly concealed and, more importantly, made acceptable to perpetrators and bystanders already brutalized by war, some scholars maintain that the course of the *Blitzkrieg* campaign in the Soviet Union had a much more direct and specific effect on the decision to implement the 'final solution'.

Two contradictory interpretations of the relationship between *Blitzkrieg* and genocide have been suggested. The first argues that the Nazi regime chose to carry out mass murder following its realization that the *Blitzkrieg* in the East, and therefore in the long run the war itself, had been lost. The recognition of the failure to defeat Bolshevism was of crucial importance, since the Nazi regime had unleashed its campaign in the East as a crusade against what it perceived to be the enemies of humanity and culture (at least its Aryan representatives). Hence the immense sense of frustration felt by the Nazis. It was this frustration at having been unable to complete the task they had set themselves, rather than any premeditated plan to annihilate the Jewish people, which made Germany turn against the Jews, the one 'enemy' they were capable of destroying. Thus the failure of the *Blitzkrieg* in Russia is presented as being at the root of the 'final solution'. Had the campaign against the Soviet Union succeeded, genocide might not have taken place at all, and probably the Jews would have been simply pushed further East, expelled from the German occupied parts of Russia.[36] This interpretation, in spite of its Marxist origins, has the curious characteristic of partly overlapping with a conservative revisionist thesis on the German war against Russia and the origins of the 'final solution'. In the latter interpretation, the argument is made that the Nazis waged war against Bolshevism out of fear, since they were certain that otherwise Stalin and his 'Asiatic Hordes' would overrun and destroy Germany. Having been informed of the atrocities committed by Stalin against his own people, the Nazi and military leadership simply adopted (or 'copied') his methods as what they believed to be self-defence measures. This revisionist thesis itself is of course anything but original, since it is closely related to the Nazis' own presentation of reality. Moreover, it both implies, and in some places clearly asserts, not merely a seemingly logical connection between the war against Bolshevism and the genocide of the Jews, but also an apparently reasonable course of action on the part of the Germans, since it claims that the 'final solution' was not 'original', but only an imitation of the real or perceived acts of the Bolsheviks, who were, after all, seen by the Nazis as identical with the Jews. Hence we are presented with a process whereby the Nazis both took an example from the enemy, and, having associated their victims with the same enemy from whom they had allegedly learned these methods, felt they had a licence to destroy them.[37]

Both the left-wing and the right-wing revisionist interpretations, which view the 'final solution' as a 'by-product' of either the failure of *Blitzkrieg* or the nature of Stalinism, are exceedingly problematic, since to a large extent they do not correspond to the evidence.[38] Thus the contrary thesis points out that the killing of the Jews began well *before* the *Wehrmacht* had suffered major military reverses. Hence it has been argued that rather than deciding on the 'final solution' out of a sense of frustration, the decision on the genocide of the Jews was taken precisely at the point when the Hitler felt that the war against the Soviet Union had been won and that therefore Germany's energies could be diverted to the next important mission, purging the world of the Jews. And, once that policy had been decided on and the first steps leading to its implementation were taken, there was no going back, due to the nature of the regime and to its previous fixation on the 'Jewish question'.[39]

It should be pointed out, of course, that some interpretations reject such clear-cut connections between *Blitzkrieg* and the 'final solution'. Thus, for instance, while the 'frustration' thesis tends to push the decision on genocide to as late as winter 1941/42, and the 'height of victory' thesis places it in the summer months of 1941, yet another thesis, though not necessarily 'intentionalist', tends to predate the decision on genocide to before the attack on Russia. Nevertheless, even this interpretation has to concede that the actual *killing* began only after the launching of 'Barbarossa'. Hence, while there is no consensus on the nature of the tie between the *decision* on mass murder and the course of the *Blitzkrieg* in Russia, there is almost complete unanimity on the connection (but not on the *nature* of that connection) between *Blitzkrieg* and the *implementation* of genocide.[40]

This brings us, however, to yet another aspect of the relationship between war and genocide. *Blitzkrieg*, as we have seen, has been presented by some scholars as a determined attempt to avoid total war. However, there can be little doubt as to the ties between total war and the Nazi version of genocide, namely, industrial killing. It was, after all, the First World War – the first modern, industrial, total war – that introduced the notion and practice of industrial killing of millions of soldiers over a relatively short span of time. The death camps of the Second World War would seem inconceivable without the mechanical slaughterhouse of the Western Front between 1914–18. Hence, I would argue that while it is important to recognize the ties between the strategic, political and ideological aspects of *Blitzkrieg*, on the one hand, and the nature of totalitarian regimes, domestic policy and genocide, on the other, we must also emphasize that this type of warfare cannot be divorced from total war as a phenomenon of modern industrialized society. Rather, *Blitzkrieg* should be viewed as an aspect, or offshoot, of total war, an attempt to revise it or make it more effective without doing away with those features of the original deemed crucial to the conduct of modern war. In this sense it can be argued that while Nazi Germany attempted to avoid total war in the military and economic sense, it certainly did all it could to accomplish a total psychological mobilization of the population, just as much as it strove for a total elimination of its real and perceived enemies. The limits on war were to be set only as far as the suffering of the population at home and the German soldiers at the front were concerned. The foe could expect either complete subjugation or total annihilation.[41]

The Nazi *Blitzkrieg* was therefore not an alternative to total war, but rather an attempt to adapt modern war to existing domestic and foreign conditions, as well as to Germany's expansionist aims and ideological ends. The Nazi conception of war predicated total domination and ruthless extermination. Hence the still-present admiration for the Nazi war machine, even when allegedly focused only on its purely military aspects, is especially disturbing, since it carries within it an implicit fascination with mass killing and total destruction. It is this issue which I would like to address in the final section of this chapter.

III   Images and representation

The image of the quick, lethal, almost clinical German *Blitzkrieg*, that combination of roaring tanks and screaming dive bombers, brilliant staff officers and healthy, smiling troops singing as they march to victory, was first propagated among both the German public and the Reich's neighbours, friends and foes alike, during the initial phases of the war. It was a powerful and persuasive image, for it closely corresponded to events as they were experienced by the various parties involved in the conflict, even if their radically different implications depended on one's loyalties. Indeed, the perceived congruity between the propagandistic image of war as disseminated in films, newsreels, photographs, leaflets, radio programmes, etc., and its reality was perhaps the most shocking aspect of *Blitzkrieg* for a public that had grown sceptical about the correspondence between image and reality. For in reality, just as on the silver screen, the tanks roared, the Stukas screamed and the *Wehrmacht*, though perhaps not made of smiling soldiers, marched on into victory.[42]

While Nazi propaganda produced such images of *Blitzkrieg* with the clear intention of both intimidating its enemies, prospective allies, and neutrals, and uplifting the spirits of a German public initially quite anxious about a possible repetition of the 1914–18 ordeal, other nations found this image just as useful in explaining their own experience of the war. Thus the French, for instance, tried to justify or rationalize their humiliating 1940 débâcle by grossly exaggerating the overwhelming numerical and techno-logical superiority of the *Wehrmacht*, drawing what seemed to a public just recovering from the actual manifestations of *Blitzkrieg* highly convincing sketches of endless streams of tanks and aircraft, followed by invincible, not to say superhuman Aryan troops (feared, even hated, but occasionally also envied and admired),[43] all descending in an unstoppable flood upon France's fair fields and towns, shrugging aside the courageous, amiable, but outnumbered and technologically outdated French *poilus* (who by implication had been betrayed by the corrupt republic). This utilization of Nazi propagandistic images was an easy way out for incompetent generals and weak or opportunistic politicians whose lack of insight, indecisiveness, and outright blunders had had much more to do with the defeat than any material, numerical, or innate superiority of the enemy. Nevertheless, since this image proved to be so useful in explaining what would have otherwise been difficult to accept, it was generally taken at face value at the time and lingered long after the end of the war.[44]

As the war went on, and *Blitzkrieg* receded in the face of a more total, and much less swift and glorious war, its German image became increasingly ambiguous, until finally it was transformed, indeed reversed, with the wielders of technology now playing the role of inhuman automatons, while those lacking *matériel* but rich in courage taking up the posture of the super-man. Thus, whereas in 1940 it was the *Wehrmacht* which won cheap victories with modern fighting machines, by 1944 it was the enemy who was flying and driving even more sophisticated machines against the increasingly (at least in relative terms) ill-equipped troops of the *Wehrmacht*. Consequently, Nazi propaganda now changed its tune, presenting the war as a struggle between the German spirit and the cold, inhuman technology of the enemy (symbolized by the strategic bomber, that one item of technology not produced by the German armaments industry). Thus, whereas in 1940 spirit and machine were welded together into the German *Blitzkrieg*, in 1944 the German spirit confronted the alien machine, and the *Geist* was naturally bound to win in this newly christened *Materialschlacht*.[45]

This, of course, never happened. Nor did the previous image ever totally vanish, since the great heroes of the latter years of the war still remained to a large extent both the *masters* of machines, such as the *Luftwaffe* pilots, the submarine crews, and the *Panzertruppen*, and the machines themselves, the superheavy 'Tiger' and 'Panther' tanks, the first jet planes such as the Messerschmitt 262, and, most of all, the V-1 and V-2 rockets, those wholly depersonalized weapons, the epitome of technological war, the *Wunderwaffen* which failed to bring about that change of fortune and total transformation of modern war itself finally accomplished in a different part of the world by the atom bomb.[46] Hence, when the war ended, the Germans (but many other participants in the conflict as well) were left with two competing images of their war. The first, closely related to the end-phase of the fighting, portrayed hordes of well-equipped enemies attacking the Reich from every conceivable direction, East and West, air and sea, held back by desperately tired but courageous troops, ill-fed, sorely lacking in modern armaments, tough and cynical and proud.[47] The second evoked better times, and compared the orderly, efficient, neat victories of German arms with the messy, destructive, chaotic defeat. Naturally, this image was derived from the German perspective, whereby the destruction of Warsaw or Rotterdam was part of a swift triumph, while that of Hamburg and Berlin served as proof of the enemy's steamroller techniques and over-destructiveness. But it was a powerful and enticing image, which cast the winner in an inferior moral role, allowing him only superiority of numbers and production capacity, not of human virtues and technological quality. Moreover, both images could to a large degree be disseminated rather easily in the West, since they played on liberal guilt feelings regarding the terror bombing of Germany and the conquest and political subjugation of Eastern Europe and Eastern Germany by the Red Army as an ally of the West. Both images also relied on the assumption, widely held in Germany and generally accepted in the West, that there was no correlation between the German soldier, who conducted a professional, 'fair' war, and the criminal policies of the regime carried out by the SS and its various agencies.[48]

Hence the image of *Blitzkrieg* continued to play an important role in the post-war period as well. Yet this role was not confined to Germany. Indeed, precisely because *Blitzkrieg* was always both a military tactic and an image, both a reality and a manner of representing that reality, it became, in a sense, the ideal (of) modern war. Thus anyone who imagined war, propagated it, represented it in film or art or fiction or conscription brochures, could draw upon this available image of *Blitzkrieg*. Although, as I have argued, in reality *Blitzkrieg* was merely a version of total war, it came to serve as a highly potent counter-image to that other memory of industrial, modern total war, that of the mechanical slaughter of the Western Front in 1914–18, and while the latter was to be avoided at all costs, the former remained horribly (whether perversely or naturally) attractive, especially to those young men of numerous nationalities and several generations who, given the opportunity, were always likely to try and re-enact it. This is, after all, the popular image of war as portrayed in countless war films and novels. It is a heroic, fast, dangerous, exhilarating, glorious and sensuous representation of a paradoxically 50-year-old futuristic war.[49]

This transformation of *Blitzkrieg* into the good war, that is, the kind of war everyone prefers to fight, at least if fighting can not be avoided, is not only the domain of overenthusiastic teenagers, but also of sober (though ambitious) generals. The Israeli tank general Tal, for instance, is said to have likened the 1967 Israeli desert war against Egypt to a *Blitzkrieg* and to have compared himself with Guderian.[50] Similarly, one cannot help feeling that the American General Schwarzkopf was portrayed (not unwillingly, one would assume) as the leader of a 1990s-style *Blitzkrieg*, which contained all the necessary elements of few losses, immense quantities of sophisticated *matériel*, quick results and massive destruction to the enemy. But while the good war has thus come down to us in German (blissfully ignoring of course those essential components of this type of warfare such as terrorizing the population by concentrated bombing of open cities), we are now experiencing yet another disturbing transformation of *Blitzkrieg* into a media spectacle.

Since *Blitzkrieg* is essentially part image and part reality, its two fundamental components are military action and media representation. Propaganda was always crucial for the success of *Blitzkrieg* campaigns, just as harmless but frightening sirens formed an inherent element of dive bombers whose demoralizing effect was much greater than their destructive power. *Blitzkrieg* itself was to some extent a frenzied, yet well planned, murderous spectacle in which the actors were supplied with live ammunition. But nowadays, since the introduction of live media coverage, we are experiencing another kind of theatre. Now we can watch battles at close range, in real time, without knowing what their outcome will be, indeed, sharing the confusion of the battle scene with the participants. This is a play without a script, and while the reporting is live, the dead really die, and the blood really flows. Yet we view all this at an immense distance from the event, and though we know that it is happening just as we observe it, there is absolutely nothing we can do about it, not even give a drink of water to the wounded, or bandage a bleeding child. If *Blitzkrieg* was the first war to blend modern images and technology, to sell itself as a media event, war in the post(modern)war age has become even more immediate and direct, happening right in front of our eyes, yet simultaneously reinforcing our sense of complete detachment from the events unfolding on the screen, since they are, precisely due to their being broadcast in real time, so far from us that they can never touch our actual existence. Hence, live reporting breeds indifference, not compassion, detachment, or empathy. We take it as a given that the war out there and our own reality are connected *only* through the television screen, and that the connection can be severed at any moment we choose by pressing a button.

By way of conclusion, I would thus like to emphasize the links between the various aspects of *Blitzkrieg* discussed in this chapter. We have noted that while *Blitzkrieg* could have been motivated by a desire to minimize the price of war as far as one's own population was concerned, it was simultaneously closely related to the unleashing of a policy of genocide toward other populations. That is, while trying to be a limited war domestically, it was a total war *vis-à-vis* real and perceived enemies. We have also seen that *Blitzkrieg*'s reliance on images was not only a necessary precondition for its success, but has also played a role in perpetuating its fascination for postwar generations. Thus we may say that there is a link between the anaesthetized image of *Blitzkrieg* disseminated in the popular media, and the current 'real-time' reporting on war and violence whose effect seems to be detached curiosity and indifference, rather than compassion and political mobilization. In recognizing these links, we would be justified to feel profound unease about the potentialities of our own civilization. To take just one hypothetical example, how would we react today to a live CNN report from Auschwitz, showing us the gas chambers in operation, the smoking crematoria, the arrival of new transports, all in real time? How would that reality affect our own? We think of the real-time reports from Bosnia, Somalia, India, China, Russia, as well as the inner cities of the United States, and we know the answer. In this sense we can perhaps argue that *Blitzkrieg* was much more than a new strategy, for it was part of a process in the development of modern humanity which perfected our capacity to participate and yet remain detached, to observe with fascination and yet remain indifferent, to focus on an extraordinary explosion of energy and passion, and then calmly switch it off and go about our business. Perhaps *this* is the essence of *Blitzkrieg*, since it was, after all, an attempt to wage destructive war while pretending that nothing of importance (at least for the domestic population) was actually going on. In this sense we may even argue that *Blitzkrieg* was the perfect manifestation of modernity, since it presupposed normality as a simultaneous and essential component of atrocity, or, in our own terms, it anticipated the phenomenon of the 'real time' report, the symbol of contemporary humanity's indifferent acceptance of, and detached fascination with, death and destruction.

Notes:

1. On *Blitzkrieg* and the economy, see T. Mason, 'Some Origins of the Second World War', and 'Internal Crisis and War of Aggression, 1938–1939', in T. Mason, *Nazism, Fascism and the Working Class*, ed. J. Caplan (1995), pp. 33–52 and 104–30, respectively; A. S. Milward, *The German Economy at War* (1965), and his *War, Economy, and Society, 1939–1945* (1977). For criticism of this literature, see below, note 3. For a highly detailed discussion, see W. Deist *et al.*, *Das Deutsche Reich und der Zweite Weltkrieg* (1979), Vol. I, esp. parts 2–4

(H.-E. Volkmann, W. Deist, M. Messerschmidt); and W. Deist, *The Wehrmacht and German Rearmament* (1981). On *Blitzkrieg* doctrine, see B. R. Posen, *The Sources of Military Doctrine* (1984), esp. chs. 3 and 6. On pre-1914 military strategy, see J. Snyder, *The Ideology of the Offensive* (1984), esp. chs. 2–5.

2. A. Speer, *Inside the Third Reich*, 5th edn. (1979), pp. 269–367, esp., pp. 299–314, 351–356. Detailed analysis in B. R. Kroener *et al.*, *Das Deutsche Reich und der Zweite Weltkrieg* (1988), Vol. V/1, esp. parts 2–3 (R.-D. Müller and B. R. Kroener). A more general case for the relationship between economy and hegemony, in P. Kennedy, *The Rise and Fall of the Great Powers*, 2nd edn. (1989), esp. ch. 6.

3. R. J. Overy, 'Germany, "Domestic Crisis" and War in 1939', and 'Hitler's War and the German Economy: a Reinterpretation', in his *War and Economy in the Third Reich* (1994), pp. 205–32 and 233–56, respectively; 'Debate: Germany, "Domestic Crisis" and War in 1939', comments by D. Kaiser and T. W. Mason, reply by R. J. Overy, *Past & Present* 122 (1989): 200–40. See also G. L. Weinberg, *The Foreign Policy of Hitler's Germany* (1980), and D. Kaiser, *Politics and War* (1990), pp. 370–92, esp. 375–84.

4. On the powerful impact of the war on contemporaries and the manner in which its image distorted their understanding of reality, see, e.g., M. Bloch, *Strange Defeat. A Statement of Evidence Written in 1940* (1968), pp. 25–125, esp. pp. 25–6, 51–4, including the notes. See also such accounts as J. Green, *La fin d'un monde: Juin 1940* (1992); H. Habe, *A Thousand Shall Fall* (1942); J.-P. Sartre, *Les carnets de la drôle de guerre* (1983), and his *Iron in the Soul* (1984 [1949]); C. Malaparte, *Kaputt* (1979 [1943]).

5. The prophets of armoured warfare included J. F. C. Fuller and B. H. Liddell Hart in England, Charles de Gaulle in France, Heinz Guderian in Germany, and Marshal Tukhachevsky in the Soviet Union. See brief discussion in M. Howard, *War in European History*, 2nd edn. (1977), pp. 130–5. The British rejected these ideas, the French preferred the Maginot Line, and Tukhachevsky was executed by Stalin in 1937. Guderian, however, became one of Hitler's darlings. See further in Charles de Gaulle, *Vers l'armée de métier* (1934); B. H. Liddell Hart, *The Tanks*, 2 vols. (1959); J. F. C. Fuller, *Memoirs of an Unconventional Soldier* (1936); J. Erickson, *The Road to Stalingrad*, 2nd edn. (1985), pp. 12–20, 30, 44–9 (on Tukhachevsky); and Heinz Guderian, *Panzer Leader*, 4th edn. (1977), esp. pp. 18–46. On French strategy, see J. M. Hughes, *To the Maginot Line* (1971); and R. J. Young, *In Command of France* (1978).

6. German *Wochenschauen* of the period, often reproduced in post-war films, provide a vivid picture of both the reality and the image of *Blitzkrieg*, especially in France. A highly intimidating German film on the *Blitzkrieg* in Poland was shown widely in European capitals. See T. Taylor, *The March of Conquest* (1958), p. 10. The panic and confusion on the French side has also been the subject of numerous representations. One of the most outstanding is the opening scene of René Clément's 1952 film *Forbidden Games*, which depicts the perverting impact of war on children. See also the outstanding novel, C. Simon, *La route des Flandres* (1960).

7. H. Boog *et al.*, *Das Deutsche Reich und der Zweite Weltkrieg* (1983), Vol. IV, esp. part 1, ch. 3 (Müller).

8. Further on the planning of 'Barbarossa,' see ibid., part 1, chs. 1 and 4 (J. Förster, E. Klink and H. Boog).

9. K. A. Maier, *Das Deutsche Reich und der Zweite Weltkrieg* (1979), Vol. II, part 6 (H. Umbreit), esp. pp. 268 and 282 for figures. See also the excellent discussion in Posen, *Military Doctrine* (1984), esp. ch. 3 (slightly different figures cited on p. 83).

10. See Maier, *Deutsche Reich* (1979), II, 244–59, 282–307 (Umbreit), and p. 282 for figures; and Posen, *Military Doctrine* (1984), esp. chs. 4 and 6 (slightly different figures on p. 84, and statement on more operational French aircraft on the Armistice than on 10 May 1940, p. 133, citing the commander of the French Air Force, General Joseph Vuillemin).

11. The risks involved are nicely articulated in Howard, *War in European History*, p. 132. For the German divisional structure on the eve of the attack, see Maier, *Deutsche Reich* (1979), IV, p. 254 (Klink). For an account of the fighting from the perspective of the German tank formations, see Guderian, *Panzer Leader*, pp. 89–117. On the French side, see G. Chapman, *Why France Collapsed* (1968); A. Goutard, *The Battle of France, 1940* (1958); Bloch, *Strange Defeat*, esp. ch. 2.

12. For figures, see Boog, *Deutsche Reich*, IV, pp. 56–76 (J. Hoffmann), and 168–89, esp. 184–88 (Müller). On prejudices and ideological determinants concerning Russians and Bolsheviks, see ibid., pp. 18–25, 413–47 (Förster).

13. On operations, see ibid., pp. 451–712 (Klink) for the German side, pp. 713–809 (Hoffmann) for the Soviet side. On the collapse of the economic 'Blitzkrieg strategy', see pp. 936–1029 (Müller). Also see M. van Creveld, *Supplying War*, 3rd edn. (1980), pp. 142–80; H. Rohde, *Das Deutsche Wehrmachttransportwesen im Zweiten Weltkrieg* (1971); W. Zieger, *Das deutsche Heeresveterinärwesen im Zweiten Weltkrieg* (1973).

14. Figures in Boog, *Deutsche Reich*, IV, pp. 62–75, 734 (Hoffmann) on the Soviet side, 183–5 (Müller) on the German side. See also Erickson, *The Road to Stalingrad*, pp. 93, 322; and Ploetz, *Geschichte des Zweiten Weltkrieges*, 2nd edn. (1960), pp. 122–7.

15. Boog, *Deutsche Reich*, IV, p. 183 (Müller). For a somewhat different calculation, see Posen, *Military Doctrine*, p. 20. See also, H. Schustereit, *Vabanque: Hitlers Angriff auf die Sowjetunion 1941 als Versuch, durch den Sieg im Osten den Westen zu bezwingen* (1988).

16. On the experience of German soldiers on the Eastern Front, see O. Bartov, *Hitler's Army: Soldiers, Nazis, and War in the Third Reich* (1991), and T. Schulte, *The German Army and Nazi Policies in Occupied Russia* (1989). On the failure of the Wehrmacht to replenish its manpower and *matériel*, see Kroener, *Deutsche Reich*, V/1, parts 2–3 (Müller and Kroener).

17. Ploetz, *Geschichte*, pp. 448–53, 471, 499, 593–4, 613; Boog, *Deutsche Reich*, IV, p. 734 (Hoffmann). Somewhat different figures are cited in Milward, *War, Economy, and Society*, p. 74.

18. For the initial phase of the controversy, see esp. the contributions by T. Mason and A. J. P. Taylor in *The Origins of the Second World War*, ed. E. M. Robertson, 5th edn. (1979); A. J. P. Taylor, *The Origins of the Second World War* (1976 [1961]); Mason, 'Internal Crisis'. For its later development, see Overy, 'Domestic Crisis' and 'Hitler's War'; 'Debate'; Kaiser, *Politics and War*, esp. pp. 375–82.

19. Most importantly, see C. R. Browning, *Fateful Months: Essays on the Emergence of the Final Solution* (1985), ch. 1, and his *The Path to Genocide: Essays on Launching the Final Solution* (1992), part 2, esp. ch. 5; A. Mayer, *Why Did the Heavens Not Darken?* (1989); R. Breitman, *The Architect of Genocide* (1991); M. R. Marrus, *The Holocaust in History* (1989 [1987]), esp. ch. 3; G. Fleming, *Hitler and the Final Solution* (1984), including the introduction by S. Friedländer.

20. Apart from works by Mason and Milward cited in note 1, see also T. Mason, 'The Workers' Opposition in Nazi Germany', *History Workshop Journal* 11 (1981), pp. 120–137, and his *Social Policy in the Third Reich: the Working Class and the 'National Community'* (1993); S. Salter, 'Class Harmony or Class Conflict?', in *Government Party and People in Nazi Germany*, ed. J. Noakes (1980), pp. 76–97; Deist, *Das Deutsche Reich*, Vol. I, part 1 (W. Wette).

21. It is interesting to note that at about the same time several important works were published dealing with the relationship between domestic crisis and Germany's role in the unleashing of the First World War. See F. Fischer, *Germany's War Aims in the First World War* (1967 [1961]), and his *War of Illusions* (1973 [1969]); H.-U. Wehler, *The German Empire 1871–1918* (1985 [1973]); V. R. Berghahn, *Germany and the Approach of War in 1914* (1973). This approach, whose origins are to be found in E. Kehr, *Battleship Building and Party Politics in Germany* (1973 [1930]), was somewhat qualified, though not wholly undermined, by G. Eley, *Reshaping the German Right* (1980), and his *From Unification to Nazism* (1986); D. Blackbourn, *Class, Religion and Local Politics in Wilhelmine Germany* (1980), and his *Populists and Patricians* (1987); D. Blackbourn and G. Eley, *The Peculiarities of German History* (1984).

22. This could also be related to the tendency of the regime toward what has been termed 'cumulative radicalization', and for its need to move constantly forward, generated at least in part by Hitler's sense of mission and fears regarding his approaching physical and mental decline. See H. Mommsen, 'The Realization of the Unthinkable', in *The Policies of Genocide*, ed. G. Hirschfeld (1986), pp. 93–144; A. Bullock, *Hitler, A Study in Tyranny*, 2nd edn. (1964), e.g. pp. 525–6, 568–9, 755–6; and J. Fest, *Hitler* (1982 [1973]), pp. 607–21, for an acute analysis of Hitler's psychological motives in unleashing the war.

23. For the controversy over the Hossbach memorandum outlining Hitler's plans for war and Germany's state of preparation for the conflict, see the various contributions in Robertson, *The Origins*. For the document itself, see J. Noakes and G. Pridham, *Nazism 1919–1945* (1988), I, pp. 675–92, esp. 680–8.

24. Mason, 'The Workers' Opposition'; Salter, 'Class Harmony or Class Conflict?'

25. For Mason's last essay on and re-examination of this debate, see his 'The Domestic Dynamics of Nazi Conquests'; for revisionist interpretations, see P. Hayes, 'Polycracy and Policy in the Third Reich'; and H. James, 'Innovation and Conservatism in Economic Recovery', all in *Reevaluating the Third Reich*, ed. T. Childers and J. Caplan (1993), pp. 161–89, 190–210, 114–38, respectively.

26. Total war was of course declared only after the debacle in Stalingrad in early 1943, which was also seen at the time as the beginning of the end for the Reich. But pressure toward total mobilization came during the first winter in Russia, just as the recognition of a possible defeat began to surface in many people's

minds. The most detailed, best documented and most reliable analysis of the transformation from *Blitzkrieg* to *Weltkrieg* and its military, economic and manpower implications is to be found in volumes IV, V/1, and VI of *Das Deutsche Reich under der Zweite Weltkrieg* issued by the Militärgeschichtliches Forschungsamt, formerly in Freiburg, currently in Potsdam, Germany, with well over 3,000 pages of tightly printed text, along with maps, charts and graphs.

27. Speer, *Inside the Third Reich*, parts 2–3. See also R. J. Overy, *Goering, The 'Iron Man'*, 2nd edn. (1987).

28. The chief criticism in the economic sphere is by Overy; see above, notes 3 and 27. See also articles by James and Hayes, above, note 25. For the increasingly more nuanced interpretations of German society under Nazism, see I. Kershaw, *The 'Hitler Myth'. Image and Reality in the Third Reich* (1987), and his *Popular Opinion and Political Dissent in the Third Reich* (1983); D. J. K. Peukert, *Inside Nazi Germany* (1987 [1982]); R. Gellately, *The Gestapo and German Society* (1990).

29. On passive resistance, everyday life, and youth, see, e.g., M. Broszat and E. Fröhlich, *Alltag und Widerstand* (1987); D. J. K. Peukert, 'Edelweisspiraten, Meuten, Swing. Jugendsubkulturen im Dritten Reich', in *Sozialgeschichte der Freizeit*, ed. G. Huck (1980), and his 'Alltag und Barbarei', in *Ist der Nationalsozialismus Geschichte?*, ed. D. Diner (1987); D. J. K. Peukert and J. Reulecke (eds.), *Die Reihen fast geschlossen* (1981); L. Niethammer (ed.), *Lebensgeschichte und Sozialkultur im Ruhrgebiet 1930–1960*, 3 vols. (1983–5); A. Klönne, 'Jugendprotest und Jugendopposition', in *Bayern in der NS-Zeit*, eds. M. Broszat *et al.* (1979–81) V, pp. 527–620; A. Klönne, *Jugendkriminalität und Jugendopposition im NS Staat* (1981), and his *Jugend im Dritten Reich* (1982).

30. However, see T. Mason, 'The Primacy of Politics. Politics and Economics in National Socialist Germany', in Mason, *Nazism*, pp. 53–76. Apart from works of criticism noted above, there had always been a trend which insisted on the centrality of foreign policy. See, e.g., in K. Hildebrand, *The Third Reich*, 4th edn. (1987); A. Hillgruber, *Germany and the Two World Wars* (1981), his *Endlich genug über Nationalsozialismus und Zweiten Weltkrieg?* (1982), and his *Zweierlei Untergang: Die Zerschlagung des Deutschen Reiches und das Ende des europäischen Judentums* (1986).

31. Note, among innumerable examples, the popular book by L. Deighton, *Blitzkrieg* (1979), which was, e.g., issued in a Hebrew translation by the publishing house of the Israeli Ministry of Defence in 1986. For a different angle on relations between the military and the regime, see the excellent study by K.-J. Müller, *Army, Politics, and Society in Germany, 1933–45* (1987). It is interesting that some of the criticism of Fischer's and Wehler's theses bears similar marks, in that it both seeks to undermine the notion of manipulation from above by investigating popular trends, and, from the opposite extreme, lays more stress on foreign policy and strategic calculations. Apart from the literature cited above, see, e.g., V. R. Berghahn and M. Kitchen (eds.), *Germany in the Age of Total War* (1981); W. Deist, *Militär, Staat und Gesellschaft* (1991).

32. T. Mason, 'Intention and Explanation: a Current Controversy about the Interpretation of National Socialism', in Mason, *Nazism*, pp. 212–30. The best available introduction to interpretations of Nazism, is I. Kershaw, *The Nazi*

Dictatorship, 3rd edn. (1993). An example of 'intentionalist' interpretation is K. D. Bracher, *The German Dictatorship* (1970 [1969]); and of a 'functionalist' one: M. Broszat, *The Hitler State* (1981 [1969]). Recent analyses of these two schools can be found in: Browning, *Fateful Months*, ch. 1, and his *The Path to Genocide*, ch. 5; and S. Friedländer, 'Reflections on the Historicization of National Socialism', in S. Friedländer, *Memory, History, and the Extermination of the Jews of Europe* (1993), pp. 64–84.

33. The foremost representative of the 'intentionalist' school as regards the Holocaust is L. S. Dawidowicz, *The War Against the Jews 1933–1945*, 3rd edn. (1986 [1975]); see also her historiographical survey in *The Holocaust and the Historians* (1981). Other important 'intentionalists' are, e.g., Fleming, *Hitler and the Final Solution*; E. Jäckel, *Hitler's World View*, 2nd edn. (1981 [1969]). Useful introductions to interpretations of the 'final solution' include: Marrus, *The Holocaust in History*; F. Furet (ed.), *Unanswered Questions: Nazi Germany and the Genocide of the Jews* (1989 [1985]); and D. Cesarani (ed.), *The Final Solution: Origins and Implementation* (1994).

34. See, esp. H. Mommsen, 'The Realization of the Unthinkable', and his 'National Socialism: Continuity and Change', in *Fascism: a Reader's Guide*, ed. W. Laqueur, 2nd edn. (1982); M. Broszat, 'Hitler und die Genesis der "Endlösung"', *Vierteljahrshefte für Zeitgeschichte* 25 (1977), pp. 753–5. See also Broszat's polemical essay on the need for a revision of German history and decentring of Auschwitz: 'A Plea for the Historicization of National Socialism', in *Reworking the Past: Hitler, the Holocaust, and the Historians' Debate*, ed. P. Baldwin (1990), pp. 77–87.

35. The best discussion is in Browning, *Fateful Months*, ch. 1, and his *The Path to Genocide*, ch. 5. See also Marrus, *The Holocaust in History*, ch. 3; and the authoritative R. Hilberg, *The Destruction of the European Jews*, 3 vols., rev. edn. (1985).

36. This is the central argument of Mayer, *Why Did the Heavens Not Darken?*

37. This argument was made by Ernst Nolte, whose main articles on this issue are now to be found in an English translation, in *Forever in the Shadow of Hitler?* (1993). Nolte has also argued that it was reasonable for Hitler to view the Jews as enemies and to treat them as prisoners of war (or internees), since Chaim Weizmann allegedly declared war on Germany. See also contributions by Michael Stürmer, Klaus Hildebrand, Joachim Fest and Andreas Hillgruber. Related to this was Hillgruber's above-cited book, *Zweierlei Untergang*. On the connection between revisionist texts of the 1980s and their Nazi origins, see: O. Bartov, 'Historians on the Eastern Front: Andreas Hillgruber and Germany's Tragedy', in O. Bartov, *Murder in Our Midst: the Holocaust, Industrial Killing, and Representation* (1996), pp. 71–88. The best discussions of the *Historikerstreit*, the German historians' controversy which set the context for these arguments, are as follows: C. S. Maier, *The Unmasterable Past* (1988); H.-U. Wehler, *Entsorgung der deutschen Vergangenheit?* (1988); R. J. Evans, *In Hitler's Shadow* (1989); Baldwin, *Reworking*.

38. On differences between 'Stalinism' and 'Hitlerism' see the chapter by I. Kershaw, '"Working Towards the Führer". Reflections on the Nature of the Hitler Dictatorship', in Ian Kershaw and Mosle Lewin (eds.), *Stalinism and Nazism: Dictatorships in Comparison* (1997), pp. 88–106.

39. This is the main argument of Browning, *The Path to Genocide*, ch. 5. In ch. 4 of this book Browning criticizes Mayer's view of the Holocaust as a 'by-product'. See also O. Bartov, 'Review of Mayer's *Why Did the Heavens Not Darken?*', in *German Politics and Society* 19 (1990): 55–7. There is a different 'by-product' interpretation of Nazi genocide policies, whereby these are seen as part of a general trend of perverted science, or even as inherent to the nature of 'normal' modern science. See. e.g., D. J. K. Peukert, 'The Genesis of the "Final Solution" from the Spirit of Science', in Childers, *Reevaluating the Third Reich*, pp. 234–52; M. Biagioli, 'Science, Modernity, and the "Final Solution"', in *Probing the Limits of Representation*, ed. S. Friedländer (1992), pp. 185–205; M. H. Kater, *Doctors Under Hitler* (1989); R. Proctor, *Racial Hygiene: Medicine Under the Nazis* (1988); R. J. Lifton, *The Nazi Doctors: Medical Killing and the Psychology of Genocide* (1986).

40. The main argument on a pre- 'Barbarossa' decision is made by Breitman, *The Architect of Genocide*. In the 17th Annual Conference of the German Studies Association (1993), Browning and Breitman debated the issue at the panel 'The Nazi Decision to Commit Mass Murder', and their positions seem now to have come somewhat closer.

41. In this context see the important chapter by M. Geyer, 'The Militarization of Europe, 1914–1945', in *The Militarization of the Western World*, ed. J. R. Gillis, (1989). A good introduction to the First World War is M. Ferro, *The Great War 1914–1918*, 2nd edn. (1987 [1969]). On total mobilization see, e.g., J. W. Winter, *The Great War and the British People* (1986); J.-J. Becker, *The Great War and the French People* (1985 [1973]); J. Kocka, *Facing Total War: German Society 1914–1918* (1984 [1973]). On cultural aspects of the first industrial war, see P. Fussell, *The Great War and Modern Memory* (1975); R. Wohl, *The Generation of 1914* (1979); E. J. Leed, *No Man's Land* (1979); M. Eksteins, *Rites of Spring: the Great War and the Birth of the Modern Age*, 2nd edn. (1990 [1989]); S. Hynes, *A War Imagined: the First World War and English Culture* (1991). On the fascist personalities forged by the war and its aftermath, see the fascinating work by K. Theweleit, *Männerphantasien*, 2 vols., 2nd edn. (1987 [1977]). The writings of Ernst Jünger, and the cinema of Fritz Lang, are both essential to understanding the post-1918 European mentality. I thank Anton Kaes for his illuminating paper on this issue, 'War, Media and Mobilization', delivered at the October 1993 New York University conference 'War, Violence, and the Structure of Modernity'.

42. See notes 4 and 6, above. Further on the French attitude to war during the *drôle de guerre* and the subsequent shock and bewilderment following the German attack, see, e.g., J.-L. Crémieux-Brilhac, *Les Français de l'an 40*, 2 vols. (Paris, 1990); H. Amouroux, *Le peuple du désastre 1939–1940* (1987 [1976]); P. Rocolle, *La guerre de 1940*, 2 vols. (1990); R. Bruge, *Les combattants du 18 Juin*, 3 vols. (1982); J.-P. Azéma, *1940 l'année terrible* (1990); P.-A. Lesort, *Quelques jours de mai-juin 40: Mémoire, témoinage, histoire* (1992); P. Richer, *La drôle de guerre des Français* (1990). A mere look at the covers of these books suffices to evoke the sense of fear, confusion, shock and anxiety to escape the enemy with which such works are concerned. A good popular account in English is A. Horne, *To Lose a Battle: France 1940*, 2nd edn. (1988 [1969]).

43. Ambiguous portrayals of fascists and Nazis can be found, e.g., in M. Tournier,

The Ogre (1972 [1970]); J.-P. Sartre, 'The Childhood of a Leader', in his *Intimacy* (1977 [1949]), and his trilogy *Les Chemins de la liberté*, published in English as *The Roads to Freedom*. Ambiguity in portraying Nazis and fascists is of course not confined to French writers, and has, for instance, featured in many post-war films, such as Cavani's *The Night Porter*, Visconti's *The Damned*, Bertolucci's *1900*, Malle's *Lacombe, Lucien*, Fassbinder's *Lili Marleen*, Syberberg's *Hitler*, Kluge's *The Patriot*, Wertmuller's *Seven Beauties*, etc. The bizarre obverse side of this tendency was Hitler's expressions of admiration for Stalin, whom he called 'one of the most extraordinary figures in world history', and 'a hell of a fellow!' See *Hitler's Table Talk 1941–44*, 2nd edn. (1973 [1953]), pp. 8, 587.

44. On lingering images from Vichy, H. Rousso, *The Vichy Syndrome: History and Memory in France since 1944* (1991). On France's soldiers, their self-representation, role in the *débâcle*, and subsequent conduct and views, see P.-M. de la Gorce, *The French Army* (1963); J. S. Ambler, *Soldiers Against the State*, 2nd edn. (1968 [1966]); P. C. F. Bankwitz, *Maxime Weygand and Civil–Military Relations in Modern France* (1967); R. O. Paxton, *Parades and Politics at Vichy* (1966). On the realities of opinion, images, and collaboration in Vichy, see, e.g., P. Ory, *Les collaborateurs 1940–1945* (1976); J.-P. Rioux, *La vie culturelle sous Vichy* (1990); P. Labories, *L'Opinion française sous Vichy* (1990). On the attempts and failures to purge France of the collaborators and to recreate an acceptable image of an indigestible past, see P. Novick, *The Resistance Versus Vichy: the Purge of Collaborators in Liberated France* (1968); R. Aron, *Histoire de l'épuration* (1967); P. Assouline, *L'Epuration des intellectuels* (1990).

45. This is one of the central arguments of my book, *Hitler's Army*, where I make use of various types of evidence such as letters, diaries and propaganda. For letters, see also W. and H. W. Bähr, (eds.), *Kriegsbriefe gefallener Studenten 1939–1945* (1952); and H. F. Richardson (ed.), *Sieg Heil! War Letters of Tank Gunner Karl Fuchs 1937–1941* (1987). For youthful images of the war, see A. Heck, *A Child of Hitler*, 3d edn. (1986); R. Schörken, 'Jugendalltag im Dritten Reich', in *Geschichte im Alltag – Alltag in der Geschichte*, ed. K. Bergmann and R. Schörken (Düsseldorf, 1982), pp. 236–46. For soldiers' post-war representations of their experience, see, e.g., G. Sajer, *The Forgotten Soldier*, 2nd edn. (1977); H.-U. Rudel, *Stuka Pilot*, 2nd edn. (1973). On propaganda, see, e.g., J. W. Baird, *The Mythical World of Nazi War Propaganda, 1939–45* (1974), and his *To Die for Germany: Heroes in the Nazi Pantheon*, 2nd edn. (1992); E. K. Bramsted, *Goebbels and National Socialist Propaganda, 1925–45* (1965); Z. A. B. Zeman, *Nazi Propaganda* (1964); D. Welch (ed.), *Nazi Propaganda: The Power and the Limitations* (1983), his *Propaganda and the German Cinema, 1933–1945* (1983), and his *The Third Reich: Politics and Propaganda* (1993). For German reception of propaganda, see M. G. Steinert, *Hitler's War and the Germans* (1977).

46. This search for the heroic individual even in mass technological war is addressed by O. Bartov, 'Man and the Mass: Reality and the Heroic Image in War', in his *Murder in Our Midst*, pp. 15–32. Representatives of this tendency in Germany, on very different intellectual levels, are, e.g., Ernst Jünger, Hans Ulrich Rudel, and the film *Das Boot*. Jünger's revived popularity among intellectual circles in Europe and the United States is especially interesting in

this context. These are examples of depoliticized, rather than depersonalized technological warfare, and of team spirit in a 'war is hell' situation where one accepts the rule that *à la guerre comme à la guerre*. See esp. E. Jünger, 'Der Erste Weltkrieg: Tagebücher I', Vol. 1 of *Sämtliche Werke* (1978), including his *In Stahlgewittern* (1920), *Das Wäldchen 125* (1925), *Feuer und Blut* (1925) and *Kriegsausbruch 1914* (1934).

47. This was the image sketched by Hillgruber in his *Zweierlei Untergang*, but of course, it is a common one in popular post-war literature and divisional chronicles. See, e.g., H. Spaeter and W. Ritter von Schramm, *Die Geschichte des Panzerkorps Grossdeutschland*, 3 vols. (1958), esp. Vol. 3. There is, however, a clear distinction between the Western Allies, portrayed mainly as carriers of deadly, inhuman technology, and the Red Army, portrayed more as barbarous hordes. The former are infantile, playing irresponsibly with dangerous toys, and stupidly indoctrinated into seeing all Germans as Nazis; the latter are primitive, savage, innumerable, irrational, but individually can be more easily pacified, especially with alcohol. Fundamentally, both are inferior to the Germans, being less cultured and sophisticated, less mature and responsible.

48. On the images and reality of the Germany army in the Second World War, see: M. Messerschmidt, *Die Wehrmacht im NS-Staat: Zeit der Indoktrination* (1969); C. Streit, *Keine Kameraden: Die Wehrmacht und die sowjetischen Kriegsgefangenen, 1941–1945*, 2nd edn. (1991); H. Krausnick and H.-H. Wilhelm, *Die Truppe des Weltanschauungskrieges: Die Einsatzgruppen der Sicherheitspolizei und des SD, 1938–1942* (1981); G. R. Ueberschär and W. Wette (eds.), *'Unternehmen Barbarossa'* (1984); J. Förster, 'The German Army and the Ideological War against the Soviet Union', in Hirschfeld, *The Policies of Genocide*, ed. G. Hirschfield; O. Bartov, *The Eastern Front 1941–45* (1985), and his *Hitler's Army*.

49. On the creation of the new American hero as a counter-image of the failed Vietnam venture, see S. Jeffords, 'War, Gender, and Identity: "Rambo", "Terminator", "RoboCop",' unpublished paper (1993). It should also be noted that anti-war films are often viewed, especially by young men, as exciting war films. See J. W. Chambers II., 'All Quiet on the Western Front (1930): the Antiwar Film and Image of the First World War', *Historical Journal of Film, Radio and Television* 14/4 (1994): 377–411.

50. On Israeli *'Blitzkrieg'* see, e.g., M. Handel, 'Israel's Political-Military Doctrine', in *Occasional Papers in International Affairs*, No. 30, Center for International Affairs (1973); and on its nemesis in 1973, see H. Bartov, *Dado: 48 Years and 20 Days* (1981).

7

The 'final solution'

Nicholas Stargardt

By the time the Nazi regime collapsed in the rubble of Berlin in 1945, between five and six million Jews had been killed. From June 1941 to May 1942, this 'final solution of the Jewish question', to use the Nazi euphemism with its nineteenth-century ring, took shape. It moved from the face-to-face killings by mobile death squads on the Eastern Front to the complex bureaucracy and industrial technology of Europe-wide deportation trains to gas chambers. When Germany attacked the Soviet Union on 22 June 1941, specially selected SS units, or *Einsatzgruppen*, and police battalions began to carry out mass shootings in the wake of the advancing German army. Initially, their victims were Jewish and non-Jewish men. Women and children were included by some units from August onwards. Shootings by relatively small mobile units continued even after the establishment of the death camps in the early months of 1942. Some 2.2 million Jews in total were shot, burned and beaten to death by such units made up of SS men, police reserve battalions and gendarmes as well as regular army soldiers and East European auxiliaries. At times, German railway and other civilian personnel assisted too. Throughout the summer and autumn of 1941, a fateful tension existed in this continuously escalating campaign of mass murder between improvised local initiatives and central control from Berlin under the direction of the SS, headed by Heinrich Himmler and his deputy Reinhard Heydrich. Local initiatives continued apace. In the autumn, a gas van was tried out at Semlin in Serbia as an automated form of killing. At Chelmno in Poland, the commander of one *Einsatzgruppe*, Herbert Lange, began to deploy mobile gas vans in December 1941, left over from the so-called 'euthanasia' action against asylum patients, this time in order to kill Jews and gypsies. His 'experiments' in gassing accounted for 145,000 deaths. Himmler authorized the extension of the use of gas. At Chelmno, Sobibor, Belzec, Majdanek and Treblinka the exhaust from static diesel engines was pumped into specially constructed chambers. At a camp for Soviet Prisoners of War, Auschwitz, a cyanide compound used as a pesticide – developed in the 1920s by the German Jewish scientist Fritz Haber – was tested on a group of inmates. This was 'Zyklon B'. The technique, in which pellets of the compound were tipped into a chamber from a vent in the ceiling, would become the standard method of mass murder. Behind it stood a complex and rapidly assembled bureaucratic and industrial infrastructure, involving inter-departmental and international cooperation between police, home affairs and economics ministries, railways and military authorities, local and national governments across Nazi-occupied Europe.

For the Jews caught in German-occupied Europe, their descent from citizens enjoying varying degrees of emancipation and civil rights to the killing sites of the 'final solution' proceeded at a varied pace in different countries. In Poland and Hungary, for instance, government measures to strip the Jews of civil liberties and property had mirrored those carried out by the Nazis in Germany in the 1930s; yet, the Hungarian Jews were not deported to the death camps until the Germans occupied their erstwhile Axis ally in 1944. In the Netherlands, Jews had enjoyed full civic rights in cities like Amsterdam since the sixteenth century and persecution began only with the Dutch defeat in 1940. Because the German military authorities worked largely through the Dutch civil administration and police, social compliance and conformity were remarkably high, resulting in the swift and near universal registration and deportation of Dutch Jews to their deaths. For European Jews a common pattern overlaid the myriad of individual variations. They were registered, separated out by being made to wear the yellow star, stripped of their property, deported to ghettos and transit camps and on to the archipelago of labour and death camps. On arrival the deportees were divided between those to be gassed immediately (including all children and the women who accompanied them) and those who might be worked to death, employed in disposing of the corpses and other *Sonderkommando* duties in the death camps themselves. Some worked alongside other categories of forced labourers in war industries, like the IG Farben works near Auschwitz or in the notorious tunnels of Mittelbau Dora in the Harz mountains where the V-rockets were built. Within the death camps themselves, gas chambers and the adjacent crematoria were often disguised as delousing stations, victims deceived into undressing for the 'showers', in order to make burning of the naked corpses and recycling of their clothing easier. After death, the victims' clothes, hair, spectacles and gold teeth were systematically collected by special squads of camp inmates, supervised by the SS and their local allies; alongside widespread individual looting of the Jews at all stages of their persecution, the hand of the central bureaucracy was present in the tallies and the takings sent back to the Reich Economic Ministry. At times, the crematoria simply could not cope with the numbers being killed: when the half million Hungarian Jews were gassed at Auschwitz-Birkenau during the summer of 1944, many of the corpses were burned in open trenches by the Jewish *Sonderkommandos*. In addition to the Jews, over a quarter of a million gypsies were slaughtered in the mass shootings and the camps. A lesser but still unquantified number of male homosexuals, perhaps 10–15,000, a smaller number of female homosexuals, and so-called 'asocials', including people who were deemed to be vagrant, drunken, or workshy, were consigned often to their deaths within the camp system.

The place the 'final solution' occupies in both academic study and wider cultural perceptions has shifted dramatically during the 55 years since the end of the Second World War. After an initial explosion of public information about the death camps, in Western Europe and the United States as well as in censorship-ruled Eastern Europe a blanket of silence descended on the actual experience of persecution. Even psychoanalysts in the United States, many of them Jewish, did not begin to recognize that survivors had undergone what Henry Krystal came to call 'massive psychic trauma' until the term could be legitimated by quite other sufferers, such as veterans of the Korean war. The Eichmann trial of 1960, with its spectacular publicity and symbolic power of being staged in Jerusalem, changed all this. Serious historical investigation and debate only began in the mid-1960s with the publication of Raul Hilberg's *Destruction of the European Jews*. But Hilberg also had great difficulty in finding a publisher. Although the 1960s and early 1970s saw a revival of academic interest in Nazism, this was set in the context of the pre-occupation of the 1968 generation of leftwing activists with the threat of neo-fascism, so that it was the rise of the Nazis or the Second World War rather than the 'final solution' which attracted their attention. During the 1980s and 1990s this balance shifted to the point where 'the Holocaust' now overshadows any other aspect of Nazism in the Western public imagination. Literature and film have played their part here, from Hollywood feature films, first highly fictionalized in *The Holocaust* and then 15 years later *Schindler's List*, to documentaries such as Claude Lanzmann's *Shoa* or Lawrence Rees' *The Nazis: A Warning from History*. In Germany there have been local productions like *Das schreckliche Mädchen* and *Jakobs Gold*, whilst the two leading museums, Yad Vashem in Jerusalem and the Holocaust Museum in Washington, have set a standard of how to communicate the experience of persecution which has been taken up by the Imperial War Museum in London and elsewhere. The concentration and death camps themselves were almost all preserved as some kind of memorial site, but were also subject to the vicissitudes of the cold war. Death camps like Auschwitz were generally dedicated to the persecution of the Anti-Fascist Resistance during the communist era in Eastern Europe and only since the revolutions of 1989 in Eastern Europe have they been reconsecrated to the memory of their Jewish victims (if anything it is the communist victims of the Nazis who are now in danger of being overlooked). The cold war also exercised its influence on Western European sites too, with the British looking to Bergen Belsen or the Americans to Dachau – neither of which were death camps – as the symbols of Nazi genocide because these were camps which their troops liberated. More importantly, it was only in the 1980s that Western scholars started to compare atrocities committed against the Soviet population with the mass murder of the Jews. So central has the Holocaust become to contemporary debates across a wide range of issues that it is hard to remember that this was not the case until relatively recently.

Despite, or perhaps even to some extent because of, the new centrality of the murder of the Jews in our common awareness of what the twentieth century stood for, a difficulty persists in finding a language in which to speak and write about it. During the 1970s and 1980s, this was particularly marked. On the one side there was the language of everyday experience to be found in the personal memoirs of survivors or their videotaped interviews; on the other, there was the abstraction of much of the language of historical debate in which historians like Hans Mommsen deployed the categories of 'systems theory' drawn from American political science. Although this gap has now narrowed considerably, in part because the testimony of survivors is considered vastly more important than it was even twenty years ago, in part because historians have rediscovered how to write about the motives and attitudes of actual human perpetrators, a significant gap nevertheless persists. This gap is being given rough institutional shape by the marking out of a line between history, whose practitioners for the most part still study the perpetrators, and Holocaust studies, centred on the victims. Even when the same methods of investigation, such as the oral history interview, are used, the assumptions and methods of interpretation tend to be very different, with the uniqueness and commemorative importance of survivor testimony being frequently deployed as arguments for suspending the normal types of analytical scrutiny oral historians would use in order to interpret their sources. Such insistence on the words of the victims as being beyond commentary and enquiry is creating a new problem for scholars. How can they do justice to survivors' testimony and experience without forsaking the questioning, probing stance on which historical analysis depends? There is a danger here of placing the victims of the Nazi Holocaust in a new intellectual ghetto where their experience and words are not communicated and assimilated into historical enquiry because historians become too timid to interpret them in the face of what Peter Novick has challengingly dubbed 'the Holocaust industry'. The oft-repeated claim by Elie Wiesel that only the survivors can comprehend what they experienced carries a deeply pessimistic undertow about what can be communicated to respectful and imaginative audiences. But perhaps we will only find out what the limits of 'cultural translation' are here if historians make more effort to work on the experience and testimony of victims as well as perpetrators. Above all, there is a need to draw together the experience of different groups of victims of the Nazis, be they Jews, Soviet prisoners of war and civilians, gypsies, homosexuals, the mentally ill, Jehovah's Witnesses, Catholic priests, or communists.

In both quantitative and qualitative terms, historical research has been transformed in the 1990s by discoveries made in the Russian archives, as German records recovered by the advancing Soviet forces have become available to Western scholars for the first time. This evidence has greatly extended what we know about both central policy making and actual activities on the ground. Since the mid 1990s a new generation of German historians has come to the fore, producing a series of invaluable local studies as well as studies of the SD–SS–police complex of power in Berlin. The questions historians now routinely ask about the Holocaust have also been broadened out. Inspiration here has come from several quite different directions. In the 1980s a number of non-professional as well as professional historians in Germany began to investigate the killing of psychiatric patients, uncovering in the process medical, political, administrative and intellectual links with the murder of the Jews. Then, in 1992 and 1996, Christopher Browning and Daniel Goldhagen each published studies of the same Hamburg reserve police battalion's participation in the Holocaust. Although both scholars drew on the same sources, namely the files compiled by Hamburg prosecutors in the 1960s, each drew diametrically different conclusions about what motivated these middle-aged part-time policemen drawn from one of Germany's least Nazified cities to perpetrate atrocities and murder. At the same time as these studies appeared, the diaries of Victor Klemperer, a well-known German-Jewish scholar of romance literature at Dresden who was protected by his marriage to an 'Aryan' from deportation, were published in Germany and became an instant literary sensation. Chronicling the entire period from 1933 to 1945, they also provide exceptionally rich material on attitudes towards Jews in everyday life which scholars like Marion Kaplan and Saul Friedländer have begun to explore. Finally, the collection and study of survivor testimony, already well-established in the 1970s and 1980s, has continued to grow dramatically, not least through older centres like the Wiener Library in London or Yad Vashem in Jerusalem and the foundation of the Washington Holocaust Museum. Here too the subjects of investigation have also widened, from an earlier concern with issues of Jewish resistance to investigations of music and art, everyday life, gender relations and the experience of children.

However much we now know about the Holocaust, it is still true that there are many aspects about which we know little or nothing. Although Auschwitz-Birkenau accounted for the greatest single toll of Jewish lives, the hurried German retreat on that sector of the Eastern Front meant that a far greater number of inmates also survived it than from camps which the Order of the Death's Head closed according to its own plans. About some camps we know far less: approximately 70 Jews survived Treblinka; only two survived Belzec, one of whom, Chaim Hirschmann, was killed by Poles during the post-war pogrom of 1946 in Lublin. Indeed, from 1943 onwards, special units of prisoners, usually composed of Jews and Soviet prisoners of war, disinterred the graves from sites of mass shootings in order to burn the remains and realize Himmler's objective of obliterating any trace of the slaughter from posterity. At the same time, there was no way that his 'great secret' could actually ever be maintained. Both the private fascination of the executioners and of the SS as an organization precipitated the creation of extensive photographic documentation. The open air executions of 1939–40 in Poland and of 1941–2 across Eastern Europe attracted many spectators and became widely known, if circum-spectly discussed, in Germany. This pattern of destroyed and retained evidence, of survivors' testimony and its absence leaves a complicated patchwork in which we know an enormous amount about many aspects of the Holocaust and very little about others. Because of the power of the visual record in an age of documentary films, we are inevitably deeply influenced by photographic records taken, in many cases, by perpetrators or their voyeuristic German colleagues.

One consequence of the exponential growth of interest in the Holocaust has been the proliferation of specialized subject areas within it, each driven by their own questions and sources, so that it is no longer possible to give an overview of the subject without inevitably concentrating on some topics to the exclusion of others. Here I shall focus on two issues that have loomed large in the scholarly research and debates of the last two decades. First, I shall consider historical interpretations of the events and decisions that paved the way from a policy of forced emigration of the Jewish population as the prime goal of Nazi policy towards the Jews in the pre-war period to a policy of European-wide mass murder, which was being implemented at the latest by May 1942. Second, I shall look at the issues of the mentality, moral framework and complicity of the perpetrators and consider how far these tie in with evidence about the knowledge and attitudes of the German population as a whole.

I   The politics of genocide

In the 1980s, the leading interpretators of the origins of the Holocaust aligned themselves either as propounding 'intentionalist' explanations or so-called 'structuralist' or 'functionalist' ones. As we shall see, both of these approaches have their intellectual and moral points of reference in arguments made by allied and exiled commentators during and immediately after the war. 'Intentionalist' historians like Lucy Dawidowicz and Gerald Fleming stressed Hitler's personal anti-Semitism as the key factor in explaining the Holocaust. For them, there is an essential continuity of ideas and programme, from Hitler's reception of pseudo-scientific notions of biological racism in pre-war Vienna – or perhaps, as Brigitte Hamann's recent study of Hitler's youth implies, during the years of the First World War – to Hitler's willingness to blame Germany's defeat in the First World War on the Jews, his formulation of his ideas in *Mein Kampf* and on finally to his ominous warning to the Reichstag on 30 January 1939, that: 'If the international Jewish financiers outside Europe should succeed in plunging the nations once more into a world war, then the result will not be the bolshevization of the earth, and thus the victory of Jewry, but the annihilation of the Jewish race in Europe' (*Dokumente der deutschen Politik*, vol. 7 (1940), pp. 476–9.

For Dawidowicz and Fleming, the pre-war acts of the Nazi regime left no doubt as to the virulence of its anti-Semitism. There were random attacks, beatings and murders of Jews by the storm troopers immediately after Hitler came to power. On 1 April 1933, the party called for a boycott of Jewish shops and businesses. Within the year Jews were forced out of the civil service and the legal and medical professions. In 1935, the Reichstag was summoned to join the annual Nazi party rally in Nuremberg to rubber-stamp new laws on German marriage and citizenship which reduced Jews to second-class citizens. Measures aimed at the expropriation of Jewish property and the forced emigration of Jews were introduced, which reached a peak in 1938, culminating, in November, in the burning of synagogues and looting of Jewish shops as Josef Goebbels ordered the party activists into a 'spontaneous action'. These major initiatives occurred against a backdrop of unremitting verbal and rhetorical violence in the Nazi press, in which the speeches of Hitler, Josef Goebbels and Julius Streicher played a key part. For 'intentionalists', Hitler is the central actor who plotted the murder of the Jews from the outset.

> Once Hitler adopted an ideological position, even a strategic one, he adhered to it with limpetlike fixity, fearful lest he be accused, if he changed his mind, of incertitude, of capriciousness on 'essential questions'. He had long-range plans to realize his ideological goals, and the destruction of the Jews was at their center.

> (Dawidowicz, 1975: p. 158)

By contrast, 'functionalists' started not with Hitler but with how the Nazi state worked. Both Martin Broszat and Hans Mommsen laid great emphasis on the ways in which the blurring of institutional demarcation lines, bureaucratic competition and, from at least the war onwards, high levels of decentralization from Berlin to the local satraps in Eastern Europe, all gave great opportunity for local initiative and autonomous decision-making from below. If the 'intentionalists' tended to share the view of the American prosecutors at the Nuremberg trials that the Nazi regime was a totalitarian monolith, guilty of a central conspiracy to wage war and commit mass murder, the 'functionalists' were often no less inspired by the search for justice. But in their case, inspiration came from the German trials of the late 1960s and 1970s of lower-ranking perpetrators, in which the defendants regularly resorted to the idea that they were trapped in a totalitarian system and would have been punished had they failed to carry out its orders. To challenge this comfortable alibi involved exploring the ways in which local initiatives had actually given shape to the Holocaust.

Behind historians' disputes over where responsibility rests for Nazi crimes lie fundamental differences in their interpretations of the character of the Nazi state itself. Those who take a strongly 'intentionalist' line, such as Fleming, hold to a rather traditional notion of totalitarianism. In this totalitarian model the regime is held to be omnipotent in relation to society as well as internally monolithic and subordinated to the unbending will of the dictator. Neither individual initiative nor dissent have a place here. The 'structuralist' interpretation, on the other hand, holds that the state was inwardly fragmented into a plurality of competing institutions, and that relationships of power within the state and between the state and society did not flow only from the top down. If the totalitarian model takes its cue from the post-war writings of Hannah Arendt and C. J. Friedrich, the idea of the Nazi state as fragmented and polycratic goes back to Franz

Neumann's *Behemoth*, an impressive and critical study of the regime while it was still in power.

Historians such as Hans Mommsen and Martin Broszat were interested in exploring the internal contradictions within the dictatorship, the competing hierarchies of power and the chaotic as well as increasingly radical 'solutions' which these internal conflicts precipitated. From this point of view, Hitler has come to be seen as a leader who ruled not by initiating but by holding back and arbitrating between different factions. Thus what appear in the intentionalist account as stepping stones towards extermination appear in the structuralist reading as a series of *ad hoc* compromises, whose logical progression only becomes obvious in retrospect. The 1 April 1933 boycott and the so-called '*Kristallnacht*' of November 1938 are understood as initiatives launched by Goebbels, in part to satisfy party radicals that the regime was in earnest, in part to win favour with Hitler. On the other hand, the framing of the Nuremberg Laws and the measures of economic expropriation show Hitler taking the more 'moderate' of the options presented to him. Each stage of persecution clearly prepared the way for more extreme measures and so formed a progression of sorts, but at what point were alternatives other than mass murder discarded by the Nazi leadership? This has meant separating the general climate of rising anti-Semitism fostered by Hitler and other leading Nazis from the specific timing and character of the decision to murder European Jewry. So, for example, Hitler's 30 January 1939 warning can be read at a number of levels. It certainly raised the pitch of general rhetorical violence against the Jews, but, as Hans Mommsen argued, it could also be interpreted as indulging in a kind of 'hostage' bargaining with the lives of Germany's Jews with 'world' Jewry; all on the basis that – according to Nazi thinking – Jews controlled international finance and politics in France, Britain and the USA. Substance is added to this case by Saul Friedländer's finding that Jewish real estate in Germany was the last asset to be 'aryanized'. It was part of pre-war plans whereby the ageing community in Germany would be held to account for the good behaviour of those who emigrated, so providing circumstantial evidence for the 'hostage' interpretation.

To a large extent, opinion among historians has swung towards this view of the Nazi state as polycratic rather than monolithic in its normal mode of operation. At the same time, there has been a growing recognition that opposite tendencies were at work which were crucial in giving the system its overall drive and dynamism. In the recent work of two of the regime's most eminent scholars, Saul Friedländer and Ian Kershaw, great importance is attached to the anti-Semitic elements of Nazi ideology and especially to

Hitler's own views in establishing the norms and commonsense consensus on which the political and administrative elite came up with their rival but increasingly murderous 'solutions'. In other words, polycracy had its limits and Hitler could still dictate whilst delegating.

As a result, the scope of the 'intentionalist–functionalist debate has narrowed amid growing consensus on how the regime worked. Most of the more recent discussion about the Holocaust as state policy has focused on the ways in which mass murder of the Jews was linked to the attack on the Soviet Union in 1941. It is generally accepted that 1941 was the crucial year, although it is still unclear whether a formal decision in favour of extermination preceded the attack on the Soviet Union, as Helmut Krausnick and Richard Breitman argued, or followed in its wake, as Christopher Browning and Philippe Burrin have posited, or was not taken until Germany declared war on the United States in December, a case made by L. J. Hartog and Christian Gerlach. Despite these differences, virtually all contributors to these discussions would emphasize continuities in murderous intentions and practices going back to before 1941. Here the work of Götz Aly and others on both the killing of psychiatric patients and the murder and forced expulsion of Jews and Poles from western Poland to make way for the settlement of ethnic Germans have been highly influential in making specific links back from 1941 to the start of the war in September 1939. This case for a fundamental continuity from September 1939 through to the fully-fledged implementation of a European-wide Holocaust by May 1942 has been made most powerfully in a recent major study by Peter Longerich.

Within the massive accumulation of circumstantial detail now available a number of issues have become clearer. First, Hitler's own role was not 'hands off'. Hitler had himself informed directly of the *Einsatzgruppen* killings through the summer of 1941, so that – even if a direct written order from him remains untraceable – there can be no doubt that he knew and approved of these actions from an early stage. Hitler's own rediscovery of his January 1939 'prophecy' about the extermination of the Jews in the event of a world war fits well with the summaries provided by Hans Frank and Josef Goebbels of his speech to party leaders, on 12 December, the day after Germany declared war on the USA. As Goebbels summarized on 13 December 1941 in recently published sections of his diary unearthed in the Moscow archives:

> With regard to the Jewish Question, the Führer has decided to make a clean sweep. He prophesied to the Jews that if they once more caused a world war, they would experience their extermination. This was not rhetoric. The world war is there, the extermination of the Jews must be

the necessary consequence. This question is to be dealt with without any sentimentality. We are not there to sympathise with the Jews but to sympathise with our German people. If the German people now has once more sacrificed 160,000 dead in the campaign in the East, then the original agents of this bloody conflict must pay for it with their lives.

(Gerlach, *Werkstattgeschichte*, 18 (1997), p. 25)

Whether or not this speech actually amounted to a basic policy decision – a *Grundsatzentscheidung* as Gerlach terms it – must remain a moot point. Hitler was speaking in his private rooms in the Chancellery and to party, not state functionaries. Hence, neither Heydrich, nor Goering (who had empowered Heydrich, on 31 July 1941, to draw up a plan for a 'final solution to the Jewish question') were present. It is possible, by contrast, given what we know of Hitler's dislike of giving decisions a formal character, that he issued no more specific instructions than this to any gathering of Nazi leaders, whatever he may have said in one-to-one meetings. Moreover, by 1941 he had good reasons for not issuing written instructions: having personally authorized the 'euthanasia action' in writing in 1939, by August 1941 protests and rumours about the killing of asylum patients within Germany had forced Hitler to retreat. So, it is likely that Hitler chose not to commit himself to paper again. In one sense, it is almost immaterial whether or not Hitler thought that this particular speech was markedly different from his earlier rhetorical assaults on the Jews: what is significant is that his listeners got the message. When Hans Frank returned to Poland, he passed on what he understood to be the gist of the speech: 'We were told in Berlin: . . . liquidate them yourselves!' (Gerlach, p. 30).

What Hitler certainly did do was discuss policy towards the Jews in private on a one-to-one basis with key figures like Heinrich Himmler, as the discovery of the SS leader's appointments' diary (newly recovered from the Moscow archives) has revealed. On 18 December for instance, Himmler noted down the conclusion of his discussion with Hitler, 'The Jewish question. To be exterminated as partisans' ('Judenfrage. Als Partisanen auszurotten'), prompting debate as to whether this referred already to all Jews or to those in Eastern Europe or the Soviet territories 'only'. For Gerlach, this document pins down a decision for the Holocaust directly; for other historians, it is one important link in a chain which began earlier and only found its full-scale implementation in the first five months of 1942. Either way, it does show that Hitler was informed and consulted at a number of key moments. In public, Hitler also did not shrink from regularly repeating his 'prophecy' about the destruction of the Jews in his set-piece speeches, thereby doing what he could to lend a cloak of ideological legitimacy to the rumours circulating within Germany about the actual mass killings without referring to them explicitly. In a sense, this was in line with what we know about Hitler's pre-war role as well, where much of his contribution was to make anti-Semitism central to the regime's self-presentation. It became a clear goal for which others had to come up with the detailed policies.

At this point, historians' answers to the date and decision question depend to a considerable extent on which elements they are most concerned to track. In terms of Hitler's own thinking, one of the most interesting interpretations has been proposed by the Swiss historian Philippe Burrin. His argument is that Hitler did eventually issue a verbal or possibly written instruction in late September or early October 1941. What Hitler really thought at any time is a deeply problematic issue, but Burrin's shrewd reading of the available evidence here is carefully contextualized and psychologically perceptive: he argues that Hitler believed the war against the Soviet Union was going badly by late August and early September, and that the worse Hitler thought the war was going, the more he returned to his 'prophecy' of January 1939 that the war would lead to the destruction of European Jewry. This, in turn, would fit well with an account that located Hitler's own radical political anti-Semitism not in his youth in pre-First World War Vienna, but to his rage at Germany's defeat in 1918. The link in Hitler's own mind between German defeat and the destruction of the Jews was one that he finally reiterated and emphasized in the political testament he penned before shooting himself in his bunker in Berlin on 30 April 1945.

Most of the evidence we have for the 'final solution' is political and administrative and concerns the actions of others. Christopher Browning, for example, has argued for the same dating as Burrin to early October by tracking the activities of the key organizers, Himmler and Heydrich. The decision to deport German and Czech Jews to the East was one Himmler passed on to Arthur Greiser on 18 September (after a round of meetings with Hitler as well as key figures in Nazi policy-making in the East on 16 and 17 September). Sometime in October, the sites for the first death camps must have been selected at Belzec and Chelmno, given that actual construction had begun there by early November. Although Belzec was initiated by the local police and SS leader in Lublin, Odilo Globocnik, the rapidity with which personnel from the 'euthanasia' action were transferred to provide their expertise on gassing technique, not to mention Globocnik's own promotion to organize the other death camps, testify to enthusiastic endorsement of his actions from above. Although these were still relatively small installations, compared with the later Auschwitz-Birkenau complex, they were already far bigger than the gassing cubicles that had been used to kill psychiatric patients in the basements of German sanatoria. For Auschwitz itself, it is still not certain whether the first 'experimental' gassings of Soviet prisoners of war and Silesian Jews took place there in late August and early September (as the invaluable camp diary of Danuta Czech recorded) or in early December. Yet, what does emerge from the great mass of circumstantial detail available is how rapid the search for a coordinated, tried and tested method for mass murder was during the autumn of 1941 which could take over from and replace the mass shootings. Since, at exactly the same time, the numbers of men being deployed to carry out mass shootings were also being increased, the speed with which experiments with gas chambers were being initiated strongly suggests a central mind solving the question as to how to kill far larger numbers of Jews than those being rounded up in the Soviet Union and Poland. Mass deportations may not have actually started from Western Europe directly to the killing centres until the late spring of 1942, but the facilities were being prepared and tested in the winter.

Against the background of this convergence of focus on the autumn of 1941 in the search for a decision and a date, Peter Longerich has recently published a hugely impressive study of the politics of extermination, in which he has argued against there having been a single decision for mass murder. Instead, he delineates four steps in the radicalization of Nazi genocidal policy: first, autumn 1939, which saw mass shootings in Poland of Jews, Polish 'intellectuals' as well as asylum patients at the same time that asylum patients in Germany were also being killed; second, summer of 1941, with the mass shooting of Soviet Jews; third, autumn of 1941, with the extension of the mass murder of the Jews to Poland; fourth, spring 1942, when the Jews deported from Western Europe were no longer being held in transit camps but were being killed on arrival. 1941-2 still remains the most important period in this account, but Longerich makes the crucial point that the war against Poland in September 1939 itself opened the gates to policies of killing. First, there was the orgy of killings in Poland; then came plans in which 'resettlement' plans clearly envisaged no longer forced emigration, but rather physical annihilation. Plans to create a Jewish reservation in Lublin in the autumn of 1939 or later to deport the Jews to Madagascar, current from 1940 till the attack on the Soviet Union, when it was temporarily replaced by a third plan to push the Jews into inhospitable areas such as the Pripyet marshes or the Arctic circle, were in reality plans for mass extermination. They were plans where nature would do the killing rather than gas chambers. But as with the actual murder of so many of the Holocaust's victims through starvation and overwork – 'destruction through labour' as the catch-phrase had it – these were schemes where nature would only be destructive because of the conditions the Nazi regime would impose upon it.

On December 1941, Longerich broadly follows one element in Gerlach's and L. J. Hartog's accounts in seeing Hitler's declaration of war on the United States as having removed the last inhibitions about killing all Jews within his power. World war spelled the end of keeping the Jews alive as possible hostages in future peace negotiations with Britain or the USA, although one might note in passing that Himmler was not above trying to revive this concept in the last phase of the war, holding groups of Jews to exchange for German prisoners of war. The link to the declaration of war against the USA is plausible in another way too: because it signalled a world war, it drew together Hitler's prophecy with his prior notions of the Jews as the wire-pullers both in Moscow and New York.

Like other serious scholars Longerich often examines the detail of killing and deportation operations to work back to reveal the central co-ordinating plans which they put into effect, and back from the plans to reveal the *latest* possible point that the policy decisions must have been made to which the plans gave form. We cannot rule out, of course, that broad decisions were taken earlier, say in the summer or early autumn of 1941, and that a longer time-lag elapsed before planning, priorities and logistics allowed them to be put into operation. But we can be fairly certain that by early 1942 at the latest the 'final solution' had been given its centralized, uniform, pan-European form. The evidence is damning partly because it is handled so cautiously. Key elements of this kind of reasoning involve pinning down the moments at which local actions were taken up from above and imposed as standard practice on other areas and when local exemptions to murder were disallowed. This is – literally – a forensic exercise. As shown by the cross-examination of expert witnesses like Christopher Browning, Richard Evans and Peter Longerich by David Irving in his failed libel action against Deborah Lipstedt and Penguin Books during the spring of 2000, historical interpretations of decision-making and the Holocaust have to be analytically rigorous enough to withstand legal testing in a fashion which is rare in historical scholarship.

II Perpetrators

Hitler, Heydrich and Himmler may have been indispensable to the series of decisions, plans and administrative orders that rapidly evolved into a system of mass extermination, but neither the rapidity with which this system came into being, nor the scale on which it operated is explicable without the hyperactive support of the bureaucracies beneath them and the many unsolicited murderous initiatives of a whole range of German authorities and individuals. Historians are generally in consensus that policy at the centre frequently evolved through initiatives from below, that is, as long as the initiatives proceeded in the desired direction. The Germans who carried out mass murder were not, therefore, in many cases merely following orders, but rather were ambitiously anticipating them.

A number of recent regional studies have contributed greatly to our understanding of how the Holocaust unfolded in the Baltic states, Serbia, Belorussia, Poland and Galicia. Much of this work has been done by a younger generation of scholars, including Thomas Sandkühler, Dieter Pohl, Christoph Dieckmann, Christian Gerlach and Martin Dean. One of the great benefits of this research is that it makes apparent the links between the Holocaust, the killing of Soviet prisoners of war, and German occupation policy in the East in general, involving as it did the planned mass starvation of the Soviet civilian population, sweeping destruction of villages and their inhabitants in reprisal for partisan activity and deportation to forced labour in Germany under appalling and often deadly conditions. It serves to remind us that the entire war against the Soviet Union was intended to be – and was – a genocidal campaign of colonization and that the highest death toll at German hands was that of Soviet civilians. Within this context the various versions of the SS's 'general plan for the East', which foresaw the need to exterminate up to 30 million people, are suggestive that the death camps would not necessarily have ceased to operate if the extermination of the Jews had been completed. Alongside the gypsies and the mentally ill, the Jews were the first target of the death camps, but they were not the only victims of a policy of mass murder that could be and was as readily carried out by shooting, burning and the deliberate imposition of starvation.

These local studies also help to reveal something of the perpetrators themselves, at least through the bureaucratic form they adapted and invented to legitimate what they were doing within the Nazi system. A number of key earlier studies also help to build up a picture of the attitudes and values of the perpetrators of the 'final solution'. On the central SD and SS personnel, Michael Wildt's study of the SD (Security Police) has shown how this group's views hardened in the pre-war years into an extreme anti-Semitic consensus. According to Wildt, this hardening of views took place during the period in which the SS and SD's influence over Jewish policy was least, namely during the 1936–7 lull, when Hitler was wooing foreign opinion for the Olympic Games and the remilitarization of the Rhineland. Ulrich Herbert's superb biography of the senior SS and police official Werner Best is very revealing about the underlying outlook of the group of key perpetrators to whom Best belonged. Herbert has characterized the outlook of the higher SS as the 'rational anti-Semitism' of a particular peer group. Born too late to fight in the First World War, these wartime adolescents belonged to a peer group of university-educated middle- and upper-class youth socialized in the Weimar Republic and in ethnic-nationalist, right-wing values of the student associations, or nationalistic parties from the early 1920s. Two thirds of them possessed university degrees (many of them in law), one third doctorates. Within the Nazi regime they also formed a distinct peer group, better educated than the party leaders and younger than comparably high-ranking civil servants. They were concerned with achieving extreme but also 'rational' and administratively orderly solutions. Men who disdained the rowdy, emotional anti-Semitism of Julius Streicher, Goebbels and even of Hitler, they none the less defined their own political radicalism primarily in terms of extreme, race-based anti-semitism. They also saw themselves as something of a 'vanguard' within the regime. Hitler spoke of the need for 'ethnic cleansing' in Poland (*völkische Flurbereinigung*) on 7 September 1939; Best had already advocated this in 1936.

Ulrich Herbert has described the outlook of these higher-ranking SS and police officials as guided more by a stance than by a clear aim, which 'enabled individuals to do "the right thing" at the critical moment without reflection or discussion, but also without benefit of direct orders, and thus select the most radical among various available courses of action in any given situation' (Herbert, 1999: 26–7).

There is a trend, however, in the recent German scholarship to take the forms of rational planning exhibited here at face value. Herbert characterizes the outlook of the SS officials as 'amoral' and 'utilitarian' in outlook, a view which he extends to the non-SS administrators and military personnel involved in the 'final solution'. As the new regional studies reveal, this preference for a language of 'utility' characterizes the reasons officials provided each other with at the time for perpetrating mass murder. A rather unimaginative 'menu' of viable pretexts was patched together: ghettos had to be cleared because of the risks of 'starvation' or 'disease'; men were killed because of the danger of 'partisan action' and 'subversion'; women and children then became 'useless mouths to feed'. Or, in the language of the demographic planners for the resettlement of the Baltic region, which Götz Aly brought to light, people simply had to 'vanish'. Christian Gerlach has uncovered the way that Ministry of Agriculture officials and military strategists alike coolly planned to inflict mass starvation on the civilian population as part of their preparation for the attack on the Soviet Union, because they saw this as a rational solution to the logistic problem of feeding the German army and German civilian population whilst waging a rapid war of movement with inevitably long lines of communication. He too interprets these plans as 'rational', again leaving the door open to seeing the men who devised them as coolly, amorally rational.

This type of interpretation seems to me to elide moral and technical issues, ignoring what is most revealing in these new sources. What these planners considered to be discussable, rational solutions in 1940 and 1941 tells us what they implicitly knew their superiors would consider *moral* and *legitimate*. Actions which left the German population hungry, arousing the spectre of the First World War defeatism at home, were not legitimate, and therefore not discussable; the deaths of millions of Soviet civilians or the murder of Jews and Soviet prisoners of war were discussable. But to elide their rationales for acting with rationality *per se* is to miss the point: these were, in Nazi terms, legitimate rationales for murder. This is the bureaucratic language of a particular profession, searching for and creating the right ways of formulating and legitimating its actions for its own internal administrative consumption – and by extension for dealing with other German agencies. It is elliptical, euphemistic, passive and mechanical. But it is not amoral: the very dependability of these field operatives rested on their mutual confidence that they shared a common set of *moral* as well as political assumptions about Jews and Slavs and gypsies (and gypsies, as Moshe Zimmermann has shown, in any case were slaughtered without resort to administrative pretexts). The SS and SD leaders were also not as distanced and utilitarian as their language would suggest. They – like so many others in the army, in the civilian administration, and in the ordinary population of the occupied territories – went to see the sites of mass killings for themselves. So, when 10–12,000 Jews were shot on Sunday 12 October 1941 at Stanislau in Galicia, many German bystanders gathered, snapping photos for their collections and, as word spread, the Governor, Hans Frank, dropped by 10 days later to view the site for himself. The dull, problem-solving language of the new bureaucracy of murder was only one way in which these people communicated the 'great deeds' in which they were involved.

III   'Ordinary' killers

Two of the most fascinating contributions to understanding the involvement of wider circles of German society in the 'final solution' were made by Christopher Browning and Daniel Jonah Goldhagen in their radically different interpretations of the activities of the same group of middle-aged part-time policemen, Reserve Police Battalion 101. Drawing on the same files, built up by the interrogation by Hamburg prosecutors of 210 former officers and men in the 1960s and early 1970s, their research reopened the question of the attitudes and motives of the mass killers of the Holocaust. Until their studies appeared in the mid-1990s, a kind of orthodoxy had been established largely by reference to the memoirs of Rudolf Höss, the commandant of Auschwitz, and through Hannah Arendt's commentary on the trial of Adolf Eichmann. This depicted the perpetrators as inwardly distanced from their actions, their emotional detachment supported by a bureaucratic division of labour and the industrial technology of the death camps. Already, studies such as Michael Burleigh's of the doctors and nurses involved in killing psychiatric patients, which appeared in the 1980s and early 1990s, questioned this rather comfortable, unproblematic picture, suggesting that levels of conscious involvement, curiosity and the exercise of free will in killing were far greater than previously supposed. Now a group of largely middle-aged men from lower-middle-class and working-class backgrounds from one of the least Nazified cities in Germany came under the spotlight. And what was interesting about them was precisely that they were deeply involved in the pre-industrial killing of the 'final solution'. In their first action on 13 July 1942 at Jozefow, in the Lublin district of Poland, they had to face their victims one to one and walk from parked lorries outside the village into the edge of the forest, make them lie down and shoot them in the back of the neck. Those who hit the head were promptly soaked with blood, brains and skull fragments. In the evening afterwards, little was said, little was eaten and a great deal was drunk, setting a pattern of using alcohol to numb nerves during and after future 'actions'.

Further research has shown that this group was not typical of the police units as a whole, which tended to be younger and more strongly tied to the regime by career ambitions or explicitly Nazi ideological commitments. But the lack of such obvious explanations in the case of this particular group of part-time policemen is precisely what makes them psychologically interesting, especially given that their own commander, Major Trapp, explicitly offered them the opportunity not to participate in shooting and to do guard duty instead. Browning offers us a situational account, borrowing the anthropological notions of 'liminality' and 'rites of passage' to explain how this first experience of mass murder turned a group of unprepared reservists into cold-blooded killers. His central argument is that they killed out of 'conformity' or peer-group pressure: to step out of line took more courage than to kill. As he shows, those few who refused to participate in the actual shooting continued in the main to be excused from actions to hunt Jews down. The moral decisions these men made at Jozefow were crucial to their future actions.

Goldhagen took the diametrically opposite view. Inverting Browning's explanation of how killers overcame their initial reluctance to kill, he proposed that what we really need to understand is how Nazism 'unleashed' Germans' murderous desires. German culture, he claims, was already saturated with 'eliminatory anti-Semitism', so that 'what Hitler and the Nazis actually did was to unshackle and thereby activate Germans' pre-existing, pent-up anti-Semitism' (Goldhagen, 1996: 443). This argument depends on accepting that German identity was defined against the Jewish 'other' from the Middle Ages to the twentieth century (and then miraculously ceased to be in the post-1945 era). Here Goldhagen invokes a two-dimensional notion of 'national character' of a kind which historians of national identity have called into serious question during the last 30 years, one which depends on an ahistorical notion of essential traits which just as mysteriously disappear again. Where Goldhagen permits the non-German guards and executioners – about whom we still know far too little – a multi-causal explanation for their participation, the Germans are reduced to a mono-causal model. This approach seems deeply flawed in a number of respects. A will to violence can occur within a single generation. Long-range explanations explain both too much and too little: why then and not before or indeed continuously? The history of anti-Semitism is long, but it is also a discontinuous history. The content as well as the social and political weight of anti-Semitism were not constant. German society did witness a revival of political anti-Semitism at the end of the nineteenth century, but the comparative perspective is lacking here. Germany was no more anti-semitic than contemporary France, very much in the grip of the Dreyfus affair, and anti-Semitic views were also indulged at both popular and elite levels, though usually less noisily, in Britain and the United States. Even in the late Weimar years, anti-Semitism seems to have been of far more importance to the 'old fighters' of the SA than to Nazi voters.

Goldhagen is on much stronger ground when he challenges how much explanatory weight can be attached to a factor like peer group pressure, as employed by Browning. As he notes, such pressure to conform always implies the conformity of a minority with a majority and therefore is inadequate for explaining the behaviour of the majority itself. The majority of these small, mobile groups of perpetrators must have been implicitly willing to expend their energies and imagination on killing unarmed Jews and Soviet citizens, even if they would not necessarily have done so in other circumstances. Browning may, indeed, have taken note of this criticism. For, in his more recent writing, he has emphasized the internal moral and emotional transformation of the killers themselves. This seems to me to be a more plausible approach to the issue, but it is one which immediately raises the question of when this transformation of values and outlook took place. Did it happen in 1941or 1942, when these men were posted to the Eastern Front? Or had key transformations already happened to them before they left Germany? Did the people who flocked to buy bargains at the auctions of Jewish goods held on the Hamburg docks during the war inhabit the same moral universe as they had in 1932 or even in 1938? To understand how big a transgression was involved in becoming a killer of unarmed civilians, we need some measure of how German society would have viewed their actions. We need to know how far mass murder set such citizens apart from the society from which they came and – repeatedly – returned. To answer this question involves making links between two histories which have largely been written and read separately, the history of the Holocaust and the social history of everyday life in Nazi Germany.

IV   German opinion and the 'Jewish war'

The scholarship which would tell us exactly how the men of Police Battalion 101 fitted into Hamburg society before, during and after their contribution to the 'final solution' still has to be undertaken. The closest proxy we can draw on is a number of studies of knowledge and attitudes towards the Holocaust within the German state and society. As David Bankier among others has shown, knowledge about mass murder was widespread. There were letters home, conversations with soldiers on leave, photographs, even home movies, as well as information from leaflets dropped by the RAF and BBC broadcasts. But these were also essentially 'private' forms of communication. Listening to foreign broadcasts or reading leaflets, though widespread, was punishable as treason. Private knowledge did not automatically imply public responsibility. There were many things in Nazi Germany that people could know 'without knowing'. This, of course, as Herbert's study of Werner Best and Gitta Sereny's of Albert Speer underline, was true of the regime itself. In the autumn of 1941, Best was posted to Paris and learned of the *Einsatzgruppen* killings from army officers returning from the Eastern Front. When Heinrich Himmler made his two speeches to party and military leaders, in October 1943 and January 1944, probably none of his audience was hearing this news for the first time: but it was the first time that they were being officially informed of it in a gathering and were therefore being made co-responsible for it by Himmler so that they could not deny their involvement later. Small wonder then that Speer went to inordinate lengths to convince Gitta Sereny that he had left the October 1943 meeting at Poznan before Himmler spoke. As in the radicalization of racist attitudes, so too in this trend towards wilful self-deception, there are strong parallels between developments in the state and in society. German society at large was never so informed by the regime: ignorance and silence would do, not approval and endorsement in this case, even if cultivating one's own wilful ignorance actually implied a degree of collusion and consent. Denying responsibility and knowledge was not necessarily only a post-war phenomenon in Germany.

In his studies of Bavarian society during the Third Reich and of *The Hitler Myth*, Ian Kershaw found that Germans did not, on the whole, want to be reminded by the regime of what they already knew about the mass murder of the Jews. So, when Goebbels brought in the newsreel cameras in April 1943 to film the uncovering of the mass graves of the Polish officers shot in the Katyn forest by the NKVD, this particular attempt to mount anti-Soviet atrocity partly backfired because of the associations the images aroused. As the security police reported from Würzburg, 'Among those associated with the Churches the view was put forward that it could be a matter of mass graves laid out by Germans for the murdered Polish and Russian Jews' (Kershaw, 1983: 365). Even if knowledge of the gas chambers did remain fairly restricted in Germany, the knowledge that Jews had been slaughtered *en masse* was widespread. When it dealt with other images, including mass female rape, Goebbels' atrocity propaganda succeeded better in stiffening German resolve to fight to the end. Here it fed existing German fears of the 'Russians', a foreboding of Soviet atrocities to come which underpinned the resistance of both German soldiers on the Eastern Front and the civilian population at home till well beyond the country's capacity to do more than delay the moment of complete defeat. In addition to their fear of the Russians, sources such as Victor Klemperer's diaries chronicle the fact that many Germans expected to be punished by the British and Americans as well as the Soviets for the mass shootings of Jews in the event of a German defeat. In the context of the war of annihilation being fought on the Eastern Front, such expectations must also have played some part in the sense of foreboding that the German nation had tied itself to the Nazi regime, which after-all was the point Goebbels was trying to make via such 'negative propaganda' in the first place.

There was a second and no less important dimension to Kershaw's findings, which did not make sense to him at the time but which more recent publications help to elucidate. To his surprise, Kershaw found that most references to the genocide against the Jews were in the context of the

Anglo-American bombing raids. Many people regarded allied bombing raids as revenge and retaliation for the treatment of the Jews, often in a very literal and parochial way: Fürth and Frankfurt were being spared air-raids because they were allegedly – even in September 1943! – 'outright Jewish cities'. This also prompted people to think that the Jews should have been kept in Germany as hostages in the city centres and as 'human shields'. Similar proposals were made in letters to Goebbels, advising the government, for example, to herd the Jews together in the cities threatened with bombing and forbid them access to the air-raid shelters; or that the Americans and British should be told that 10 Jews should be shot for every German civilian killed (Kershaw, 1983: 368–9). So too, when Dresden was bombed on 13 February 1945, Victor Klemperer tore off the Jewish star – out of fear that any Jew would be murdered on the street in revenge for the 'terror bombing' of the city.

Such literal-minded and blood-thirsty adoption of the Treitschkean slogan of the Nazis, 'The Jew is your misfortune', added up to a profoundly different public consciousness from that before the war, let alone before 1933. Even if such extreme manifestations were never characteristic of the majority of the population, they none the less signified a profound transformation of basic social commonsense. The recent publication of the diaries of Victor Klemperer, a German-Jewish academic who survived the Nazi period largely thanks to his 'privileged' Aryan marriage, help to make sense of these attitudes of fear of bombing and hatred against the Jews which Kershaw noted. Klemperer's diaries show how his own social identity was gradually transformed from 'Herr Professor Klemperer' to 'the Jew Klemperer' by the outbreak of the war. Keenly interested from the outset in the impact of Nazism on language and ideas, Klemperer developed the thesis that Nazi language worked by simplification – taking terms already in use and redefining them by juxtaposition and opposition. Above all, it worked by endless variation and repetition. What struck him forcibly during the war years was the way that the notion of the war as a 'Jewish war' was absorbed into the commonsense of everyday life and repeated by those who were not Nazis or were even highly critical of the regime. The slogan 'the Jewish war', of course, was replete with ambiguity – a war against the Jews, started by the Jews, or conducted on behalf of the Jews against Germany? All of these emphases surface in his examples. As Rudolf Schottlaender, another middle-aged, German-Jewish academic in a similar position to Klemperer noted in his memoirs, such outbursts of this key anti-Semitic axiom could come quite unexpectedly, as a kind of mental reflex to anger and fear. While Schottlaender was doing forced labour as an unskilled factory worker in Berlin in late 1942,

A worker above me in rank, one of those old union types, always very objective, never anti-Jewish, was walking next to me, and we could see the flames from an air raid on Berlin. Suddenly he blurted out: 'Those are your friends up there!' All I said was: 'I didn't invite them.' Yet I was deeply affected by this, since the alienation from all the others, which I was aware of as a daily thing, came this time very unexpectedly, and had been directed toward me personally.

(Frank Stern, 'Antagonistic Memories' in Luisa Passerini, (ed.), *Memory and Totalitarianism*, (1992), p. 26; Rudolf Schottlaender, *Trotz allem ein Deutscher*, (1986), p. 48ff)

Klemperer's ideas are beginning to make their way into academic study, having recently been taken up by the Israeli historian Frank Stern in tracing the antagonistic memories of Germans and Jews regarding the bombing of the German cities. The underlying assumption, which shocked the German nationalist and assimilationist Victor Klemperer again and again, that Jews and Germans had come to be regarded as fundamentally different must count as one of the longer-lasting cultural effects of the Third Reich; discernible even in the wave of German philo-Semitic cultural interest of the 1990s, with its underlying assumption that Jews are different and exotic, rather than simply one of the formative influences on and within German culture itself.

During the war years, thousands of Germans took part in the forced auctions of Jewish property on the Hamburg docks, wore fur coats distributed by the Winter Relief, heard specific details about mass executions, listened to Hitler's repetition of his 'prophecy' that the Jews would be annihilated, and lived in cities where the dirty jobs were done by forced and starving foreign labourers, many of them from the Soviet territories. Many knew too that the war on the Eastern Front was brutal and destructive beyond compare, and lived in the expectation of Soviet atrocities in the event of a German defeat. To know all these things, but not to know what they meant, to invest the unconscious effort not to draw obvious but uncomfortable conclusions, to blame the war inflicted by the allies on Germany (not of course the other way around) on the Jews all bespeak a society which had been profoundly transformed by Nazism. This lack of interest in the Jews was not 'disinterested'. It was callous; a far cry from the world of 1933 or even of 1938. The war was lived and experienced through the language of Nazism. What Michael Burleigh and Wolfgang Wippermann dubbed the 'racial state' became part of the intellectual and emotional commonsense of very many people's lives. In the autumn of 1939, individual army officers protested against the atrocities committed by the SS and their auxiliaries against Poles and Jews in Poland. The campaign against the Soviet Union was accompanied at home in Germany by public protests against the murder of *German* psychiatric patients in 1941. But as information filtered through about the murder of the Jews later that summer and autumn virtually no voices were raised against such acts any more. The answer to the riddle of what motivated the men of Police Battalion 101 to kill may partly lie in this broader transformation in the values of society at large. Society may have lagged behind the enthusiasms of the Nazi old guard, expressing mixed feelings about the murders, burning and looting of *Kristallnacht*, fearful too of revenge for the murder of the Jews in 'the East'. Much has been made of the way that the regime used negative propaganda in the second half of the war to sustain civilian morale to fight on to the end – the fear of Soviet 'atrocities' should the Red Army reach Germany. But the regime would not have been able to maintain the axiom that Nazism and German identity were inextricably linked until the final defeat if it had not been able to count on the conformity of its population, a conformity informed in some part too by a widespread – if not universal – sense of complicity in the murder of the Jews.

Select bibliography

General

Saul Friedländer, *Nazi Germany and the Jews: The Years of Persecution, 1933–1939* (1997).

Christopher Browning, *The Path to Genocide: Essays on Launching the Final Solution* (1992).

Christopher Browning, *Nazi Policy, Jewish Workers, German Killers* (2000).

Christian Gerlach, 'The Wannsee Conference, the Fate of the Jews and Hitler's decision in principle to exterminate all of the Jews', *Journal of Modern History*, 12 (1998), 759–812.

Ulrich Herbert (ed.), *National-Socialist Extermination Policies: Contemporary German Perspectives and Controversies* (1999).

Götz Aly, *The 'Final Solution'* (1998).

Hans Mommsen, *From Weimar to Auschwitz* (1991).

Lucy Dawidowicz, *The War against the Jews, 1933–1945* (1975).

Michael Marrus, *The Holocaust in History* (1987).

David Cesarani (ed.), *The Final Solution: Origins and Implementation* (1994).

Raul Hilberg, *The Destruction of the European Jews*, 3 vols. (1961).

Gerald Fleming, *Hitler and the Final Solution* (1986).

Omer Bartov (ed.), *The Holocaust: Origins, Implementation, Aftermath* (2000).

Perpetrators

Daniel Goldhagen, *Hitler's Willing Executioners: Ordinary Germans and the Holocaust* (1996).
Christopher Browning, *Ordinary Men: Reserve Police Battalion 101 and the Final Solution in Poland* (1992).
Martin Dean, *Collaboration in the Holocaust: Crimes of the Local Police in Belorussia and Ukraine, 1941–44* (2000).
Michael Burleigh, *Ethics and Extermination* (1997).
Omer Bartov, *The Eastern Front, 1941–1945: German Troops and the Barbarisation of Warfare* (1985).

German society

Victor Klemperer, *I Shall Bear Witness: Diaries, 1933–1941* (1998).
Victor Klemperer, *Till the Bitter End: Diaries, 1942–45* (1999).
David Bankier, *The Germans and the Final Solution: Public Opinion under Nazism* (1992).
Ulrich Herbert, *Forced Foreign Labour in the Third Reich* (1997).
Frank Stern, *Whitewashing the Yellow Badge* (1992).
Ian Kershaw, *Popular Opinion and Political Dissent in the Third Reich: Bavaria, 1933–1945* (1983).

Part II

Germany since 1945

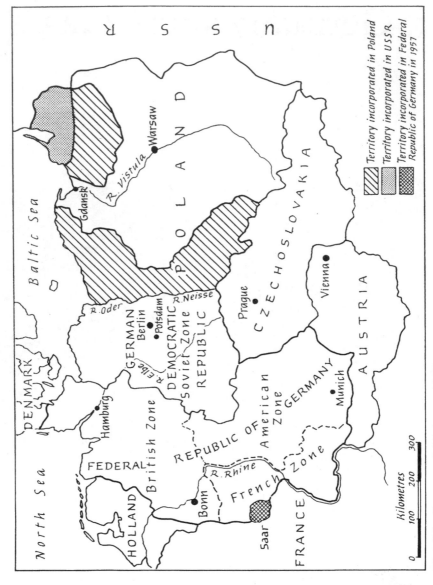

Map II.I Germany divided, post-1945

8

Division and stability: the Federal Republic of Germany, 1949–1989

Mark Roseman

Unlike the historiography of the Wilhelmine, Weimar or Nazi periods, the literature on West German history offers no prevailing orthodoxy or defining controversies. There is no equivalent to a *Sonderweg* theory, no central debate like that between functionalists and intentionalists for the Third Reich. This may be because West Germany's history ended too recently for scholars yet to have gained a clear perspective. Indeed, we are not even sure whether the unification of 1990 really was the end of an era: after all, though *West* Germany as a separate state has ceased to exist, the Federal Republic as a set of institutions continues. Alternatively, the key point may be that the (happy) absence in this period of a catastrophe akin to the outbreak of the First World War or the rise of Nazism means that there is no single overriding issue to which all other questions can be subordinated. Whatever the reason, the outcome is that we have to approach a survey of West German history without that convenient armoury of theories and interpretations available to the historian of earlier epochs.

However, even if we lack the grand debates, we can at least identify two sets of questions which in one shape or another inform a great deal of the writing about the post-1945 period. What interested many scholars was the question of how it was possible that such a well-functioning and stable democracy could be created on the same soil that had allowed Weimar to wither and die, had proved so receptive to the ideas of National Socialism and had committed so much energy and so many resources to the demonic projects of *Lebensraum* and the Holocaust. Was the FRG's success perhaps thanks to the constraints and support provided by the new external environment – by the Allied presence, the cold war and the division of Germany? Or were institutional innovations within West Germany itself responsible? How central was the 'economic miracle' and what put the dynamism into the Deutschmark? These questions were often asked in wonder or admiration, but also tinged with anxiety. At each stage of West Germany's development fears were expressed that some prescriptive German flaw might re-emerge and bring the whole edifice crashing down. In the 1960s many observers thought the end of the economic boom would be the FRG's downfall; in the 1970s, others believed terrorism and the political disaffection of the young could spell the end of democracy. Those particular anxieties were rapidly confounded by the republic's continuing solidity, but today observers are asking whether the end of the division – of Germany and of Europe – has at last undermined the special post-war framework for stability.

Alongside the issue of stability, the other recurrent question has been about restoration, continuity or new beginnings. During the 1970s and 1980s, a great deal of historical research was carried out into the FRG's formative years. Historians wanted to know whether the emerging institutions, social structures, elite composition and value systems were essentially Weimar revivals or even continuations from the Third Reich or whether they constituted something genuinely new. More recently, historians have cast their gaze beyond the occupation period and asked whether the 1950s, in turn, were characterized by conservatism and restoration, or instead constituted a period of dramatic social change.

The following survey of West Germany's history thus focuses on these two themes of the balance between restoration and change, and the origins and nature of West German stability. Because the historiography is so diffuse, it is not possible to identify every point where the survey draws on or differs from established interpretations. However, in one respect the present essay does take a clear-cut position in relation to the existing literature, in that it argues that recent research on early West German history has produced something of a paradox. On the one hand, West German historians of the post-1968 era have indisputably shown the enormous amount of institutional, social and personnel continuity or restoration that initially characterized the FRG. Yet at the same time, because many of these historians have been critical of the existing political order, they have been less willing to acknowledge that this was a republic which almost from the start was dramatically more successful and stable than its hapless Weimar predecessor. The paradox is, therefore, that we are left with a story where remarkably limited innovation seems nevertheless to have generated an enormously different outcome.

To solve this puzzle, the present survey begins by arguing that (important geopolitical changes apart) there were indeed few decisive structural, personnel or cultural differences between Weimar and Bonn. What initially favoured the Bonn republic was instead that its peculiar and protracted birth under Allied occupation, and in the aftermath of Holocaust and total war, meant that it emerged without the antagonisms, instabilities and fears which so burdened Weimar from the beginning. Thus 'restoration or new beginning' when applied to the republics themselves, rather misses the point. It was the different kind of baptisms by fire from which Weimar and Bonn emerged, rather than any niceties of their internal structures, that was initially crucial. Second, it will be argued here that, whilst Bonn in many respects returned to Weimar habits, it also witnessed subtle but vital changes in the discourse and outlook of the population. The experience of war and defeat led to the construction of different historical and political narratives, pushing some political alternatives (nationalism and revanchism, for example) off the agenda. However, really radical social and economic change came only in the late 1950s and 1960s, in the wake of economic growth and the expansion of mass consumerism. Against the background of these changes, and the student revolts which they helped to bring about, a genuinely new and liberal political culture emerged in the 1960s and 1970s.

I The emergence of the new political order, 1945–1949

I.1 The zero hour and new beginnings

For most Germans who lived through it, the 1945–9 years were the most traumatic period of their lives. Defeat had been total and overwhelming, destroying the last vestiges of illusions about the Third Reich's invincibility. The enormous psychological impact of total defeat was reinforced and exacerbated by the almost total disruption of social life. By the end of the war, many German towns were just piles of rubble occupied by a tiny remnant of their former inhabitants. Population mobility was staggeringly high – perhaps as many as half the population was on the move in 1945. Expellees, refugees, prisoners of war, displaced persons, evacuees and many others thronged the roads and packed the few operating trains. In contrast to the wartime experience, food supplies collapsed and in spring 1946 and 1947 rations levels in industrial areas fell to starvation levels. Food shortages, Allied restrictions and other problems kept the economy in a near vegetative state.

Most Germans were preoccupied with their survival, and merely passive recipients of what was decided on the political stage. For a small but crucial minority of Germans, however, including many returning exiles, the early post-war years saw new ideas and the revival of hopes for reform. The reformed Social Democrats (SPD) aspired to the creation of a new more humane society, coupling the old dreams of responsible public control over the economy with a more explicit emphasis than their Weimar forebears on the importance of parliament and the rule of law. Even more significant was the decision by bourgeois politicians to form a non-denominational Christian Democratic Party (CDU), bridging that division between Catholics and Protestants which had undermined the centre-right of German politics since the nineteenth century. For leaders of both political parties, many of whom had already played important roles in the Weimar Republic, the Allies were an important source of hope – and this impulse towards co-operation was to be a crucial foundation of the eventual settlement.

1.2   The cold war and its impact

The period 1946–7 saw the cold war lay its glacial hand on Europe. From the summer of 1947, the USA and Britain moved over to a policy of rapidly reconstructing western Germany as a prelude to any future agreement with the Soviet Union. Icy stand-off metamorphosed to high drama in 1948 when the Soviet Union blockaded Berlin (which although under Four-Power control was located within the Soviet zone of occupation) in response to the introduction of a new currency, the Deutschmark, in the Western zones. The cold war increasingly dominated Allied behaviour towards western Germany and the perceptions and behaviour of West Germany's own statesmen and population. For many Germans, the cold war's powerful psychological impact derived not just from the objective threat posed by the presence of Soviet troops just across the zonal border but also from the resonances of past experiences, including class conflict in the Weimar period, Nazi anti-Bolshevik propaganda and the expellees' direct experiences of Soviet brutality (few reflected on how Russia had been treated under Nazi tyranny). At the same time as being a time of fear, the cold war also represented a psychological and political opportunity for Germany to be counted among the free world against the communist threat.

Between 1947 and 1949, the international order began to take on a radically different cast to the inter-war period. In geoeconomic terms, a world of more open trade and closer European integration was just beginning to emerge. The creation of the International Monetary Fund and the first General Agreement on Tariffs and Trade signalled the US desire to create a functioning multilateral world economy. On the European level, the Marshall plan – and the creation of the Organization of European Economic Cooperation to administer it – was encouraging greater trade between the western European powers. On the political and military side, these new economic structures were paralleled by the formation of ever closer military cooperation. In April 1949 the NATO agreement was signed, holding out the promise to Europe of being protected under the American nuclear umbrella. Though by 1949, when the FRG came into being, many of these new structures or trends were still very far from being firmly established, they were nevertheless to form a crucial ingredient in the FRG's success.

I.3   Institutions and structures in the new West German state

Whilst it was encouraging the development of new institutional forms on the international stage, the cold war was in many ways narrowing the options within Germany itself. The American urgency for creating an economically viable and politically self-contained western German entity led them to drop many of their earlier reform and denazification measures. The British were similarly dissuaded from engaging in social experiments. Those military government reform initiatives that remained often met with opposition from entrenched German groups, and had to be dropped in the interest of the rapid creation of a West German state. The result was that the new constitution was remarkably similar to that of Weimar. Both were federal capitalist systems, based upon a proportional representation system in the lower house, and a regionally based upper house. In almost every branch of law, the Weimar precedent represented the orientation point. In civil service and judiciary there was a remarkable degree of institutional and personnel continuity.

However, the new state did incorporate a number of important changes, some of them the result of lessons drawn from the Nazi era, some the logical consequence of the German division. First, there was the simple fact that this was conceived explicitly as a provisional state, created in anticipation of the emergence of a reunited Germany. In recognition of this provisionality, the constitution was called simply the Basic Law and never put to popular vote. Whilst not necessarily encouraging strong identification with the new state, this provisional status did at least make it easier for the parties involved in drawing up the constitution to bury their differences; it also made it easier to exclude the public and thus deracinate much of the constitutional debate.

*On the political front, the most crucial innovation was that the destruction of Prussia and the reorganization of the other states within the western zones created the basis for a far more balanced federal system.*A second important set of reforms concerned the way in which the popular will was expressed. As far as the electoral system was concerned, the list voting of Weimar was replaced with a mixed two-vote system. An electoral hurdle denied representation to parties with less than 5 per cent of the vote. The plebiscitary elements of Weimar's constitution were scaled down. There were also changes concerning the way parliament itself operated, most importantly the introduction of the constructive vote of no confidence. Finally there was the major institutional discontinuity: the German army was initially not re-established, re-emerging only after an extended period of absence and explicitly subordinated to NATO.

Some important modifications were introduced to the economic and financial system as well.*The creation of a central bank independent of political control ensured public confidence in the stability of the currency.* Following the introduction of the DM in June 1948, Ludwig Erhard, soon to become the FRG's first Economics Minister, not only rapidly dismantled much of the control apparatus which had hitherto administered the post-war economy, but also went further in the direction of a market economy than the framework of the inter-war period: cartels were now outlawed and the protectionist trend of the inter-war years was replaced by a consistently free trade approach.

Another, less obviously propitious, contrast between the new republic and that of Weimar was that the Allies exercised and retained so many powers.*The Federal Republic of Germany could not conduct its own foreign policy, indeed had no Foreign Minister, relating to the outside world almost exclusively through the medium of the Allied High Commission.*The output of the Ruhr, the FRG's industrial heartland, was controlled by the International Ruhr Commission, a body created in 1949 to meet French anxieties that Germany's economic weight might be deployed against it. West Germany was not allowed its own armed forces. In short the new republic was at best semi-sovereign. *

I.4   The radicalization that did not take place

For all the lessons learned from the past, the republic was thus born in circumstances that were at least as constrained and ignominious as those faced by Weimar. In addition to the limits on its sovereignty noted above, the economy had been consolidated by a currency reform and deflation every bit as harsh as that which had ended the hyperinflation of 1923; the cold war phase had led to a disappointing of the left's hopes for reform just as far-reaching as the failure of socialization initiatives in 1918–20; the losses of territory in the east and the presence of millions of expellees and refugees on German soil created a potential for revanchism far greater than had the Versailles Treaty. And yet, by dint of the shock effect of war and defeat, the role and function of the Allies, and the pro-western élites who had managed to position themselves as makers of public opinion, neither public behaviour or attitudes, nor the results of the first federal elections in September 1949 pointed to the public alienation, disaffection or radicalization which had been such a feature of the Weimar period. The radical right had been so discredited (and, it has to be said, discriminated against by Allied electoral practices) and the Communists marginalized that the politicians of the centre ground had emerged at least as strong as they had ever been. True, there were no simple majorities – the proliferation of parties (12 were represented in the first federal parliament) showed that the new constitutional provisions had not succeeded in ending the problem of political fragmentation. But Germany in 1949 seemed to be a far less openly embittered or divided society than it had been at the end of its post-First World War stabilization in 1924. The real question, though, was whether this was merely an artificial product of the shock, exhaustion and Allied control of the occupation years. How would the system develop as Germany gradually regained its independence?

II   The stabilizing of the political order, 1949–1957

II.1   Germany becomes part of a western order

German history had shown that stability at home was unlikely to be achieved without a set of secure external relationships. Yet, although the cold war had undoubtedly created a psychological and strategic climate facilitating West Germany's acceptance among the western powers, key obstacles remained. How could German politicians join the western club without selling out the goal of German reunification? How could the West German desire for a speedy return to sovereignty be reconciled with European, particularly French desires to exercise continuing political and economic control? How could the American insistence that the FRG make a major contribution to the defence of Europe be squared with opposition to German rearmament both within Germany and in the rest of Europe?

Despite these challenges, West Germany rapidly attained a secure place within the western club. The formation of the European Coal and Steel Commission by the Paris Treaty of 1951 ended the inequality of the Ruhr

control, and reassured Germany's neighbours that German resources
would not be used against them. It also started the ball rolling towards
closer European integration, culminating in the formation of the European
Economic Community in 1957. On the military front, after a failed attempt
to form a joint European army, Germany was invited into NATO in 1955,
and with its membership came the return to near full sovereignty – though
the Allies retained rights over Berlin, the stationing of troops on German
soil, and considerable emergency powers. Finally, the London Claims
Conference and the agreements with Israel produced an acceptable debt
settlement, even if it fell far short of the true cost of German crimes.

The relative ease of the process had, of course, much to do with the
common fear of the Soviet Union. The security guarantees provided by the
large number of US troops stationed on German soil were another factor.
The continental powers were helped by past negative experience and
American encouragement to see the virtues of economic integration as a
source of both stability and prosperity. The absence of nationalism within
Germany was another vital ingredient. Even so, the rearmament issue
proved particularly contentious for the FRG, and the SPD's concerted
campaign against it enjoyed support both from those who opposed any new
military commitment and those who feared that it would seal the division
between East and West Germany. Here Konrad Adenauer played a crucial
role in 'selling' the FRG's involvement to the West German public – a point
to which we will return below.

II.2   Legitimating the social order

Another lesson of history was that a republic which failed to solve the
'social question' had little chance of success. Here the opening situation
was paradoxically more auspicious than that of Weimar, despite the
enormously greater challenges of reconstruction faced by Bonn. For one
thing, there was a recognition on all sides that the constitution should not
make Weimar's mistake of promising what could not be delivered. The
cold war, and the fact that the hardships of the immediate post-war
period had dampened popular expectations, all reduced the pressure
labour was able to bear or willing to apply for more radical reforms.
Moreover, again unlike Weimar, war veterans or their widows did not
enjoy the political or moral status to allow them to form a vociferous
claimant community.

Yet, there remained a large gulf between the emphasis of the government
parties and their allies on a fairly unfettered market economy and the
labour movement's determination to introduce at least some of its dreams

for the creation of a more socially responsive socioeconomic system. Labour's demands came to a head in 1950 with the call for formal representation of labour within management of industrial enterprises, or 'codetermination'. In the end, a variety of circumstances, not least the fact that the government was dependent on trade union cooperation in the Schuman plan negotiations, produced a compromise which all sides could live with. Labour's success in getting equal representation on the supervisory boards of the iron and steel industry in the 1951 Act, and a weaker right to speak in other industries in 1952, was enough of a symbolic achievement to prevent the alienation of the left from the new system.

The other major social problem needing resolution was the position of millions of refugees and expellees on West German territory. Here, the problem was solved by effective law-making and above all by economic growth. The Law for the Equalization of Burdens made large transfers of resources to the expellees but because the levies could be paid over an extended period and thus were in effect a tax on growth they were at little cost to the established population. Fairly rapidly, government-assisted expellee businesses were to be an important source of innovation and growth in the relatively underdeveloped rural areas of Bavaria, Lower Saxony and Schleswig-Holstein.

These measures were important in legitimating the new order, particularly as they were passed at a time when prosperity had not reached the majority of the population and unemployment remained high. But in the course of the 1950s there was little doubting what was the main cement of the Federal Republic's social fabric – extraordinary and sustained economic growth. Factors contributing to the growth included a propitious international environment, the considerable scope for catching up on innovation opportunities wasted in the inter-war and immediate post-war years, the fact that despite the heavy bombing much of German capacity had remained intact, the steady stream of highly qualified labour in the form of expellees and migrants from the GDR and the favourable fiscal and monetary framework. At first, growth was accompanied by high unemployment and some price increases, giving rise to considerable unease. But the slowly but steadily rising wage levels of the 1950s created perhaps the new republic's biggest claim to popular support and gradually dispelled the deep-seated suspicion held by many Germans that democracies were incapable of running society effectively. Though the 'social' in Erhard's 'social market economy' was initially more claim than substance, in 1957 the welfare state was able to make a quantum leap forward in the form of the new pensions law, which created dynamic pensions linked to the general growth rate of the economy.

II.3   Emergence of the *Kanzlerdemokratie*

A striking fact of the Federal Republic's life was that despite the many limits to Germany's sovereignty and freedom of action the government was able from a very early stage to speak and act with an authority denied to any German government or leader since Bismarck, with the exception of Hitler. In part this was because the Nazis had crushed the centrifugal tendencies within German society – the ability of army leaders, civil service, business-men, labour, Prussian aristocrats and other groups to defy the government. In part it was because the Allied presence and the dissolution of the German army had protected the nascent German administration in the immediate post-war period from having to do the sort of deals with other power groups which had so undermined Weimar leaders. The destruction of Prussia also eliminated the confusions and resistances built into the uneven federal structure of pre-Nazi Germany. Finally, of course, the distribution of power within parliament itself, and above all the very substantial position enjoyed by the CDU even in the first electoral period was a crucial prerequisite of decisive action.

But on top of these factors there was Konrad Adenauer's personal authority. Despite taking office well after retirement age, Adenauer exuded a mixture of patriarchal but determinedly civilian authority and a canny, on-the-level and unbombastic rhetorical style. His control over cabinet and parliament was so marked that it was said he had invented a new political system: the 'Chancellor-Democracy'. His most important contribution was in the area of foreign policy. Adenauer's commitment to close western integration, his belief that it was only through such western ties that Germany could restyle itself into a stable democracy, coupled with his personal authority, allowed him to 'deliver' the western strategy at home, despite the fact that it was clearly pushing the prospects of unification with East Germany ever further into the distance.

II.4   Values and attitudes in the new republic

How far had attitudes and values changed within the new republic? Many critical observers felt that few Germans had learned much from the past. Opinion polls for much of the 1950s suggested that the population was not much more influenced by democratic ideas than it had been a generation earlier.

It was understandable that left-wing critics should talk of a 'restoration'. And yet the political and ideological climate in Bonn was very far from being a replication of Weimar. The biggest break was, of course, in the

marginalization of nationalism and the emergence of new attitudes towards
Germany's place in the wider world. The sense of the new realities of world
power penetrated to every aspect of German life. When it came to attitudes
on more domestic matters, it is true, there were many continuities – in
middle-class anti-communism, for example, and a strong desire for order.
Yet, whereas in Weimar the bourgeoisie had shown itself willing to embrace
a culture of violence in order to crush the left, restore order and re-establish
Germany's place in the world, after 1949 there was a very conscious effort
to return to old niceties. Guides to etiquette and good behaviour, to *guten
Ton*, sold in hundreds of thousands. Whilst for left-wing critics this
emphasis on decency and order was both stifling and hypocritical and was
often not particularly democratic (aiming to produce the decent, loyal state
citizen rather than the active democrat), it gave the old civic virtues of the
bourgeoisie a place they had not enjoyed in Weimar.

In Weimar, many on the right had sought to unify society by crushing the
organized left. In post-'49 Germany, a strong, anti-pluralistic yearning for
unity remained. But instead of aspiring to create unity by force there was an
almost wilful desire to believe that German society was *already* unified. The
popular sociologists of the time – Geiger, Schelsky and others – reflected
and reinforced the desire to believe that here was a society where class
divisions were a thing of the past. As a result, even when the rhetoric of
political leaders still had a strident Weimar tone, contemporaries often
experienced this rhetoric as being out of keeping with the times, a 'ghost-
like' reminder of social divisions that no longer existed.

Overstating the case, one could argue that it was precisely the restora-
tiveness, the return to bourgeois values of decency and civility, that
marked Bonn out from Weimar. What was new, too, was that conservatism was so successful. In 1957 the CDU managed to get an absolute
majority of the votes, achieving something that Hitler had been unable
to do even in the unfree elections of March 1933. Stifling as the cold
war climate may have been, by the second half of the 1950s, German
society was probably more united in ideology and values than at any
time in its history.

II.5   Germany in denial

There is no doubt that there was considerable obfuscation of the past,
denial of involvement, indeed a conspiracy not to mention it. Most German
people were unwilling to confront their role in Germany's crimes. But the
hegemonic myths of the post-'45 era were far more constructive than those
which had held sway in the inter-war period. After all, the twists and turns

that allowed a whole generation of civil servants and businessmen to emerge with careers intact from the denazification panels, nevertheless at the same time did involve each individual distancing themselves from their pasts. This was very different from the glorification of tradition or the stab in the back legend which had so undermined Weimar. The kinds of narratives that Germans privately and publicly constructed after 1945 to make sense of what had happened revolved round the lessons that had been learned from the defeat – lessons such as the ability to put your shoulders to the wheel and build a better society, or the ability of European nations to work together. They did not involve denying the defeat or plotting ways to overturn the terms of the post-war settlement.

And yet there was a brittle, exaggerated quality to life in the 1950s which could not be healthy in the longer term. You could see it in the intensity with which an entire generation threw itself into work and personal enrichment; you could see it in the strained silences of family life. Indeed, families in this period suffered in many respects from a double burden. On the one hand, the very different experiences of home front and battle front had created communication gaps and distances between husbands and wives. Cramped housing conditions and long working hours added to the strain. On the other hand, there was the communication gap between the generations about the politics of the past. Youngsters growing up in the 1950s often felt they were living a double lie – the lie of happy families, and the lie of a society that would not face up to its past – both of which led them in the 1960s to denounce what they saw as bourgeois hypocrisy.

III   Challenge and reform, 1957–1974

III.1   Into the 1960s: the surface of stability

At the end of the 1950s the FRG presented a picture of stability and success. Continued economic growth now began to bring truly unparalleled prosperity to the whole population. The implications for the patterns and rhythms of everyday life were probably more far-reaching than in any phase of economic growth since industrialization. Consumerism entered with a vengeance. The self-service shop rapidly replaced across-the-counter service; the German public began to travel abroad in their millions, the car became the dominant form of transport, television took over in the living room, the laid-back culture of rock and roll invaded the youth scene and so on.

Against this background, the political scene converged on the middle.

The SPD responded to the CDU's success with the famous Bad Godesberg party programme of 1959, in which it formally jettisoned much of the Marxist ideology which in any case had long ceased to influence party policy. As well as now embracing the market economy (though still calling for more state intervention) the party also endorsed Adenauer's broad pro-western international framework. Since a number of influential figures within the CDU began to accept the need for somewhat greater state intervention in economic and social policy, the ideological gap between the two major parties was now very small indeed. In 1966, when the combination of a very minor recession and a more serious crisis in the mining industry led temporarily to great anxiety about Germany's economic development, the CDU and SPD joined together to form the Grand Coalition – a government which lasted for three years.

Yet in the course of the 1960s it became apparent that this stable surface was in some ways rather misleading. For one thing, the massive overreaction to the 1966 recession indicated that Germany's political stability might still be very dependent on the economy's capacity to deliver. The Weimar-style reflex of the Grand Coalition suggested that the economic difficulties were being stylized as a national emergency. Brief successes for the far-right Nationaldemokratische Partei Deutschlands (NPD) in regional elections were another worry. However, more significant than the immediate impact of recession were a series of broader changes at home and abroad that were beginning to challenge the consensus.

III.2   Losing faith in cold war logic

The clear logic which Adenauer had drawn, and persuaded his fellow countrymen to draw from the international scene began to lose its plausibility. In the first place, the erection of the Berlin Wall in August 1961 discredited the magnet theory that West Germany could undermine East Germany by its own attractiveness. It began a tortuous and conflict-ridden process within West Germany's political establishment towards finding some sort of *modus vivendi* with the GDR. For Konrad Adenauer, still in office when the Wall was created (he was replaced by Ludwig Erhard as Chancellor in 1963), the Berlin crises also reinforced a growing disillusionment with American leadership, which the Germans felt had been ineffectual. There was a growing sense that America no longer had West German security needs at the heart of its strategic objectives. This view was to intersect over the following decades with a different strand of criticism which emerged in the wake of the Vietnam War, namely, that American imperialism was in fact a greater threat to peace than Soviet expansionism. In the second half of the 1960s, bitter public conflicts over foreign policy broke out for the first time since the struggle over rearmament in the 1950s.

III.3   The birth of a protest movement.

The explosion of protest that took place above all among university students towards the end of the 1960s was, however, motivated only partially by the Vietnam War. As elsewhere in the western world, the rise of affluence began for the first time to reveal its slightly ambiguous implications for the stability of public order. Though it had helped to deal with the classical 'social question', it began to throw up new needs and discontents. 'Post-material' values began to emerge, not least exported from the USA via its new youth culture. In Germany, perhaps even more important was that protest culture interacted with a far more deep-seated sense of unease at the FRG's failure to confront its past. On top of all this, there was a problem of chronic underfunding in the university sector. In the period of the Grand Coalition there was no genuine opposition to articulate people's discontents; the result was the rapid growth of the APO or Extra-Parliamentary Opposition. In 1967, the student Benno Ohnesorg was shot dead by a policeman during a protest against the Shah of Iran and this triggered a wave of demonstrations, sit-ins and other actions. Every aspect of the Federal Republic became subject to question, its bland cold-war self-assurance denounced as lies and deceit.

III.4   Revolts, reaction and reform

Youthful protest seldom enjoys much impact unless the adult generation has in some sense or another delegated to young people the task of shaking things up. This was certainly the case in the 1960s where, under the surface, a sense of the need for more openness and liberality had been steadily developing, particularly among the educated bourgeoisie. Perhaps a first indication of the changing intellectual climate had been the *Spiegel* affair in 1962, when the government had heavy-handedly infringed the rights of the press and had then deceived parliament in the process. Public reaction showed that the characteristic German middle-class reflex of approving any government action if it kept the peace was now being replaced by a commitment to constitutionality and civil liberty. Franz-Josef Strauss, the then Defence Minister, had to go, and Adenauer's own prestige never recovered – he was replaced the following year. Henceforth governments were to be increasingly constrained by the informal constitution of public opinion. More specifically, 1963 saw a number of leading

thinkers calling for fundamental reform of Germany's education institutions – giving a clear signal to the student community that change was
required. There was thus a kind of symbiosis between a slow liberalization
of the thinking public and the growth of student protest.

It is true that the student movement itself was often illiberal and
dogmatic. Even sympathizers such as Jürgen Habermas warned against a
left-wing fascism. Moreover, the direct result of student protest and subsequently of terrorism was often to provoke the state to measures of greater
illiberality. The joint decision of *Bund* and *Land* in January 1972 to tighten
the existing controls on the political activities and attitudes of applicants for
the civil service (*Radikalenerlass*), and the subsequent huge expansion of
individual screening and checks, showed the state at its rigid worst. It is
possible that even without the student movement liberalization would have
accelerated and thus that the only direct results of protest were the negative
ones of state control. To most observers then and since, however, the
collision between protest movement and a Federal Republic still in many
respects dominated by the cold war is seen as a decisive step towards
greater democracy and pluralism. In the new climate there was an
explosion of reform at all levels, resulting not least in the emergence of a
new Social-Liberal government coalition in 1969. The clarion call of the
new Chancellor, Willy Brandt, for inner reform, more democracy and
codetermination enjoyed a wide resonance.

III.5   *Ostpolitik* and *Vergangenheitsbewältigung*

It was both symptom and result of the greater openness and liberalism that
emerged in the 1960s that the Federal Republic was able to kick aside two
of the ideological props which had been essential to its stability in the
1950s. One was the total embargo on recognition of the GDR. After some
early moves by the Freie demokratische Partei (FDP) during its period of
opposition, the new Social Liberal Coalition of 1969 initiated a series of
measures which saw talks in Moscow in 1969 and treaties with Moscow
and Poland in the following year, brought the heads of government of the
two German states together for the first time in 1970 and culminated in the
new Basic Treaty of 1972. Following a series of improvements in transit
arrangements between the states and a Four-Power agreement in 1971
which clarified (though did not resolve) the status of Berlin, in the Basic
Treaty the two states recognized each other as separate states, although the
Federal Republic did not renounce its aspirations to national unification or
accept the GDR as a separate *nation*.

The other 'prop' or taboo of the 1950s to be broken was the silence about the past. The creation in 1958 of a new Central Office for Prosecution of National Socialist Crimes had been a first step in this direction. The 1960s saw a series of profound analyses from German scholars about the workings of the Third Reich and a growing willingness on the part of schools to tackle this difficult period. Willy Brandt's famous gesture, in December 1970, of falling to his knees before a monument to those who died in the Warsaw uprising, made such an impact because it publicly brought together these two strands: the new amity with the Warsaw Pact powers and the willingness publicly to acknowledge Germany's responsibilities in the past.

IV Crisis and consolidation, 1975–1989

IV.1 The end of the miracle

Many observers have seen for Germany, as for France, the events of the late 1960s and their impact as marking 'the end of exceptionalism'. And in many respects such challenges as confronted the Federal Republic in the post-1973 period have been comparable to those facing other western states. Like most other states, the stormy growth of the post-war decades came to an end. In 1974–5, West Germany hit its first serious post-war recession. Henceforth, mass unemployment was a permanent feature, rising from the million mark in the post-1975 years to over two million after the second major recession in 1979–80. The economic slowdown was not a sign that West Germany had lost its earlier abilities; rather the oil crisis, the ending of a special post-war 'catch-up' period, and the emergence of a new set of geoeconomic conditions (the weakening of the dollar, the emergence of competition from Far East and newly developed countries) created a more unpredictable and challenging growth environment for all European countries.

Under these conditions the bubbling reform atmosphere of the late 1960s and early 1970s rapidly lost its fizz. After the fall of Willy Brandt (his private secretary turned out to be a GDR spy) in 1974, the new Chancellor Helmut Schmidt rapidly came to lay increasing emphasis on consolidation rather than reform. The hope that had emerged, after Erhard's fall, that demand management by the federal government could prevent recessions, proved illusory. Instead, the problem of stagflation reared its head in the 1970s. Particularly after 1979, all attention came to be devoted to controlling state spending, a struggle which continued when the CDU returned to government in 1982 and which lasted through the 1980s. Aside from the intensifying economic constraints, the checks and balances of a federal system in which the *Länder* were largely in the hands of the opposition, as they were in the 1970s, also set limits to reform. Under these conditions, the SPD increasingly lost its way. In gradually dropping any aspirations to control demand and unemployment levels, the SPD in many ways anticipated the so-called *Wende* – the return to CDU control which followed the FDP's defection in 1982.

Similarly, the student movement fragmented, its most radical advocates descending during the 1970s into the terror of the Red Army faction. A series of spectacular actions including the attack on the German embassy in Stockholm in 1975, the 1977 murders of the Attorney-General Siegfried Buback and Hanns Martin Schleyer, president of the German Employers' Association, and the abduction of a Lufthansa flight to Mogadishu, all confronted the West German state with difficult challenges but had little in common with the reformist enthusiasm of the earlier period. The only more positive expression of that spirit was the emergence in the 1980s of the Green Party as a major political movement, in many regions threatening or eclipsing the FDP as the third force between the major parties.

The 1980s, as elsewhere, saw considerable public disaffection with the political process. On top of the reduced freedom of manoeuvre imposed by the new financial and economic situation there were other reasons for the new much-commented-upon alienation from the established parties. In a global world, the centres of decision-making seemed to many people more and more remote. Political scandals came to light that might have remained under the carpet in more deferential times, and several senior German politicians had to resign in the wake of dirty tricks allegations or of accepting improper payments. The growth of television created a false openness, with politicians ostensibly answering questions, but in reality staking out bargaining positions in ongoing decision-making processes. The result of such exposure was that, as elsewhere, politicians became slicker and slicker and less and less credible.

And yet even if it shared in certain common western problems of attrition, in comparative terms the West German state proved its durability and strength. It remained one of the strongest economies in the world. It controlled the inflationary pressures of the post-oil-crisis period far better than most other developed economies. True, the economic difficulties in conjunction with the large number of foreign 'guest workers' now on German soil did give rise to some racist protest, but in general the political impact of deep recession, contrary to many fears, gave little comfort to the extremist parties of left and right. In short, in a changed world, West Germany remained a pillar of stability.

IV.2   Problems of national identity

In many ways, then, West Germany had by the mid-1970s completed the transition from maverick to model state. But in other respects its situation remained distinctive and troubled – and as always the criss-crossing of history and geopolitics was at the heart of the specific German problem.

First the difficult past would not go away. For a long time, one of the key demands of the CDU had been to combat the growing lack of any link to the notion of Germanness on the part of the younger generation with a renewed historical consciousness of the *Vaterland*. Helmut Kohl, Chancellor since 1982, wanted to realize this vision, as did a number of prominent conservative-minded historians such as Michael Stürmer. But the celebrated *Historikerstreit* of the mid-1980s revealed that, although the passing of time and the weakening of the cold war meant that some things which had been left unsaid on the right were now sayable again, it was impos-sible to resurrect a 'wholesome' or 'usable' past for easy national identification.

Secondly, the FRG's geopolitical position remained highly individual and complex and a source of considerable contention and division. As a front-line power, the FRG continued to experience the special vulnerability of being the probable battleground of any future war, and the territory most likely to be subject to Soviet blackmail and pressure. In the post-Vietnam era this led many Germans, notably Helmut Schmidt, to be particularly sensitive to signs that the Americans were pulling back from their global commitments. President Carter's stance at the SALT talks of allowing the Soviets a clear conventional and tactical nuclear superiority in Europe for the sake of parity in strategic nuclear weapons at the global level, met with particular criticism. It was Schmidt whose proposals led to the NATO twin-track decision of 1979, which threatened to station tactical nuclear missiles on European soil if negotiations with the Soviet Union failed to reduce the number of SS20s aimed at Europe. On the other hand, again as a front-line power and as a power with developing relations with the GDR, the FRG saw itself as having a special interest in *détente*. The twin-track decision was thus notably divisive, since it ranged those who believed that NATO and the USA should be doing more for Europe against those, including very many young people, who believed the growth in nuclear armaments was itself the biggest danger to their security. The stationing of the first Pershing missiles on German soil in the early 1980s led to massive protest marches. It was not least on this issue that the SPD became deeply divided.

Nevertheless, one should not exaggerate the threat posed to West

German stability by these issues. The CDU, despite its somewhat more national-minded rhetoric, in fact pursued the same *Ostpolitik* as the SPD. Like the SPD, too, the CDU sought closer ties with the FRG's western neighbours to reassure them about its *rapprochement* with the east. In the continuing West German foreign policy conception, German unification, if it were ever achieved, had to go hand in hand with closer European union. For most West Germans of the younger generations the national issue was of very secondary importance. The GDR was far more of a foreign territory than France, Britain or Italy. Whilst conservative thinkers worried that the lack of national awareness would ultimately deny the Federal Republic the kind of inner resources necessary to weather a serious crisis that were available to other classic nation states, West Germany in fact seemed to other observers in fact to benefit from the 'post-national' consciousness of many its citizens.

V   Division and stability

During the 1980s statesmen as varied in their views as Andreotti, Mitterand and Thatcher all directly or indirectly expressed a wish that West Germany should retain its separate existence and not aspire to recreating a single German nation. That showed how successful the FRG had been – but it also showed that there was a fear that reunification might undo all that had been achieved. Was this justified? Were the FRG's successes based on shaky foundations, likely to be undermined once unification took place?

There was little doubt that the divisions – of Europe and of Germany – had together simplified the task of creating a stable republic in the post-war period. For one thing, the proximity of a Soviet threat, whether real or perceived, had created a commonality of interest between West Germany and its neighbours. Most Germans eschewed nationalism in favour of the idea of a common western interest; similarly, Germany's neighbours had to subordinate their animosity towards the former enemy to a recognition of their mutual interdependence and vulnerability in the age of the superpowers. Second, the division of Germany had made for a more manageable state: the destruction of Prussia created the basis for a more balanced federal structure; the new more equal confessional balance facilitated the emergence of a non-denominational Christian Democratic Union.

Yet at least as important in creating and consolidating the new order were the changes Nazism, war and defeat had bequeathed to Germany. The combination of the exhaustion and disillusionment of the broad population, on the one hand, and the active political minority's awareness of the need for reform, on the other, provided the crucial prerequisite for the success of democratic rebirth in Germany.

In any case, West Germany rapidly outgrew dependence on the conditions of its birth, acquiring in the 1960s a pluralistic and democratic political culture, a post-nationalist liberalism that often put to shame the nations that had helped bring the new state into being. This was particularly apparent in the 1980s. In Britain and the USA, that decade saw entire regions and social classes simply cast on the scrap heap by the policies of Thatcher and Reagan. In France, it saw extreme racism become part of the political mainstream. In the Federal Republic of Germany, by contrast, the sensitivity to social harmony, the incorporation of regional interests, the pressure to compromise, all of which were built into its formal and informal political systems, made such developments unthinkable. It was and is not plausible that the end of the cold war and the end to division would simply undo these changes.

Even if one ignores the quality and strength of the FRG's political culture, the argument that the new geopolitical situation of a post-cold war world would inevitably revive the old temptation to look eastwards and perforce create instabilities in Germany is implausible. Even without the cold war, the world is very different from the inter-war period. To take one very obvious example, in a world of nuclear weapons any thought of a 'Barbarossa' – waging the knockout blow against Russia to create a stable German empire in east Europe – is clearly a non-starter. But far more significant is the change in geoeconomics. The slogans of central European empire-building or *Lebensraum* made sense only in an imperialist and highly protectionist world, where each nation had to secure and control its own hinterland of markets and raw materials. The end of the cold war has done nothing to revive this scenario – on the contrary, it has contributed to a further opening of world markets and trade.

In short, it is hard to accept the view that the Federal Republic's stability was dependent on its remaining a divided state. In one crucial sense, however, West Germany's very success did leave it ill-equipped to cope with the challenges of reunification. Precisely because it was so well able to win the support of its citizens and foster what was in many cases a clearly non-nationalist identity, it has lacked the broad public sympathy and legitimacy for the sacrifices required to complete the national unification process. There are dangers inherent in the resulting tensions and conflicts, but they are dangers with which the Federal Republic, with its durable political institutions, powerful economy, and ability to accommodate regional interests, is able to cope at least as well as any of the maturer democracies of Europe.

Table 8.1 Bundestag election results, 1949–1994 (000s)

In this table results are not given for insignificant party affiliations, which generally gained less than 1 per cent each, so that figures below do not add up to 100 per cent. The only exception was the election of 1949, where such other groups gained, taken together, 6.2 per cent.
a) Total votes gained in the whole country, b) percentage of total votes, c) number of seats, before 1990 excluding deputies of West Berlin, because Berlin was under an especial international status, d) disappeared later from the German system of political parties.

| | 14.8.1949 31.2 mill. 24.5 mill. 78.5 | | | 6.3.1953 33.1 mill. 28.5 mill. 85.8 | | | 15.9.1957 35.4 mill. 31.1 mill. 87.8 | | | 17.9.1961 37.4 mill. 32.8 mill. 87.7 | | |
Eligible / Turnout / % voting	a	b	c	a	b	c	a	b	c	a	b	c
CDU/CSU[d]	7,359	31.0	139	12,440	45.2	243	15,008	50.2	270	14,298	45.3	242
SPD	6,935	29.2	131	7,945	28.8	151	9,496	31.8	169	11,427	36.2	190
FDP	2,83	11.9	52	2,628	9.5	48	2,307	7.7	41	4,029	12.8	67
KPD/DKP (Kommunistische Partei Deutschlande)	1,362	5.7	15	0,607	2.2	—	—	—	—	—	—	—
DP[d] (Deutsche Partei)	0,94	4.0	17	0,898	3.3	15	1,007	3.4	17	GPD	2.8	—
BHE[d] (Bund der Heimatvertriebenen und Entrechteten)	—	—	1,614	5.9	27	1,374	4.6	—	0,871			
Centre[d]	0,723	3.1	10	0,217	0.8	2	0,086	0.3	—	—	—	—
Bavaria Party[d]	0,986	4.2	17	0,466	1.7	—	0,168	0.5	—	—	—	—
WAV[d] (Wirtschaftliche Aufbau Vereinigung)	0,682	2.9	12	—	—	—	—	—	—	—	—	—
SRP/NPD (Sozialistische Ruchspartei)	0,429	1.8	5	0,296	1.1	—	0,309	1.0	—	0,263	0.8	—
DFU (Deutsche Friedens-Union)	—	—	—	—	—	—	—	—	—	0,61	1.9	—

Table 8.1 *continued*

	19.9.1965 38.50 mill. 33.4 mill. 86.8			28.9.1969 38.7 mill. 33.0 mill. 86.7			19.11.1972 35.4 mill. 31.1 mill. 91.2			3.10.1976 42.0 mill. 38.1 mill. 90.7			5.10.1980 43.2 mill. 38.3 mill. 88.7		
Eligible Turnout % voting	a	b	c	a	b	c	a	b	c	a	b	c	a	b	c
CDU/CSU	15,524	47.6	245	15,195	46.1	242	16,794	44.8	225	18,397	48.6	244	16,900	44.5	226
SPD	12,813	39.3	202	14,066	42.7	224	17,167	45.9	230	16,099	42.6	213	16,262	42.9	218
FDP	3,097	9.5	49	1,903	5.8	30	3,129	8.4	41	2,995	7.9	39	4,030	10.6	53
KPD/DKP	—	—	—	0,197	0.6	—	0,114	0.3	—	0,141	0.4	—	0,080	0.2	—
GDP	—	—	—	—	—	—	—	—	—	—	—	—	—	—	—
Centre[d]	—	—	—	—	—	—	—	—	—	—	—	—	—	—	—
Bavaria Party[d]	—	—	—	—	—	—	—	—	—	—	—	—	—	—	—
WAV[d]	—	—	—	—	—	—	—	—	—	—	—	—	—	—	—
SRP/NPD	0,664	2.0	—	1,422	4.3	—	0,207	0.6	0,122	0.3	—	0,067	0.2	—	—
DFU[d]	0,434	1.3	—	—	—	—	—	—	—	—	—	—	—	—	—

	6.3.83 44.08 mill. 39.2 mill. 89.1			25.1.87 45.3 mill. 38.2 mill. 84.3			2.12.90 60.4 mill. 46.9 mill. 77.8			1994 60.4 mill. 47.0 mill. 79.1		
	a	b	c*	a	b	c*	a	b	c*	a	b	c*
CDU/CSU	18.9	48.8	244 (+11)	16.7	44.3	223 (+11)	20.3	43.8	319	19.5	41.5	294
SPD	14.8	39.2	133 (+5)	14.0	37.0	186 (+7)	15.5	33.5	239	17.1	36.4	252
FDP	2.7	7.0	34 (+1)	3.4	9.1	46 (+2)	5.1	11.0	79	3.1	6.9	47
Greens	2.1	5.6	27 (+1)	3.1	8.3	42 (+2)	1.7	3.8	—			
NPD	0.09	0.2	—	0.2	0.6	0.1	0.4	—	—			
DKP	0.06	0.2	0.2	—	—	—						
PDS (Parteides Demokratischen Sozialismus)	1.1	2.4 0.4	1.2	8**	—	3.4	7.3	49				
REP (Republikaner)	1.0	2.1	—	0.8	1.9	—						

* +11 Berliner MdB

** The parties got seats although they did not gain 5 per cent of the total votes because of special provisions for the former GDR where they got more than 5 per cent. In 1994 th s will no longer be the case.

Source: C.C. Schweitzer, Detlev Kausten, et al. (eds) Politics and Government in Germany 1944–1994. Basic Documents (Oxford: Berghahn Books, 1995), p. 442.

Table 8.2 Real growth of the West German economy, 1951–1980 (%)

Year	%	Year	%
1951	10.4	1966	2.9
1952	8.9	1967	–0.2
1953	8.2	1968	7.3
1954	7.4	1969	8.2
1955	12.0	1970	5.8
1956	7.3	1971	3.0
1957	5.7	1972	3.4
1958	3.7	1973	5.1
1959	7.3	1974	0.4
1960	9.0	1975	–2.7
1961	5.4	1976	5.8
1962	4.0	1977	2.7
1963	3.4	1978	3.3
1964	6.7	1979	4.5
1965	5.6	1980	1.8

Source: V.R. Berghahn, *Modern Germany* (Cambridge: Cambridge University Press, 1982), p. 262.

Table 8.3 Structure of the labour force by sector, 1907–1972 (%)

Year	Agriculture	Industry and handicraft	Tertiary sector Total	Tertiary sector Commerce/ Banking
1907	35.2	40.1	24.8	12.4
1925	30.5	42.1	27.4	16.4
1933	28.9	40.4	30.7	18.5
1939[a]	25.9	42.2	31.9	17.5
1950[b]	23.1 (26)	(45)	(29)	
1960	13.2 (19)[c]	(48)	(33)	
1962	12.5	46.0	41.2	17.5
1970	8.3			
1972	7.7	46.1	46.2	16.5
1975	(12)	(49)	(37)	

Notes: [a] Reich Territory of 31.12.1937.
[b] Fed. Rep.; figures for GDR in brackets.
[c] GDR figure for 1959.
Sources: V.R. Berghahn, *Modern Germany* (Cambridge: Cambridge University Press, 1982), p. 263.

Table 8.4 Exports of major industrial nations as a percentage of GDP from 1913 to 1987

Country	1913[1]	1928[1]	1938[1]	1950[1]	1958[2]	1960[2]	1970[2]	1980[2]	1987[2]
Germany	19.3	14.4	5.4	8.5	15.1	19.0	21.2	26.5	28.7
UK	23.4	17.2	9.2	16.9	23.0	20.0	22.5	27.2	26.3
Italy	9.7	8.8	6.3	7.9	11.6	14.6	15.4	21.8	19.7
US	6.6	6.0	3.7	3.8	4.3	4.9	5.6	10.2	7.6
Japan	14.3	14.5	14.9	8.4	11.8	11.1	11.3	14.9	13.2

Notes: [1] Goods only.
[2] Goods and services.

Source: Weidenfeld, H. and Zimmermann, H., eds., *Deutschland-Handbuch* (1989), p. 623.

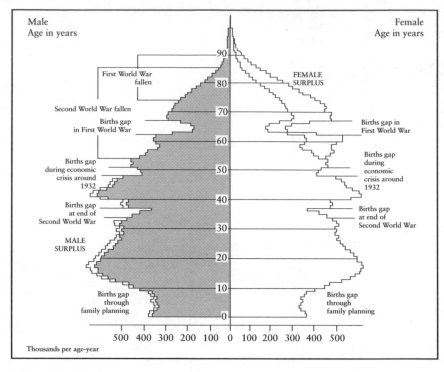

Figure 8.1 West German population structure in 1981

Select bibliography

Balfour, Michael, *Germany, the Tides of Power* (1992).

Berghahn, V. R., *The Americanisation of West German Industry, 1945–1973* (1986).

Berghahn, V. R., *Modern Germany: Society, Economy and Politics in the Twentieth Century* (1987).

Dahrendorf, Ralf, *Society and Democracy in Germany* (1968).

Fulbrook, Mary, *The Divided Nation: A History of Germany 1918–1990* (1991).

Kramer, Alan, *The West German Economy* (1991).

Larres, Klaus and Panayi, Panikos, eds., *The Federal Republic of Germany since 1949: Politics, Society and Economy before and after Unification* (1996).

Nicholls, A. J., *Freedom with Responsibility* (1995).

Pulzer, Peter, *German Politics, 1945–1995* (1995).

Smith, Gordon, *Democracy in Western Germany: Parties and Politics in the Federal Republic*, 3rd edn (1986).

Rogers, Daniel, *Politics after Hitler. The Western Allies and the German Party System* (1995).

Schwarz, Hans Peter, *Adenauer. From the German Empire to the Federal Republic* (1995).

Smith, Eric Owen, *The German Economy* (1994).

Turner, Henry A., *The Two Germanies* (1987).

Turner, Ian, ed., *Reconstruction in Post-War Germany: British Occupation Policy and the Western Zones, 1945–1955* (1989).

9

The failed experiment: East German communism

Mark Allinson

The German Democratic Republic may eventually rate merely a historical footnote, having occupied little of Germany's geography and chronology. In the 1990s, however, the wealth of historical material suddenly available, and the personal and political need to exorcise the latest German dictatorship, have produced an outpouring of work on the GDR, and a variety of interpretations of its history and place in the wider context of German history.

Dispassionate assessments of GDR history are difficult, essentially for political reasons. During its lifetime (1949–90), the GDR's own accounts were almost exclusively one-sided and adulatory, while western reports, particularly in the earlier years, highlighted the GDR's repressive nature. Only from the later 1960s were these publications regularly balanced by more analytical works which accepted the GDR's existence, such as those by Hermann Weber and Dietrich Staritz.

After the collapse in 1989 of the Socialist Unity Party of Germany (SED), the GDR's ruling communist party, much historical work was based on the premiss that the GDR was an illegitimate dictatorship and morally an *Unrechtsstaat* ('a state based on injustice'). The legal legitimacy of SED rule and the GDR's existence is still sometimes questioned just as it was during the Cold War.

The first stated aim in the hitherto most extensive investigation, the *Bundestag* report commissioned after unification, illustrates well the spirit of such politicized history:

> By a precise analysis of the totalitarian power structures of the SED dictatorship, the Inquiry Commission should help to ensure that those forces which were decisive in organizing the repression of people in the GDR never again receive a political chance in united Germany.[1]

The commission also intended to highlight the SED's 'deformation' of individuals' lives and to allow the 'victims' at least 'historical justice'.[2] Much attention was devoted to establishing the relative 'political responsibility' of those involved in the GDR's political structures.[3] The dramatic language and the investigation's avowedly political aims suggested that the authors reached their conclusions in advance.

The commission's chairman, Rainer Eppelmann, a long-standing opponent of the SED, was a leader of the 1989 revolutionary movement. Was this history written by the 'victors'? Much GDR history has been written by active opponents of the SED, or by those with an interest, often based on political conviction, in stabilizing the expanded FRG's structures, and must be seen in this perspective. Since 1990 bitter rows have raged over who may write GDR history, with attempts made to discredit historians regarded as too close to the old regime.

Apart from heavy criticism of the GDR's systems and structures, much attention has centred on the Ministerium für Staatssicherheit (Ministry for State Security), the infamous Stasi, effectively the GDR's secret police. Here the boundary between history and current politics is most blurred, as the Stasi files, now administered by a government agency, have been used to discredit many linked to the ministry, particularly those still active in political life. However, the validity of the Stasi (or any other) files is uncertain: some individuals were unaware of their classification as Stasi 'informal informants', and whether prepared by the Stasi or another official source, reports of societal dissatisfaction may have been cleansed or exaggerated before being passed upwards. Interpreting the GDR's enormous paper legacy is highly problematic.

Those who identified with their former state have taken a different approach. The SED's successor party, the PDS (Party of Democratic Socialism) is a good example and has published (among much else) its response to the Bundestag report. These authors' aims were also clearly stated: 'to oppose *from left-wing standpoints* this attempt to claim the power of interpretation over a significant part of German history'.[4] Generally such work has not exclusively defended SED policies or denied power abuses, but has tried to analyse where the SED's interpretation of socialism failed. Typically, such authors have incorporated a critically comparative approach to the FRG.

However, not all historical writing on the GDR is avowedly politicized, though even the absence of a clear condemnation of the SED has sometimes been criticized. Much work has analysed the GDR's political and societal structures and scrutinized particular episodes from a more objective academic perspective. Equally clearly, GDR history-writing did not emerge from a void in 1989–90, but built on earlier foundations, augmented by newly available material. For instance, the SED's repressive nature was already well documented, notably by Karl Wilhelm Fricke. This tradition continues in work on the Stasi and the post-war Soviet internment camps. However, practically all historians distance themselves from the style of pre-1989 GDR publications, written as self-legitimation and for explicitly party political purposes.

Leaving aside the various motivations for GDR histories, what key issues are involved? Much disagreement centres on the comparison, implied or direct, between the GDR and the Third Reich as totalitarian dictatorships, and the claim that East Germans lived under unbroken dictatorship from 1933 to 1989. Left-wing writers sharply reject such comparisons as a falsification of GDR history and a relativization of Nazi atrocities which attempts to mask continuities between the Third Reich and the FRG, and to discredit socialism by association with Nazism. Totalitarianism has re-emerged as a concept in historical and political science. However, even the Bundestag report noted that to compare was not to equate, and that important differences, such as the Second World War and genocide, existed between the two states. Beyond such theoretical debates, more empirical approaches attempt to establish means of comparing and distinguishing the political and social structures of both periods. How was SED rule maintained – purely by a strong Soviet military presence, or by tacit popular acceptance of the party? Why did so many participate in the structures established by the communists who attained political ascendancy after 1945? Why did SED rule then collapse so quickly? How stable was SED rule, and how and why did this vary over time?

A further, associated argument centres on the GDR's long-term independent viability and, by extension, of communist political systems (particularly since the USSR's collapse). Could the GDR have survived, or was it doomed to fail? The view was advanced by Mitter and Wolle in *Untergang auf Raten* ('Downfall by Instalments') that the GDR was essentially doomed after the popular uprising of June 1953 was crushed: 'We are dealing with a state party which was already politically finished in June 1953 and nonetheless ruled for a further 36 years.'[5] Other writers, such as Thomas Neumann, see Stalinism and eventual collapse as the inevitable outcome of Marxist politics. Was the GDR's fate really sealed at any specific point before 1989? If so, why did stability last and arguably grow into the 1980s? Could any realistic alternatives have saved the country or speeded its demise? These debates are linked to economic history and the GDR's international situation. Did *Ostpolitik* precipitate collapse or delay it? Did the GDR ultimately exist merely at the Soviets' whim? The international dimensions are crucial to understanding the GDR's internal dynamics.

The periodization of GDR history remains essentially unchallenged, falling into five major periods: first, direct Soviet occupation from 1945 to 1949, while the basic political structures were created; second, from the GDR's creation in 1949 to the Berlin Wall's erection in 1961, during which period socialist political and economic structures were strengthened and developed under the SED's Walter Ulbricht (despite the June 1953 uprising and the emigration of over two million citizens). Third, between 1961 and 1971, with the population secured behind the Wall, the system consolidated and experienced a relatively golden age and limited economic liberalization. In 1971 there was another rupture when Erich Honecker assumed power. International economic crisis and growing internal dissent dashed initial hopes of a GDR which fulfilled citizens' needs. The final period, from mid-1989 to 1990, marks the disintegration of SED rule and the surrender of GDR sovereignty.

While this periodization accurately reflects political developments, it masks various ongoing structural trends. For instance, the internal organization of the SED and the other parties and mass organizations developed progressively until the late 1950s, after which a high degree of stability essentially endured until late 1989. Conversely, popular attitudes were already altering years before the GDR collapsed. We clearly need a more differentiated approach to GDR history.

Bearing in mind these interpretative problems, this chapter attempts to explain the GDR's structures and to explore the system's apparent stability against the background of the threats it regularly experienced throughout the 1945/49–1989 period.

I Establishing the structures

Nobody imagined in 1945 that the Soviet zone of defeated Nazi Germany, heavily war-damaged and with a population long exposed to anti-Bolshevik propaganda, would become a stable communist state. The essential prerequisites were Germany's Cold War division, and occupation by the Soviet Military Administration in Germany (SMAD), which used its sovereign power to advantage the German communists, especially those returning from Moscow exile with plans to establish a powerbase.

Until 1989 the communists exploited not only their Soviet protection, but also the moral superiority of their anti-fascist past. Many Communist Party (KPD) members had suffered greatly while actively opposing Nazism. After 1945 this apparently unimpeachable record was used to legitimize socialism. The communists further argued that Nazism derived from capitalism, that returning to the Weimar Republic's political and economic system would threaten a fascist revival, and that the division of democratic forces during Weimar had facilitated the NSDAP's power seizure. Thus political unity should underpin Germany's future. Those who disagreed were branded Nazi sympathizers.

Believing Marxism–Leninism was scientifically proven, many communists sincerely hoped to avoid renewed catastrophe. However, to be a credible antidote to Nazism the party could not ignore democracy and impose a one-party system. Walter Ulbricht summarized KPD strategy in May 1945: 'It must look democratic, but the power must be in our hands.'[6]

This strategy constantly guided the communists. The first German officials appointed to head city and provincial governments were mainly bourgeois. However, the crucial posts (education, law and order) were usually assigned to reliable communists. The SMAD also permitted the re-establishment of 'democratic' political parties. Alongside the KPD, the SMAD licensed the SPD, a Christian Democratic Union (CDU) and a Liberal Democratic Party (LDPD). However, these parties' autonomy was limited as the overriding 'unity' principle required the parties to agree policies unanimously in a 'Democratic Bloc', effectively guaranteeing a KPD veto. When KPD proposals were rejected, the communists' anti-fascist credentials were used to accuse the other parties of endangering democratic reconstruction. By late 1945 many CDU and LDPD members reverted to more conservative policies. Consequently the SMAD regularly intimidated and removed politicians who opposed socialism too vociferously. While many politicians moved west, those who stayed usually remained silent to preserve their positions. For decades the CDU and LDPD officially proclaimed socialism while many grass-roots members remained unconvinced but could only attempt to influence politics by remaining within their parties.

While the CDU and LDPD were quite easily controlled, the SPD, as an alternative workers' party, posed greater difficulties. Many Germans feared communism and associated the KPD with the hated Soviets; unsurprisingly the SPD became more popular. Fearing defeat in free elections, the communists and the SMAD campaigned to unite the two parties to preserve communist influence, citing the anti-fascist imperative and the need to avoid the allegedly damaging division of the workers' parties during Weimar.

Though many social democrats feared communist domination, by Easter 1946 the campaign succeeded – at least in the Soviet zone where the SPD voices warning against a *Zwangsvereinigung* ('forced merger') were drowned

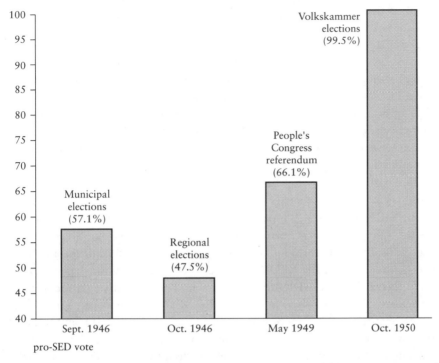

Figure 9.1   Stabilization of the voting system: how the pro-SED vote was ensured

out by emotive anti-fascism. The merger was approved not by ballot but by delegates who either genuinely backed the merger or were pressurized by the Soviets. Many socialists felt these machinations presaged an undemocratic system. The new Socialist Unity Party of Germany (SED), apparently a broad party, was initially constituted with total parity between communists and social democrats and inherited the KPD's privileged position in the Soviet zone's civil government. Yet by 1948 socialist unity was abandoned as, under Soviet protection and amid Germany's deepening division, the communist element transformed the SED into a Leninist 'party of a new type', and abandoned parity. The SED expelled the many committed social democrats and others who rejected the new Moscow-inspired line. This ideological overhaul was achieved with the agreement of senior former SPD leaders, notably Otto Grotewohl, whose motives ranged from self-preservation to conviction about communist policies. By 1948, with the zone's state apparatus and economic management mainly in SED hands, career considerations encouraged many social democrats to conform quietly. As the Soviets forbade an independent SPD, committed socialists had to choose between the SED or illegal opposition and probable punishment.

The SED's creation and subsequent communist domination still excites controversy. This development was arguably the first sign of renewed dictatorship, and that the SED's coercive, deceptive nature was predetermined. Clearly the merger resulted from pressure on individuals, while its SPD opponents were denied equivalent publicity. The SED's creation invited vitriolic attacks from the western SPD. Yet the notion of *Zwangsvereinigung* in 1946 is too broad: many social democrats (and communists) wanted and believed in workers' unity; even after the purges of the early 1950s, the SED still included ideologically committed members as well as careerists and opportunists.

The SED completed the party system in 1948 by creating two satellite parties. The Democratic Farmers' Party (DBD) reflected the SED's failure to unite workers and farmers, but attempted to integrate rural communities into political life on the SED's terms. Similarly, the National Democratic Party (NDPD) enabled reformed Nazis and conservative nationalists to participate in reconstruction within the SED's framework. The Soviet forces ensured no competing parties emerged. The DBD and NDPD therefore presented socialist policies to their target groups without challenging SED hegemony, and additionally attracted CDU and LDPD voters, enabling the SED to 'divide and rule' within the framework of political unity; both new parties joined the Democratic Bloc, strengthening SED control. As the bloc parties' political autonomy was weakened by moral blackmail and SED or Soviet coercion (particularly at the highest levels), so they acquired a role as 'transmission belts' to convey the SED's policies to the particular societal groupings they represented (Christians, farmers, etc.).

Alongside the parties, the SMAD also licensed various mass organizations, each firmly under KPD/SED control. On the unity principle, only one organization was permitted for each population sector. Through the Free German Trades Union Fedation (FDGB), the Free German Youth (FDJ), the Democratic Women's Association (DFD) and numerous similar organizations, the SED reached most of the population, including the many who otherwise distanced themselves from socialist politics, and prevented the development of independent movements which might challenge SED hegemony. Though membership of such organizations was never obligatory, their officially unimpeachable democratic, anti-fascist principles made refusals to join politically suspect. For instance, failure or refusal to join the FDJ might jeopardize university entry.

Structurally, the theoretically pluralist party system differed from the

Third Reich, while the mass organizations system was extremely similar. Despite being apparently democratic, the political system was firmly under SED control and supervised by the Soviets, the ultimate powerbrokers. No alternative avenues remained for potential opponents, whatever their anti-fascist credentials. By the early 1950s, every party and organization formally acknowledged SED supremacy. Functionaries who refused such loyalty were forced out in campaigns against 'reactionary, backward elements', or saw the impossibility of opposition and simply withdrew, sometimes to West Germany.

The GDR's establishment on 7 October 1949 further guaranteed SED power as the constitution outlawed attacks on 'democratic' institutions and politicians, creating a legal framework to neutralize opponents. Media control, underpinned by a licensing system, was also firmly in the 'democratic' hands of SED trustees.

Table 9.1(a) Distribution of seats in the Volkskammer, 1963–1989

Party	Seats	%
SED (Socialist Unity Party)	127	25.4
FDGB (trades union)	68	13.6
FDJ (youth organization)	40	8.0
DFD (women's organization)	35	7.0
Cultural League	22	4.4
CDU (Christian Democratic Union)	52	10.4
LDPD (Liberal Democratic Party)	52	10.4
NDPD (National Democratic Party)	52	10.4
DBD (Democratic Farmers' Party)	52	10.4

Source: DDR Handbuch, vol. 2 (Cologne: Verlag Wissenschaft und Politik, 1985), p. 1440.

Table 9.1(b) How the SED engineered a majority in the Volkskammer: many members of the mass organizations were also SED members

Party	Seats	%
SED	271	54.2
CDU	54	10.8
LDPD	52	10.4
NDPD	54	10.8
DBD	52	10.4
Members of no party	17	3.4

Source: DDR Handbuch, vol. 2 (Cologne: Verlag Wissenschaft und Politik, 1985), p. 1440.

The unity principle behind SED control also underpinned the electoral and government systems. Officially to prevent fascism's re-emergence, the Democratic Bloc parties and organizations presented a joint electoral ticket; the distribution of seats in the Volkskammer ('People's Chamber') was agreed beforehand. The population simply voted for or against the unity list. As those using the available, but usually inaccessible, booths were suspected of voting against the official candidates and therefore against democracy, even the first 'unity' elections of 1950 achieved a 'Yes' vote of 99.72 per cent on a 98.73 per cent turnout, a precedent which endured (largely without manipulating results) until 1989. Referenda in the 1950s merely underlined these structural parallels to the Third Reich.

Though the GDR's structures resembled a parliamentary democracy (People's Chamber, prime minister, president/Council of State), in practice the state apparatus merely shadowed the SED's own organization, which included policy departments equivalent to every ministry. This apparatus developed policy initiatives which were formally proposed to the government and parliament. In line with party discipline, which bound every member to execute party policies, the SED's government officials then implemented party decisions. This system of party control was repeated at regional and district level and guaranteed by 'democratic centralism', which required every level of party and state to obey decisions taken higher up. Thus the GDR's power structures varied significantly from the Third Reich's comparatively shambolic organization (see Chapter 5, above). The close cooperation of state and party bodies, the frequent interchange of personnel between both hierarchies and the marriage of state and party functions in key officials at each level generally ensured party superiority over the state without conflict. The Third Reich's competing offices and unclear command lines were replaced with a plurality of strictly ordered vertical hierarchies (SED, state, mass organizations, bloc parties), within which the SED hierarchy was ultimately paramount. The system did not depend on a leadership personality: neither Ulbricht nor Honecker presented himself as a charismatic leader comparable to Hitler, though the trappings of status (e.g., portraits in public buildings and newspapers) continued a long tradition, not peculiar to Germany. By the Honecker era these structures had stabilized and stagnated. Administratively, the country was effectively on automatic pilot.

However, despite the SED's cleansing and the other parties' and organizations' avowals of loyalty, many still preferred different options. In the late 1940s and early 1950s, before the system stabilized, many spoke out in local meetings. Within the SED, however, the principle of 'party discipline' was so established that most critics nonetheless supported the national leadership. An atmosphere of intimidation based on internal party cleansings and the developing Stasi progressively neutralized most waverers, at least publicly. The SED leadership's control over its apparatus and its allies was, however, never total inasmuch as many instructions were never realized by often inefficient or apathetic local groups. Although this undermined SED attempts at totalitarian rule, before 1989 it never threatened the party's overall authority.

Two further factors enhanced the SED's early hegemony. First, many East Germans loyally supported socialism and were not yet disillusioned by later political and economic crises. Second, most Germans were initially too concerned with rebuilding their lives to take much interest in politics. When normality returned, the political structures were already so entrenched that most people could only act within them. This was, for many, the price of defeat and occupation.

II   The road to socialism

As noted above, Marxism identified capitalism as the principal precursor of fascism; consequently capitalism must be eradicated. Over 20 years eastern Germany was transformed and divided from West Germany.

In 1945–46 a thorough land reform was enacted, and business owners with Nazi connections and wartime profiteers forfeited their firms, which were nationalized, along with banks and essential industries, or became 'Soviet limited companies'. Thus some 40 per cent of East Germany's industrial capacity came under state control. These economic changes heralded radical socialist development. The new SED-controlled economic ministries extended party influence beyond the purely political arena.

From July 1948 the zone's economy was coordinated in overly ambitious central plans, though the attempt was fraught with difficulties. As trade with the West faltered following the 1948 currency division, the GDR attempted greater autarky by establishing a new heavy industrial sector alongside huge projects to mine the inferior brown coal, its only abundant natural resource, and to replace wartime building losses. Such major investment in heavy industry and mechanical engineering left little capacity for consumer needs. Increasing demands were made on workers, who were encouraged to work extra shifts and to continually overfulfil production targets while food and other commodities remained in short supply and often expensive. Few workers identified with a workers' government which appeared to exploit them.

In July 1952 Ulbricht announced 'the building of socialism', predicting a 'class struggle' against opponents of socialism's historic mission. Various austerity policies were introduced and farmers who resisted the agricultural cooperatives (LPGs) paid tax penalties; food shortages worsened as some farmers fled before collectivization. The SED also introduced Marxist–Leninist school curricula, strengthened border security and undermined churches' influence over young people.

Most contentious was the unremunerated 10 per cent productivity increase with which the 'workers' government' incensed most workers. The SED stuck rigidly to this policy, despite eventually rescinding (at Soviet insistence) the other harsh measures introduced since July 1952. When a group of builders marched on the GDR's ministry building they were joined by thousands of disgruntled Berlin workers for whom the productivity demands were the final straw after years of toil for little reward. Though the government reluctantly recanted, these protests provoked widespread uprisings the following day, 17 June 1953. Though most rioting occurred in Berlin, many other areas were affected by strikes (though only a minority participated). Some SED offices were ransacked and members feared to display their party badges. The demonstrators were originally enraged by the 10 per cent quota increase and poor living standards, but many quickly demanded German unity and the SED leadership's removal, effectively questioning the GDR's socialist identity. However, no natural leaders emerged, reflecting the SED's successful monopolization of political structures and opportunities, and the police efficiently dealt with individual ringleaders. Finally Soviet tanks suppressed the uprising.

The 1953 uprising clearly demonstrated the importance of Soviet military presence in upholding SED power. None the less, once the initial uprising was quashed normality quickly returned. Already many party and state careers depended on the GDR's continued existence, and many activists remained loyal to the state's anti-fascist credentials, though few believed the official explanation of the uprising as a Western-inspired counter-revolutionary *putsch* attempt. Within the party, and therefore state, leadership the uprising ironically strengthened Ulbricht's position against a grouping in the party hierarchy plotting his removal. As Moscow was unwilling to appear to be surrendering to the demonstrators, the SED's leader was secure. In any case, Ulbricht's SED opponents mainly did not wish to endanger the party's rule.

SED hegemony was never seriously challenged again before 1989. Both party and people learned from the events. Those who had hoped to contest the political system guaranteed by the USSR's occupation rights acknowledged the SED's strength and either left the country or, more commonly, resigned themselves to the situation. Disturbances elsewhere (Hungary and

Figure 9.2   Numbers leaving the GDR, 1949–1961
*1961 value refers to January–August only

Poland in 1956, Czechoslovakia in 1968) caused significant ripples of dissent (particularly among intellectuals and the young, though mainly not workers) but no organized opposition, arguably because of the residual fear Soviet tanks had inculcated in 1953. Yet popular perceptions of SED rule were not exclusively and negatively shaped by 17 June 1953 until the autumn of 1989. The rebellion's crushing did not imply that most GDR citizens spent 36 more years awaiting, let alone plotting, the SED's downfall. While 17 June 1953 clearly established the boundaries of permissible political activity in the national consciousness, popular reactions and behaviour patterns were also shaped by later consolidative developments, notably improving living conditions, the emergence of a generally reliable welfare state and better career prospects. As Niemann has pointed out, far fewer people left the GDR after 1953. Skilled workers were particularly underrepresented among those arriving in the West. The 1953 uprising effectively cleared the air.

Meanwhile the SED developed arguably less abrasive methods of achieving its social, political and economic aims after June 1953, though the essential structures remained. Although some economic progress was achieved and living standards rose, they lagged behind the FRG's (always the GDR population's reference point). Political motivations apart, this lack of relative prosperity still caused hundreds of thousands to emigrate every year. The GDR economy could not survive this manpower loss indefinitely. As most of those 'fleeing the republic' left via the open border to West Berlin (the borders to the FRG were closed in 1952) Ulbricht recommended to the Soviet leader, Khrushchev, that the border to West Berlin also be sealed. Thus the Berlin Wall was erected on 12–13 August 1961 and travel to the West was forbidden to most GDR citizens until 1989.

Although the Berlin Wall was viewed internationally as an admission of failure by the GDR and Soviet governments, some GDR citizens, alarmed by the open border's potential dangers, initially welcomed it. Few imagined the Wall's longevity. Though a radical measure against previous failures, it secured new successes. The economic progress of the late 1950s was consolidated by a more stable labour market, more reliable economic planning, and a growing popular acceptance that, with the borders closed, one might as well make the best of things.

Meanwhile, the building of socialism progressed apace. Destalinization after 1956 notwithstanding, Ulbricht succeeded in ousting the remaining threats to his power within the SED hierarchy by 1958. Following industrial socialization during the 1950s agriculture was almost totally collectivized in 1960, with farmers' widespread opposition overcome by a concerted campaign by party and state agitators and Stasi threats. Small traders, artisans and service industry businesses were also encouraged to join cooperatives. (The final wave of socialization overtook small businesses in 1972.) Economic socialization and collectivization gave the SED-controlled ministries more direct power, while stifling private initiative and potential economic pluralism. An attempt to allow groups of 'People's Own Companies' (*Volkseigene Betriebe,* VEBs) more autonomy in the 'New Economic System' of 1963 was abandoned in 1970 as the SED realized that it was undermining its political control.

Not content with socializing the economy, Ulbricht also attempted popular ideological conversion. Though his attempt to impose Ten Socialist Commandments in 1958 was mainly unsuccessful, the more dedicated shunned religious ceremonies to perform socialist naming ceremonies and socialist burials. More effective was the education system's overhaul. Within the obligatory ten-class 'polytechnical' system, all pupils studied Marxism–Leninism and visited workplaces to experience socialist economics and working methods. Marxism–Leninism also became obligatory in higher education. The introduction of national service in 1962 exposed all young men to socialist ideology for a further 18 months. The SED isolated the churches from young people by effectively banning religious education in state schools and introducing a secular coming-of-age ceremony, the *Jugendweihe*, in which young people pledged themselves to the socialist fatherland, its leading party and its (atheist) ideology. Practically all young people participated in this ceremony by the late 1950s. Though the SED successfully distanced much of the population from religion, commitment to socialism was only superficially achieved, and began to disintegrate in the deteriorating economic situation of the mid-1980s.

In all areas of state and society, including the legal system, socialist measures were introduced during the 1950s and 1960s. Finally a new constitution was promulgated in 1968, defining the GDR as a 'socialist state' and legally enshrining the SED's leading role. The new constitution preceded the replacement in 1971 of the ageing Ulbricht as SED First Secretary by Erich Honecker. His accession was greeted optimistically, and coincided with the FRG's new *Ostpolitik*, enabling the GDR's increasing international recognition. The SED's failure, however, to implement the human rights stipulations of the 1975 Helsinki Accord, designed to ensure freedom of movement between countries, was regarded with disappointment and bitterness by many, as was the 1976 cultural crackdown, in marked contrast to Honecker's original protestation of 'no taboos' in cultural life.

Honecker aimed to maintain the SED's power monopoly, but attracted unfavourable comparisons with Gorbachov's reformist Soviet Communist Party after 1985. Under Honecker, political life became routine, punctuated every five years by SED congresses which simply re-elected the leadership. Political objectives and legitimations remained unchanged; the leadership grew older; life simply continued. Honecker did, however, embark on an ambitious programme to improve living standards. Subsidies for essential goods and social security benefits were increased. The highlight was a scheme to provide modern housing: by the late 1980s the SED claimed to have built or modernized three million flats.

These popular schemes with tangible results were, however, highly costly and exacerbated a financial crisis. The failure of economic reform in the late 1960s and the concentration of resources in a few new technologies left the GDR economically unstable. High social welfare costs, alongside draining commitments to defence and inflated bureaucracies, resulted in neglect of capital maintenance and investment. Rising fuel costs in the mid-1970s aggravated the GDR's indebtedness. The country was living beyond its means and even substantial foreign loans only temporarily alleviated the situation, while the long-term causes were not addressed. Though socialism was financially imperilled by the 1980s, the population hardly noticed the deepening crisis as Honecker maintained his social policies, ignoring the debt mountain. Meanwhile, popular opposition emerged, particularly directed at the environmental costs of the attempts to avert economic collapse; even within the party apparatus alternative economic policies were formulated in the late 1980s. The leadership, however, resisted calls for economic liberalization, fearing the ramifications for SED power. Worsening economic conditions and the GDR's indebtedness clearly helped provoke the 1989 uprisings and the state's eventual collapse.

III   Winning hearts and minds

We have seen how the post-war situation and SED policies created a costly 'real existing socialism' within a political straitjacket. What of the millions within this system? The sudden collapse of 1989–90 suggests that GDR citizens shared the predominant Western evaluation of an illegitimate state imposing its ideology on an unwilling population. However, widespread GDR nostalgia subsequently emerged, not only amongst the recently disempowered carriers of the system. Initially, unification created bitterness amongst many East Germans who wished to contribute to a united Germany and felt their life's work was being ignored. Relatively strong support for the Party of Democratic Socialism (PDS) and the contrast with the clear support for radical change during 1989–90 suggest a more complex relationship of citizens to state and party than simple resentment.

It is perhaps often forgotten that Germany in 1945 was a defeated nation, expecting to pay for defeat. Furthermore, although many East Germans feared Soviet occupation and associated the KPD/SED with it, some still venerating Hitler, many others hated Nazism and welcomed the opportunity to start afresh. Most Germans therefore initially felt obliged to tolerate the new regime, while a significant proportion actively supported an anti-fascist and/or socialist future. Encouraged by land reform and nationalization, optimism gripped many East Germans. Most, detached from developments in the West, viewed their zone's early development as a logical progression; the extent of SED hegemony was not immediately apparent (though some quickly drew parallels with the NSDAP's power mechanisms).

Public opinion reports rarely mention the GDR's legitimacy directly, though the GDR's foundation was welcomed by many who erroneously hoped it would ease eventual German unification. However, in the 1950s there were frequent reports of individuals who regarded Adenauer as Germany's true leader or who revered their 'Führer, Adolf Hitler'. General optimism about German unity persisted into the 1960s, encouraged by the SED, though the population often complained that socialist policies deepened Germany's division. Those expelled from Germany's eastern territories long resisted emotional integration with the GDR. Thus, many citizens failed to identify closely with the state they accepted in practice. GDR identity and socialist commitment were closely linked, but the German question was never forgotten. In a 1968 survey 65 per cent of East Germans regarded the GDR as their fatherland, but 33 per cent still thought of 'Germany' first.[7] During the 1970s and 1980s only about 50 per cent of young people identified with the GDR, and during the 1980s, particularly post-Gorbachov, Marxist–Leninist commitment declined sharply.[8] Even SED functionaries recognized in 1989, as socialism was overthrown, that a non-socialist GDR had no legitimate role.

Some historians believe that East Germans learned how to behave under a dictatorship during the Third Reich and therefore accepted the GDR more readily. This thesis is supported by early opinion reports which reveal much popular cynicism. Agricultural collectivization was predicted, long before 1960, by landworkers suspicious of communism. Many felt they would gain little from protesting, as the ruling party was bound to win. Rumours predicting the worst regularly spread in the 1950s and 1960s. During international crises panic buying occurred alongside rumours that 'the war' had started. In the earliest years youngsters on work camps or outings were sometimes reported to have been deported to Siberia. That such erroneous reports were widely regarded as part of the natural order suggests both that many did not regard their country as a normal democracy and that they were resigned to their fate. The lesson of the Third Reich and the post-war imposition of socialism seemed to be that one must accept the prevailing political atmosphere while hoping for change; the Hungarian uprising produced little open protest in the GDR but much unwarranted optimism about impending reform.

Nevertheless, opposition also existed alongside resignation. The expulsions from the border areas in 1952–3 outraged many, while the *Jugendweihe*'s introduction was fiercely opposed by active church-goers. Anti-SED graffiti, swastikas and oppositional leaflets regularly appeared, particularly in the earlier years. However, open opposition was relatively rare and concentrated on specific grievances and everyday conditions rather than existential questions. Only once, in 1953, did this ill feeling develop into a general uprising. Otherwise the widespread resentment was experienced individually rather than collectively. The standard SED line that the economic difficulties were principally bequeathed by Hitler did not impress a population aware even after 1961, via Western television and other sources, of considerably better conditions in the FRG. Travel restrictions were themselves a long-standing irritant.

Despite the daily annoyances and restrictions on freedom of movement, most GDR citizens accepted their situation and lived within it. Like people everywhere, they built families and strove to further their careers and improve their surroundings. The population was encouraged to be active within the SED-dominated social and political framework, and involvement in the organizations and political parties was taken to indicate support for the SED and socialism. However, the genuinely popular mass organization activities generally involved sport, holidays or other material advantages and cannot imply ideological commitment to the SED; those desiring personal advancement could not exclude themselves from the FDJ or FDGB, nor refuse national service. The mass organizations' rapid collapse in 1989–90 demonstrated that most members lacked true devotion. The huge votes for the Westernized CDU and the long-derided social democracy in March 1990 suggested that 40 years of ideological education and propaganda had hardly affected most East Germans.

In the early years most non-socialists simply distanced themselves from the mass organizations which were run by a small, overburdened nucleus. As career opportunities became increasingly dependent on socialist commitment through 'social activity', most people began to participate, but once they had gone through the motions they withdrew into a world which neglected SED values. Before 1961 it was still possible to leave the GDR, but thereafter there remained only internal emigration, centred on family life and, increasingly, Western television. Under Honecker the SED tacitly accepted that complete control, the hallmark of true totalitarianism, was impossible, and the SED even came to accept the population's essentially apolitical nature. The pressure to display constant socialist commitment diminished; even Western television became less of a taboo. Thus was established the 'niche society' in which most people, and even many SED members, combined public conformity and private indifference. By the 1980s, over two million were party members, but despite ideological training many were principally motivated by career development and outward appearances. The sharp membership decline during 1989–90 demonstrated the opportunism: the PDS retained only 10 per cent of its members.

The SED achieved little more than socialization to particular behavioural norms. The population grew accustomed to comprehensive kindergarten provision, FDGB holidays, workplace collectives, and to flag parades on national holidays. The SED even succeeded in divorcing most people from active Christianity. Certainly the population grew accustomed to 'real socialism', but general acceptance of broad socialist principles did not imply support for the SED once alternatives became possible. Had the bulk of the population been truly committed to socialism, instead of paying lip service to it for want of other options, the collapse of 1989–90 could never have occurred.

Alongside the true believers, the opportunists and the apolitical majority were those who consistently opposed SED rule. Initially these were mainly groups who lost status from the economic reorganization, but also traditional conservatives and liberals, many moderate social democrats, and unrepentant Nazis. The SED presented its opponents as a threat to anti-fascist democracy and established vigorous police control and repression to counter opposition, however mild, by groups or individuals.

Alongside the Soviet troops, which were particularly active in the first years, the principal organ was the Stasi, which considered itself the 'shield and sword of the party'. The Stasi infiltrated practically every sphere of life with undercover officers or 'informal colleagues' who reported dissident comments or activities. Knowledge of the Stasi's potential omnipresence prevented the public expression of most negative opinion and stifled much opposition at birth. The Stasi also actively coerced individuals and groups to loyalty to the SED. Even the churches, the only permitted organizations outside direct SED control, were infiltrated by Stasi officers.

The Stasi was ultimately unable to prevent the emergence in the 1970s and 1980s of new, more politically dangerous opponents angered by the contradiction between the SED's avowed peace policy and the GDR's role in the arms race, and by ecologists concerned about cavalier environmental policies. Protest also focused on human rights issues. Most dangerously, these opponents often appropriated socialist terminology, challenging the SED's ideological monopoly. In the 1980s many pastors allowed opposition meetings in the sanctuary of church buildings and made the churches' internal communications systems available. Though the Stasi succeeded in infiltrating many groups, it could not prevent enthusiasm for nuclear disarmament and environmentalism spreading amongst younger people for whom the SED's original anti-fascist legitimations appeared increasingly irrelevant.

Though the peace and environmental groups became known in the GDR, thanks largely to the Western media, hindsight has often over-estimated their importance. The groups' significance lay in their very existence as assembly points for the mass protests of late 1989. Public protests such as those in Leipzig in early 1988, though small-scale, demonstrated that not all opposition could be doused. However, the vast majority did not participate in such protests and remained unconcerned by the issues involved, reflecting the Stasi's enduring intimidatory strength and the abiding memory of June 1953. Despite widespread dissatisfaction among many of the inactive, for most citizens the causes remained linked to the increasing difficulties of everyday life and the continuing arbitrariness of bureaucratic decisions, particularly concerning visits to the West.

IV   Conclusions

In hindsight, it seems indisputable that the GDR's existence was guaranteed only for as long as this coincided with the USSR's interests and the Berlin Wall protected the economy against a mass exodus to the West. The repressed dissatisfaction felt by many who never openly protested before 1989 is reflected not only in the many applications for exit visas despite the personal disadvantages of such applications, but also in the rush to emigrate via Hungary in 1989. None the less, most of those already holidaying in Hungary when the borders opened returned home. Despite real socialism's difficulties, the GDR had become a home. While German unification or the end of SED rule seemed impossible, most people were prepared to live and work within the framework, and a significant proportion were dedicated to preserving it. Over 40 years a common identity developed; many citizens experienced pride in their country's achievements, without necessarily supporting the SED. The dichotomy between GDR identity and rejection of the SED found expression after 1989 in GDR nostalgia alongside the majority's clear desire to abandon 'real socialism'. This sense of community, fostered in adversity, must principally explain the GDR's enduring stability within the context of divided Europe, despite the distance between the SED and many of its subjects.

In explaining the GDR's relative long-term stability we must not neglect the many sincere adherents of socialism. The KPD/SED's claims to anti-fascist legitimacy achieved widespread acceptance both inside and outside the party, particularly immediately after 1945 when many saw salvation in a socialist future which would outlaw fascism; many felt the end was far more important than the means. Even in the early 1960s many remained optimistic that the SED could successfully build socialism and that the future belonged to the GDR, not the FRG. Only later, when the power structures and behaviour patterns were already established, was it apparent that socialism would not bring great material welfare. Many socialists nonetheless remained committed to the SED and almost unquestioningly accepted that a return to capitalism would mean less social welfare and raise the spectre of a fascist revival. This dedication to socialism was shared by many in the security services. Their role, alongside those who served the party and state apparatus for more opportunistic reasons, should not be overlooked. A stable GDR would not have survived for long if the majority of the population had continually and actively opposed it. This was a dictatorship in which many connived and with which most made their peace. So ingrained was the system after 40 years that even many who instigated the 1989 revolution envisaged reforming rather than overthrowing the GDR, which they hoped would retain a form of socialism. Against this background, questions of guilt and responsibility for the GDR as a political entity seem misplaced.

It is tempting to assume that the GDR was doomed to failure almost from the outset as a state founded and maintained against the will of its subjects. Certainly the GDR can be regarded as a dictatorship: the SED leadership and its many loyal and disciplined agents exerted fierce control over the rest of the population's lives, from frustrating careers to shooting would-be escapees at the border. However, historians who regard the June 1953 revolt as the root of eventual collapse neglect the fact that it was after 1953, if not 1961, that the GDR properly stabilized, at least in terms of individuals' outward conformity, if not of their inner commitment. The later economic collapse resulted from external pressures as well as the SED's economic mismanagement, which sacrificed much to ideological demands and the USSR's interests, even when these clashed with the GDR's. Meanwhile, social and political stability essentially remained until Gorbachov's accession in the USSR, his policies wilfully refuted, despite popular aspirations to a freer society, by Honecker, who correctly perceived in them the seeds of the system's destruction. Ultimately it was this external impetus which disrupted and ended SED rule in 1989, just as it had established it 43 years earlier.

Notes:

1. Deutscher Bundestag, 12. Wahlperiode 12/7820, 31.5.1994, 'Bericht der Enquete-Kommission, 'Aufarbeitung von Geschichte und Folgen der SED-Diktatur in Deutschland', p. 5.
2. *Ibid.*
3. See, for example, *ibid.* pp. 24–7, 33.
4. *Ansichten zur Geschichte der DDR* (1994), vol. 5, p. 7 (italics added).
5. Mitter, A., and Wolle, S., *Untergang auf Raten* (1993), p. 551.
6. Leonhard, W., *Die Revolution entläßt ihre Kinder* (1990), p. 440.
7. Niemann, Heinz, *Meinungsforschung in der DDR* (1993), p. 323.
8. Henderson, K., 'The Search for Ideological Conformity', *German History*, 10:3 (1992), pp. 321–2.

Select bibliography

Baring, A., *Uprising in East Germany* (1972).
Černý, J., Keller, D., and Neuhaus, M., *Ansichten zur Geschichte der DDR* (1994).
Childs, D., ed., *Honecker's Germany* (1985).

Childs, D., *The GDR. Moscow's German Ally* (1988).

Dennis, M., *German Democratic Republic. Politics, Economics and Society* (1988).

Fulbrook, M., *The Divided Nation: Germany 1918–1990* (1991).

Fulbrook, M., *Interpretations of the Two Germanies 1945–1990* (2000).

Fulbrook, M., *Anatomy of a Dictatorship. Inside the GDR 1949–1989* (1995).

McCauley, M., *The GDR since 1945* (1983).

Niemann, H. *Meinungsforschung in der DDR: Die geheimen Berichte des Instituts für Meinungsforschung an das Politbüro der SED* (1993).

Scharf, C.B., *Politics and Change in East Germany* (1984).

Sontheimer, K., and Bleek, W., *The Government and Politics of East Germany* (1975).

Staritz, D., *Geschichte der DDR, 1949–1985* (1985).

Thomanek, J.K.A., and Mellis, J., eds., *Politics, Society and Government in the German Democratic Republic: Basic Documents* (1988).

Weber, H., *DDR: Dokumente, 1945–1985* (1986).

Weber, H., *Die DDR 1945–1986* (1988).

Woods, R., *Opposition in the GDR under Honecker, 1971–85* (1986).

10

Ossis and *Wessis*: the creation of two German societies, 1945–1990

Mary Fulbrook

German society after the war was in a state of crisis. The images of ruined sky-lines, jagged shells of hollow buildings etched against the sky, and women and children in rags pushing cartloads of possessions through the heaps of rubble, are perhaps the most compelling visual summaries of this moment. Demographically, it was utterly skewed by the loss of men in the war (see Figure 10.1). German society was also a society on the move. The shifting of the eastern border to the Oder–Neisse frontier, and the loss of territories further east to the Soviet Union and Poland, unleashed the greatest population migration in central Europe for several centuries – a migration which had already started in the closing months of the war, as Germans fled in front of the advancing Red Army. And while refugees and expellees trekked westwards, numerous displaced persons, former prisoners of war, foreign workers and forced labourers, sought to return to their homes. In the first decade after the end of the war, around 12 million people who had formerly lived elsewhere were accommodated on the soil of West Germany – around one-fifth of the population of the Federal Republic were essentially 'immigrants'.

Nearly half a century later, when the Berlin Wall, that infamous symbol of the Cold War, was finally breached on 9 November 1989, Germans celebrated a sense of national reunification. Yet, within days – even hours – of the opening of the Wall, it became clear that West and East Germans had effectively become strangers to one another. Affluent, fashion-conscious Westerners gazed at East Germans in jeans and cheap black leather jackets queueing eagerly for taken-for-granted Western goods such

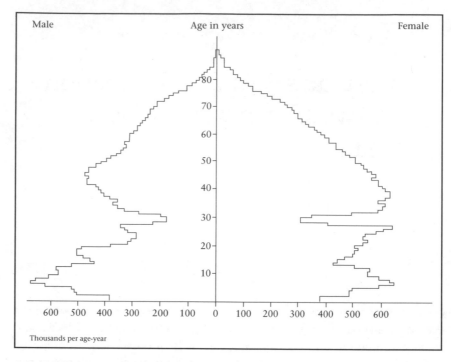

Figure 10.1   Age and sex structure, 1946

as bananas, oranges and stereo equipment. The differences were symbolized by the cars characteristic of each side: BMWs and Volkswagens versus Wartburgs and Trabants. Jokes about Trabis and bananas, about Deutschmark nationalism and the elbow society, proliferated as East and West Germans realised how little they appeared to have in common. The contrasts were not only with each other, but also with the common past. Both German societies had changed a great deal since the early post-war days.

There is as yet no established set of controversies over the comparative social history of the two Germanies – indeed, there is as yet no synthesis of East German social history at all, as relevant research materials have only become available since unification. Both public and scholarly attention has tended to focus on the political structures of the dictatorship. Any new approach to East German social history must both take seriously the impact of this dictatorship on society – indeed, the very deep impregnation of society by the state – but at the same time examine the ways in which society was resistant to political intrusion, or changed in directions which were unintended by the regime. This chapter first sketches general changes in the overall shape of society in the two German states, and then looks at the impact of these societal changes on different groups within society.

I Political division and societal history

Key societal differences were initially effected by the occupying powers. In the West, for all the problems with the term 'restoration', continuity rather than change was the rule. Although the major war criminals were brought to some kind of justice at the Nuremberg Trials, the more general denazification policies were of little long-term effect. By March 1946, denazification had been reduced to a matter of individual self-justification, and the process was essentially wound up with few long-term effects by the early 1950s. Similarly, by 1946 Britain and the USA had come to the view that it was in their interest to rebuild the West German economy. The announcement of the Marshall Plan in June 1947, and the introduction of the currency reform on 20 June 1948, consolidated this shift. There was only minimal restructuring of the capitalist system. Pressures for socialization of the mining industry were resisted and the measures proposed by the *Land* governments of Hesse and North-Rhine-Westphalia were vetoed. Despite an early determination to break up the highly cartelised German economy, there was effective resistance on the part of German entrepreneurs. The 'social market economy' associated with West Germany's first Economics Minister, Ludwig Erhard, differed in many respects from the much more state-directed economy of Nazi Germany; nevertheless, general continuities in the capitalist industrial system as a whole are more striking than specific differences.

Meanwhile, far more radical measures for restructuring were effected in the Soviet zone. In September 1945, about 7,000 agricultural estates of over 100 hectares (around 250 acres) in size were expropriated from their previous owners, and the land was divided and redistributed as small peasant plots or taken into state-owned farms. This land reform laid the basis for later collectivization of East German agriculture, and abolished the economic base – and the very existence – of the historically significant Prussian Junker class. Similarly drastic measures were adopted with respect to industry and finance, starting with the centralization of banking and insurance in July 1945. Over the following two years, many major industrial enterprises were expropriated (partly legitimated by a plebiscite in Saxony in 1946). Some industrial enterprises were taken into Soviet ownership as joint-stock companies (SAGs) as a part of their reparations policy; others became, from April 1948, state-owned *Volkseigene Betriebe* (VEBs). The SAGs were phased into East German state ownership as VEBs from 1949 to 1954. At the same time, denazification policies were deployed as a means to achieve significant shifts in personnel, particularly in areas which were of strategic political importance.

With the creation of two separate German states in 1949, early divergences were consolidated. West Germany was – primarily for political reasons at the start – tied into Western European economic arrangements (starting with the European Coal and Steel Community) which were the precursors of the European Economic Community in 1957 (later the European Community and eventually the European Union). In the 1950s the Federal Republic enjoyed its renowned 'economic miracle', with average annual growth rates of around 8 per cent. The early, rapid economic growth began to stabilize, and even falter, in the mid-1960s, and the German economy was adversely affected by the oil crises of 1973 and 1979 and the more general recession of the 1980s. Nevertheless, the West German economy continued to perform strongly in comparative terms, with the Deutschmark – almost a national monument – providing a benchmark of currency stability in Europe.

Economic development was accompanied by significant shifts in West German social structure. The old, heavy industries of the Ruhr were displaced in significance by the rise of high-tech industries. The European Common Agricultural Policy was accompanied by a decline in the proportion of the population working on the land. Thus the traditional blue-collar and agricultural sectors of society shrank in proportion to the number of white-collar workers and those employed in the service sector. From the later 1950s, but particularly after the flow of refugees from the GDR was stemmed by the erection of the Berlin Wall in 1961, there was a significant influx of foreign labour from the Mediterranean countries. By the late 1980s, West German society was marked by a combination of widespread affluence with pockets of poverty, particularly among the 'guest worker' communities. It was a much more urbanized society, with a majority of the population living in cities or large towns. It was, too, an ageing society: a declining birth rate, and the rising life expectancies of an older generation, put in jeopardy the implicit social contract of the insurance schemes covering West German health and well-being from cradle to grave.

The East German regime, under the leadership of the Communist SED, energetically pursued policies designed to transform the structure of East German society in rather different directions. In the summer of 1952, the building of socialism was announced. This included the first wave of the collectivization of agriculture, followed in 1960 by a second wave. By the later 1960s, most of the agriculturally productive land in the GDR was in fully collectivized farms (LPGs), which became increasingly specialized in the course of the 1970s and 1980s. At the same time, industry was subjected to state ownership and central planning and control. While major industrial enterprises had already been expropriated during the occupation period, in the 1950s remaining private enterprises were subjected to adverse, discriminatory measures, such that they shrank to a relatively insignificant sector of the East German economy. In 1958, many small enterprises were transformed into a rather curious category of mixed enterprises 'with state participation'; in 1972 these mixed enterprises were finally taken into state ownership. Only a few artisanal occupations remained in private hands in the 1970s and 1980s. Centralized economic planning was reformed in the New Economic System (NES) introduced in 1963, which gave more leverage to intermediate management levels. The political backwash of 1968 led, however, to a recentralization of the East German economy from 1970, although with a higher degree of specialization and more importance attached to consumer goods than was evident in the 1950s. Attention was focused on adequate housing and social policies.

Honecker's proclaimed 'unity of economic and social policy' was, however, ill-equipped to face the international economic crises of the 1970s and 1980s. The GDR had a number of advantages due to its unique situation in the Soviet bloc as a kind of stowaway in the EEC and poor twin of the affluent West. The GDR's economic difficulties were nevertheless only massaged and camouflaged, not cured, by injections of Western help such as the Strauß credit of 1983; and Honecker was increasingly unwilling to face up to the real economic problems. From the early 1980s, evidence of economic decline and, indeed, impending national bankruptcy, was largely ignored, as Honecker pursued his own blinkered policies at the expense of sober proposals for achieving economic viability. From both above and below, recognition of growing economic and environmental damage played a role in the implosion of the GDR in late 1989.

Differences in economic organization and levels of material affluence were not the only important factors shaping societal divergence. Just as important were differences in state/society relations. While West Germans enjoyed a diversity of political parties, social institutions, leisure clubs and so on, in East Germany the ruling communist party, the SED, sought to dominate society through state-run organizations. There was no area of work, social life or leisure which was not in some way controlled by one of the official institutions of party and state. The only partial exceptions were the churches, which, after an early period of persecution and hostility, eventually enjoyed a unique status as officially tolerated (if politically constrained) 'autonomous social institutions in socialist society'. Increasing control of East German society by the communist state was attempted with

some difficulty in the 1950s, but was one of the keys to the apparent
stability of East German society from the 1960s to the early 1980s.

Thus, over the 40 years from the foundation of the two states in 1949 to
the collapse of communist domination in the GDR in 1989, major
differences in political systems, regime policies, and roles in the international system had produced indelible marks on the two German societies.
At the same time, secular trends – industrialization, mechanization, the
shift away from heavy industry and from labour-intensive agricultural
techniques, the expansion of the service sector, the growth of computer
technologies – led to certain lines of development shared, although at
different speeds and to different extents, by the two German societies (see
Figures 10.2 and 10.3). What was the impact of these wider trends and
broader contexts on the constitution of particular social groups?

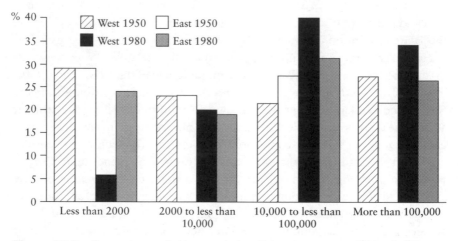

Figure 10.2 Percentage of the population living in communities of different
sizes in East and West Germany, 1950 and 1980

II   Elites and 'middle classes'

Striking differences in the social history of the two Germanies are evident
among the more privileged and elite groups. Despite the theoretical
'dictatorship of the proletariat' and associated 'withering away of the state'
predicted in Marx's theory of pure communism, the actually existing GDR
found itself in the 'transitional stage' of a Marxist–Leninist dictatorship of
the vanguard communist party. And despite the theoretical equality of
citizens in a Western democracy, real power, wealth and privilege remained
unequally distributed in the Federal Republic of Germany.

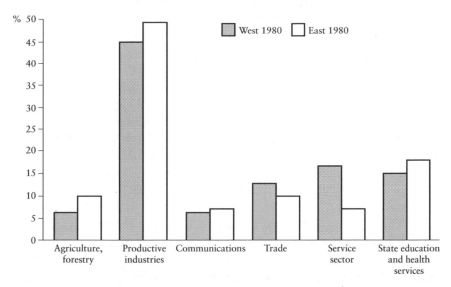

Figure 10.3   Employment by occupation type in East and West Germany (percentage)

At the apex of GDR society were, undoubtedly, the political bigwigs. Top politicians enjoyed a lifestyle and privileges to which the majority of the population were denied access. Many lived in the exclusive compound of Wandlitz, a little way north of Berlin, where – within walls – they could enjoy a relatively luxurious lifestyle, with Western goods available in well-stocked supermarkets, and leisure and sports facilities denied to the rest of the population. This compound was popularly known as Volvograd, on account of the chauffeur-driven Volvos; top individuals also had a variety of other 'perks of the job', such as exclusive hunting lodges and private country retreats, which (although essentially modest and petty-bourgeois by Western standards) unleashed a good deal of fury among East Germans when revealed in late 1989.

Below the truly powerful elite were far larger numbers of political and organizational functionaries, or official carriers of the regime. Closely associated with and under the control of the ruling communist SED were the affiliated bloc parties and mass organizations, the various levels of state and government, and the organs of control and coercion (see Chapter 9, above). The officials of these organizations formed a broader, but still relatively closely defined, functional elite under central SED control. Promising young people might find themselves caught in a complex situation: upward mobility was inevitably tied to a high degree of political conformity. Promotion was determined by political commitment, subordination to the vicissitudes of party discipline, and the selection mechanisms of *Kaderpolitik* (cadre politics). In the late 1940s and 1950s, this was preferably combined with a previously *dis*advantaged social background. In the 1960s, in particular, rapid upward social mobility was possible; but from the 1970s, social mobility was much less marked, and the East German elite began to reproduce itself, combined with a degree of ageing and stagnation. By the 1980s, some scholars have suggested that middle-rank functionaries were experiencing considerable frustration at the blocking of their career prospects by the older generation.

What of the broader middle classes? Given the GDR's changed social structure, the term 'intelligentsia' is often used rather than 'bourgeoisie'. Many traditionally 'bourgeois' occupations obviously shrank to relative insignificance in the GDR: small, independent shopkeepers, private firms, and other elements of what used to be called the *Besitzbürgertum* (property-owning bourgeoisie) disappeared almost by definition (although a very small number of independent enterprises managed to cling on). But other 'bourgeois' occupations in the GDR – traditionally the preserve of the *Bildungsbürgertum*, the professional or educated bourgeoisie – showed interesting lines of continuity, with some groups affected more than others.

Those professions which were highly politically relevant experienced the greatest changes. There was, for example, considerable turnover in legal personnel in the GDR, in marked contrast to West Germany. Although crucial to the regime's socialization policies, it took somewhat longer to weed out the educational profession. Despite a quite extensive early turnover of teachers, with rapidly trained *Neulehrer* (new teachers), barely older than their pupils, installed in the early months of the occupation period, unwelcome vestiges of a previous era nevertheless lingered in the 1950s and 1960s. However, over time, changes became apparent. Political control of schools became ever more intense, with active FDJ groups within schools and the careful vetting and disciplining of staff. Similarly, in higher education increasing political surveillance and control ensured a growing conformity, as well as fostering a degree of provincialization among the professoriate. Apart from the so-called *Reisekader*, those conformists with permits to travel, most academic staff had only restricted access to international publications and international conferences.

Members of the East German technical intelligentsia found themselves in a complex position: the regime both needed, and also to some extent feared, them. Insofar as they were prepared to toe a minimalist line of conformity, they enjoyed a relatively privileged position. In the course of the 1950s, incentives – such as higher incomes – were offered to highly skilled people (such as medical doctors) who might otherwise have been tempted to join the flow of refugees through the still-open border of Berlin to the West. In the 1960s, following the building of the Wall, Ulbricht's policies of modernisation were predicated on a belief in the 'technological-scientific revolution', and again technical expertise was accorded a relatively high status. The records suggest that, on the whole, members of the intelligentsia – in the broad sense used by GDR officials in compiling their own opinion reports – retained a rather cautious political stance in the GDR, tending to remain quiet on matters of political contention.

As far as the cultural sphere is concerned, the picture is also differentiated. There were many who were prepared to work on behalf of the regime through newspaper and magazine journalism, and the production of propaganda. Equally, in the more rarified sphere of 'highbrow culture' a significant handful explicitly supported the regime (such as Anna Seghers or Hermann Kant), in addition to those few who maintained a critical distance, but were sufficiently supportive, or useful for the regime's image abroad, to retain a high profile and relatively privileged status within the GDR (Stefan Heym, Christa Wolf). Others maintained some sort of disaffected distance from the regime, but clung on in some form within the GDR, while a prominent but comparatively tiny minority were forced or chose to leave (Wolf Biermann, Monika Maron, and others). If one includes pastors and priests under the cultural intelligentsia, then a quite complex picture emerges: the churches were left to denazify themselves after the war, which meant in the event a startling continuity of clerical personnel after the end of the Third Reich. But from the 1950s onwards, the SED adopted a highly proactive stance *vis-à-vis* the Protestant Churches in particular, seeking to infiltrate and influence their policies and personnel. By the 1980s, a highly ambiguous picture had emerged, in which state-sustaining as well as more dissident Christians could be found in prominent positions in the Protestant Churches (contrast Manfred Stolpe and Rainer Eppelmann, for example).

The price of any pursuit of professional interests – the prerequisite for which was appropriate higher education – was a degree of conformity. Those who refused to conform were excluded from straightforward career paths (often having to study theology and opt for a career in the church instead); outspoken critics suffered imprisonment or exile; but the majority chose to remain within defined parameters. It should also be remembered that an important and substantial minority of the GDR elite felt some enthusiasm for at least the ultimate goals, if not always the immediate means, of the Marxist–Leninist state. In any event, over time 'actually existing socialism' attained an air of permanence (accepted even in the West, with *Ostpolitik* and subsequent agreements) in which people made the best lives they could. By the 1980s, one in five of the adult population were members of the SED – a clear measure of outward conformity if not ideological commitment.

In the more open political conditions of West Germany, there was not the same degree of political constraint: nevertheless, despite multiple centres of power and social influence, this was far from being a completely egalitarian or genuinely pluralist society. Despite the explicit political break with Nazism in West Germany, there were marked continuities of personnel in the early post-war years. Many entrepreneurs and financiers who had known of, helped to finance, and benefited from the exploitation of slave labour in Nazi concentration camps, survived the momentary hiccups of denazification to continue their economic successes under democratic auspices in the 1950s. A striking continuity of personnel within the legal profession was also – or should have been – something of a moral blight for the new *Rechtsstaat* (state based on law). The restoration of jobs and pensions to civil servants who had served under Hitler was ensured under a controversial piece of legislation in 1951.

Quite apart from the question of continuities with the Nazi period, which inevitably faded in salience over time, there were powerful inbuilt tendencies towards the reproduction of social inequalities. Although the old Prussian/German aristocracy had lost its social basis as a landowning caste, its prestige and influence lingered on, bearing witness to the power of 'cultural capital': many historically resonant names (often prefaced by 'von') could be found among leading professional, economic and political circles of West Germany. Moreover, in a country where many *Länder* (regional states) retained a tripartite (rather than comprehensive) school system, educational qualifications often served as credentials legitimating the reproduction of social status: high school leaving qualifications (the *Abitur*), a university degree, and often also a doctorate, were strongly correlated with a privileged social background. West German employers, managers and politicians – and even trade unions – enjoyed a degree of structural and cultural closeness, often institutionalized (as in the preparation of policies for parliamentary legislation). The importance of political parties in making nominations for key posts (even including university chairs and directors of institutes) also tended to reproduce an establishment.

Generational and cultural changes, particularly after the eruptions of the later 1960s, began to erode these patterns, while the rise of new social movements and citizens' initiatives in the 1970s and 1980s challenged the inbuilt structures of power and decision-making. Moreover, creative writers, film-makers, visual artists and other culturally creative spirits adopted an explicitly and self-consciously critical role. Controversies over the character of West German society and identity were often played out in the highbrow media, with contributions from writers such as Günter Grass, the left-liberal philosopher Jürgen Habermas, and (as in the so-called historians' dispute of 1986–7) philosophers and historians ranging from Ernst Nolte and Michael Stürmer on the right to scholars of a more left-liberal persuasion such as Hans-Ulrich Wehler, Jürgen Kocka and others.

At the same time, the more general socioeconomic changes described in the previous section led to changes in the character of the middle classes. Rapid economic growth in West Germany was accompanied, at the lower levels, by a significant expansion of the proportion of employees in white-collar work and the service sector compared to traditional blue-collar jobs. This led to a widespread perception of upward social mobility which was, in fact, a function of changes in the shape of the social structure as a whole, rather than increased mobility (both upwards and downwards) across dividing lines within a static social structure. Thus it was possible that by the late 1980s – particularly for those blind to the presence of a largely foreign underclass – West Germany appeared to be a predominantly affluent, urban and well-educated society.

III   Workers and peasants

The GDR claimed to be a 'workers' and peasants' state'. The workers, in particular, were allotted a leading role – but only through their vanguard party, the Marxist–Leninist SED, whose task it was to try to transform the actually existing consciousness of the East German working class into what it ideally ought to be. Hence, in practice, the experience of most workers in the GDR was not quite along the idealistic lines originally envisaged by Karl Marx. The psychological experience of alienation was not removed at one stroke of the philosopher's pen as private enterprises were transformed into 'people's own enterprises' (VEBs). But, at the same time, the experience of blue-collar work in the GDR was more complex and multifaceted than might be thought when the only comparison is with the obviously more affluent and liberal West.

Wages and standards of living were much lower than in the West. But job security was assured: there was no official unemployment. Both the right and the duty to work were enshrined in the 1968 constitution. Sociological surveys of workers in the 1970s show that a sense of *Geborgenheit*, or security, was rated rather highly by workers who otherwise showed a quite realistic sense of adverse comparisons with the West on factors like wages and working conditions.

Having a job did not necessarily mean actually working at full capacity; there were many bottlenecks in supplies, for example, of raw materials or spare parts, which meant that production was often faltering and long periods of under-employment were experienced. Both wages and conditions of work varied quite widely with the sector of industry. In some areas, particularly highly sensitive fields such as uranium mining, appalling conditions of work and an almost wilful disregard for health and safety considerations were accompanied by high rates of pay and short-term benefits. In others, a long and tedious day in poor conditions was matched only by the pinched miseries of a low income and poor housing conditions, ameliorated only marginally by the high level of state subsidies for basic foodstuffs, transport and rent.

The representation of workers' interests in the workers' and peasants' state was also somewhat ambiguous. Many felt that the official trade union, the FDGB (which enjoyed a membership covering, according to the official statistics, slightly more than the total number of people officially in work) hardly represented their interests, and the FDGB's records are full of complaints about paying membership dues when there was no chance of affecting wages and conditions through union action as in the West. And, despite frequent unofficial work stoppages (most spectacularly on 17 June 1953), there was no right to strike in the GDR. On the other hand, some research suggests that workers' brigades performed useful functions as transmission belts for the representation of interests, and the FDGB records also reveal on occasion a real concern with ironing out problems in the workplace and listening to workers' complaints: there is no automatic conception of management always being right.

Many workers too seem to have continued a long-standing tradition in Germany of pride in their work, and enjoyment of the companionship of comrades: the workplace cannot be viewed as simply a location of oppression. Feelings of solidarity among workplace colleagues – who did not have to compete with one another for scarce jobs, or fear redundancy – were one element of the post-1989 'ostalgia', or nostalgia for at least partly 'good old days'. But some aspects were less welcome, such as the constant campaigns for increased productivity (which mostly meant enhanced exploitation of labour) in which an enforced collective competitive spirit was to take the place of market forces or real incentives. And ultimately – as 1989 showed – many workers were prepared to vote with their feet and head for higher wages and living conditions in the West if offered the opportunity.

In West Germany, a shrinking working class enjoyed increasing affluence and shorter working hours in a society where inequalities of wealth remained large. Implicitly, workers agreed that it was better to make a bigger cake than to argue over the way the cake was cut. Early post-war trade union radicalism was tamed under the influence of the Marshall Plan and the Americanization of industrial culture. The new, streamlined system of trade unions cooperated with management to ensure the smooth functioning of the capitalist economy. Although agreements in 1951, 1952 and 1976 relating to co-determination and works' councils were by no means uncontroversial – seen by some employers as too much of a concession, and by many workers as not enough – labour relations in the Federal Republic were comparatively smooth. In the 1950s, demands for wage increases were restrained, and over the following three decades the Federal Republic enjoyed a reputation as a relatively low-strike economy. Moreover, factors such as mechanization, computerization, and the shift away from heavy industry, as well as the fact that many of the lowest paid jobs were taken by *Gastarbeiter*, meant that ever fewer West Germans identified themselves as members of the blue-collar working class.

With the mechanization of agriculture and EC subsidies, flight from the land was the most marked feature of West German rural life, with a dramatic decline in the proportion of the population working on the land to little over 5 per cent in the 1980s. Many farmers found it more profitable to turn over at least some of their land and rooms in their farmhouses to a growing tourist industry – bed-and-breakfast accommodation and leisure pursuits took the place of tilling the fields. As the percentage of people living in small villages and hamlets shrank, from a little under a third (29 per cent) of the population in 1950 to only 6 per cent of West Germans in 1980, so too the character of these small communities changed. No longer relatively cut off from the outside world, they were increasingly linked up by improved communications: fast roads, television and the telephone combined with tourism to transform the character of rural life in West Germany.

The character of rural life was transformed in East Germany, too, but in rather different ways. For one thing, there was not the dramatic shrinking of the rural population experienced in the West: the percentage of the East German population living in communities of less than 2,000 declined only marginally, from 29 per cent in 1950 (the same as West Germany) to 24 per cent – still around a quarter of the population – in 1980. Nor did communications improve so dramatically: roads remained somewhat parlous and potholed in many areas, public transport was irregular and infrequent (if cheap), and although the possession of television sets increased in the 1970s and 1980s, only a small percentage of the population (9 per cent in 1988) had a telephone at home – and most of this 9 per cent was to be found among the political elite in towns. On the other hand, while to all outward appearances rural society in East Germany looked remarkably unchanged (the villages retaining a dusty, old-fashioned appearance, with cobbled, relatively traffic-free streets and little appearing to be happening), as far as the social organization of agriculture and the character of peasant life was concerned the changes were far-reaching. The expropriation of large estates, and later collectivization of agriculture, significantly affected the character of rural life. Agricultural workers were no longer tied to the estates of particular landowners, nor were they peasants in their own right, but rather they worked on collectivized farms which were essentially run as increasingly specialized enterprises. In comparison at least with the peasant agriculture of neighbouring Poland, the much more mechanized

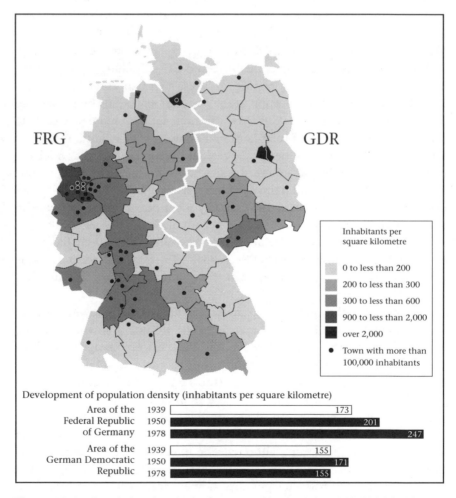

Figure 10.4   Population density and towns with more than 100,000 inhabitants

and large-scale agriculture of East Germany was relatively productive, although it could not compare with West German agriculture's sheltered and privileged position in the European Community.

IV   Cross-cutting patterns of social identity

Many social identities, such as gender, youth, generation, region, ethnicity and religion, cross-cut socioeconomic classes. While the Federal Republic introduced policies directly affecting some of these areas, more strenuous efforts were made by the GDR regime, often with unintended and even counter-productive consequences.

In West Germany, once the early post-war heyday of the *Trümmerfrauen* (women working in the rubble) was over, women's roles tended to revert to the traditional 'three Ks' of children, kitchen, church (*Kinder, Küche, Kirche*). Despite constitutional and legal commitments, and despite an increasingly vocal middle-class women's movement in the West, simple factors such as lack of sufficient affordable childcare worked against full equality in the workplace: women remained predominantly in part-time and lower-paid occupations, and often worked out of economic necessity rather than for self-realization or career fulfilment (although there were key changes over time, as in political participation and visibility). In the GDR, economic priorities combined with ideological commitment to dictate the full participation of women in the paid labour force. A combination of factors including extensive child care facilities (crèche, kindergarten, after-school care, even boarding facilities), abortion on demand within the first 12 weeks of pregnancy (introduced in 1972), and – to reverse the declining birth rate – the subsequent introduction of generous maternity leave and benefits meant that, by the 1980s, fully half the workforce was female. However, despite rough numerical equality as far as participation in education, training and employment was concerned, women remained predominantly in lower status jobs, in lower positions within hierarchies, and (with one or two notable exceptions) never gained a serious foothold in the higher echelons of politics. Moreover, many East German women continued to bear the brunt of domestic responsibilities in the privacy of their own homes (where a traditional division of labour proved rather reluctant to wither away). For many women the lack of real personal choice, and the combination of a traditional domestic role with paid employment, were experienced less as 'emancipation' than as a 'double burden'.

As with gender, biological age may have very different meanings for different social classes, under different circumstances. Babies and toddlers in the GDR were more likely to experience institutional care and enforced conformity (even in such matters as being lined up in crèche like a work brigade for potty training) than to enjoy the more child-centred, individualized early socialization of West German youngsters who tended to stay at home until starting school at the age of six. While the West German young were exposed to a self-conscious and sometimes awkward attempt at active democratization, East German schoolchildren learned to repeat the official shibboleths and never step out of line. Heavy priority was given to seeking to capture the minds and hearts of the rising generation, through a wide variety of organizations (the Ernst Thälmann Youth Organization, Young Pioneers, Free German Youth) and indoctrination. As early as 1954, a secular state ceremony, the *Jugendweihe*, was introduced as an alternative to confirmation in church and, through very serious sanctions against those who refused, a means of pressurizing children to conform. But the SED's attempts at the enforced production of socialist personalities were not entirely successful. Youth non-conformity was a constant thorn in the flesh of the East German authorities. Fighting the cultural (and hence political) influence of the decadent West, from the Elvis Presley/rock 'n' roll crazes of the 1950s via beat music and jazz in the 1960s to the rock concerts of the 1980s, was a perpetual preoccupation of the East German regime, reflected in extensive records in the Central Party Archives. Youth disaffection and youth revolt were, in different ways, of political importance in West German social history, too, particularly in the 1960s, with the student revolts, youth demonstrations, and challenges to the *spießbürgerlich* amnesia of a repressed past, and – in very different vein – later with a rising concern about drug abuse among the young.

Generation in both Germanies proves to be an important and often overlooked category of analysis. In Germany after 1945, there are certain key generations which may be delineated, even if rather crudely and in inchoate terms. There is the generation of those who experienced the Third Reich as adults, which one might call the deeply divided KZ (concentration camp) generation, including as it did both those *Mitläufer* who sustained the Nazi regime, and those of their opponents who had survived incarceration or exile. This generation was crucial to the establishment of the two German states, and it was the bitter experiences of the latter, the anti-fascists, who stamped their mark on the legitimating credentials of the GDR, while it was the former who lent an aura of uneasy suspicion to the democratic virtues of the first years of the Federal Republic. The 'HJ-generation' consisted of those slightly younger Germans socialized under the Third Reich through such organizations as the Hitler Youth (hence 'HJ') or its sister organization, the League of German Girls (*Bund deutscher Mädel*, BdM). Some analysts have argued that it was this 'HJ generation' that proved to be particularly reliable and conformist 'carriers' of the two new German regimes. It is possible that many GDR functionaries of this generation, whose political conformity was rewarded with rapid promotion in the 1960s, proved particularly loyal in state service until, in middle age in the 1980s, they found their paths to the very top blocked by a generation of elderly politicians. There was, then, in the GDR, what might be called the FDJ generation, socialized through the East German Free German Youth organization, perhaps paralleled by the '68'ers' of the Federal Republic; both were stamped by formative socialization experiences within (and often in reaction against) the opposing political systems; it was, interestingly, the FDJ generation that spearheaded the revolution of 1989. Of course, it should be added, not everyone born in certain years would necessarily identify with everything (or even anything) implied by these generational labels.

Germany has historically been characterized by great regional variations (see earlier chapters in this book). The federal structure of West Germany allowed many regional differences and identities to be preserved through the decentralized *Länder*. The geographically smaller, less densely populated and politically highly centralized East German state started to

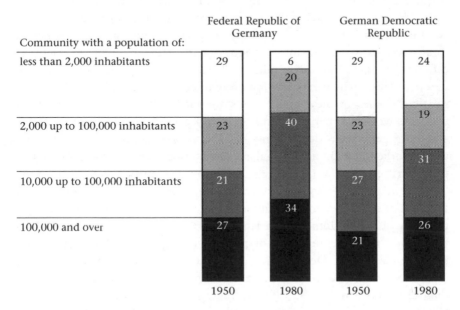

Community with a population of:	Federal Republic of Germany		German Democratic Republic	
	1950	1980	1950	1980
less than 2,000 inhabitants	29	6	29	24
		20		
2,000 up to 100,000 inhabitants	23	40	23	19
				31
10,000 up to 100,000 inhabitants	21		27	
		34		
100,000 and over	27			26
			21	

Figure 10.5 Distribution of population by percentage in communities of different sizes

iron out regional differences, particularly after the *Länder* were replaced by the smaller *Bezirke* in 1952. Nevertheless, some regional cultures in the GDR proved resistant to change, particularly where rooted in socio-economic differences (rural Mecklenburg versus the industrial south) or where fostered by the state (for reasons of tourism or international respectability). The Sorb community in the southeastern region of the GDR enjoyed a special status, with dual-language signs and the protection of local customs, although urbanization and assimilation into the industrial working class tended to dissolve the conditions for the survival of an essentially rural culture and language community. Regional identities can be (re-)created: it was relatively easy, after the fall of the Wall, for areas such as the Catholic Eichsfeld – previously severed by the Iron Curtain – to resurrect its distinctive Catholic identity, or for a re-established Thuringia to claim that it was the 'heart' of Germany.

As far as minority communities were concerned, the position in West Germany was one of ambiguity and mixed messages. West Germany's citizenship laws were based on the Law of 1913, and consolidated by the loss of territories in 1945: they embodied an essentially ethnic/cultural concept of 'German-ness', which bestowed rights of citizenship on those who had been citizens of Germany in the borders of 31 December 1937 (i.e. prior to Nazi expansion) and their descendants; qualifications for acquiring citizenship included tightly defined cultural and economic criteria. Although those excluded from citizenship on racial grounds in 1935 were given some priority in regaining their citizenship, officially ordained 'philo-Semitism' (being nice to Jews, while still stereotyping them as different) in the 1950s ran at odds with widespread popular anti-Semitism in a population where very few Jews remained in any event. And the rather restrictive rules on new applications for citizenship left even long-term residents who had been born and bred in West Germany, such as second- and third-generation descendants of *Gastarbeiter* (euphemistically termed guest workers), without political representation, while 'ethnic Germans' from territories lost to Germany after 1945 were entitled to 'return' to the 'homeland', even if they and their ancestors had never set foot on the soil that became the Federal Republic. At the same time, West Germany's uniquely liberal asylum laws (a legacy of the guilt incurred by the Third Reich) led to rising numbers of people seeking political asylum in the Federal Republic. Despite the substantial numbers involved, West Germany's conservative political elites continued to maintain the stance that 'Germany is not a country of immigration'. In a sense, they were right: Germany had a long tradition of relying on migrant labour for economic reasons, while preserving a restrictive definition of citizenship. But it was at

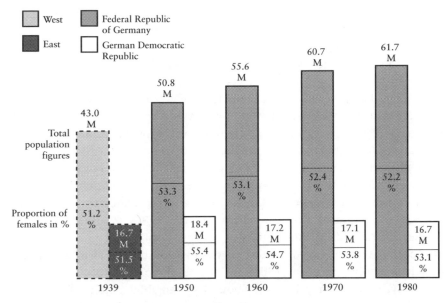

Figure 10.6   Population growth (in millions)

a considerable social, economic and political cost as far as the immigrant communities were concerned.

Despite its proclaimed internationalism, the numbers of foreign workers in the GDR were very much smaller and were largely kept apart from the local population. Workers from countries such as Mozambique and Cuba were kept in segregated hostels. Occasional workplace incidents involving foreigners which are reported in the FDGB files suggest a residual degree of racism among East German workers (which included rather traditional anti-Polish sentiments), but under the restrained political conditions obtaining in the GDR this never attained the degree of public impact experienced in West Germany. Nor did the GDR define citizenship in such restricted ethnic/cultural terms, particularly after its shift to a class definition of nation in the 1970s, although it has to be added that the GDR never enjoyed quite the same pressure from immigrants for citizenship as did its more affluent Western twin – rather the reverse.

Religion is, and has been for centuries, a key aspect of identity in Germany. Here too, political division determined a marked divergence in the social meaning of religion and the roles of the churches. In West Germany after the war, the massive influx of refugees diluted previously relatively homogenous and insulated Catholic and Protestant communities, which had in some areas virtually preserved the religious–political boundaries of 1648. Although the churches as institutions retained considerable importance in West German life, processes of secularization tended to make religious practice (if not belief) less widespread among the population over the following decades. In the GDR, which had a predominantly Protestant population in 1949 (around 15 million Protestants and one million Catholics in a total population of around 17 million), massive campaigns against Christianity in the 1950s were followed by a more muted, but no less insidious, attempt to co-opt the churches. This culminated in the separation of the East German Protestant churches from their all-German links in 1969, the development of the notion of a 'church within socialism', and the church-state agreement of 6 March 1978. The latter, however, backfired as far as the state was concerned, and gave religion a heightened political salience in the 1980s (countering earlier tendencies towards secularization as in the West), and in turn led to significant involvement of Protestant pastors and other Christians in the dissident movements of the 1980s and the revolution of 1989.

Finally, a word may be said about less tangible matters. Given the intrusion of the state into virtually every aspect of East German life, including the high politicization of leisure activities and sport (which was less a matter of individual enjoyment than national prestige), there was no area of life entirely free from a degree of collectivization and pressure. This inevitably had its effects on social psychology. Restraint and suspicion (at times based in fear of Stasi surveillance), along with feelings of solidarity rather than competition, were widely prevalent (though far from universal) and ambiguous modes of being among citizens of the GDR. These patterns of interpersonal relations were in some contrast to varying behavioural patterns evident in the very different political conditions in the West. The old definition that 'social history is history with the politics left out' could hardly be less apposite.

V   The fractured nation

This brief survey has sought to sketch some of the ways in which society in the two German states diverged over 40 years of separation. There were, of course, common elements, relating not only to a common past, but also to general trends such as industrialization, revolutions in technology, a changing international culture, and the prevalence of the mass media (with television insidiously invading through a porous Iron Curtain). Family links were maintained, with particular salience for those living on the eastern side of the Wall. There were common interests in peace and *détente* in central Europe. The remilitarization of both states in 1955–6 was accompanied on both sides of the Iron Curtain by distinctive pacifist voices, if more muted and suppressed in the GDR (where, following the introduction of conscription in 1962, the church was able to win an alternative form of military service in 1964, not bearing weapons). The social movements and identity politics in the West in the 1970s found parallels in the new political activism of peace initiatives, environmentalist and human rights groups in the far more difficult political conditions of the GDR in the 1980s.

But for all the refractions of similar trends through different political prisms, perhaps the most striking feature of German social history after 1945 is the growing divergence of the two German societies. Despite some limited but clear breaks with the Nazi past in the West immediately after defeat (particularly with respect to political and military elites), in its first two decades West German society was essentially marked by continuity, followed eventually by delayed processes of rupture and change from the later 1960s. East German society followed a different timescale: massive early structural transformation was followed from the 1960s by social stabilization, even – by the 1980s – stagnation. Ultimately, a common language, a common heritage, and a residual sense of common national identity, were fractured by deep-rooted and extensive differences in the very constitution of social classes, life chances, cultural attitudes and patterns of behaviour. In short, the people had been constituted to become quite different social beings in the two German states.

Select bibliography

With the opening of the East German archives, there is much new research on the social history of the GDR: however, the early fruits of this research are still largely available only in German. This select bibliography therefore includes some slightly older English-language classics and textbooks which have not as yet been replaced by new syntheses, as well as a selection of recent German publications including some excellent collections of essays and source materials.

Baylis, T., *The Technical Intelligentsia and the East German Elite* (1974).
Berghahn, V., *The Americanisation of West German Industry* (1986).
Bessel, R. and Jessen, R., eds., *Die Grenzen der Diktatur* (1996).
Budde, G.-F., ed., *Frauen arbeiten. Weibliche Erwerbstätigkeit in Ost- und Westdeutschland nach 1945* (1997).
Childs, D., ed., *Honecker's Germany* (1985).
Dennis, M., *Social and Economic Modernization in Eastern Germany from Honecker to Kohl* (1993).
Fulbrook, M., *Anatomy of a Dictatorship: Inside the GDR, 1949–1989* (1995).
Helwig, G. and Nickel, H. M., eds., *Frauen in Deutschland 1945–1992* (1993).

Hennlg, W. and Friedrich, W., eds., *Jugend in der DDR. Daten und Ergebnisse der Jugendforschung vor der Wende* (1991).

Hübner, P. and Tenfelde, K., eds., *Arbeiter in der SBZ-DDR* (1999).

Hübner, P., ed., *Eliten in Sozialismus. Beiträge zur Sozialgeschichte der DDR* (1999).

Hübncr, P., *Konsens, Konflikt und Kompromiß. Soziale Arbeiterinteressen und Sozialpolitik in der SBZ/DDR 1945–1970* (1995).

Jarausch, K., ed., *Dictatorship as Experience* (1999).

Kaelble, H., Kocka, J. and Zwahr, H. eds., *Sozialgeschichte der DDR* (1994).

Kleßmann, C., *Die doppelte Staatsgründung* (1982).

Kleßmann, C., *Zwei Staaten, eine Nation* (1988).

Kleßmann, C. and Wagner, G. eds., *Das gespaltene Land: Leben in Deutschland 1945 bis 1990: Texte und Dokumente* (1993).

Kocka, J., ed., *Historische DDR-Forschung* (1993).

Kolinsky, E., *Women in West Germany* (1989).

Krejci, J., *Social Structure in Divided Germany* (1976).

Ludz, P. C., *The Changing Party Elite in East Germany* (1972).

Maaz, Hans-Joachim, *Behind the Wall: The Inner Life of Communist Germany*, transl. (1995).

Mayer, G., *Die DDR-Machtelite in der Ära Honecker* (1991).

Naimark, Norman, *The Russians in Germany* (1995).

Ostow, Robin, *Jews in Contemporary East Germany* (1989).

Vollnhals, C., ed., *Entnazifizierung* (1991).

Wallraff, G., *Lowest of the Low* (1988).

Winkler, G., ed., *Frauenreport '90* (1990).

11

Culture, history and national identity in the two Germanies, 1945–1999

Erica Carter

It is late August 1992, and the attention of the international press fixes on the port town of Rostock on the Baltic coast. On 24 August, a group of youths begin a campaign of violence against asylum seekers housed in hostels in the Lichtenhagen suburb of the city. Over the next few days, the hostel and neighbouring buildings will be ransacked, cars will be torched, police and 'foreigners' physically assaulted – all to an accompanying chorus of 'Germany to the Germans: foreigners out!'

But what press reports will emphasize is not only the damage done in Rostock to buildings and material possessions, or even the physical aggression that has by 1992 become so much a part of life for immigrants and asylum seekers in post-unification Germany. Public anxiety will centre instead on the bizarre response to the riots from the ordinary citizens of Lichtenhagen. In anti-foreigner riots in the Saxon town of Hoyerswerda one year earlier, crowds of local residents had gathered to support the rioters with shouts of encouragement, applause, or other gestures of approbation. In Rostock, too, it is not until Thursday 29 August that 2,000 demonstrators will register a protest against the racist excesses of the riots. For now, the rioters are accompanied by a crowd of bystanders whose stance towards the events appears as one of staunch, if muted approval. The Austrian news magazine *Profil* sums up the outrage of commentators at home and abroad when it writes of the Rostock riots: 'not only have several hundred marauding skinheads and violent youths seen themselves as justified in taking the law into their own hands; their actions have been accepted, indeed welcomed by the people of Lichtenhagen.' This is, concludes the magazine, 'a caesura in postwar German history'.[1]

In both Germanies after the war, mainstream culture at least paid lip service to a prohibition on behaviour that recalled the anti-Semitic and racist excesses of National Socialism. In the GDR, which claimed an identity as an anti-fascist state, popular xenophobia and anti-Semitism (of which there were certainly numerous instances) were officially suppressed. In the Federal Republic, the state's position was more contradictory. While on the one hand, far-right parties that publicly preached racism (the nationalist NPD or the new right Republikaner Party) were officially tolerated, as was widespread popular hostility to so-called guest workers, the 1949 constitution, on the other hand, outlawed discrimination on grounds of sex, descent, race, language, homeland, origin, faith, religion or political opinions.

When this constitutional promise of tolerance was flouted in Hoyerswerda, Rostock and elsewhere, many observers made connections with the nationalist fervour that had surrounded unification in 1990. The Federal Republic had demanded of its citizens a loyalty to the constitution and the rule of law. Events in the early 1990s suggested, however, a swing in popular allegiance to more archaic forms of national belonging. Many in Germany seemed now to identify most strongly, not with visions of Germany as a modern nation state founded on democratic government and the rule of law, but with primordial appeals to an ethnically pure *Volk* whose identity was sustained by the exclusion of alien or foreign elements: witness the Rostock slogan, 'Germany to the Germans – foreigners out!'

I   National culture and identity in the two Germanies

It has been a regular contention of political history that nationalism was a spent force in post-war Germany. Certainly, political nationalism was actively suppressed in the GDR, and remained in the FRG the preserve of fringe parties on the far right. In the context of that analysis, however, something of a historical riddle is presented by the resurgence in the early 1990s of right-wing nationalism, in the guise not only of anti-foreigner violence in Rostock and elsewhere, but of increased popular and electoral support for the ultraright. The far right garners much of its support from groups at the socioeconomic margins: from disaffected youth, the unemployed, the socially disadvantaged. But what gave their politics of despair its nationalist inflection, if post-war nationalism was indeed as effectively suppressed as existing historiography would claim?

In the rest of this chapter, we will trace some of the ways in which a cultural history of post-war Germany might begin to answer that question. The hypothesis that frames the following account is that, while the ethnic nationalism that made such a disturbing reappearance in the early 1990s was for many decades suppressed, or at least marginalized from political life, both post-war Germanies experienced persistent difficulties in overcoming the problematic *cultural* legacy of authoritarian nationalism.

That argument is advanced in full cognizance of the pitfalls of ascribing to the two Germanies after 1945 a common national culture or shared national identity. After unification in 1990, it became clear that 40 years of separate development had produced sharp cultural differences between so-called *Ossis* and *Wessis* (inhabitants of the GDR and FRG respectively – see Chapter 10 above). The distinctions begin at the level of language; thus studies in comparative linguistics have registered, not only lexical differences, but national (as opposed to regional and dialect-based) variations in grammar, spoken and written style and register. East–West divisions were further cemented by the emergence of distinct education systems: the one, in the FRG, based on a three-tier structure that tended to cement class-cultural hierarchies from secondary level; the other, in the GDR, structured according to strictly egalitarian principles (though these were not always realized in the often authoritarian classroom practice of GDR schools). Some of the divergent tendencies in the literature, arts and mass media of the GDR and FRG will be traced later in this chapter; and these will illustrate – as does, at greater length, Mary Fulbrook's chapter in this book – that there is good reason for caution about attributing to the former GDR and FRG a common national culture, or a shared national identity. The organization, not only of the political systems of the two German states, but also of cultural forms, practices and institutions around the opposing philosophies of socialist collectivism versus Western liberal individualism, produced an apparently ever-widening gulf between the cultural identities of the two Germanies East and West.

II   Two Germanies: a common cultural heritage

Or did it? While German division produced a clear divergence between socialist and capitalist cultural forms, the FRG and the GDR continued to share a common – and highly problematic – cultural heritage. Cultural debates in both states returned repeatedly to German fascism, and focused on the extent to which the Nazi past had been 'overcome'. The issue of *Vergangenheitsbewältigung* (overcoming the past), moreover, was not only related in those debates to Nazism and the Third Reich. The Nazi vision of a racially pure culture embodying the spiritual essence of *Volk* and Reich was certainly the most repugnant version of cultural nationalism that German history had produced: but it was by no means without historical precedent. From the late eighteenth century, aspirations for a German nationhood achieved politically, through the formation of a democratic nation state, existed in tension with a cultural nationalist and Romantic vision of a German identity grounded in folk, blood and soil. That *völkisch* conception of national identity, though officially rejected by both post-war German states, continued even after 1945 to shape popular conceptions of national belonging and citizenship. In the GDR, which claimed for itself a supranational identity as a state rooted in international socialism, political nationalism was officially reviled; but a cultural nationalist structure of feeling survived in policies and practices that suppressed social difference in all its various forms. Homosexuality, for instance, was decriminalized in the GDR in the early 1970s – unlike the FRG, which retained Paragraph 174 of the Civil Code that rendered homosexuality a criminal offence. The everyday experience of lesbians and gay men in the GDR, by contrast, was one of official intolerance and public vilification. Similarly, the largest indigenous ethnic minority, the Sorbs, were officially feted for their contri-bution to national culture in the GDR; yet in reality, Sorb communities were uprooted and local cultures fragmented by large-scale resettlement through the 1970s and 1980s, when the regime identified Sorb territory in the southeast GDR as the main source of raw materials (lignite, or 'brown coal') to feed post-1971 industrial expansion. A further example: the tiny minority of foreign workers and students from socialist states in the developing world (Angola, Mozambique, Vietnam) was in theory more politically integrated in the GDR than in the West. Thus they enjoyed a right to vote in local elections that was never granted to migrant workers in the West. In fact, however, since they lived largely in hostels or barracks, and since integration programmes in schools, universities or local communities were non-existent, migrant minorities remained on the social margins. As one post-1989 commentator on minority issues in the former GDR put it 'the exclusion of everything "alien," or more precisely, of everything defined as alien, is by no means a new phenomenon or a western import, but a reaction familiar from the old days of the SED – just one of the many means by which GDR society sought to sustain its own identity'.[2]

In the FRG, the same tension between official guarantees of minority equality, and actual sociocultural exclusion, was visible for much of the post-war period. Here however, that contradiction is explicitly inscribed in two conflicting passages of the constitution. On the one hand, the opening articles of the Basic Law embraced liberal-democratic definitions of the citizenry as a political community enjoying equal rights and civil liberties.

Yet this sociopolitical model of citizenship was undermined by later sections of the constitution which proffered instead an ethnically based and culturally exclusionary definition. The Federal Republic was until the late 1990s unique among Western European states in basing access to citizen status, not on *ius soli* (citizenship by territory), but *ius sanguinis* (citizenship by blood). Thus Article 116 of the Basic Law defined as an FRG citizen 'everyone ... who, as a refugee or expellee of German ethnicity [*Volkszugehörigkeit*], or as a spouse or descendant of such a person, has been admitted to the territory of the German Reich as it existed on 31 December 1937.'

Even the Basic Law, then, failed to resolve the contradiction between classical liberal models of the nation state as a political community of equal citizens, and Romantic nationalist conceptions of an ethnically defined nation. The effects of that contradiction were most keenly felt in the post-war Federal Republic by the large migrant minority that, by the mid-1990s, constituted over 8 per cent of the German population. This substantial minority was lauded by successive post-war governments for its economic contribution to national life. As the CDU apologist for multiculturalism, Heiner Geißler, put it in 1991 'the German economy ... needs foreigners as a labour force, as consumers and as taxpayers'.[3] And yet this public celebration of migrant minorities as participants in the national economy was rarely matched by the sociopolitical recognition of 'foreigners' as equal citizens. Unlike second- or third-generation ethnic Germans from eastern Europe – the so-called *Aussiedler* whose linguistic and cultural links to Germany were tenuous, but whose ethnic German origins granted them immediate access to FRG citizenship – 'foreigners' born and raised in Germany had no automatic right to naturalization.

The situation of migrant minorities stands, in other words, as a pointed reminder of the continuing oscillation in definitions of German identity between liberal Enlightenment models of the nation as a pluralist collectivity (in which, amongst others, migrant workers who settled in Germany would be included as equal citizens), and Romantic visions of an internally homogeneous *Kulturnation* stripped of 'foreign' influence.

III The Allied response to fascism, 1945–9

In an effort to trace some of the historical shifts and tensions between these polarized conceptions of national culture and identity, let us turn first to the period after 1945: the brief interregnum under Allied control, before Germany was divided into two opposing states. On 7–8 May 1945, Germany submitted its unconditional surrender to the four Allied powers:

France, Great Britain, the USA and the Soviet Union. Thus ended 12 years of National Socialist rule in Germany and six years of a world war that had left millions dead, and Germany itself physically decimated. A provisional government was set up in the first weeks of May 1945 under Admiral von Dönitz; but on 23 May, the Dönitz government was dissolved, and the Allies assumed supreme power in Germany.

The stated aim of Allied military government was three-fold: demilitarization, denazification and democratization of a country which, under fascist rule, had orchestrated a bloody war, and perpetrated unprecedented horrors in the concentration camps and gas chambers. Allied government began, then, with an apparent consensus on the general thrust of policies for reconstruction. The rather abstract formulation on which that consensus was based, however, produced an increasing divergence in denazification policy and practice amongst the four occupying powers. The sharpest distinctions were those produced by philosophical differences in understandings of the origins of German fascism. The Western Allies subscribed to a liberal individualist view of fascism as a manifestation (albeit a highly corrupted one) of political will. In this view, it was to the distortion of German collective and individual consciousness that National Socialism was most centrally to be attributed. The Law for Liberation from National Socialism (*Befreiungsgesetz*), which came into force in the Western zones in March 1946, shifted the emphasis of denazification definitively away from a Soviet-style structural purging of Nazis from public life, and towards an examination of the predispositions of individual Germans to fascism. Under the terms of the *Befreiungsgesetz*, German citizens were to submit to tribunals questionnaires on all aspects of their political activity under the Third Reich. That information was used as a basis for the categorization of individuals under one of five possible headings: major offenders, offenders, lesser offenders, followers or fellow-travellers, and the exonerated.

The denazification tribunals were accompanied by initiatives for democratic re-education, ranging from film screenings on such issues as wartime atrocities or the Holocaust, through academic exchange programmes, mobile libraries and school visits, to an extensive reform of the press and media system. It was in this latter area that Western cultural policy arguably made its greatest impact. Following the introduction of a licensing system that allowed cultural production by Germans to recommence, individuals were licensed to publish newspapers in the Western zones. Most of these were regionally based and politically independent; and such titles as the *Frankfurter Rundschau*, the *Süddeutsche Zeitung* and *Die Welt*, or the liberal weeklies *Die Zeit* and *Der Spiegel* – all of which emerged under Allied occupation – were stable enough to survive the rigours of political and economic change after 1949, and to become the leading 'quality' publications of post-war West Germany. In the words of two recent commentators: 'the period of Allied control of the press was decisive in shaping the longer-term pattern of the press up to the present day'.[4]

The same was true of the long-term development of broadcasting in West Germany. Here again (at least until the advent of new communications technologies and the broadcasting reforms of the 1980s), the medium remained regionally based in broadcasting stations initially established under Allied control. The denazification and re-education policies of the Western Allies, in other words, left their mark on post-1949 West Germany in the form of a diversified, decentralized and (at least theoretically) politically independent cultural sphere.

To the GDR, Soviet denazification delivered a very different cultural legacy. According to the economistic Marxist analysis that underpinned denazification in the Soviet zone, fascism was the outcome, not centrally of the psychological dispositions of the German people, but of capitalist politico-economic development. The focus of denazification in the Soviet zone was thus not individual but structural; it centred on the dismantling of such sections of the military–industrial complex as were located in eastern Germany, as well as on the erasure of National Socialist influence from public life. Thus, along with land reform, the dismantling of large sections of East German industry and the transportation of plant and raw materials as reparations to the Soviet Union, the Soviet military command concentrated its energies on removing ex-Nazis from public office, and on promoting communism. In the political arena, the drive towards Soviet-style communism was most visible in the forced merger in April 1946 between the Social Democratic Party in the Eastern zone (SPD), and the communist KPD. The party that emerged from that union, the Socialist Unity Party (SED) moved quickly to the position as the Soviet Union's political mouthpiece that it was to sustain until the founding of the GDR in 1949, and indeed throughout the country's 40-year history.

IV German cultural intellectuals: humanism and its limits

Mary Fulbrook has described denazification in the four zones of occupation as polarized between a Western focus on rehabilitation, and a Soviet concern with structural transformation.[5] There was, however, a third prevailing tendency in this period that emanated, not from the occupying powers, but from indigenous cultural intellectuals. In the Soviet zone, a coalition of socialist writers and intellectuals came together as early as July

1945 to form the Cultural Association for the Democratic Renewal of Germany (*Kulturbund zur demokratischen Erneuerung Deutschlands*). Under the leadership of the writer Johannes R. Becher, who took up the presidency after returning from Soviet exile, the *Kulturbund* committed itself to a revival based on the 'true German cultural values' represented by Enlightenment humanism, and embodied in the writings of such figures as Goethe, Schiller or Lessing. In late 1940s Germany, that tradition was seen as having survived in the work of exiled writers – Anna Seghers, Arnold Zweig or Bertolt Brecht (all of whom returned after 1945 to the Soviet zone) – or in such powerful post-war anti-fascist statements as Wolfgang Staudte's 1946 film *The Murderers Are Among Us (Die Mörder sind unter uns)*. That film – the first production of the Deutsche Film-Aktiengesellschaft (DEFA) under whose monopoly GDR film production was later organized – ends with a demand for the pursuit of war criminals in the context of a democratic restoration of the rule of law. 'We have no right to judge', says the protagonist Dr Mertens (Wolfgang Borchert), 'but we have a duty to accuse.'

Mertens is led to that insight by his lover Susanne (Hildegard Knef), whose love convinces him that human values can survive despite the immensity of Nazi crimes. The film evinces, in other words, a commitment to a new moral and political order grounded in the humanist tradition – a commitment typical of cultural responses to fascism from German intellectuals both East and West. The *Kulturbund*'s manifesto demanded, for instance, the 'rediscovery and promotion of the democratic humanist tradition that is the national heritage of our people'. In the West, the same call for a humanist revival echoed through the founding statements of key post-war cultural initiatives. In April 1946, the writers Hans Werner Richter and Alfred Andersch launched the periodical *Der Ruf (The Calling)* which aimed – as indicated by its sub-title, 'Independent Writings from the Young Generation' – to act as mouthpiece for a rising generation of democratic Germans. Like the founders of the *Kulturbund*, the editors of *Der Ruf* saw in Enlightenment humanism a specifically German source of post-war cultural transformation. In one important statement from *Der Ruf* in 1946, Alfred Andersch for instance called for 'a new socialist humanism' rooted in an alliance between 'young Germany' and the youth of Europe.[6]

From the beginning, *Der Ruf* opposed Allied re-education policies, which it saw as unjustly tainting the German majority with the stain of guilt for 'the crimes of a minority'.[7] This, coupled with the journal's support for democratic socialism, led quickly to Allied censure, and finally to the banning of *Der Ruf* in April 1947. Its successor in the literary sphere, the group of left-liberal writers brought together in September 1947 to form the *Gruppe 47*, reiterated in its founding principles *Der Ruf*'s demand for home-grown forms of cultural democratization. Indeed that demand was one that echoed across the field of cultural production in the West. The immediate post-war period saw, for example, a wave of so-called rubble films (*Trümmerfilme*): productions by German directors set amongst the ruins of a defeated Germany, and thematizing the nation's cultural destruction and future renewal. Titles like Helmut Käutner's *In Those Days* (*In jenen Tagen*, 1947), Harald Braun's *Between Yesterday and Tomorrow* (*Zwischen gestern und morgen*, 1947) or Rudolf Jugert's *Film Without a Title* (*Film ohne Titel*, 1948) used Germany's ruined cities as a visual metaphor for the demolition of German cultural tradition and identity. In life stories from the inhabitants of that ruined landscape, however, they found traces of a humanity that could provide the basis for moral reconstruction in a post-fascist Germany. *In Those Days*, for instance, is a retrospective of the Third Reich, told from the perspective of a car whose life-span exactly parallels the twelve years of National Socialism. The stories of the car's owners make up a patchwork tale of everyday resistance and petty heroism: a narrative which, as the voice-over (the car) tells us at the end, points the way to a rediscovery of human values and thus to a viable future for the post-war nation.

Equally indebted to the new humanism was the philosopher Karl Jaspers, who wrote in his seminal analysis of German guilt, *The Guilt Question* (*Die Schuldfrage*, 1946) that 'we know ourselves to be first and foremost part of humanity; we are in the first instance human beings, then Germans'.[8] But there is, ultimately a contradiction in Jaspers' work – one that dogged post-war humanism in all its manifestations. Cultural renewal was seen by Jaspers and others to depend on the revival in Germany of such universal values as tolerance, respect for the dignity of human life, and free and open communication. Paradoxically, however, universal humanity was invoked in the context of an appeal to a very particular and limited community, the German nation. Witness for instance Jaspers' use of the first person plural in the opening paragraphs of *Die Schuldfrage*: 'We want to learn to talk together ... not simply to reiterate our own opinions, but to hear the thoughts of the other.'[9]

Jaspers' appeal here to 'we the Germans' as a national community of the guilty produces (as do arguably all cultural constructions of communal identity) a division between self and other, 'us' and 'them', that undermines his demand for universal free communication. His preoccupation with a specifically German form of national guilt threatens, in other words, to privilege a German perspective, and to marginalize that of the 'others' who were the victims of National Socialism. That this is the result, moreover, not just of failings in Jaspers' rhetoric, but of a broader philosophical weakness in post-war humanism, is evidenced by a similar ethnic exclusivity in other cultural representations. Despite the denunciation of anti-Semitism in most *Trümmerfilme*, for instance, the films only rarely feature Jewish characters. More telling still are the narrative conventions that developed around such Jewish representation as was present in post-war film. Though certainly shown as the victims of Nazi persecution, Jewish figures in the *Trümmerfilme* are without exception removed by their own hand from the narrative; invariably, they commit suicide, usually at a moment when capture and deportation to the death camps seem inevitable.

This cinematic stereotype of the suicidal Jew highlights the ultimate inadequacy, not only of the *Trümmerfilme*, but of post-war humanism in general, as a vehicle for the engagement with the other that such as Jaspers demanded. Philosophical critiques of humanism have regularly noted its incapacity to grasp what might be termed the other within the self; and certainly the *Trümmerfilme* seem unable to confront, either the racist pathologies of its German characters, or the brutalization that was the product of Nazi persecution of the Jews. These films not only falter on the threshold beyond which they must portray their German characters as the perpetrators of racist murder (the Jews kill themselves): they also never dare represent the torture and humiliation that would transform deported Jews from fully rounded characters loaded with melodramatic pathos, to dehumanized camp inmates.

It was, moreover, not only the ethnic other – the Jew – who was omitted or repressed from historical narrative. The post-war Enlightenment subject (Dr Mertens in *The Murderers Are Among Us*, or such writers as Becher, Richter or Andersch) was in the majority of cases not only ethnically marked as German; he was also gendered, the male heir to a masculine tradition. Feminist historians of post-1945 Germany have shown how central was women's contribution to economic and cultural regeneration. The so-called rubble women (*Trümmerfrauen*) were put to work in their thousands after the war to clear the ruins of the bombed-out cities; they took on the heaviest of 'male' manual labour, working as crane drivers, coal miners or industrial labourers. Women were politically active, too, in local women's committees and peace groups; they denounced, amongst other things, their men's penchant for war, and demanded a woman-oriented transformation of culture and politics in Germany. Some of those calls were answered, by equality clauses in both 1949 constitutions for instance. And yet, in the philosophical texts, the films and literature of the period, it is men – from Goethe to Brecht, from Lessing to Böll – who figure as the bearers of Enlightenment, culture and history. As one recent history points out, there was widespread resistance in the West in particular to women's participation in cultural and intellectual life: there were almost no women film or theatre directors: women artists, though active, received little recognition: and even such well-known writers as Elisabeth Langgässer or Luise Rinser were largely shunned by the literary establishment and cultural critics.[10]

In terms of Germany's attempted rupture with fascism, the period from 1945 to 1949 presents, in sum, a contradictory picture. Denazification in the Soviet zone in the end only paved the way for a regenerated dictatorship masquerading as democratic centralism. In the West, denazification by questionnaire and tribunal proved overly bureaucratic and open to abuse. Many former Nazis escaped sanctions, and party members were in any case universally rehabilitated under the FRG's general amnesty in 1951. Cultural intellectuals in all four zones created their own, specifically German response to fascism; but that response seemed compromised, ultimately, by its intellectual rooting in a Germano-centric and gender-exclusive version of the humanist tradition.

V German history as other – its repression and its return

It is a reflection of the limitations of post-war denazification that in 1976, three decades after the end of the Second World War, the prominent GDR novelist Christa Wolf could still strike a chord when she wrote, 'What is past is not dead; it is not even past. We cut ourselves off from it; we pretend to be strangers'.[11] So began Wolf's monumental autobiography *Patterns of Childhood* (*Kindheitsmuster*), first published by the GDR's most significant literary publisher, the *Aufbau-Verlag*, and released in West Germany one year later. Previous works of fiction, including *Divided Heaven* (*Der geteilte Himmel*, 1963) and *The Quest for Christa T.* (*Nachdenken über Christa T.*, 1968) had established Wolf, both as a committed socialist, and as a modernist whose practice was often at odds with the GDR's official socialist realist aesthetic. *Patterns of Childhood* extended Wolf's experimentation with modernist form; her autobiographical narrative of a childhood under National Socialism was continually fractured by a second story – the narrative of a two-day visit to Wolf's former home in what is now Poland – as well as by discursive passages debating the nature of autobiographical writing and historical memory.

The book, in other words, set out not only to recapture a lost past – the history of the often ambivalent relationship of post-war generations to German fascism (Wolf herself was born in 1929, four years before the Nazi seizure of power). *Patterns of Childhood* also impressed upon its readers the necessity of debate on the relationship between their own (often highly contradictory) memories, and official histories of the Third Reich. That the book was indeed hailed as stirring back into life 'a whole swathe of the past' is in part a testament to the special status of Wolf and other literary intellectuals in the GDR.[12] In what came to be known as the East German 'land of readers' (*Leserland DDR*), novelists and poets enjoyed a privileged cultural status. Officially celebrated as the socialist heirs to Germany's great literary tradition, writers were at the same time held in high regard by the GDR populace. In a situation in which the press and broadcasting were dominated by party dogma, and where the popular arts – popular music, television, fashion and so on – often offered little more than pale imitations of Western models, literature (as sales and readership figures amply testify) was valued for its capacity to lend authenticity to the representation of GDR experience.

But readers' enthusiasm for *Patterns of Childhood* cannot only be explained by the high profile of literary works *per se* in the GDR. In its concern with personal memory as the source of a new form of knowledge about the national past, the novel was symptomatic of a broader sea change in post-war cultural responses to German fascism. Post-war humanism, as we have seen, had called for a return to Enlightenment values as the source of a regenerated German identity. In Wolf's novel, by contrast, the writer delves into the recesses of her own (enlightened socialist) identity, and finds buried here the residues of other selves – the exile nostalgic for a lost Polish home, the child born under and formed by National Socialism. These figures from a barely suppressed past are at one and the same time alien to, but also embedded within the narrator's present-day identity; we 'cut ourselves off' from a past which, however, 'is not dead; it is not even past'.

VI The flight from the past: two paths to modernity

This perception that fascist history enjoyed a lively afterlife in the subjectivities of individual Germans, was, even by the mid-1970s, a recent one. For over a decade after German division in 1949, both Germanies had given every appearance of turning their faces from the past, and had focused instead on building futures beyond National Socialism. In the GDR of the 1950s, the SED continued structural transformations begun under Soviet military rule. The building of socialism after 1949 involved, amongst other things, the restructuring of the education system along Marxist–Leninist lines; the formation of a socialist mass culture, through the youth and women's organizations, for example (the Free German Youth, the Pioneers, the Democratic Women's League of Germany and others), or through the staging of mass rallies and other spectacles to celebrate occasions of historical note (May Day, the anniversary of the October revolution, and so on). A further plank in socialist cultural planning was the secularization of all areas of public life; thus religious instruction in schools was abolished, and in 1954 the state introduced the *Jugendweihe*, an adolescent initiation rite designed to replace religious confirmation. In literature and the arts, socialist realism was enshrined as the official state aesthetic; and a highly ramified system of state censorship was put in place with the creation in 1951 of the Bureau for Literature and Publishing (*Amt für Literatur und Verlagswesen*) and the State Commission for Artistic Affairs (*Staatliche Kommission für Kunstangelegenheiten*).

That the pathway to socialism was a rocky one is indisputable: witness, for instance, the June uprising of 1953, when demonstrations spread across the GDR in protest against increases in productivity targets ('work norms') for industrial workers. Witness too the considerable diversification of socialist cultural practices during the post-Stalinist 'thaw' of 1953–6: a period in which such prominent figures as Bertolt Brecht and Stefan Heym were able, despite the constraints of censorship, to voice at least some of the most urgent arguments for political reform.

And yet efforts to revisit and reassess the fascist past were obstructed throughout these early years by the GDR's (highly questionable) definition of itself as an anti-fascist state that, in the transition to socialism, had definitively severed links with the Third Reich. Not until 1990, during the interregnum between SED rule and unification with the West, did the then Prime Minister, Hans Modrow, publicly admit the GDR's equal historical responsibility with the FRG for German fascism. On the one hand, then, historical continuities between Nazism and East German state socialism were officially disavowed. This did not on the other hand produce a conception of the GDR as arising *ex nihilo* from the ruins of 1945. Against the 'zero hour' rhetoric of some West German intellectuals, the SED regime posed a Marxist vision of the GDR as heir to a hitherto suppressed tradition of progressive forces in history. Thus, while modernist high art, for instance, was officially rejected – for its formalism, its 'decadent' preoccupation with marginality, and most centrally, for its insistence on radical rupture with the historical past – the SED on the other hand embraced cultural forms expressive of a historically rooted socialist modernity. Hence, for example, the SED's early enthusiasm for architectural modernization on a grandiose scale; for, as stated, for example, in July 1950 in the government's Sixteen Principles of Town Planning, the modernized GDR city would stand as an emblem of 'the social order of the German Democratic Republic, the progressive traditions of our German people and the great aims which are set for the construction of Germany as a whole'.[13]

This self-identification of the GDR regime with progressive historical forces – foremost amongst these the revolutionary working class – had contradictory cultural effects. At times, it produced a clear cultural pluralization. There are still, for instance – despite the activities of the *Gruppe '61* and the *Werkkreis Literatur der Arbeitswelt* – few Western equivalents of the workers' writing circles and industrial residencies for writers that began after the Bitterfeld writers' conference of 1959. The so-called *Bitterfelder Weg* embarked upon at that event produced some genuine cross-fertilizations between 'high' and 'low', bourgeois and working-class cultures. Christa Wolf's portrayal of factory life in *Divided Heaven* (1963), and Erwin Strittmatter's portrait of agricultural labour from the same year, *Ole Bienkopp*, are two examples.

If, however, the GDR's achievement after fascism was to reinstate subordinate class groupings as modernity's heirs, then one of its chief historical failings lay arguably in its inattention to those other identities that Nazism had so brutally excluded from the historical process. To be sure, cultural practitioners in the post-war GDR produced some compelling portraits of the fascist persecution of cultural difference: Bruno Apitz's Holocaust novel *Naked amongst wolves* (*Nackt unter Wölfen*, 1958) for instance, or Konrad Wolf's film of a German-Jewish love affair *Stars* (*Sterne*, 1959). Yet the range of forms in which engagement with the cultural other might occur, was strictly limited. According to official doctrine, one primary feature of the socialist realist work of art was its so-called solidarity with the people (*Volksverbundenheit*). Potentially, this commitment to the *Volk* might have produced an infinite cultural diversification. In reality, however, 'the people' were defined, not as a heterogeneous body with potentially diverse forms of cultural expression, but as a collectivity that should at least aspire to a unitary class identity. Literature, visual art, the mass media and other cultural forms were given a key role in fostering working-class identification; hence official calls for the socialist realist work of art to adopt a partisan (*parteilich*) perspective that would allow it to approach questions of social life from the standpoint of the working class.

This equation of 'progressive' culture with working-class identity produced some unfortunate blindspots in official cultural representations. The GDR was putatively a state from which social inequality was on the way to being expunged; but the privileging of class in GDR culture produced a blindness to equally persistent inequalities – of gender, sexuality or ethnicity for instance – which survived intact in the GDR despite that state's formal commitment to egalitarian principles. To take the example of gender: while women were granted formal equality at work – and by the late 1980s, over 90 per cent of GDR women were in full-time employment – cultural stereotypes of femininity and masculinity were pervasive, and women and men remained largely confined to conventional social roles. In the over-whelming majority of households, for instance, women continued, despite their commitment to waged work, to bear primary responsibility for childcare and domestic labour; and the GDR workplace too was marked by traditional hierarchies that confined women to the lower echelons (Margot Honecker, Education Minister and wife of the SED leader Erich Honecker, was a notable but rare exception).

The official myth that a class-identified GDR populace had become the bearers of a uniformly progressive socialist modernity had problematic consequences, too, for the GDR's relation to the recent past. Officially, fascism belonged to a past epoch which the GDR had overcome in the transition to socialist modernity. That this position was untenable was later demonstrated by writers, artists and intellectuals who, from the late 1960s, began more vigorously to explore the GDR's historical continuities with fascism. That it had seemed sustainable until that point was due in no small measure to the GDR's symbolic projection of what psychoanalysis would term the 'bad other' of Nazi history onto West Germany. If socialist modernization was seen by the SED regime to have produced in the GDR a radical break with Third Reich barbarism, the Federal Republic, by contrast, was vilified for its continued commitment to capitalist regenera-tion; for in the Marxist–Leninist view, it was precisely capitalist modernity that had been the wellspring of German fascism.

The Federal Republic, of course, countered with its own myth of progressive modernity versus barbaric tradition. On the one hand, the post-war Western state – unlike the GDR – did formally acknowledge its historical responsibility for German fascism. That acknowledgment took various forms, including compensation for (some of) the victims of Nazi terror, privileged access for Jewish immigrants to German citizenship, political and economic support for the state of Israel, and an open door policy on political asylum, the latter designed to repay West Germany's debt to an international community that had given refuge to Germans fleeing Nazi persecution. But these compensatory gestures in no sense implied a recognition of the FRG state's continuity with German fascism. On the contrary, post-war governments were as vociferous as their GDR counterparts in claiming that modernization had produced a definitive rupture with National Socialism.

Modernization began at the constitutional and political level with the institutionalization in 1949 of the structures of Western-style representative democracy: a two-tier parliament, an electoral system based on proportional representation, a strong constitution designed to safeguard basic rights, and a separation of powers between the Federal government in Bonn (*Bund*) and the federal states (*Länder*). Federalism in particular had important implications for cultural policy and practice in the post-war state. Unlike the GDR, where the Leninist interpretation of democracy as 'democratic centralism' had produced a centralization of culture under state and party control, the so-called cultural sovereignty (*Kulturhoheit*) of the *Länder* produced a refreshing regional pluralism. The distinctive identities of regional urban centres from Hamburg to Munich were nourished throughout the 40 years of German division by generous subsidies from *Länder* governments to theatre, film, music, the visual arts and literature. This regionalization of identities was further cemented by education policies which, though nationally coordinated through the Standing Conference of Ministers of Culture (*Ständige Konferenz der Kultusminister*), preserved important local structural and pedagogic distinctions. Thus, for instance, confessional schools in the Catholic and conservative-dominated states of Bavaria, the Rheinland Palatinate, North-Rhine Westphalia and elsewhere tended in the early post-war years to view the curriculum as a vehicle for the promotion of the Christian faith, while the Protestant-dominated and social democratic states of Baden-Württemberg, Hamburg and Schleswig-Holstein, by contrast, favoured a fully secularized primary and secondary education. Post-1960s experiments with secondary-level comprehensives were similarly more pervasive in the SPD states (most prominently in Hesse) than in conservative regions where the traditional and highly selective three-tier system remained the norm. That regional differences fostered at school level did, moreover, continue to structure individual and collective identities in the FRG is perhaps best illustrated by patterns of cultural consumption in adult life. Thus, for instance, in West German broadcasting, the regional audience remained a key target group – and this even after the advent of new technologies (satellite and cable) that might have seemed to privilege audiences constituted at national or indeed supranational level. A final instance is the West German press. There have been in the post-war period some successful national publications: the tabloid *Bild*, or the right-of-centre quality titles *Die Welt* and the *Frankfurter Allgemeine Zeitung* (*FAZ*). But it is a measure of the success of cultural decentralization that the daily newspaper found on breakfast tables across the Federal Republic is still statistically more likely to be a local or regional title – the *Süddeutsche Zeitung* in Munich, in Berlin the *Berliner Morgenpost* or *Der Tagesspiegel* – than a national publication.

Modernity in the form espoused in government policy had, then, a distinctly regionalist flavour. There was, however, a second thrust to modernization in the FRG whose cultural implications were rather different. Under Adenauer's Economics Minister, Ludwig Erhard, the Federal Republic in the 1950s pioneered the model of the so-called social market economy, which – as Mark Roseman's contribution to this volume shows in more detail – combined a 'hands-off' approach to state economic planning with an embracing of the free market as a route to democratization. Post-war observers were divided on the implications for culture of this embracing of enlightened capitalism as a route to post-fascist modernity. Conservative apologists for a free market system modelled on the 'American way' pushed hard for an Americanization of the economic system through the liberalization of markets, the academic and commercial development of the business disciplines – management, marketing and public relations – and a reorientation of economic policy towards consumer-led growth. These were, for instance, the ingredients of West Germany's so-called economic miracle as presented in Ludwig Erhard's self-congratulatory volume *Prosperity for All* (*Wohlstand für Alle*, 1957). Erhard was, however, cautious about the cultural benefits of Americanization. In a climate of conservative hostility to mass culture American-style – a hostility exemplified by moral panics over the effects of popular film, youth culture and popular music (the first and most notorious film target was Willi Forst's apparently sympathetic portrait of prostitution in *The Sinful Woman/Die Sünderin*, 1951: in relation to music, jazz, swing and rock 'n' roll especially were denounced as offensive and un-German) – Erhard too urged restraint in the cultural realm. Thus his writings promoted a nationally specific mode of cultural commodification that, while certainly drawing on American mass market models, would preserve 'German' traditions of quality, good taste and technological excellence.

Left-wing observers were yet more sceptical of the cultural benefits of capitalist development. In 1962, the social philosopher Jürgen Habermas published what was to become a pivotal text in left-liberal cultural debates, *Structural Change in the Public Sphere (Strukturwandel der Öffentlichkeit)*. In Habermas's neo-Marxist analysis, the rise of capitalism and the concomitant emergence of the bourgeois class were linked with the development of an enlightened public culture whose key vehicles included the press, the bourgeois novel, and public discourse in the salons and coffee houses of the eighteenth-century intelligentsia. Marxist thinkers after 1949 were divided on the fate of the classical bourgeois public sphere. Habermas himself saw it as threatened by advancing commodification, but, especially in his later writings of the 1970s and 1980s, he sustained a belief in the possible survival of the

Enlightenment tradition through a commitment to democratic values as embodied in the Basic Law (hence Habermas's famous defence of what he terms 'constitutional patriotism'). The older generation of Western Marxists were more sceptical. The Frankfurt School Marxists of the early post-war period (so-called because of their affiliations to the Frankfurt-based Institute of Social Research, closed by the Nazis after 1933) saw capitalist development as having produced a cultural order in which aesthetic, moral, cultural and spiritual values were subordinated to the demands of capitalist accumulation. Capitalist domination had reached its apotheosis in the collusion under Nazism between monopoly capital (Krupp, Thyssen, Siemens *et al.*) and the fascist state: a collusion that had produced the extraordinary excesses of slave labour in the munitions factories, and mechanized mass slaughter in the death camps at Auschwitz and elsewhere. Enlightenment traditions had finally died in the gas ovens at Auschwitz; thus, the Frankfurt School philosopher Adorno famously concluded, critical cultural activity survived at best in the realm of an autonomous art that radically distanced itself from the means-ends rationality of the market.

The commitment to highbrow modernism that was the logical conclusion of Adorno's arguments was not shared by less politically pessimistic figures on the liberal left: the writer Heinrich Böll for instance, whose work was notable for its combination of critical political engagement with a more accessible realist aesthetic. But what was common, not only to Adorno, Habermas and Böll, but to conservative theorists of modernization, was their perception of the nature of the forces underpinning historical development. Erhard's free market conception of the liberal individual (the entrepreneur unfettered by market regulation, the free-spending consumer) as the motor of historical progression was of course radically opposed to the Marxist championing of the (working-class) collectivity; but for both, it was the rationally constituted subject born in the age of Enlightenment that had been – and would in some accounts continue to be – the bearer of progressive developments in modern history.

VII 1968 and after: modernity's subject fragmented

On 2 June 1967, a demonstration was staged in West Berlin to protest against an official visit by the Shah of Persia. The protest culminated in confrontations between demonstrators and police, and with the shooting of a student, Benno Ohnesorg. Those events were to become a turning point in West German cultural–political development. The left-liberal intelligentsia had for some time expressed unease over the failure of a putatively modernized Federal Republic to sever links with National Socialism. The

Auschwitz trials of the early 1960s had shocked the country with their revelation of the numbers of war criminals who lived on unpunished as apparently ordinary citizens. The Grand Coalition of 1966 had installed ex-Nazis in high office: Kurt-Georg Kiesinger as Chancellor, with the somewhat compromised Heinrich Lübke continuing as President. All this, combined with the lack of effective opposition under the all-party Grand Coalition, and a series of scandals exposing ex-Nazis in public life, had by the late 1960s fuelled a spirit of hostility to the status quo. This disaffection, most keenly felt by a rising generation too young to have experienced fascism, crystallized in the student unrest of the late 1960s and early 1970s. Ohnesorg's death especially gave new impetus to leftist student groups such as the Socialist League of German Students (Sozialistischer Deutscher Studentenbund – SDS); it confirmed their Marxist analysis of post-war West Germany as a state dominated – as was the Third Reich – by the dehumanizing forces of capitalist accumulation and state control.

The response of the student left was an energetic commitment to the Marxist utopia of working-class revolution. But the grass-roots unrest fomented in the so-called extra-parliamentary opposition after 1967 involved much more than a class-based challenge to post-war cultural–political consensus. The emergence through the 1970s and 1980s of new social movements across the political spectrum – the women's movement, the ecology and peace movements, single-issue citizens' initiatives (*Bürgerinitiativen*), squatters' groups – revealed a West German polity fractured, not only along lines of class, but of gender, sexuality, region and generation.

The identity politics of the period posed two kinds of challenge to the Enlightenment mythology on which the FRG was founded. The ecology and peace movements in particular, with their warnings of nuclear catastrophe and ecological collapse, raised key doubts over the vision of historical progress that had underpinned socioeconomic development in both post-war German states. That challenge to rationalist conceptions of a progressive history was reinforced by a new scepticism over Enlightenment rationalism's capacity to represent the multiple identities in and through which history was made. From feminism, for instance, came insights into the gender blindness of existing histories: witness the efforts of feminist historians, writers, artists or film-makers to recapture the lost narratives of women 'hidden from history'. The fracturing of the subject of German history which those feminist efforts entailed was echoed across the spectrum of cultural production in the period. The renaissance of West German film under a new generation of *auteurs* – Rainer Werner Fassbinder, Wim Wenders and Werner Herzog were the most enduring –

was characterized by a new concern with the complexities of subjective encounters with German history, in Fassbinder's historical melodrama *The Marriage of Maria Braun* (*Die Ehe der Maria Braun*, 1979), for instance, in Helma Sanders-Brahms' autobiographical portrait of her mother, *Germany, Pale Mother* (*Deutschland, bleiche Mutter*, 1980), or in Alexander Kluge's idiosyncratic *The Patriot* (*Die Patriotin*, 1979).

The emphasis in films from the so-called New German Cinema on recent history as a post-modern patchwork of competing narratives and identities was paralleled in contemporary historiography by a turn to local and oral history, which produced a similarly pluralized picture of German historical experience. It was, moreover, not only the *collective* identity of 'Germany' that began now to fragment. We saw in Wolf's *Patterns of Childhood* one example of how literature of the period used conceptions of the fractured self to explore a new *subjective* relation to German identity and history. The pervasiveness of this historical subjectivism was evidenced, too, by the engagement amongst younger intellectuals with the post-modern philosophies of Lyotard, Baudrillard and Foucault, or with psychoanalysis as a tool for understanding psychic attachments to political formations. Klaus Theweleit's 1977 study of the psychology of the fascist male, *Male Fantasies (Männerphantasien)* was a key text in this regard; more significant still was Alexander and Margarethe Mitscherlich's *The Inability to Mourn* (*Die Unfähigkeit zu Trauern*, 1967), now part of the recognized canon of historical writing on the post-war period. The Mitscherlichs' social-psychological account of the FRG as a nation incapable of over-coming its psychic investment in fascism was warmly received in a West Germany whose younger intellectuals seemed obsessed with the same search to unearth the residues of fascist history in contemporary German identity.

Post-1968 interiority, moreover, was not confined to the West. Ulbricht's replacement in 1971 by Erich Honecker as First Secretary of the SED ushered in a period of unprecedented cultural openness in the GDR. The new liberalism was evidenced by official toleration of previously vilified popular cultural forms (rock music, Western dress, discotheques, etc.), as well as of literary works exploring individual conflicts with state socialism, from Ulrich Plenzdorf's youth cultural lament *The New Sorrows of Young W.* (*Die neuen Leiden des jungen W.*, 1972), through Irmtraud Morgner's picaresque fantasy of a woman's life, *Troubadora Beatriz* (1974), to Monika Maron's bleak account of environmental pollution and state censorship, *Flight of Ashes* (*Flugasche*, 1981). *Flight of Ashes* appeared after the 1976 expatriation of the dissident singer-songwriter Wolf Biermann, an affair that marked the beginning of a renewed clampdown on cultural opposition.

Maron's novel, accordingly, was banned in the GDR; but the centring of the narrative on the psychological torment of a woman journalist caught in the conflict between the political demands of socialism and a more personal ethical and emotional agenda made the novel none the less typical of a decade or more of GDR literary subjectivism.

VIII 1983–1996: the return to nation?

The legacy of the cultural movements of 1968 and after was, then, a newly diverse, 'post-modern' conception of German identity. The German 'nation', it had now to be acknowledged, was an unstable and internally heterogeneous construction, an entity fractured by differences of class, gender, sexuality, region, ethnicity, etc., and (in the perception of GDR intellectuals especially) marked by contradictions between subjective desires and collective ethico-political demands.

In the face of such cultural instability, there was from the early 1980s something of a retrenchment to apparently more comfortable conceptions of unitary nationhood. The conservative *Wende* (turning point) that followed Helmut Kohl's election as West German Chancellor in 1983 involved what many saw as a problematic reassertion of national values. One notorious example was Kohl's comment early on in his term of office on the 'grace of belated birth' that supposedly distanced post-war generations from responsibility for National Socialism, and allowed them to look towards a more positive future for late twentieth-century Germany. Parallel controversies raged through the 1980s in the cultural realm: witness, for instance, the heated debates sparked by Edgar Reitz's 1984 epic *Heimat* over the new patriotism in contemporary West German film; witness too the historians' debate (*Historikerstreit*) of 1986–7, which featured such prominent figures as Ernst Nolte and Jürgen Habermas in conflict over the legitimacy of reclaiming patriotic values from some corners of the history of National Socialism.

The GDR, too, witnessed from the early 1980s a re-engagement with hitherto denigrated national traditions, in the reinstatement of the Prussian legacy in official history, for instance, or in the exploration within dissident movements of points of convergence East and West (the networking activities of the women's and peace movements are one example). But it was the 'quiet revolution' of 1989 that most forcefully reasserted the centrality to German identity of concepts of *Volk* and nation. When the crowds on the streets of Leipzig, Dresden and Berlin changed their slogan from 'we are *the* people' to 'we are *one* people' (*Wir sind ein Volk*), and when, in the elections of spring 1990, they chose the Conservative

Christian Democrat (CDU) and Christian Social (CSU) coalition as the political force that promised the most rapid route to unification, commentators abroad and at home (the writer Günter Grass was amongst the most persistent) feared that Germany was set to abandon the liberal dream of pluralist democracy in a Germany ruled by and for the people, in favour of an all-too-familiar authoritarian and monolithic vision of nation.

The truth, at the time of writing, is that Germany remains as ever balanced between these competing national models. On the one hand, as the 1992 Rostock atrocities amply demonstrate, unification did indeed provoke a resurgence of right-wing nationalism and racist violence. On the other hand, the German model of federal democracy remained amongst the most successful in Europe in guaranteeing civil rights and social justice to its citizens. More than this, cultural trends are inexorably towards a pluralization of cultural forms and identities. Grass-roots pluralism is perhaps most strikingly evident in the cultural productions of Germany's most politically and economically marginal group, the migrant workforce. Some of the most vibrant literary works of the 1990s were penned by first- and second-generation migrant writers: Emine Sevgi Özdamar, whose novel *Life Is a Caravanserai* (*Das Leben ist eine Karawanserai*, 1992) received the Walter Hasenclever literary prize in 1992; or the poet and essayist Zafer Senoçak, whose essay collection *Atlas of Tropical Germany* (*Atlas des tropischen Deutschland*, 1993) offers an especially eloquent plea for a multiethnic and multicultural Germany. Turkish-German hip-hop – surely amongst the most startling of contemporary cultural creolizations – blossomed in the last years of the twentieth century in the inner cities of a Germany that still refused to recognize Turkish migrants politically as citizens, but which had long since acceded to their cultural influence. As ever, then, the question of what is 'German' remains open, and German identity a site of contestation over competing constructions of nation.

Notes:

1. Misik, Robert, 'Die Dämonen ziehen ein', *Profil* 36 (31 August 1992), p. 43.
2. Krüger-Potratz, Marianne, *Anderssein gab es nicht. Ausländer und Minderheiten in der DDR* (1991), p. 2.
3. Geißler, Heiner, 'Kein Grund zur Angst. Ein Plädoyer für eine multikulturelle Gesellschaft', *Der Spiegel* 41 (1991), p. 2.
4. Bullivant, Keith, and Rice, C. Jane, 'Reconstruction and Integration: the Culture of West German Stabilization 1945 to 1968', in Rob Burns, ed., *German Cultural Studies. An Introduction* (1995), p. 219.
5. Fulbrook, Mary, *The Fontana History of Germany 1918–1990. The Divided Nation* (1991), 141–50.

6. Andersch, Alfred, 'Das junge Europa formt sein Gesicht', *Der Ruf*, 15 August 1946. Reproduced in Klaus Wagenbach *et al.*, eds., *Vaterland, Muttersprache. Deutsche Schriftsteller und ihr Staat seit 1945* (1994), p. 55.
7. *Ibid.*, p. 57.
8. Jaspers, Karl, *Die Schuldfrage. Von der politischen Haftung Deutschlands* (1965), p. 16 (first edn., 1946).
9. *Ibid.*, p. 7.
10. Bullivant and Rice, 'Reconstruction', pp. 224f.
11. Wolf, Christa, *A Model Childhood*, transl. Ursule Molinaro and Hedwig Rappolt (1983), p. 3. The translation 'Patterns of Childhood' is preferred by many critics, since it avoids the didactic connotations of the term 'model': connotations that the author herself resisted, since the identity she portrays herself as having assumed as a child under National Socialism is presented as deeply problematic.
12. Anonymous participant in a public debate on *Patterns of Childhood* following a reading by Wolf at the GDR Academy of Arts, 8 October and 3 December 1975. Reproduced in Karin McPherson, *The Fourth Dimension. Interviews with Christa Wolf* (1988), p. 62.
13. The sixteen principles of town planning are reproduced in Ian Latham and Jane Brierley, eds., *Architectural design profile* (1982), p. 3.

Select bibliography

Burns, Rob, ed., *German Cultural Studies. An Introduction* (1995).
Carter, Erica, *How German Is She? Postwar West German Reconstruction and the Consuming Woman* (1997).
Clyne, Michael, *Language and Society in the German-speaking Countries* (1984).
Eley, Geoff, 'Modernity at the Limit: Rethinking German Exceptionalism before 1914', *New Formations* 28 (spring 1996), pp. 21–45.
Elsaesser, Thomas, *New German Cinema: A History* (1989).
Fulbrook, Mary, *The Fontana History of Germany. 1918–1990, The Divided Nation* (1991).
Fulbrook, Mary, *Interpretations of the Two Germanies 1945–1990* (2000).
Goodbody, Axel, and Tate, Dennis, eds., *Geist und Macht. Writers and the State in the GDR* (1992).
Humphreys, Peter J., *Media and Media Policy in Germany: The Press and Broadcasting since 1945* (1994).
Kaes, Anton, *From Hitler to Heimat. The Return of History as Film* (1989).
Kolinsky, Eva, *Women in West Germany: Life, Work and Politics* (1989).
O'Brien, Peter, 'Identity Crisis in the New Germany,' *Debatte* 2(1) (1994), pp. 64–81.
Pommerin, Reiner, ed., *The American Impact on Postwar Germany* (1995).
Suhr, Heidrun, 'Ausländerliteratur: Minority Literature in the Federal Republic of Germany'. *New German Critique* 46 (1989), pp. 71–103.

I2

The end of the GDR: revolution and voluntary annexation

Jonathan Osmond

I The German question and the legitimacy of the GDR

Writing in 1844 in *Germany: A Winter's Tale*, Heinrich Heine characterized the smell of Germany's future as 'old cabbage and Russian leather'. Add to these the fumes of burning lignite and the exhausts of Trabant two-stroke engines, and one might in a sour-tempered moment claim to have captured the scent of the German Democratic Republic. Heine was writing a while before the first unification of Germany. The GDR existed only in division until its unification with the Federal Republic of Germany on 3 October 1990. Since that date the smells, sounds and sights of eastern Germany have altered in numerous ways, drawing the land closer to its mighty western neighbour, but there remain elements of unease, discontent and even anger on both sides of what had been the most fortified border in Europe. The revolution in the GDR – for revolution it surely was – brought immediate joy to many East Germans but it did not succeed in bringing lasting reform to the state. Instead it paved the way for the absorption of the GDR into an enlarged Federal Republic, a course which certainly meant for many people enhanced freedoms, opportunities and living standards, but also levels of insecurity unfamiliar from GDR days.

The ambiguities of these events have been reflected in their treatment by politicians, intellectuals, journalists, political scientists and historians. Portrayals have ranged from the exultant and self-satisfied to the angry and complaining, usually – but by no means always – observing a west–east demarcation. Along this line are the political memoirs of Wolfgang

Schäuble, proud to have negotiated the unification treaty for Chancellor Helmut Kohl but crippled by a would-be assassin nine days after German unity; the plangent self-justifications of GDR leaders Erich Honecker, Egon Krenz, Günter Mittag and Hans Modrow; the uncompromising warnings against unification by novelist Günter Grass; and the depiction of psychological devastation by East German psychotherapist Hans-Joachim Maaz.

The panoply of issues in current debates includes: the nature of the revolution and its appropriation; the legitimacy of retribution against those in authority in the GDR; the balance between economic freedom and social justice; the extent of popular collusion in the communist system and the ways of confronting it now; the respective contributions to union of the old and new federal states; and the ownership and interpretation of the GDR's history. Put in these general terms, the disputes may appear anodyne and remote. In practice, they involve real people in bad and in good situations: a woman being refused an abortion on religiously defined grounds she does not share; members of a farming family losing their house and employment to a West German claimant; a border-guard being imprisoned for disobeying orders to shoot escapees; a wife learning that for years she has been spied upon by her husband for the security service; a worker in the Saarland on the French border facing a tax increase to finance the unification of Germany up to a Polish border he has never seen; the reuniting of a family; the opening of a profitable new business; the renovation of a street; a first Mediterranean holiday; and the opportunity to read and discuss critically. All these experiences are laden with the meanings of unification, and it will be a long time before they can be analysed dispassionately, especially in Germany itself. From a racist attack on the street to an academic discussion of the continuities of German history, the revolution in the GDR and German unification have opened up the German question once more, but added to it new clauses.

In the autumn of 1989 hundreds of thousands of GDR citizens took to the streets of the major cities, demanding the political and social changes of which others, fleeing to the Federal Republic via third countries, had despaired. This two-fold popular pressure played its part in bringing about change in the party and state leadership and the opening of the GDR's borders. Thereupon the very nature of the GDR came into question, democratic elections were held, and a swift process of economic, social, and then political unification with the Federal Republic was set in train. To understand these events, however, one must first look back further: to the very status of the GDR and to the tensions building within it by the 1980s.

From its foundation, the GDR was subject to the criticism that it was an 'artificial' state, defined only by the original Soviet occupation and by the political purposes of the German communists. Such a viewpoint was not restricted to those in the Federal Republic who disputed the legitimacy of the state. In the GDR in August 1989 Otto Reinhold, the rector of the Academy of Social Sciences of the party Central Committee, was writing of the GDR: 'It can be conceived only as an anti-fascist, socialist state, a socialist alternative to the FRG. What right would a capitalist GDR have to exist beside a capitalist Federal Republic? None, of course.' This equation of the state with its political system was to prove a liability in 1989–90, despite the fact that all states are in a sense 'artificial', in that they are created out of particular historical circumstances. The shape of Poland since 1945 or the creation and re-creation of the Austrian Republic in the twentieth century are both related instances of states defined in territory and political system by warfare and power politics, but their integrity has not been challenged in the way that the GDR was challenged and annulled. The fact that the GDR was based almost entirely upon a political project meant that the state itself was vulnerable when the political system collapsed, but primarily because there was an alternative resolution to the crisis, namely unification with the hugely successful Federal Republic next door.

This is not to deny that the GDR had over 40 years established an identity of its own and a degree of loyalty amongst large numbers of its citizens. In part this identity was based upon regional particularities; the role of the Saxons, Thuringians, Mecklenburgers, Brandenburgers and Berliners should not be underestimated. In part it rested on pride in the achievements of the GDR after the calamity of world war and in the face of Western hostility. In part it was due to the high degree of social protection afforded to the working population. The political authorities themselves made great play of the distinctive nature and contribution of the GDR, and by the 1980s had distanced themselves from expectations of German unity, while at the same time linking the GDR to the wider German past, both 'progressive' and – in the cases of Martin Luther, Frederick the Great, Otto von Bismarck, and the Prussian conspirators of July 1944 – the less obviously 'progressive'. If a separate GDR identity was being fostered, it was, of course, reinforced by the isolation of the GDR from the West after the building of the Berlin Wall in 1961.

In 1989–90 these elements of 'artificiality' and vulnerability of the state on the one hand and distinct identity and citizen loyalty on the other combined to produce the volatile mixture of pressure for reform from within, population haemorrhage and a rising clamour of demands for German unity. That they did so was dependent, however, on events outside Germany.

II The GDR and the wider world

The limited scope for political change in the states of the Warsaw Treaty Organization had been demonstrated most pointedly in 1953 in the GDR, in 1956 in Hungary, and in 1968 in Czechoslovakia. On all three occasions Soviet troops had been instrumental in crushing popular revolt and/or communist reformers. The Poles had a more varied experience, but General Jaruzelski's declaration of a State of War in 1981 to combat the independent trade union Solidarity was intended in part to prevent Soviet military intervention. In Rumania Nicolae Ceauşescu managed to detach himself somewhat from Soviet tutelage, but only by being more ghastly than the party leaders elsewhere. The famous crisis points were matched by numerous other instances when Soviet pressure was brought to bear on domestic politics. In the GDR, Walter Ulbricht's ejection from the party leadership in 1971 was due to Moscow's connivance with his domestic opponents, foremost amongst whom was Erich Honecker. Honecker, who succeeded Ulbricht, in his turn faced Soviet obstruction. In 1984 his proposed visit to the Federal Republic was scotched by a cautious Kremlin. It was shortly thereafter, however, that the reliance of the East Berlin leadership upon Soviet military might began to be thrown in doubt. The selection of Mikhail Gorbachev as General Secretary of the Communist Party of the Soviet Union in March 1985 ushered in a period of attempted openness and restructuring in the USSR which was to culminate in a clear message from Gorbachev that his forces would not intervene in the affairs of fellow Warsaw Treaty Organization members and his encouragement of those in the GDR Politbüro who wished to push out Honecker and save communist rule through reform, albeit of an ultra-cautious type.

The talk of reform in Moscow, the worldwide acceptability of Gorbachev, and the withdrawal of ultimate Soviet military support were accompanied by other, often contradictory messages from fellow communist states. Polish striving for change and the resultant political and economic instability of the 1980s were not generally admired in the GDR, either by the party leadership or the population at large. Unsavoury prejudices played a large part in this. Greater economic leeway in Hungary, on the other hand, was viewed positively by the many East German holiday-makers to that country, if not by the East Berlin regime. Much further afield the Chinese communists' savage treatment of the student protesters on Tiananmen Square in June 1989 outraged reformers and moderates in the GDR, especially when the party leadership went out of its way to congratulate its Beijing counterpart. Within the Politbüro, however, there were also those who hoped to avoid recourse to such tactics within the

GDR. The implicit threats from Honecker, State Security (Stasi) head Erich Mielke and others were real enough, but they served to generate anger, instability and a search for other solutions, even within the Socialist Unity Party of Germany (SED).

The GDR looked westward as well as eastward, and if anything the Federal German contribution in the 1980s appeared to be one of bolstering the GDR. Massive bank loans, brokered in part by the Catholic conservative Prime Minister of Bavaria, Franz Josef Strauss, pulled the GDR out of the worst of its economic difficulties at the beginning of the decade and allowed the regime to continue its social policy of heavily subsidizing necessities. Then in 1987 Honecker's rescheduled visit to Bonn was permitted by Gorbachev, and he revelled in this assertion of the separate identity and political parity of the GDR. Meanwhile the Federal Republic over the years performed another useful function for the GDR leadership by buying out substantial numbers of GDR *émigrés*. From the perspective of East Berlin these were malcontents whose departure could only strengthen socialist rule.

III   Origins of domestic grievance

There were indeed causes for discontent at home, although most of them were not new and had not since June 1953 led to a major challenge to the regime. The economy of the GDR, though lauded as a success story at home and within the communist camp and respected even in the West, was built upon flawed foundations and was unable to provide the standard of living glimpsed nightly by the population on West German television. Heavy dependence upon Western loans, misdirected investment in already outdated high technology, inflexible trade patterns within the Council for Mutual Economic Assistance (CMEA), and cumbersome planning mechanisms marred further by deceit and corruption all contributed to an economy characterized by long but inefficient working weeks. A well-educated and generally hardworking population could not compensate for unreliable old plant and production bottlenecks. The provision of consumer goods was nothing like as dire as in Poland during the 1980s, but choice was poor, quality was low, and there were long waits for motor cars and other major purchases. The obvious deterioration of the physical environment, both through neglect and pollution, contributed nothing to people's sense of well-being. The economic trajectory was also not reassuring: even on the basis of the questionable official figures, growth in net material product declined from 5.5 per cent in 1984 to 2.1 per cent in 1989. It would be mistaken to suggest a simple link between economic slowdown and political protest, although the economic situation restricted the choices available to those at the top in the GDR when the political crisis hit.

Political issues and matters of personal liberty shaped the relatively small dissenting groups of the 1980s, groups which were to provide an important focus for the large-scale protest in 1989. From the beginning of the decade two aspects of militarization were challenged: the stationing of American and Soviet missiles in Europe, and the emphasis on armed preparedness propagated in GDR schools amongst children from a very early age. In January 1986 a small illegal group was founded, the Peace and Human Rights Initiative, the founders of which were intellectuals and artists. They faced harassment and even expulsion from the GDR, but returned to speak out once more in 1989. Another strand of opposition concerned itself primarily with the environmental issue. This was by no means a politically neutral agenda, bearing in mind the GDR's heavy energy dependence on dirty lignite, the over-use of chemical fertilizers in agriculture, and the secretive, largely Soviet-controlled uranium mining in the south of the country. The security forces were even prepared to invade ecclesiastical premises in their 1987 raid on the Berlin Zion church's environmental library. The churches, particularly the Protestant churches, were indeed the only officially permitted alternative forum for debate, and – sometimes against the wishes of the church hierarchy – they came to represent a focus for dissent. Not to be neglected either were those who used the democratic rhetoric and constitutional provisions of the GDR to criticize the regime in practice. In January 1988 and January 1989 the words of the early communist Rosa Luxemburg, murdered in that month in 1919, were taken up by demonstrators: 'freedom is always the freedom of others who think differently'. And in May 1989 unofficial observers attempted to monitor the process of local elections, coming to the unsurprising conclusion that the authorities were deliberately underestimating the growing numbers of those expressing opposition to the official list of candidates of the so-called National Front.

The unofficial peace movement, the environmentalists, the activists within the churches, and the political protesters – amongst whom there was a high degree of overlap – represented nevertheless a very thin stratum of GDR society. Not only that: their ranks were depleted by the voluntary departure or expulsion of many active individuals. Those who remained were under constant scrutiny by the Stasi not only in their purportedly political activities, but in their working, social, private and sexual lives. The spies were not primarily full-time Stasi operatives, but unofficial informers who were often members of the dissenting groups themselves. The writer

Sascha Anderson, for example, was thought by his associates to be a mainstay of the alternative cultural scene in the Prenzlauer Berg district of Berlin. Perhaps he was, but he was also a Stasi informant. Similarly, several figures who emerged in the new oppositional political parties of 1989 – Wolfgang Schnur of Democratic Awakening and Ibrahim Böhme of the SPD, for example – were irretrievably compromised by their connections with the Stasi. Church leaders were not immune, although the prominent lay figure, Manfred Stolpe, survived as post-unification Prime Minister of Brandenburg, despite admitted contacts with the security forces.

The Stasi might feel that it was in complete control of potential opposition, but it could not prevent long-term dissatisfaction on the part of the population at large. The particular focus of an individual's or a family's disgruntlement might vary, but the imposition of the tight border and the day-to-day behaviour of the bureaucracy took their toll on people's patience. For the upsurge to come, however, it required extraneous factors, and these were to emerge in 1989.

IV   The revolution of 1989

The process began in Hungary, which had progressed so far along the path of reform that the communist leadership agreed with neighbouring Austria to dismantle the fortifications on the common border from 2 May. This decision affected the GDR because a large number of East German holiday-makers realized the possibility of crossing into Austria and thence to the Federal Republic, where they could claim automatic citizenship. Through the summer, crowds built up in the Hungarian resorts and near the border, swollen by East Germans who had travelled to Hungary not for a holi-day but in order to emigrate. They were not at first allowed through the border officially, although illegal breaches did take place, and then – under pressure and financial cajolement from Bonn and against the express wishes of their allies in East Berlin – the Hungarians on 11 September let the East Germans out without hindrance. Their trembling joy and the warm reception they received in the Federal Republic – initially at least – were flashed around the news bulletins of the world. West German television kept the population of the GDR fully informed.

Meanwhile the compound of the Federal German embassy in Prague was occupied by large numbers of would-be emigrants, and smaller numbers ensconced themselves in its Warsaw counterpart and in the Federal German mission in East Berlin. The Federal German Foreign Minister, Hans-Dietrich Genscher, negotiated with East Berlin a resolution of the mounting problem in Prague, and on 30 September personally announced to a rapturous reception outside the embassy building that trains would leave Prague for the Federal Republic. Erich Honecker had insisted that they pass through GDR territory – causing violent scenes outside the railway station in Dresden when the local population realized what was happening and tried to get into the station premises – but there was no attempt to prevent the departure of these citizens. Indeed the official GDR response was that this was good riddance, an attitude which further inflamed feelings against the regime.

Escape was but one response to the growing crisis. From September, at the Nikolaikirche in the centre of Leipzig, Monday evening services began to be followed by ever-growing demonstration marches. The participants had a variety of demands: permission to travel outside the GDR, but also freedom of speech and assembly at home. There were those who chanted 'We want out!', but increasingly the marchers declared that 'We are staying here!' In their further assertion that they, and not the party hierarchy, were 'the people' in whose name the GDR existed, the emphasis had shifted to demands for political reform. This was potentially a very dangerous situation. The security forces waded in on many occasions to seize placards and to arrest marchers, but as the size of the demonstrations grew from several hundred to hundreds of thousands the threat grew of armed suppression in imitation of the Chinese. Only narrowly was mass bloodshed avoided on 9 October, although the responsibility for the crucial intercession has been claimed by a number of individuals, least convincingly by SED security secretary Egon Krenz himself.

The instability of population exodus and political protest was compounded by crisis within the SED itself. At the top Erich Honecker was sick with a gall bladder complaint for most of the summer, and it was unclear who, if anyone, was now in charge. Günter Mittag, the Party Secretary for the Economy, was Honecker's nominee, but – complained other members of the Politbüro – he took no action to stave off the deepening crisis. Not only in the Politbüro, but also in the further reaches of the party at district level opinion began to harden that Honecker had reached the end of his career. He took up work again on 25 September, hosted the celebrations of the fortieth anniversary of the GDR on 7 October, and was voted out of office by the Politbüro on 17 October and by the Central Committee the following day.

The anniversary festivity was indeed a crucial juncture, which brought together popular discontent, stirrings within the SED and the influence of Gorbachev. What had been intended by Honecker as a ringing endorsement of the success and stability of the GDR turned into the beginning of its final crisis. There were serious scuffles in Berlin between demonstrators and the security forces, and even the massed uniformed youth of the GDR were more enthusiastic about the reformer Gorbachev than they were about the hard line of the GDR leadership. Honecker looked completely out of touch with reality and was an embarrassment to Gorbachev and to most of the SED Politbüro. Quite what Gorbachev remarked on the eve of celebrations is contested by the eye-witnesses, but his message was clear: there had to be changes at the top. This was an encouragement in particular to Politbüro members Egon Krenz and Günter Schabowski, who conducted behind-the-scenes discussions with most of their comrades. At the meeting of 17 October it was Prime Minister Willi Stoph who interrupted Honecker to propose his dismissal, along with that of Mittag and Propaganda Secretary Joachim Herrmann. Honecker, Mittag and Herrmann in loyal communist fashion joined the rest of the Politbüro in voting in favour of the motion, and Egon Krenz was confirmed next day as new SED General Secretary by the Central Committee.

The ousting of Honecker did not bring the crisis to an end. Rather the reverse: demonstrations for wide-ranging political reforms and against the power of the Stasi took place now in towns and cities throughout the GDR. The Leipzig events dominated, but by 4 November the numbers on the streets in the capital were now the highest yet: estimates began at 500,000. A number of new parties and organizations had been founded in September and October, the most important and broadest of which was New Forum. Krenz and Schabowski meanwhile attempted to present a new face of the SED, the former appearing on television engaging in debates in the street with ordinary citizens and the latter facing the cameras at a nightly press conference. They both stressed that democratic reforms were possible and they promised a new travel law. When this appeared on 6 November it excited nothing but disappointment and contempt, and was rejected next day by a committee of the GDR parliament, the People's Chamber. Events were now moving very swiftly. The Stoph government resigned that day and the Politbüro immediately afterwards on 8 November, opening the way for the Central Committee to elect a new one. For the first time the votes cast for and against candidates were made public, and some did not find favour. An important new face also appeared in the Politbüro: Hans Modrow, the district Party Secretary for Dresden and a man who had been considered for several years as a possible reformist leader of the GDR. He was recommended as successor to Stoph as prime minister, while Krenz continued as effective head of state and General Secretary of the party.

The most exciting events were about to occur. Krenz had arranged for the drafting of yet another travel law, this time making it possible for GDR citizens to venture westward after only routine and short-notice application for an official visa. He hoped thereby – in curious reverse logic to that employed back in 1961 when the Wall was built – to ease the crisis in the GDR by allowing its citizens out. The assumption – broadly correct as it turned out – was that most would return home. In the early evening of 9 November Krenz gave Schabowski, who was departing for his regular briefing of the international press, a summary of the new regulations for him to announce. They were intended to come into force the next day, but Schabowski told those who questioned him that as far as he knew they applied with immediate effect. This was a televised response and the consequences were felt at once in Berlin. Crowds gathered at the border crossing points and demanded to be let through. The mood was generally good-humoured, but the crush of people and the uncertainty of the security forces meant that calamity was possible. Without a clear chain of command any more but showing good sense in an emergency, the border guards opened the barriers and the crowds surged through. On the Western side the wider section of the Wall by the Brandenburg Gate was scaled by revellers. Through the small hours of 10 November Easterners swept into West Berlin and caroused in the cafés of the Kurfürstendamm, while Westerners moved through the bleak dark Friedrichstrasse down to Unter den Linden and a view of the Brandenburg Gate from the other side.

If the effects of this night were to be felt worldwide, its first characteristic was of a divided city coming once more together. The (West) *Berliner Zeitung* on 10 November carried a banner headline of 'The Wall has gone! Berlin is Berlin again!' Its second characteristic was then, perhaps, the window-shopping exodus of the following days, and the alacrity with which Western business set about creating brand loyalty. At the Chausseestrasse crossing point in Berlin, Kaiser's supermarket from the back of a container lorry dispensed free coffee and chocolate bars, packaged in branded carrier bags. At Checkpoint Charlie the youth branch of the West Berlin CDU handed out leaflets declaring 'Unity, Justice and Freedom' and 'Self-determination for all Germans'. Attached was a token for 'one small drink' at McDonald's, generously valid for three days.

Egon Krenz reaped little reward. The political crisis deepened, while the potential economic consequences began to exercise the authorities east and west of the broken Wall. As Krenz began to establish dialogue with representatives of the Bonn government and Modrow installed his new government, the demonstrations continued. It was not going to be possible for the debate to take place solely within the SED. Federal Chancellor Helmut Kohl seized the initiative in late November when he put forward his ten-point plan for German unity, and then in early December pressure from within the SED as well as from without forced Krenz into resignation and brought Modrow into negotiation with a wide range of old and new parties at the so-called Round Table. Events in Berlin were matched by widespread purges of the SED throughout the GDR and the establishment of local round tables.

V   Crisis and unification in 1990

From this point evolved a divergence into two political perspectives. On the one hand the democratic renewal of the GDR began painfully to take shape, as New Forum, Democracy Now, Democratic Awakening, the Peace and Human Rights Initiative and other new movements and parties set an agenda for change. The emphasis was as much on social responsibility and justice as on personal freedom; the socialist ideal was still at the forefront, but now in a democratic context. These developments were matched by processes of reform – part idealistic, part opportunistic – within the old parties of the GDR, including the SED, which in December took as its sub-title 'Party of Democratic Socialism'. This appellation of PDS in February supplanted the old name entirely. On the other hand, popular pressure on the streets and diplomatic manoeuvre by some governments of the West were pushing strongly in the direction of German unity, even if at this stage it was considered to be a distant rather than an immediate goal. As the crisis of population loss and economic instability continued, the latter strand of unity began to be the dominant one. The crowds now declared not 'We are the people' as they had done in the autumn, but 'We are one people', and just before Christmas 1989 gave Helmut Kohl an ecstatic welcome in Dresden. Although the British, French and Russians were concerned about the effects of over-hasty moves towards unification, Kohl saw an opportunity to seize the inter-German initiative and behind him from an early stage were the Americans.

Within the GDR the economic situation was running out of control. Production was suffering from a continued haemorrhaging of labour, and West German goods and money were entering the country. Smuggling and an illegal currency market were preventing economic stabilization. The political situation was as confused. Modrow was trying simultaneously to maintain the old power structures while granting concessions, a recipe for further conflict. One example was his attempt to replace the Stasi with a downgraded national security office, which promptly acquired the unfortunate nickname of 'Nasi'. He was forced to back down, but this did not reduce popular anger about the activities of the Stasi, revealed daily in the press. On 15 January 1990 the Stasi headquarters in Berlin were stormed by protesters, some of whom were probably Stasi operatives anxious to destroy incriminating files. Another example was Modrow's foundation in March of the Treuhandanstalt, a trustee agency originally intended to take over the economic assets of the GDR and maintain the bulk of them in the state sector. Only later did it take on the opposite role of selling enterprises off to the private sector.

The SED-PDS was disintegrating, as members left or were expelled, but the new political movements were just as fractious. New Forum, the largest of the new groupings, failed to seize the initiative as an alternative political party, choosing to remain as a broad loose movement. This helped to open the way into GDR politics for the Federal German political parties, although this would no doubt have been a characteristic of the situation anyway. As the sense of political crisis deepened, the proposed elections to the People's Chamber were brought forward from the original May to 18 March, and the Western CDU, SPD and FDP sought out for themselves appropriate Eastern partners. Helmut Kohl's CDU hedged its bets by forging an Alliance for Germany with the old Eastern CDU, a new conservative German Social Union (DSU) from Saxony, and Democratic Awakening; the SPD joined forces with its new and weak namesake in the East; and the FDP brought together old and new 'liberals' in the League of Free Democrats. New Forum teamed up as Alliance 90 with the much smaller Democracy Now and Peace and Human Rights Initiative, but in doing so failed to make a connection with the Greens environmental lobby or the Social Democrats.

All these groups and parties, plus others, were represented in the new coalition and purportedly non-party government conceded by Modrow on 5 February. The opposition parties had no specific portfolios, however, so there was no sense of real responsibility. The PDS was still perceived as the main obstacle to real reform, but none of the new players could exert much positive influence. They began to lose ground, and the elections of 18 March saw a resounding victory of the Alliance for Germany, spearheaded by the CDU. With 192 seats out of 400, it did not quite reach an overall majority and brought the SPD (88 seats) and League of Free Democrats (21 seats) into government. The PDS – now unacceptable as a coalition partner – survived with 66 seats, but the representatives of the citizens' initiatives which had been at the forefront of the revolution were nowhere, with only 12 seats in the new parliament. On 9 April Lothar de Maizière, leader of the Eastern CDU since November 1989, formed a cabinet dominated by the CDU, but with Social Democrats as Foreign Minister (Markus Meckel) and Minister of Finance (Walter Romberg).

The success of the CDU, which had not been indicated by earlier opinion polls, can be attributed to the efforts of Helmut Kohl's party to promise rapid economic integration of the GDR into the Federal Republic and to the growing international acceptance of the notion of German unity. Already in February it had been agreed in Ottawa that 'Two-Plus-Four' talks would take place, bringing together the two German states and the four former occupying powers, who had important residual rights not only in divided Berlin but also in Germany at large. Margaret Thatcher and Mikhail Gorbachev were still broadly hostile to the rapid creation of a large politically united Germany, but the momentum for an agreement of sorts was hard to stop. The desperate economic situation in the GDR had prompted even Modrow in February to agree to move toward monetary and economic union, and his attempt to create a neutral Germany had been blocked firmly by Kohl. Once the de Maizière government had taken over, Kohl could proceed rapidly with his plans for first economic, then political unity, and he had the full support of US President George Bush.

The appeal of the Deutschmark to the population of the GDR was crucial in the discussions of German unity. It was a lure to large- and small-scale currency speculators and also to those seeking better employment. To the Kohl government it was clear that the current situation had to be stabilized and that it was better to take the Deutschmark to the East Germans than to have them come westwards to the Deutschmark. There remained the question of the exchange rate, however, which must not be allowed to weaken the powerful Federal German currency and awaken memories of the inflation of the early 1920s and late 1940s. In the event, Bonn ignored the advice of the Federal Bank and gave way to pressure from the East German population and its new government. On 23 April – only two weeks after the formation of the de Maizière government – it was announced that a 1:1 exchange rate would apply to East German wages and to the first tranche of private savings. The following day Kohl and de Maizière agreed that 1 July 1990 would be the date of monetary, economic and social union, and less than a month later – on 18 May – the treaty was signed in Bonn which provided the detail. The necessary legislation was moved through the People's Chamber in the GDR and the Bundestag and Bundesrat in the Federal Republic in June. From midnight on 30 June/ 1 July the inter-German border was open, the currency was shared, and when shops opened in the GDR on Monday, 2 July, West German produce was already in place. Saxon butter had disappeared, and Bavarian butter was on display instead.

The speed of these events should not disguise the considerable but minority opposition to them in both GDR and Federal Republic. In the former it was to be expected that the PDS would object to what it saw as the sell-out of the GDR, but there were those in the other non-coalition parties who saw the opportunities for a non-aligned, democratic and socialist GDR being thrown away in favour of hard-currency consumerism. There was no let-up in the economic melt-down of the GDR, especially after 1 July, when demand for East German produce slumped. Domestic consumers were understandably attracted to new attractively packaged Western goods, and the former export markets of the GDR in eastern Europe fell away drastically. Industrial workers and farmers in the GDR began to protest about their predicament. Meanwhile in the Federal Republic the Social Democrats, led by Oskar Lafontaine, Prime Minister of the Saarland, adopted a strategy towards economic union which managed to antagonize both the western and eastern electorates. Lafontaine correctly accused the Kohl government of underestimating the problems and costs of unification, but gave the impression of trying to sabotage the national cause. At the same time he made the East German working classes feel as if they were regarded as unwanted second-class Germans. There were, to be honest, many West Germans who felt precisely this, but for the trade-union-oriented SPD to take this line was for the party a political disaster in the making.

Kohl's haste in the summer of 1990 must be understood in its international setting. He knew that the Americans would not tolerate a Germany outside NATO, nor did he wish any such thing himself. On the other hand, he had to have the agreement of the Soviet Union, and if negotiations took too long there was no guarantee that the relatively accommodating Gorbachev would still be in place. It therefore came to him as an immense and astonishing relief when at the meeting of the Chancellor and the Soviet President in the Caucasus in mid-July 1990 the latter agreed to all-German NATO membership. This was not the last hurdle in the way of German unification, but it was the most important one and the subsequent negotiations – though hectic and hair-raising at times, as the accounts by Kohl's main negotiator Interior Minister Schäuble and by Bush's aides Zelikow and Rice attest – could proceed with energy. By this stage the wishes of the GDR government, represented after the mid-August sacking of the SPD ministers by Lothar de Maizière himself, were of little consequence. Kohl's dealings were primarily with the Federal Republic's Western allies and with the Soviet Union. The Poles, anxious about the inviolability of the Oder–Neisse border, were brought in briefly to the Two-Plus-Four meeting in Paris in July, but even their concerns were put off until German unification was in place. On the last day of August the 900-page unification treaty was signed in East Berlin, on 12 September the Two-Plus-Four talks were concluded in Moscow, the following day signatures were appended to a German–Soviet cooperation treaty on Soviet troop withdrawal and German economic assistance to the USSR, and at midnight on 2/3 October 1990 the territory of the GDR became part of the Federal Republic of Germany and Berlin was restored as the capital city.

Two days later 144 representatives of the GDR joined an enlarged Bundestag, pending federal elections in December. Meanwhile, on 14 October the five reconstituted East German federal states (Mecklenburg/ West Pomerania, Brandenburg, Saxony-Anhalt, Saxony and Thuringia) held elections, which emphatically confirmed CDU dominance. Only in Brandenburg did the SPD emerge with the largest percentage of the vote. The federal results on 2 December painted the same picture, with the CDU and its Bavarian ally, the CSU, taking 43.8 per cent and the SPD only 33.5 per cent. Exceptionally for these elections the 5 per cent hurdle for getting into the Bundestag had been applied separately to the 'old' and the 'new' federal states, in order to give some recognition of the specific political circumstances in the former GDR, and this meant that the PDS and Alliance 90 (now coupled with the East German Greens) did win seats. The PDS presence, however, limited the advance of the weak East German SPD, which also faced a resurgent East German FDP. Helmut Kohl had a commanding majority in the first parliament of the united Germany. Even in the House of Representatives of the newly united federal state of Berlin, holding its election on the same day, the CDU was the major party, even if without an overall majority.

VI   The new Germany adjusts

A historiography of the final phases of the GDR has already begun to emerge, fuelled not least by the availability of East German and to a lesser extent Russian and American archival sources. Participants in the events – busily producing their memoirs – have themselves had recourse to the documentary evidence which they helped create. In the summer of 1993, for instance, former GDR head of state Egon Krenz was to be seen daily in the reading room of the former SED party archive, working through the Politbüro files of 1980. In the archives of the so-called Gauck Authority, which holds the Stasi files on innumerable individuals, shocking revelations have appeared to those daring to read what colleagues, friends and relations had reported on them. This instant access to the historical record – even greater than that of the immediate post-Nazi period – has not lessened the disputes between participants and historians about the course and interpretation of events. Let two examples here suggest typical areas of debate. The East German historians Armin Mitter and Stefan Wolle engaged in sometimes sharp exchanges with West German historians not only about the history of the GDR but also about the survival of the historical profession and use of the archives in the new federal states. Their book *Untergang auf Raten* ('Downfall in Instalments') in turn met with the criticism that it took selective chunks from the documentary legacy of the GDR in order to chart a steady decline, thereby misrepresenting the historical development of the state and society. Looking at the GDR from a very different perspective, the West German political scientist Jens Hacker's *Deutsche Irrtümer* ('German Errors') took a very critical view of the role played by Federal German politicians and intellectuals in an alleged legitimation of an illegitimate dictatorship in the East.

To complicate matters further, so many aspects of the end of the GDR represent still unfinished business. The after-effects of unification are to be felt most keenly in the 'new federal states', but they influence developments in the old Federal Republic too, and the ways in which they are interpreted depend very much upon attitudes to the old GDR and to the processes of unification itself. To give one example of many, a judgement today on the wholesale reorganization of agriculture in the former GDR since unification is coloured by one's approach to some or all of the following: to the validity of the land confiscation and redistribution of the mid-1940s, to flight westward in the late 1940s and 1950s, to the forced collectivization of 1960, to the Common Agricultural Policy of the European Community/ Union since the 1950s, and to the exploitation of market opportunities by West German supermarket chains in the 1990s. Justice is claimed both by those East Germans who have lived and worked on the land for decades and by the West German descendants of former owners expropriated or impelled to flee and leave their property behind.

Such issues make it difficult as yet to make definitive historical judgements about German unification. At every turn there are surprises and ambiguities as the situation continues to develop. Despite official jubilation and signs of conservative desires now to draw a line under aspects of the German past, many Germans in the west and south of the country felt apathetic or even hostile to the incorporation of the east. Beyond the circulation of unfunny jokes about *Wessis* and *Ossis*, however, antagonism has yet to be significant. Massive unemployment in eastern Germany seemed to threaten social stability and the very coherence of the new Germany, but opinion polls then suggested that most East Germans looked favourably upon unification and saw their living standards rising. There is no doubt that the working-class – and unemployed – presence in Germany is now more pronounced, without that helping the SPD automatically, Gerhard Schröder's 1998 victory notwithstanding. Just when it seemed in the late

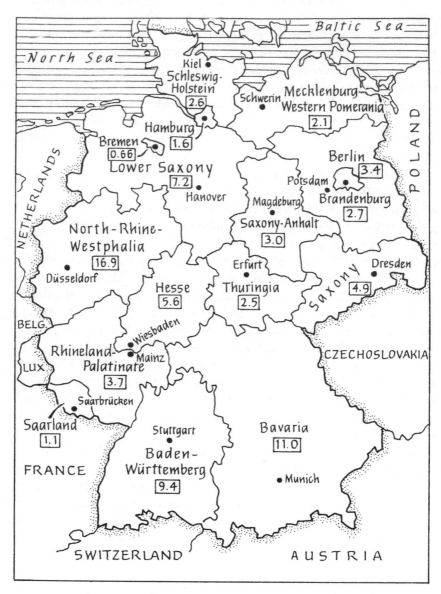

Map 12.1 Germany re-unified, 1990. Numbers shown in boxes refer to population in millions

1980s that the extreme right was about to establish itself again as a significant political force in the Federal Republic, its support fell away in West
Germany and failed to develop beyond some foul racist gangs in the former
GDR which emulated those in the West. At the other end of the political
spectrum, the PDS seemed doomed to extinction in the 1994 Bundestag
elections, when the split 5 per cent rule no longer applied. In the event it
survived, and continued to make impressive local gains as a representative
of the social complaints of the East German population. In the Bundestag
election of 1998 it even improved on its 1994 poll showing. It nudged over
the 5 per cent barrier, though the bulk of its support is in the East. In the
economy there has been devastation in many areas of the former GDR, but
there are signs that in certain respects the region could emerge with an ultra-
modern infrastructure. The overall financial costs of unification continue to
be immense – giving the lie to facile governmental promises in 1990 – but
the German economy, even in a period of less vigorous growth, is more able
than any other in the world to cope.

Generally speaking, the old Federal Republic has imposed its structures
on the old GDR, not always against the wishes of the latter's population,
although some issues such as the abandonment of the more liberal GDR
abortion law have proved divisive. There have had to be adjustments on the
part of West Germans too, however, some of them uncomfortable. The
Bonn region is already feeling the economic and social effect of the
government moving to Berlin, and other parts of West Germany are seeing
important administrative functions being transferred to cities in the east in
accordance with federal principles. It is too soon to judge how the incorporation of the relatively small and poor East German federal states will affect
the political system, but it is unlikely to remain unchanged. It may be that
the federal organs will acquire more power, and almost certainly the
political clout of Bavaria and Catholic Germany in general will be
diminished. With territorial expansion to the east and the revival of Berlin
the emphasis of German concerns will shift more toward central and
eastern Europe again. Much will depend too on the progress of monetary
union in the European Union, which Chancellor Kohl did so much to
pursue, at the cost – it would now seem – of his party and of his own reputation. The second unity Chancellor does not yet face the imprisonment
experienced by the men who deposed Honecker and opened the Wall,
Krenz and Schabowski, but his image has been tarnished. In the CDU's
attempt in 2000 to escape the consequent implosion it turned – at least in
the short term – to a politician from the East. The new leader of the CDU,
Angela Merkel, could not be more of a contrast to Helmut Kohl: a young,
slight, Protestant, eastern woman.

Revolution and unification have moved in such mysterious ways, and there are too many imponderables to yet have a proper assessment of the new Germany. This must wait awhile. The smell of Germany's future in the twenty-first century is as much a blend as it was in 1844, but the components are different and difficult to detect, even with a keen nose.

Select bibliography

Andert, Reinhold and Herzberg, Wolfgang, *Der Sturz: Erich Honecker im Kreuzverhör* (1990).

Dennis, Mike, *Social and Economic Modernization in Eastern Germany from Honecker to Kohl* (1993).

'German History and German Nationalism after Unification: Seven Historians Give their Views', *Debatte*, 1 (1993).

Glaessner, Gert-Joachim, *The Unification Process in Germany: From Dictatorship to Democracy* (1992).

Glaessner, Gert-Joachim and Wallace, Ian, eds., *The German Revolution of 1989: Causes and Consequences* (1992).

Hacker, Jens, *Deutsche Irrtümer 1949–1989: Schönfärber und Helfershelfer der SED-Diktatur im Westen* (1992).

von Hallberg, Robert, *Literary Intellectuals and the Dissolution of the State: Professionalism and Conformity in the GDR* (1996).

James, Harold and Stone, Marla, eds., *When the Wall Came Down: Reactions to German Unification* (1992).

Jarausch, Konrad H., *The Rush to German Unity* (1994).

Jarausch, Konrad H. and Gransow, Volker, eds., *Uniting Germany: Documents and Debates, 1944–1993* (1994).

Joas, Hans and Kohli, Martin, eds., *Der Zusammenbruch der DDR: Soziologische Analysen* (1993).

Kolinsky, Eva, ed., *Between Hope and Fear: Everyday Life in Post-Unification East Germany: A Case Study of Leipzig* (1995).

Kopstein, Jeffrey, *The Politics of Economic Decline in East Germany, 1945–1989* (1997).

Krenz, Egon, *Wenn Mauern fallen: die friedliche Revolution: Vorgeschichte – Ablauf – Auswirkungen* (1990).

Larres, Klaus, 'Collapse of a State: Honecker, Krenz, Modrow, and the End of the German Democratic Republic', *European Review of History*, 1 (1994).

Lewis, Derek, and McKenzie, John R. P., eds., *The New Germany: Social, Political and Cultural Challenges of Unification* (1995).

McAdams, A. James, *Germany Divided: From the Wall to Reunification* (1993).

Maaz, Hans-Joachim, *Behind the Wall: the Inner Life of Communist Germany* (1995).

Maier, Charles S., *Dissolution: The Crisis of Communism and the End of East Germany* (1997).

Merkl, Peter H., ed., *The Federal Republic of Germany at Forty-Five: Union Without Unity* (1995).

Meuschel, Sigrid, *Legitimation und Parteiherrschaft: Zum Paradox von Stabilität und Revolution in der DDR* (1992).

Mittag, Günter: *Um Jeden Preis: im Spannungsfeld zweier Systeme* (1991).

Mitter, Armin and Wolle, Stefan, *Untergang auf Raten: Unbekannte Kapitel der DDR-Geschichte* (1993).

Modrow, Hans, *Aufbruch und Ende* (1991).

Modrow, Hans, *Ich wollte ein neues Deutschland* (1999).

Osmond, Jonathan, ed., *German Reunification: A Reference Guide and Commentary* (1992).

Philipsen, Dirk, *We Were the People: Voices from East Germany's Revolutionary Autumn of 1989* (1993).

Pond, Elizabeth, *Beyond the Wall: Germany's Road to Unification* (1993).

Popplewell, Richard, 'The Stasi and the East German Revolution of 1989', *Contemporary European History* 1 (1992).

Schabowski, Günter, *Der Absturz* (Berlin: Rowohlt, 1991).

Schäuble, Wolfgang, *Der Vertrag: wie ich über die deutsche Einheit verhandelte* (1991).

Sinn, Gerlinde and Sinn, Hans-Werner, *Jumpstart: The Economic Unification of Germany* (1992).

Southern, David, 'Restitution or Compensation: The Open Property Question', *German Politics* 2 (1993).

Wolle, Stefan, 'In the Labyrinth of the Documents: The Archival Legacy of the SED-State', *German History* 10 (1992).

Zelikow, Philip and Rice, Condoleezza, *Germany Unified and Europe Transformed: A Study in Statecraft* (1995).

Chronology: Germany, 1918–1990

1919   January: Spartacus rising, murder of Karl Luxemburg and Rosa Liebknecht; election of a National Assembly. February: Ebert elected President; formation of 'Weimar coalition' government (SPD, Centre, DDP). June: signing of Treaty of Versailles. August: Weimar constitution proclaimed.

1920   March: Kapp–Lüttwitz *putsch*. March/April: communist uprisings. June: Weimar coalition loses its majority in the general election, SPD goes into opposition.

1922   Treaty of Rapallo between Germany and USSR.

1923   January: occupation of the Ruhr by French and Belgian troops; passive resistance by Germany. Summer: peak of great inflation. November 9: Hitler Beer Hall *putsch* in Munich. New currency, end of inflation.

1924   Hitler imprisoned in Landsberg; writes *Mein Kampf*. Dawes Plan to deal with reparations.

1925   Death of Friedrich Ebert; election of General Field Marshal von Hindenburg as President. Locarno Treaty.

1926   Berlin Treaty with the USSR. Germany enters the League of Nations.

1928   Grand Coalition (SPD, Centre, DDP and DVP) under SPD Chancellor Müller.

1929   Young Plan on reparations. Death of Foreign Minister Stresemann. Wall Street Crash inaugurates economic depression.

1930   Collapse of Müller cabinet, replaced by minority government under Brüning. French troops leave Rhineland. NSDAP make big gains in September elections.

1931   Harzburg front formed.
1932   Hindenburg re-elected President after second ballot. Resignation of Chancellor Brüning; formation of minority government under von Papen. SPD government in Prussia overthrown; in the July general election, NSDAP becomes largest party in Reichstag. Hitler refuses offer of vice-chancellorship. November: NSDAP loses votes in general election; resignation of von Papen. December: General von Schleicher appointed Chancellor.
1933   January: Schleicher resigns; Hitler appointed Chancellor on 30 January, heading a mixed cabinet. February: Reichstag burnt, state of emergency declared. March: NSDAP still fail to gain overall majority in general election, but parliament passes Enabling Act after the 'Day of Potsdam'. Dachau founded. March/April: beginnings of dismantling of *Länder* powers. April: organized boycott of Jewish shops and businesses. May: independent trade unions banned, replaced by DAF; burning of Jewish and other banned books on Unter den Linden. June and July: all parties except NSDAP banned or disbanded. July: Concordat with the Vatican. October: Germany leaves League of Nations.
1934   January: Reichsrat (upper house of parliament) and federal system abolished. June: SA (Sturmabteilung) is beheaded, and key politicians (including Schleicher) assassinated in the 'Röhm *putsch*', or 'night of the long knives'. August: death of Hindenburg; army swears oath of allegiance to Hitler, who becomes 'Führer and Reich Chancellor'.
1935   January: Saar plebiscite; returns to the Reich. September: Nuremberg Race Laws.
1936   March: German troops march into demilitarized Rhineland. August: Olympic Games in Berlin. October: Four-Year Plan announced, under Goering; treaty with Italy, forming 'Berlin–Rome Axis'. November: pact between Germany and Japan.
1937   November: Hitler harangues army leadership ('Hossbach memorandum').
1938   Purge of army leadership (Blomberg, Fritsch). March: *Anschluß* with Austria. September; Munich Treaty; Sudetenland ceded from Czechoslovakia to Germany. November 9: organized pogrom against Jews in *Reichskristallnacht*.
1939   March: German invasion of Czechoslovakia; establishment of Protectorates of Bohemia and Moravia; Memel territory returned to Reich. August: non-aggression pact between Germany and USSR

('Hitler–Stalin pact'). September: Germany invades Poland; Britain and France declare war on Germany. Euthanasia programme officially begins. German *Blitzkrieg* campaigns.

1940   April: occupation of Denmark; invasion of Norway. May: German invasion of Belgium, the Netherlands, Luxembourg and France. June: Franco–German ceasefire.

1941   June: Germany attacks USSR; special units (*Einsatzgruppen*) round up and murder Jews in USSR. August: euthanasia programme officially terminated. Autumn: beginning of organized killing of selected Jews taken from ghettos in Poland; first use of gassing in vans at Chelmno. December: Japan bombs American fleet at Pearl Harbour; Germany declares war on USA; Hitler accepts Brauchitsch's resignation and assumes personal command of the army in the field.

1942   January: Wannsee Conference to coordinate the 'final solution' under Heinrich Himmler. Founding of the extermination camps of the 'Reinhard Action' (named after Heydrich); extension of Auschwitz with the construction of the extermination centre at Birkenau. June: successes for Axis forces in North Africa under General Rommel. Autumn: successful Allied counter-offensive in Africa.

1943   January: Casablanca Conference between Roosevelt and Churchill, demanding unconditional surrender of Germany. German army defeated at Stalingrad. July: Allies land in Italy. Mussolini deposed. Summer/ autumn: Allied bombing raids on Germany. November/ December: Teheran conference.

1944   Allies land in northwest France. July 20: failure of 'July Plot' to assassinate Hitler.

1945   January–April: Allied armies advance and occupy Germany from west and east. February: Yalta Conference. April: death of Roosevelt. Hitler marries Eva Braun and commits suicide in his Berlin bunker. May: German surrender; winding up of short-lived Dönitz government. Allied occupation begins – four occupation zones. July/August: Potsdam conference. September: land reform in Soviet zone.

1946   April: amalgamation of KPD and SPD to form SED in Soviet zone. September: Byrne's speech in Stuttgart. October: Nuremberg war crimes trials end. December: USA and Britain agree to form Bizone.

1947   January 1: Bizone comes into effect. February: state of Prussia officially dissolved. March/April: Moscow Foreign Ministers'

Conference. Truman doctrine about 'roll-back of communism' enunciated. June: Marshall Plan announced; Munich Prime Ministers' Conference; establishment of Economic Council of Bizone. November/December: London Foreign Ministers' Conference.

1948 March/April: Six-Powers Conference in London; recommendation to set up separate West German state. June: currency reform in western zones; Berlin blockade begins. September: establishment of parliamentary council in Bonn.

1949 May: lifting of Berlin blockade; West Germany's Basic Law announced. August: election of first West German parliament. September: Theodor Heuss (FDP) elected President, with Konrad Adenauer (CDU) as Chancellor. October: establishment of the German Democratic Republic; Wilhelm Pieck as President, Otto Grotewohl as Prime Minister, Walter Ulbricht retaining effective power as leader of the ruling SED.

1950 February: Ministry for State Security founded in GDR. June: start of Korean War.

1951 Treaty on European Coal and Steel Community signed in Paris.

1952 March: first Stalin Note proposing reunification. May: German Treaty signed in Bonn; European Defence Community treaty signed in Paris; five kilometre border zone cleared in GDR. July: SED pronounces the 'building of socialism' in the GDR; creation of the *Bezirke* to replace the *Länder*. Collectivization of agriculture begins.

1953 March: death of Stalin; 'New Course' announced. June: uprising with widespread strikes and demonstrations in GDR is suppressed by force. July: ceasefire in Korea.

1954 Treaty of Paris signed, allowing West Germany to join NATO, following French rejection of EDC. *Jugendweihe* (secular youth ceremony) introduced in GDR as part of SED campaign against the churches.

1955 Paris Treaty comes into force; ending of Occupation Statute for FRG, which becomes a member of NATO. Founding of the Warsaw Pact, of which the GDR is a member. October: plebiscite in Saarland.

1956 National Peoples Army (NVA) founded in GDR. Stalin cult denounced at XX Congress of the CPSU. Uprisings in Poland and Hungary, but not in GDR.

1957 January: Saarland joins Federal Republic. March: Treaty of Rome establishes European Economic Community (EEC).

September: CDU/CSU win absolute majority in Bundestag election.

1958   Khrushchev's Berlin Ultimatum.

1959   July: Heinrich Lübke (CDU) elected President of FRG. November: SPD Bad Godesberg Conference renouncing radical rhetoric.

1960   Collectivization of agriculture speeded up in GDR. Wilhelm Pieck dies and is replaced by a new collective head of state, the Council of State.

1961   August: Berlin Wall erected.

1962   GDR announces compulsory conscription. Cuban crisis. 'Spiegel affair' in West Germany.

1963   Franco-German Friendship Treaty signed in Paris. Adenauer resigns, Ludwig Erhard (CDU) elected Chancellor. First agreement on transborder travel West Berlin/GDR. New Economic System (NÖS) introduced in GDR.

1964   *Bausoldatenerlass* in GDR allows alternative military service as construction workers without bearing weapons.

1966   FDP leaves West German government over budget differences: 'Grand Coalition' of CDU/CSU and SPD formed under Kurt-Georg Kiesinger (CDU) as Chancellor.

1968   Student demonstrations in West Germany. Bundestag passes Emergency Decree. GDR adopts new constitution enshrining leading role of SED. Warsaw Pact troops invade Czechoslovakia and suppress 'Prague Spring'.

1969   Gustav Heinemann (SPD) elected West German President. A major watershed in West German politics is crossed with the formation of the SPD/FDP coalition government under Chancellor Willy Brandt (SPD).

1970   Brandt (SPD) and Willi Stoph (SED) meet in Erfurt and Kassel. August: German–Soviet Non-Aggression Pact signed in Moscow. December: German–Polish Treaty signed in Warsaw. Winding up of New Economic System in GDR.

1971   Ulbricht replaced by Erich Honecker as SED leader in GDR. Signing of Four Powers' Agreement on Berlin. Brandt receives Nobel Peace Prize.

1972   Failure of CDU/CSU attempt to unseat Brandt's government by a constructive vote of no confidence. Bundestag ratification of Moscow and Warsaw Treaties. SPD/FDP coalition government re-elected with a clear majority. Signing of Basic Treaty between GDR and FRG.

1973	Basic Treaty ratified by Bundestag. GDR and FRG become members of the United Nations. World oil crisis.
1974	Brandt resigns and is replaced by Helmut Schmidt (SPD). Walter Scheel (FDP) elected Federal President. GDR revises its constitution to build up the concept of a 'GDR nation'.
1975	Helsinki Final Act of Council for Security and Cooperation in Europe (CSCE).
1976	Exile of Wolf Biermann to West Germany, followed by protests from East German intellectuals. Self-burning of Pastor Brüsewitz in GDR.
1977	Terrorist attacks and assassinations (Buback, Ponto, Schleyer) by Red Army Faction in FRG.
1978	Church/state agreement in GDR.
1979	Karl Carstens (CDU) elected Federal President. Decision to deploy nuclear missiles on German soil. Soviet invasion of Afghanistan. Second world oil crisis inaugurates a further period of economic difficulties.
1982	FDP leaves governing coalition over budget differences and votes in Helmut Kohl (CDU), in a constructive vote of no confidence, as Chancellor of a coalition between the FDP and the CDU/CSU.
1984	Erich Honecker's attempted visit to FRG cancelled.
1985	Mikhail Gorbachev becomes Soviet leader. Kohl and US President Reagan meet over SS graves at Bitburg.
1987	Honecker makes an official visit to FRG. Olof Palme Peace March in GDR. Stasi raid on *Umweltbibliothek* (Environmental Library) in East Berlin.
1988	January: Mass arrests by Stasi at Luxemburg/Liebknecht demonstration in East Berlin.
1989	East German dissidents observe falsification of May election results. Summer: Hungary begins to dismantle its border with Austria; refugee crisis as East Germans flee west. September: foundation of New Forum; Monday demonstrations in Leipzig. October: Gorbachev visits Berlin for GDR 40th anniversary and warns Honecker that it is time to reform; Honecker is deposed and replaced by Egon Krenz; demonstrations grow all over GDR. November: Politburo resigns; Berlin Wall opened on 9 November; Kohl announces 'Ten-Point Plan' for German unification on 28 November. December: SED renounces its claim to leadership. Formation of interim Round Table government.

1990   'Two-plus-Four talks' take place to consider international aspects of the reopened German question. March: elections in GDR bring in conservative-dominated coalition government. July: currency union with West Germany. October 3: unification of Germany by means of accession of newly recreated East German *Länder* to Federal Republic of Germany. December: Kohl re-elected Chancellor of united Germany.

Notes on the contributors

Mark Allinson is Lecturer in German at the University of Bristol. His publications include *Politics and Popular Opinion in East Germany, 1945–1968* (2000) and his research interests include the politics and society of the GDR and modern Austria.

Omer Bartov is the John P. Birkelund Professor of European History at Brown University. He was an Alexander von Humboldt Fellow, a Visiting Fellow at the Davis Center for Historical Studies in Princeton University, and a Junior Fellow at Harvard's Society of Fellows. He is also General Editor of the series *Studies on War and Genocide* at Berghahn Books. Publications include *The Eastern Front, 1941–45: German Troops and the Barbarisation of Warfare* (1985); *Hitler's Army: Soldiers, Nazis, and War in the Thrd Reich* (1991); *Murder in Our Midst: the Holocaust, Industrial Killing, and Representation* (1996); *Mirrors of Destruction: War, Genocide, and Modern Identity* (2000); (ed.) *The Holocaust: Origins, Implementation, Aftermath* (2000); and (ed. with Phyllis Mack) *In God's Name: Genocide and Religion in the Twentieth Century* (2000).

Richard Bessel is Professor of Twentieth Century History at the University of York and co-editor of the journal *German History*. His publications include *Political Violence and the Rise of Nazism: the Storm Troopers in Eastern Germany, 1925–1934* (1984); *Germany after the First World War* (1993); (ed.) *Life in the Third Reich* (1987); (ed.) *Fascist Italy and Nazi Germany: Comparisons and Contrasts* (1996); (ed. with Ralph Jessen) *Die Grenzen der Diktatur. Straat und Gesellschaft in der DDR* (1996); and (ed. with Clive Emsley), *Patterns of Provocation: Police and Public Disorder* (2000).

Erica Carter is Senior Lecturer in German Studies at the University of Warwick. Her publications include *How German is She? Post-war German*

Reconstruction and the Consuming Woman (1997). She has written widely on German cinema, and is currently researching the history of stars in the Third Reich.

Niall Ferguson is Fellow of Jesus College and Professor of Political and Financial History at Oxford University. He is the author of *Paper and Iron: Hamburg Business and German Politics in the Era of Inflation* (1995) which was shortlisted for the History Today Book of the Year award; *The World's Banker: a History of the House of Rothschild* (1998), which won the Wadsworth Prize for Business History and *The Pity of War* (1998). He is also the editor of *Virtual History: Alternatives and Counterfactuals* (1997).

Mary Fulbrook is Professor of German History at University College London. Her publications include *Piety and Politics: Religion and the Rise of Absolutism in England, Württemberg and Prussia* (1983); *A Concise History of Germany* (1990); *The Divided Nation: Fontana History of Germany 1918–1990* (1991); *The Two Germanies 1945–1990: Problems of Interpretation* (1992); *Anatomy of a Dictatorship: Inside the GDR, 1949–1989* (1995); *German National Identity after the Holocaust* (1999); *Interpretations of the Two Germanies, 1945–1990* (2000); (ed.) *National Histories and European History* (1993); (ed. with David Cesarani) *Citizenship, Nationality and Migration in Europe* (1996); (ed. with Martin Swales), *Representing the German Nation* (2000); (ed). *Short Oxford History of Europe since 1945* (2000).

Elizabeth Harvey is Senior Lecturer in the School of History at the University of Liverpool. Her publications include *Youth and the Welfare State in Weimar Germany* (1993); (ed. with Jennifer Birkett) *Determined Women: Studies in the Construction of the Female Subject, 1900–1990* (1991); and (ed. with Lynn Abrams) *Gender Relations in German History* (1996). She is currently carrying out research on women's involvement in National Socialist Germanization policies in the 'German East'.

Ian Kershaw is Professor of Modern History at the University of Sheffield. He was elected a Fellow of the British Academy in 1991; he is also a Fellow of the Royal Historical Society. Publications on German history include: *Der Hitler-mythos. Volksmeinung und Propaganda im Dritten Reich* (1980); English version: *The 'Hitler Myth'. Image and Reality in the Third Reich* (1987); *Popular Opinion and Political Dissent in the Third Reich: Bavaria, 1933–45* (1983); *The Nazi Dictatorship. Problems and Perspectives of Interpretation* (1985; 4th edn., 2000); *Hitler. A Profile in Power* (1991); (ed. with Moshe Lewin) *Stalinism and Nazism: Dictatorships in Comparison*

(1997); and (ed.) *Weimar. Why did German Democracy Fail?* (1990). His biography of *Hitler* was published as two volumes: *Hubris: 1889–1936* (1998) and *Nemesis: 1936–1945* (2000).

Jonathan Osmond is Professor of Modern European History at Cardiff University. He is author of *Rural Protest in the Weimar Republic: the Free Peasantry in the Rhineland and Bavaria* (1993) and editor of *German Reunification: a Reference Guide and Commentary* (1992). His current research is on rural society in the Soviet Zone and GDR and on modern German art and politics.

Mark Roseman is Professor in Modern History at the University of Southampton. He has written widely on post-war West Germany and the Third Reich. His publications include *Recasting the Ruhr (1945–1958): Manpower, Economic Recovery and Labour Relations* (1992), *The Past in Hiding* (2000) and he has edited *Generations in Conflict: Youth Revolt and Generation Formation in Germany 1770 1968* (1995).

Nicholas Stargardt is Fellow and Tutor in Modern European History at Magdalen College, Oxford. He has written *The German Idea of Militarism: Radical and Socialist Critics, 1866–1914* (1994), as well as on the intellectual history of nationalism. He is currently writing a study of children's lives in Nazi Germany.

Jill Stephenson is Reader in History at the University of Edinburgh. She is the author of *Women in Nazi Society* (1975), *The Nazi Organization of Women* (1981) and numerous articles and essays on women in twentieth-century Germany and Württemberg in the Second World War. From 1986 to 1996 she was joint editor of *German History*, the journal of the German History Society. She is completing a new book on *Women in Nazi Germany*.

Index